Like a Hurricane

Like a Hurricane

*The Indian Movement
from Alcatraz
to Wounded Knee*

Paul Chaat Smith
&
Robert Allen Warrior

THE NEW PRESS

New York • New York

Library of Congress Cataloging-in-Publication Data
Smith, Paul Chaat.
Like a hurricane: the Indian movement from Alcatraz to Wounded Knee /
Paul Chaat Smith and Robert Allen Warrior.
p. cm.
Includes bibliographical references and index.
ISBN 1-56584-316-9 (hardcover)
1. Indians of North America—Government relations—1934– . 2. Alcatraz
Island (Calif.)—History—Indian occupation, 1969–1971. 3. Wounded Knee
(S.D.)—History—Indian occupation, 1973. 4. Trail of Broken Treaties, 1972. I.
Warrior, Robert Allen. II. Title.
E98.S655 1996
979.4'61—dc2095-48025
CIP
Published in the United States by The New Press, New York
Distributed by W. W. Norton & Company, Inc., New York

Established in 1990 as a major alternative to the large, commercial
publishing houses, The New Press is a full-scale nonprofit American book
publisher outside of the university presses. The Press is operated editorially
in the public interest, rather than for private gain; it is committed to
publishing in innovative ways works of educational, cultural, and
community value that, despite their intellectual merits, might not normally
be commercially viable. The New Press's editorial offices are located
at the City University of New York.

Book design by Misha Beletsky

Printed in the United States of America

9 8 7 6 5 4 3 2 1

Contents

Preface

Bob Dylan once described the decade he reluctantly owned this way: "It was like a flying saucer that landed. Everybody heard about it, but only a few saw it." If that was generally true for the often surrealistic, flesh-and-blood carnival of the 1960s, it was a particularly dead-on description for the fast and furious campaign American Indian activists waged during that time.

For most of those who did not directly experience the surge of activism it has all but faded from memory. If it is recalled at all, it is as a series of photojournalistic images of Indians with bandannas and rifles courtesy of television reports from the presatellite age. For others it is only known through Hollywood reconstructions like *Thunderheart* or the permanant celebrity status of movement leaders like Russell Means and John Trudell.

A great many books written about American Indians have shared two characteristics. They have been written by people who were not Indians, and they usually sought to persuade readers that government policies were cruel and misguided. That tradition has on occasion produced important, even brilliant books, but it is not a tradition that guides this work.

We came to write *Like a Hurricane* out of a profound dissatisfaction with the existing narratives of this crucial period in Indian and

American history, one that we believed too often saw Indian people as mere victims and pawns. Our focus is not on the U.S. government's failed policies or on police repression, but on how Indian people, for a brief and exhilarating time, staged a campaign of resistance and introspection unmatched in this century. It was for American Indians every bit as significant as the counterculture was for young whites, or the civil rights movement for blacks.

As coauthors, we came to this project from different places, but with a shared fascination to understand as much as we could the people and organizations that comprised the story of *Hurricane.* Coauthor Smith participated in the aftermath of the story chronicled here, traveling to South Dakota in 1974 at the age of nineteen to work on the Wounded Knee trials. He stayed with the movement through most of the 1970s, joining the staff of the American Indian Movement's International Indian Treaty Council in 1977. Coauthor Warrior also knew of these events, but from a greater distance. While a graduate student, he wrote in the alternative and Native presses about Indian community issues and kept running into questions that represent the legacy of the watershed years featured here. Though not related to Clyde Warrior, whose life is told in the pages that follow, he has heard many stories of the Ponca leader from friends and relatives in Oklahoma.

We have relied on a wide range of sources, including more than sixty interviews; archives in California, Minnesota, New Mexico, and Washington, D.C.; contemporary press accounts from Indian and mainstream news organizations; memoirs; and other records. We have chosen to focus the book on three key events that took place from November 1969 through May 1973. Other events are, arguably, equally significant, and other personalities might have been included, but in the end we felt the student landing on the abandoned prison at Alcatraz, the fumbled, nearly catastrophic occupation of the BIA in Washington, and the siege at Wounded Knee a few months later best illustrated the character and substance of the Indian movement.

We look forward to future works that will engage these questions from other points of view and with different emphases. Certainly many of the figures chronicled here merit full-scale biographies. We hope others will more deeply explore the Red Power activists of the early 1960s, the student movement, and the deep connections between Iroquois and Hopi traditionals and the militants of Alcatraz and later of AIM, to cite only a few examples.

We have tried to provide an honest account of the period, through
the eyes of urban Indian rebels, conservative tribal chairmen, Bureau
of Indian Affairs officials, White House aides, and others. The decision to write a book where not everything is red or white means that
some of what follows reflects negatively on the Indian struggle. Indeed, much of *Hurricane* is a continual education in the missteps and
errors of that movement, which like all others, often fell short of its
goals. At the same time, it is also true that this undertaking has only
increased our admiration for the imagination and daring displayed by
so many courageous Indian people.

As we write, in late 1995, the most profitable casino in the world is
run by the Pequots of Connecticut, and Russell Means, the hard-
line leader of the American Indian Movement, stars in one of the
year's biggest movies, a Disney picture called *Pocahantas.* For those
tempted to reach facile, ironic conclusions, it should be noted that
some consider Indian gaming a sophisticated, effective demonstration
of Indian sovereignty, and as for Russell Means, he believes his commitment to radical transformation has only strengthened over time.

Such outcomes would have seemed fantastic to those who
dreamed of indigenous revolution two decades ago. But perhaps no
more so than the story that follows would seem to people who only
know resistance leaders as movie stars, or casinos as flashpoints of Indian rebellion. From today's perspective, the tale of one Mohawk's
plunge into the cold waters of San Francisco Bay—and the ensuing
wave of insurgency that led to a military confrontation between the
federal government and Sioux Indians only forty-two months later—
seems no less incredible.

It all makes predictions dangerous, verdicts uncertain, and accounting difficult. We have chosen instead to be observers in search of
an honest telling of a fabulous story. We are deeply indebted to the
many people who shared their memories with us of the time when Indian people, on an almost daily basis, shocked themselves and the
world.

Washington, DC
Redwood City, California
December, 1995

Acknowledgments

We would like to thank the following individual librarians and archivists who went out of their way to assist us in researching this work: Katharine Martinez, Green Library, Stanford University; Richard Koprowski, Archive of Recorded Sound, Stanford University; Richard Burdick, National Archives, Washington, D.C.; Cathy Creek, National Anthropological Archives, Smithsonian Institution, Washington, D.C.; and Sue Lobo, Community History Project, Intertribal Friendship House, Oakland, California. We are also appreciative of the people on the staffs at the Center for Southwest Research, University of New Mexico; Special Collections and California History Room, San Francisco Public Library; Minnesota Historical Society, Minneapolis, Minnesota; The Nixon Presidential Papers Project, which, when we worked there, was in Alexandria, Virginia; National Archives—Pacific Sierra Region, San Bruno, California; Pacifica Radio Archives, North Hollywood, California; Rapid City Public Library, Rapid City, South Dakota; Television News Archive, Vanderbilt University, Nashville, Tennessee; and Meyer Media Center, Crown Law Library, Jonsson Library of Government Documents, and Hoover Institution Library and Archives, Stanford University.

Two Stanford undergraduates, Marissa Flannery and Clay Akiwenzie, did excellent work as researchers on the project. Students in several Stanford courses listened to presentations and otherwise worked with the material. Students, staff, and alumni connected to the American Indian Program at Stanford, including Benny Shendo, Betty Parent, and Wilson Pipestem, helped create a wonderful context in which to do this work. Faculty and staff of the English Department at Stanford, especially Jay Fliegelman, David Halliburton, George Dekker, Ramon Saldivar, Al Gelpi, Dagmar Logie, Ranita Lochan, Margaret Minto, and Alyce Boster provided various kinds of support. We are grateful to several people who were gracious enough to read the manuscript along the way, including Mark Trahant, Jace Weaver, Steven Pitti, Steven Ray Smith, Audra Simpson, and Jolene Rickard (all the mistakes, of course, belong to us).

The Funding Exchange, New York, provided valuable early financial support for the project. The Office of Technology Licensing at Stanford awarded us a substantial grant, which helped sustain the research and writing. Our agent, Charlotte Sheedy, and her associates at the Charlotte Sheedy Literary Agency, New York, provided crucial support.

One of the greatest regrets of telling a story like this is having so much excellent material to use and such limited space to use it in. So we thank the following people for sharing more stories than we could tell: Bette Crouse, Karen Northcott, Gerald Brown, Wolf Smoke, Pete Jemison, Ken Tilsen, Chuck Trimble, Sam English, Lenny Foster, Richard Ray Whitman, George Big Eagle, Jeff Sklansky, Janet McCloud, Ramona Bennett, Gerald Vizenor, Denise Quitiquit, Kathryn Red Corn, Jeri Red Corn, Dennis Jennings, Elizabeth Clark Rosenthal, Sue Morales, Della Warrior, Alfonso Ortiz, Gladys Ellenwood, Georgia Bratt, Hank Adams, Darlene Albert, Regina Brave, Kurt Peters, Dick LaGarde, Lehman Brightman, Bobbie Green Kilberg, Mitchell Bush, Grace Thorpe, Ed Castillo, Bernie Whitebear, Donna Chavis, Jimmie Durham, Anthony Garcia, Rose Robinson, Leonard Garment, Rayna Green, Keever Locklear, LaNada Means, Sid Mills, Suzette Mills, Brenda Mitchell, Reaves Nahwooks, Clydia Nahwooksy, Jim Burress, Bruce Oakes, Jesse Cooday, Bradley Patterson, Luwana Quitiquit, Robert Robertson, C. D. Ward, Murray Wax, Colin Wesaw, Troy Yellow Wood, Bonnie Fultz, and Curly Youpie.

It's hard to imagine a harder working, more patient editor than the incomparable Dawn Davis. André Schiffrin, Grace Farrell, David Sternbach, Jerome Chou, Michael Cisco, Diane Alexander, Jim Levendos, Misha Beletsky, Hall Smyth, and others at The New Press were marvelous to work with.

Coauthor Warrior has relied on too many friends to name, but will at least single out Ray Cook, Carla McDonough, Eduardo Mendieta, Lance Friis, Geoff Johnson, and Tahlee Red Corn. His parents, Judy Warrior and Allen Warrior, as well as other family members, deserve lost of thanks. Margaret Kelley, who was there from the early days of the authors deciding to write a book, deserves special mention. Since then, she has spent a lot of time listening, reading, and breathing it in various stages in the midst of her own important work. A thank you seems hardly enough for taking on those tough tasks.

Coauthor Smith also wishes to thank his parents, Clodus and Paula Smith, and many friends who listened patiently to lengthy explanations of the various ways in which writing a book is harder than it looks. Lynora Williams already knew that, and still never doubted these pages would be completed. Her extraordinary assistance is a major reason they were. Special thanks, for their inspiration at crucial moments, to Grace, Anna, and Jane Senko, and to Lakota Harden, whose stories about her Uncles Russ and Ted and their battered leather briefcases, which made him want to know more.

To all of these people and the many others who made this work possible, we express our deepest thanks.

Part One

Thunderbird University

Chapter 1

Leap of Faith

unning without lights to avoid detection, the trawler all but disappeared into the night as it left the docks of Sausalito behind and moved into the spectacular, foreboding waters of San Francisco Bay. The passengers—there were about a dozen—tried not to think about the possibility of being crushed by an oil tanker that didn't see them, or intercepted by a Coast Guard cutter that did. One of them felt like a soldier about to face combat for the first time. There wasn't much conversation.

During the early morning hours of November 20, 1969, the trawler, along with several other boats carrying dozens more young people, headed due southeast, bound for the abandoned prison island of Alcatraz. Breathtaking views appeared on all sides. During the forty-minute journey, the boats glided past the Golden Gate Bridge, thousands of suburban homes in the East Bay, and the hulking shadows of the Marin Headlands. San Francisco's unmistakable skyline—Coit Tower, the shimmering lights of Fisherman's Wharf, and the skyscrapers of the financial district—glimmered in the distance.

Wet sea winds from the Pacific, harsh and salty, swept over the boats. Those on board anxiously searched for the few lights that marked out their seventeen-acre island destination. From San Francisco, Alcatraz appeared a mysterious place, frequently enveloped in mist and fog. Most knew little of it but the familiar legends. Al Capone and Machine Gun Kelly. The Bird Man. The most impenetrable, escape-proof prison ever built, reserved for the nation's most dangerous criminals. The Rock. Only a cruel mile and a quarter from Fisherman's Wharf, but for those looking out through iron bars it might as well have been ten thousand.

The trawler from Sausalito landed on the east side of the island, where a water barge was docked to the wharf. Ed Castillo and the other passengers disembarked and quickly took off into the darkness. They were among the first to arrive.

Castillo, from the Juaneño tribe, taught Native American Studies at UCLA and had flown up from Los Angeles only that morning. Expecting the warm temperatures of his native southland, he wore a corduroy sports coat, jeans, a ribbon shirt, and a pair of moccasins. His luggage consisted of a blanket, a sleeping bag, a pillow, a toothbrush, and a backpack filled with books.

Castillo and three others wended their way to a fence by the exercise yard on the southwest side of the island. Scaling the high fence, they proceeded through the length of the beige cellblock on the highest point in the center of the island and made their way to the abandoned warden's house. Others from their boat were already there, warming themselves around a blazing fireplace. Periodically someone would sacrifice another chair to keep the flames alive.

Castillo was happy to see the fire. Alcatraz was cold.

As the first group arrived on the island, Anthony Garcia, an Apache student from Berkeley, and Dennis Turner, a UC Santa Cruz student from the Rincon tribe, boarded the schooner of an anesthesiologist to begin their thirty-mile journey from suburban Redwood City to Alcatraz. Turner and Garcia had met at a statewide Indian education conference at Cal State Chico in the summer of 1969. There, a contingent of college students decided to form their own organization, which had its first meeting at UC Santa Cruz in October.

They were young people whom the educational system neglected and, increasingly, they desired for themselves the same opportunities others had. They wanted programs, Indian faculty slots, and course offerings that highlighted the contributions of American Indians to knowledge and culture. They rallied to the suggestion of using Alcatraz as a way to dramatize their issues. Students from all over the state left their names and addresses with Garcia and Turner at the end of the conference, excited about the prospect of having their second meeting on Alcatraz. As Turner and Garcia landed on Alcatraz they could see no evidence that anyone else had preceded them.

"Anthony," said Turner as both of them became more and more jangled, "do you think anybody's here, or do you think we're it?" Garcia didn't know.

They passed cyclone fences by a stairway. As their eyes followed the stairs upward, they noticed an orange glow piercing the blackness. They stopped, transfixed by the light. The two slowly realized it had to be from a cigarette.

Laughter emanated from the darkness. Spooked, Turner demanded to know who was there. The cigarette smoker identified himself as a student from Santa Cruz. Turner and Garcia asked if the others had made it.

"Yeah, we're here," said the man with the cigarette.

The three waited together at the dock. "It's so quiet," Garcia said.

Through the night, boats had arrived, filtering in slowly from various routes. There in the darkness and cold, most people had their first experience of the treacherous concrete stairway that leads to the second tier of the island.

Garcia, a Vietnam vet with a passion for order, noticed most people had ignored his careful instructions to bring warm clothing and blankets. For now, few seemed to mind the cold as they sat by the furniture-fueled fireplace and traded stories of their amazing landings. If some forgot the suggested provisions, they remembered to bring others. Wine and marijuana turned the warden's house into a dorm room party.

Later, drums and singing from a victory powwow filled the air. The adrenaline rush of their feat kept it going for hours, and night turned to day with few of the seventy-eight occupiers getting much sleep.

When the sun rose they got their first good look at the place. And they must have marveled that they had made it safely to the top of the island, a virtual obstacle course of hazardous paths and crumbling stairways and buildings even in daylight.

Garcia, who had curled up in a dusty corner of a second-floor room in the early hours of the morning, was jolted awake by an un-welcome, disturbingly familiar thumping noise. For a blurry second he thought he was back in Vietnam. He moved to the window and saw a white and red helicopter hovering in the sky.

It disappeared, but not for long. The helicopter returned and seemed to be preparing to land on the large parade ground below the main cellblock area. "Don't let him land," Garcia yelled to the throng of occupiers who raced down to meet the craft, "we're not ready for them yet." Garcia and others quickly rolled trash cans onto the pa-rade ground to prevent the chopper from landing. The maneuver worked. Cheers rose from the yard as the uninvited visitor flew back to San Francisco.

Not ready yet, indeed.

As the sound of the helicopter's rotors faded, the spring break at-mosphere of the previous night gave way to a sobering reality. For the most part, the island's new residents were strangers to each other. Various sets of them had worked together for months planning for the landing, but many signed on at the last minute, dressed more for a weekend at a friend's house than what would become an extended oc-cupation of a crumbling prison. Food would become a crisis almost immediately, and other problems were not far behind.

The group assembled in the chapel of the main cellblock for their first meeting. They knew it wouldn't be long before more vis-itors arrived. Boats were probably already on their way, loaded with reporters, police, and government officials. The students wanted at-tention, and attention had arrived.

The seventy-eight young Indians—most of them college students—shivering on Alcatraz that November morning had to choose someone to speak for them. This decision, unlike others that would follow, proved to be easy. Few would argue that the man to stand in the spotlight was a charismatic Mohawk from San Francisco State, Richard Oakes. He would be their representative, and through him—in theory—they would speak in a single, unified, and defiant voice.

Like so many in California, Richard Oakes came from somewhere else. In this case, somewhere else was the St. Regis Reserve in New York, near the Canadian border. In the eleventh grade he quit school to become an ironworker, the profession of his father and uncle. For more than ten years he traveled all over the Northeast, earning good money, sometimes living on the reservation and sometimes in cities like Syracuse.

"I was working in Newport, Rhode Island, when I decided to go out to California," Oakes said in a magazine article on the occupation. "I was building a bridge at that time, working a long shift. I just decided to go to California, gave up everything, and drove right across the country."

His trip included visits to Indian reservations. "I had done a lot of reading about Indian people when I was back home, but I saw little of what I'd read about. There was a lot of talk about love and friendship for your fellow man, but I never saw it. What I saw instead was the bickering and barroom fights between the Indians; the constant drinking." Oakes theorized about why this was so. "Drinking seems to fill a void in the lives of many Indians. It takes the place of the singing of a song, the sharing of a song with another tribe. . . . Drinking is used as a way to *create* feelings of some kind where there aren't any. . . . I saw the end of the rainbow; the wrong end."

Ironically, his second job in San Francisco—after a brief stint driving a truck—was tending bar at Warren's, an Indian hangout in the Mission District. He found more drunks, more bar fights; but whether by design or accident the bar was also an ideal place for social investigation of the Bay Area's Indian community. Oakes claimed to be the only sober Indian at Warren's, and for him the job became a crash course in the many problems facing urban Indians.

He poured drinks and listened to sad tales of welfare dependency, bad housing, terrible pain, and isolation.

In early 1969 he enrolled at San Francisco State College. It was a season of chaos and revolution, and a Third World Strike raged on campus. Students demanded an education relevant to a world in crisis. Soon Oakes found himself recruiting his customers into becoming students in the college's new Native American Studies program.

Oakes possessed a natural boldness, good looks, and a commanding physical presence. People knew him as easy-going and friendly, a sympathetic guy with broad shoulders and a dazzling smile. But he had more than just that. Richard had depth. He was the genuine article, one of those fearless high-steel Mohawks you always heard about, standing above the clouds on the beam of a half-finished Manhattan skyscraper, not afraid of heights or much else, for that matter. He used to box, and you could tell from the way he carried himself that he probably wasn't just a bystander in all those tavern brawls he complained about. In addition to everything else, Oakes was a family man, married to a woman named Anne from a California tribe. Anne had five children when they married, and Richard loved those kids as if they were his own.

As a student leader, he traveled the state in 1969, meeting with others who were also pioneers in this new program called Native American Studies. They were a tiny part of the ethnic studies revolution, being offered just a few faculty spots while African-American students got dozens. Oakes, like lots of others, dreamed of bigger things.

The Bay Area Indian community Oakes joined was one of the largest in the nation, and that was no accident. The American government developed programs during the 1950s to move Indian people from reservations to cities, to assimilate them as quickly as possible, and to undermine reservation life.

This was a departure from earlier policies. Only a few decades earlier, Franklin Roosevelt's New Deal proposed an agenda for Indians so unique that some in Congress attacked it as communistic. John Collier, a progressive New York social worker, served as Roosevelt's Indian Commissioner. An admirer of Indian culture, he believed that not only should Indians be encouraged to maintain traditions but even proposed legislation that would have provided funds for tribes to expand their land base. Those reforms, once they finally emerged underfunded and scaled back from a Congress that did not share Collier's enlightened views of native civilization, were a mixed blessing for Indian people. But there was little ambivalence in the policies that followed.

President Truman appointed Dillon S. Myer to be Commissioner of Indian Affairs in 1950 on the strength of his performance as head of the War Relocation Authority during World War II. Under Myer's direction, the federal government interred more than 120,000 Japanese Americans in harsh conditions for the duration of the war. Myer made a special point of widely distributing these camps around the West in order to prevent the creation of "Little Tokyos" after the war.

As Indian Commissioner, Myer stepped up efforts to end the government's involvement in Indian work and assimilate his changes into American life as rapidly as possible. Using lists that like-minded people in Congress had drawn up in 1946, the agency targeted tribes it considered ready to survive on their own. Indian reservations, with an acknowledged government-to-government relationship to the United States, would disappear, and the areas would fall under the jurisdiction of whatever states and counties they were in—a policy ominously named termination.

Simultaneously, the government pursued a related policy called relocation, through which it encouraged Indians to abandon their lives on reservations for supposedly brighter futures in America's booming cities. At Bureau of Indian Affairs (BIA) field offices on reservations, posters showed Indians in hardhats building airplanes and going home at night to new homes with modern kitchens, sparking appliances, and television sets. The BIA offered a one-way bus ticket, assistance in finding work, and housing and free medical care for a year.

Commissioner Myer and his successors also aggressively promoted the adoption of Indian children by white families. There was no attempt to place Indian children with Indian families; instead Myer appealed to church groups to understand the need for Indian children to "have the advantages of a normal home and family environment, which should be the birthright of every American youngster."

One BIA official in Washington state reported on the reaction of people at the Colville reservation to Myer's efforts: "They seem to feel that the program is a government means to move the Indians from the reservation in order to allow white operators to exploit the reservation and eventually force all Indians from the reservation areas."

Earl Old Person, a leader of the National Congress of American Indians, the largest national Indian organization, spoke for many. "It is important to note that in our ... language the only translation for termination is to 'wipe out' or 'kill off.' We have no ... words for termination. . . . Why is it so important that Indians be brought into the 'mainstream of American life'? . . . The closest I would be able to come to 'mainstream' would be to say, in [my language], 'a big, wide river.' Am I to tell my people that they will be 'thrown into the Big, Wide River of the United States?'"

Opposition came from others as well. Harold Ickes, who had been Secretary of the Interior under both Roosevelt and Truman and who had been John Collier's boss in the 1930s and 1940s, wrote "So far as our American Indians are concerned, Commissioner Dillon Myer of the Bureau of Indian Affairs is a Hitler and Mussolini rolled into one."

The criticism had little impact. The wish to terminate, relocate, and assimilate Indians had powerful support in the U.S. Congress. Myer would be gone by 1953, replaced by a banker from New Mexico, but during the 1950s the process of terminating several tribes would begin, with disastrous results. More than thirty-five thousand Indians moved to urban areas between 1952 and 1960. Originally the BIA sent them to Denver, Los Angeles, Phoenix, and Salt Lake City. By 1957 the program included Albuquerque, San Francisco, Chicago, Dallas, Tulsa, and Oklahoma City.

The program rarely lived up to the promises in the BIA propaganda. Jobs were hard to find and hard to keep, housing expensive. The cities were lonely places, and Indians generally ended up in ghetto neighborhoods. Nearly a third of those who rode the bus on the Bureau's dime returned to the reservation. Most, however, stayed, for reasons that had little to do with the grand designs of Dillon Myer and his fellow assimilationists. And why not? Reservation life was hard, and no Indian needed a BIA program to learn that.

Adam Nordwall was the kind of Indian the federal bureaucracy hoped relocation would create. A Red Lake Chippewa from Minnesota, he moved from his reservation home to the Bay Area in 1951. A temporary job with an exterminating company led to promotions and a state license. By 1969 he owned his own business, the First American Termite Company. Nordwall lived in suburban San Leandro with his wife Bobbie, a Shoshone from Nevada, and three children. He drove a Cadillac and employed fifteen people.

His story may have proved it could be done, but as it happened, the Bureau had nothing to do with it. He came to the Bay Area in the early 1950s, not because of the BIA's relocation program but because of the Korean War. Expecting him to be drafted, Nordwall's mother asked her son to move to San Francisco and be with her during his remaining time in civilian life. The call never came. Nordwall stayed.

He emerged as one of the local leaders responsible for developing programs for newcomers from reservation communities since the 1950s, when the only Bay Area meeting places for Indians were bars or government offices. In 1961 the Quakers, a denomination with a long and mixed history with Indians, established the Intertribal Friendship House in Oakland, and for the first time the community had a center for its activities. This inspired Nordwall and others to create an Indian organization called the United Bay Area Council of American Indian Affairs, Incorporated (United Council, for short). The group prided itself on sound fiscal management and strict adherence to parliamentary procedure. Existing social clubs made up most of the membership, and they included the Navajo Club, the Haskell Alumni, the Haida Tlingit Club, and the Four Winds Club. The groups offered fellowship and traditional singing and dancing, and a chance to speak one's tribal language or learn it. The United Council threw parties at Christmas and feasts at Thanksgiving. They tried to cushion the shock reservation people experienced when the tough realities of the relocation program pushed the new arrivals to despair and drink.

The growing group of transplanted Indian people Nordwall and other middle-class leaders worked to keep organized and stabilized were Navajo and Pomo, Eskimo and Comanche. Plenty of Sioux still hated their ancient enemies, the Crows, and many Crows didn't think much of the Sioux. Some of the established ones believed the newer arrivals from reservations were just looking for a handout, not willing to work hard the way they did. Most were Christians; others maintained urbanized versions of tribal traditions or followed the Native American Church. Sometimes, invisibility and isolation seemed to be all they had in common. But over the years, at Indian centers in San Francisco, Oakland, and San Jose, and at powwows and down-and-out bars, they forged a community. By 1964, plenty of people in the community were ready to make at least a dent in their invisibility.

In 1962, after the federal government decided to close the federal prison on Alcatraz, citing the facility's high maintenance cost and deteriorating condition, Nordwall and others took notice. At United Council meetings people brought up treaty provisions that promised surplus or abandoned federal property to Indian tribes. With surplus federal property in plain sight, further research led them to conclude this right was not universal to all Indians, but specific to the Sioux, whose Fort Laramie Treaty of 1868 granted the tribe surplus federal land.

On March 8, 1964, forty Indians traveled to Alcatraz by boat and claimed the island. A Sioux housepainter named Allen Cottier, a descendant of Crazy Horse, read a statement offering forty-seven cents per acre to purchase Alcatraz. This was the same amount California was then offering Indian tribes in the state for land claims dating back to the past century. Joining him were other Sioux people, including two welders named Richard McKenzie and Mark Martinez. Walter Means, who worked at the navy shipyard at Mare Island, brought his twenty-six-year-old son, Russell. They marched slowly behind an American flag. Some wore feathered headdresses.

They, frankly, saw the action as a publicity stunt, and never thought of a long-term occupation. They likely knew the treaty claim was tenuous in its specifics, but they were quite serious about the central point: treaties were not irrelevant and Indians had not forgotten them. Nordwall marched with them. His job was to arrange press coverage.

The next day's *San Francisco Examiner* and *Oakland Tribune* carried stories about the event that discussed treaty rights and the insulting forty-seven-cent solution the state offered its natives. And although one article called the invasion "wacky," what the Indians remembered, especially the increasingly savvy Ojibway—more often called Chippewa, especially in the 1960s—businessman Adam Nordwall, is that the stories ran at all.

The promised lawsuits to acquire title never materialized, and few outside the American Indian community in the Bay Area thought much of the event. But that ephemeral protest electrified many Bay Area Indians. Alcatraz captured their imagination and never let go. The 1964 landing became part of the community's oral history.

Nordwall and others brooded about Alcatraz when they drove across the Golden Gate Bridge and saw it through the fog, empty, just waiting there, or at night when the lighthouse cut through the dark; foghorn blowing. Reformed, the island with a bad reputation now warned ships of disaster. Yet, it seemed capable of so much more. It was a potential crown jewel in one of the planet's most legendary and beautiful cities.

By the middle of 1969, the question of what should be done with Alcatraz had become one of San Francisco's hottest parlor games. The suggestions included the construction of a West Coast version of the Statue of Liberty, a refuge for abandoned pets, and a gambling casino.

H. Lamar Hunt, an oilman from Houston, Texas, proposed a vast complex of apartments, shops, and restaurants. He would offer tours of a restored prison and build a futuristic museum on space exploration. That spring, the San Francisco Board of Supervisors voted to consider Hunt's concept, launching a wave of protests from Bay Area citizens and moving the issue to the front pages of the newspapers.

Hunt's plan threatened to interfere with nebulous plans Adam

Nordwall and his confederates at the United Council had been devising for the island. Over the years since the 1964 landing, they had
planned to write up a proposal and file applications in the hope that
this abandoned federal site could be used as a community center
for Indian people. All that changed as they found themselves in
competition with one of the richest men in America. Clearly, their
proposals wouldn't have a chance next to his. Other measures would
be required.

For months during the summer of 1969, Adam Nordwall, a community leader, and Richard Oakes, a student activist, became independently obsessed with winning the island for Indian people. In
their respective circles, they talked up the idea, and kept tabs on each
other from afar. The two knew each other only by reputation, and
made no attempt to meet or work together. Oakes could not have
been impressed with the businessman and his big car, nor his organization, which was tame by his campus radical standards. Nordwall
seemed like precisely the kind of leader that had failed Richard's
customers at Warren's. And for Nordwall, with decades of civic work
behind him, the sudden appearance of this student militant—only
recently arrived from New York—could only have raised all sorts of
yellow flags.

Although the two had little in common, they both took seriously
an idea that on its face seemed dubious, if not incredible. Oakes and
Nordwall may have imagined sharply different visions of the kind
of center they wanted on the island, but they agreed on the basic concept. Faced with a problem some would see as modest (after all,
Indians were one of many minorities seeking a building to provide
services to their people in a modern, progressive city), they believed
the best course of action was to invade and occupy a decaying prison
reached only by boat, a place the federal government itself couldn't
afford to maintain. This was the place Indians planned to build a
community center for people who counted themselves lucky if they
owned a car. It was almost as if a collective hallucination had drifted
over from the Haight.

If the planners needed a goad, they got one on October 10, when
the San Francisco Indian Center burned to the ground. The loss was

devastating; mourned almost like a death in the family. Suddenly Indians had no place of their own. The nagging problem of facilities to meet the needs of the area's expanding Indian community became a crisis.

A few weeks later, Nordwall and Oakes finally met. The occasion had a touch of the bizarre about it. For one thing, it was at a Halloween party. For another, the party was at the home of a *San Francisco Chronicle* reporter, Tim Findley. Nordwall told a roomful of journalists all about the planned invasion, including the date, and then swore them to secrecy. Richard Oakes was there only because Findley invited him.

Findley knew Nordwall from covering Indians for the *Chronicle*. When Nordwall had asked for advice on how to publicize an upcoming event, an event he promised would be "something big," Findley had suggested the party, since reporters would be there from other newspapers as well as radio and television. He added that he planned to invite Richard and Anne Oakes as well.

At the party, Nordwall told Oakes of his plans and asked if he would join the effort. Oakes immediately said he would. Then Nordwall briefed the reporters, warning that if the news broke before November ninth—the date of the action—the landing would be called off.

The reporters seemed interested and sympathetic. But Nordwall wondered about his new ally. He was taken aback at how quickly Oakes agreed to join forces. He also felt the student leader handled himself badly, drinking too much and becoming belligerent.

Despite that unpleasantness, the evening accomplished everything the older leader hoped for. The students were on board, and the news media was alerted. It was all falling into place. Nordwall could begin making phone calls to arrange the boats. As for Oakes, he may have left the party a little inebriated, but he was clear on one thing: He had no intention of being a bit player in some Adam Nordwall–led, media-sanctioned event.

Oakes continued to organize in the student network for an action independent of Nordwall's. Most of the planning took place at San Francisco State and UC Berkeley. At one meeting Oakes brought a lawyer, Aubrey Grossman, to help them sort out the legal questions. Did they really have a leg to stand on with this Sioux Treaty argument? Could they argue that Indians had a generic right to abandoned federal property? Would they be arrested? Could they end up with a prison sentence? Grossman, a progressive involved in land issues of the Pit River tribe north of San Francisco, encouraged them to stage the occupation and told them to let attorneys like him worry about all the legal implications later.

Meetings and logistics were not among Oakes's strengths. For these, Anthony Garcia, among others, carried the ball. In personality they were opposites, and their differences complemented each other. Where Oakes craved the spotlight, Garcia stayed in the shadows. Garcia loved order and planning and attention to detail, while Oakes focused on the big picture.

Others had good organizational skills and were reliable and level-headed, but Oakes grew impatient with explanations of why it would require weeks to find boats, attract sympathetic reporters, and make sure everyone had enough warm clothes and food. He wanted to get it on. Now. The student network moved into high gear. In classrooms late at night, students filled blackboards with maps of the Bay, lists of staging areas, and contingency plans.

All too soon the calendar read November 9, D Day for Nordwall's occupation plan, and Oakes, despite being a ringleader in other plans for the island, had to deal with the promise he had made at Tim Findley's party.

On that morning, Adam Nordwall drove with his family from his home in San Leandro to San Francisco's Fisherman's Wharf, got dressed head to toe in his best powwow clothes, and was confident that five charter boats, gassed up and ready to go, were waiting at Pier 39.

He arrived to find the worst scenario imaginable: a large and restless press corps, an anxious crowd of Indians, and the shouted question, "Where the hell are the boats?"

Their transports were supposed to be at the Harbor Tours dock but were nowhere in sight. Nordwall stalled for time trying to find a solution. Richard Oakes suggested that students read the Proclamation—a document that explained the action—to the news media. Nordwall agreed, then looked for a phone.

He didn't have long. As if to underscore the obvious, Tim Findley walked over and pointed to a boat on the water near Alcatraz, and told Nordwall film crews were already in position on board to record the actual landing.

The students dragged out the reading of the proclamation as much as they could, using three different speakers, but even that lengthy exercise came to an end. Singing and dancing followed, but the media knew something was up, and clearly would not wait much longer.

Nordwall's phone calls finally produced a willing boat, and the skipper promised to be right over, but long minutes passed and he failed to appear. People were starting to leave. The November sun, low in the western sky, cast long shadows over the pier.

As Nordwall contemplated his seemingly imminent disgrace, he noticed a beautiful, perfectly restored three-masted schooner preparing to cast off. Bearing the name *Monte Cristo* and gleaming with polished brass, it might have sailed straight out of a movie screen. The captain, an attractive man dressed in white, matched the boat perfectly. His ruffled shirt, tight-fitting pants, and long blond hair made Nordwall think of Erroll Flynn.

With nowhere else to go, the Indian in beads and buckskin and moccasins padded over to the captain dressed like a pirate, and asked for help.

Thirty minutes later they were off, literally to the sound of cannons. The *Monte Cristo* even had those. Spectators cheered and waved. The Indians brought a drum, and soon the high pitch of Plains war songs floated across the water as they headed to Alcatraz, escorted by boats filled with reporters on each side.

Nordwall marveled at his swift change in fortune. The press coverage would be awesome, and their splendid ship guaranteed fabulous pictures. There would be no landing—the captain, a Canadian named Ronald Craig, would agree only to circle the island—but this symbolic claim on Alcatraz was a lot better than nothing. Landing or no landing, Nordwall thought, what a marvelous event, what an exhilarating day.

As the boat neared the island and the Ojibway businessman

reflected on how quickly things could change, Richard Oakes quietly removed his shirt and jumped over the railing.

His plunge into the Bay stunned those watching from the deck of the *Monte Cristo*. Shouts filled the air. The captain, panicked at the sight of the thrashing Mohawk, insisted everyone stay put.

They ignored the captain. Splash. Another one, then two more Indians jumped.

As Oakes knifed his way through the frigid waters toward Alcatraz, shocked by the strength of the current and the temperature of the bay, all he could dare think about was making it to the shore. The island was 250 yards away. He swam desperately, fighting just to survive.

The *Monte Cristo* turned away from the island, preventing further disobedience, but it was too late. Richard Oakes had jumped ship. He was having none of the "symbolic" claiming of the island. He insisted on the real thing. He was tired of doing things only for publicity.

In an hour he and the others would be back at Fisherman's Wharf, still shivering, returned by the Coast Guard. Instead of failure, Oakes felt exhilaration. Taking Alcatraz suddenly became real, possible, even inevitable. Until then, Alcatraz had been a dream. His leap of faith was extraordinary, but what really mattered is that other people followed him. At that moment the long occupation of Alcatraz could be said to have begun. Richard Oakes changed the rules. The carefully scripted media event was out of control, and he, not Adam Nordwall, would write the next act.

Tim Findley's story in the *San Francisco Chronicle* ran just below the fold on page one. It called the four who jumped from the yacht "braves," quoted generously from the proclamation, gave Nordwall his due, and made no mention of the Halloween party.

Oakes and thirteen others returned to Alcatraz the very night of the *Monte Cristo* episode, taking a boat from Sausalito and spending the night hiding from the caretaker and his dog. They left the next morning, after claiming the island and telling the federal administrator who arrived with reporters that they would be back.

They hailed the two unsuccessful attempts at occupation as

scouting expeditions. The experience also taught Oakes that he needed more people to make an occupation work, so he traveled to UCLA and talked to forty members of the student group there into joining in. One person, however, he could do without. Adam Nord-wall, as it happened, would be out of town on November 20, attending a national conference on Indian education.

That would be the date of the real assault.

Chapter 2

We Won't Move

ichard Oakes's leap into San Francisco Bay was but one strand in the tangled web of multiple landings, competing leaders, and last-minute recruiting trips to expand the number of occupiers that led to the landing on Alcatraz of seventy-eight Indian people on November 20, 1969. In contrast to the complications of getting there, the week or so following that morning when the students chose Oakes as their spokesperson was remarkably straightforward. Almost immediately, the Coast Guard blockaded the island, making reinforcements and fresh supplies difficult to come by. On a few occasions, the Coast Guard attempted to land at the dock, but the young radicals—including a healthy number of combat-seasoned Vietnam vets—held them at bay.

Beyond those standoffs at the dock and the momentary excitement of an occasional boat attempting to run the blockade, the main activity on the island was coordinating the task of making Alcatraz liveable. As the occupiers did so, their stated ideal was unity, perhaps reflected best in the name they chose for themselves—Indians of All Tribes. To Luwana Quitiquit, a Pomo who worked as a secretary in the Native American Studies office at Berkeley, "That's exactly what it was. We all had things to offer each other. Brotherhood. Sisterhood."

Their choice of Oakes as their spokesperson rather than their leader on the first morning was a reflection of their ideals of unity and consensus and a rejection of the idea of hierarchy. And, when it became clear in the first few days that they would need more structure, they agreed to have a coordinating council that would organize people into groups to do the work necessary to keep seventy-eight people fed and safe.

But plenty of the young occupiers had drunk deeply from the well of anarchism popular among student radicals of the time, and even the nebulous structure of a coordinating council was, to them, too much. Why should just one person talk to the press, they thought, when they were all risking their lives and enduring the hardships? Almost as if programmed to defy authority in any form, the group would appoint someone to coordinate an activity such as unloading supplies from the dock, then shun the newly anointed coordinator's pleas for assistance. Who was he to boss them around? In a telling move, the group elected Ed Castillo, the young professor of Native American studies at UCLA, to be in charge of "security." Weighing in at 115 pounds, he was supposed to go around and tell groups of strapping young Indian guys not to drink or do drugs. After a few days, and one too many threats of bodily harm, he resigned.

But whatever problems existed were relatively minor, and the first few days were full of activity as people found places to sleep, prepared meals, talked to the hordes of reporters, and got the lay of the land. Kids played. Those with a stash—and a lot of people had one—got stoned after the reporters left each day to make their deadlines. Mostly, the emerging celebrities sat around a drum or in small groups, and sang and talked until they were ready for bed.

Couples, many of whom had met on the island, would sit and watch the sunset, then find a spot where they could see the lights of Bay Bridge go on one by one. To Quitiquit it felt like, "Here we are, we are free. There's no laws here. We don't have to conform to any laws. Only the laws we make for ourselves." With the Coast Guard blockade limiting access to the island, their anarchic utopia was fairly benign. Some scuffles, some bad feelings. And if someone had managed to sneak alcohol onto the island with them, it certainly was not enough for things to get out of hand—just enough to add a layer to the mellow zone of a pot high.

From the press they were getting, though, they didn't need anything much to get them high. From the start, most Bay Area newspapers loved the occupation, offering as it did a colorful escape from bad news such as shocking revelations of the Song My and My Lai massacres in Vietnam. As the federal government garnered its forces for what many expected to be a counterinvasion and ouster of the occupiers, UC Santa Cruz student leader Dennis Turner told the press that the young Indians wouldn't put up a fight. They wouldn't need to, he said. Since they were the "invisible Americans," no one would be able to find them.

With the San Francisco Board of Supervisors talking about passing legislation in support of the occupation, the cast of the musical *Hair* passing a hat at performances in support of the action, and donations of food, clothing, and money pouring into a new San Francisco Indian Center that was a temporary replacement for the one that had burned down in October, no one was too eager to make a misstep. And as each day passed, the idea that they might stay and make something useful out of this crumbling piece of real estate made more and more sense.

As people began settling in, Luwana Quitiquit, the secretary from Berkeley, couldn't believe that some people were actually choosing the dank, cold cells in the main cellblock as homes. With other families, she moved with her children into the warden's house. Still later, those families, including Richard and Anne Oakes and their five children, would move into apartments that had once housed prison guards and their families.

Quitiquit, along with Linda Aranaydo, a Creek and a student at Berkeley, was in charge of feeding the occupation forces. On a concrete plaza that led to the visiting and administration areas, less than one hundred yards from a kitchen full of stoves, ovens, and other appliances, the two women cooked over an open fire. It wasn't for cultural reasons. Rather, all the utilities were off and the kitchen was behind heavy iron bars.

Like the others, she did find time in those first days to do some exploring of the more than a dozen standing buildings on the island. In a room housing a power generator that kept duty rosters for guards, she found a blank, army-green logbook.

Quitiquit realized it would be perfect for registering people. She felt convinced that the occupation would be a historical event, and that the book would someday be a valuable artifact. She took the book, wrote some words to the effect of the historical importance of what it would record, and wrote her own name, her tribe, and the date—November 22, 1969.

The press shared the sentiment that the occupation was history in the making. Alcatraz rode an ocean of goodwill that seemed boundless. The whirlwind of media attention left Indians of All Tribes with a growing tide of donated money, food, and clothing, a steady influx of permanent and weekend reinforcements, and press clippings from far away places like England. They were a sensation, and so far had overcome every obstacle with pluck and creativity.

With all of the good feelings, the occupiers decided an open house was in order. They would invite the world to see true civilization amidst the ruins of barbarism, dignity and grace overcoming the childish war games of a brutish and uncaring government. A day for the new nation to shine. For the people of the Rock, for whom no amount of irony could ever be too much, the perfect date for this event was coming right up—Thanksgiving.

When the day arrived, Indians from around the Bay Area streamed onto the island for a feast and to see it all for themselves. Gladys Ellenwood, her kids dressed in dance clothes, waited patiently in line for the boat from Pier 39. She was one of thousands of Bay Area Indian residents who had migrated over the previous decade through the Bureau of Indian Affairs relocation program. She and her husband had come from Idaho with the promise of vocational training, a job, and all the trappings of American upward mobility.

But the Bureau never sent her husband to vocational school, and instead of building airplanes or some other high-paying job, he worked as a busboy in San Mateo. Like other relocatees, the disappointments of relocation led him to Warren's and the other Indian bars that sprang up in the hard-luck sections of San Francisco. They eventually ended what was becoming a more and more abusive relationship. Gladys remarried and had four more kids to add to the three she already had. After that didn't work out, she ended up raising the children, "pretty much on my own. I didn't want to go on welfare, but eventually I did. I had a good job, but couldn't find anyone to baby-sit."

She and her sons became involved in the burgeoning powwow and Indian Center scene that drew Indian people together from all over the area. Families like the Ellenwoods gathered at community centers in Oakland, San Francisco, and San Jose, and camped together at powwows up and down the coast. Her sons became popular and competitive dancers, even spending a summer in a traveling show.

For people like the Ellenwoods, Alcatraz would become an extension of the city life they had developed. On Thanksgiving and on the later weekends when she would bring her kids over, Gladys sat and talked with other Indian people while the children ran around like mad.

Thanksgiving was her first trip to the island. When she arrived, she saw a sea of cooked turkeys—turkeys on the dock, turkeys in the exercise yard where the feast was laid, turkeys everywhere. And she heard the sound of drums. Hundreds of Indian people celebrated their sudden fame and the offering of goodwill by people and organizations in the area.

A local restaurant, Bratskellar's, had volunteered to cater the affair. Non-Indians showed up at the dock bearing gifts of food and water. It was clear that the Indians of All Tribes had touched a soft spot in the heart of many in the Bay Area.

Castillo and the other occupiers greeted those coming across. They would share the standard information—their names, where they were from, what tribe—and the students who had come from far away beamed in another spotlight, this time that of the local Indian people whom they had come to support.

Beyond being elated at the prospect of a feast, Castillo and the others believed all the stronger in their dreams of what their actions meant for them and other Indians around the country. Then, as Castillo was using his halting French to speak to a foreign reporter, a cry came up from the dock. The press left their interviewees in mid-sentence and went to see what the commotion was.

Approaching the island was another boatload of Indians. This one had Adam Nordwall on its prow, standing like George Washington crossing the Delaware, as if to reassert his place of prominence in the occupation. He was wearing his powwow dance outfit—lots of bangles, a beaded headband with strings of beads that looped from the middle of his forehead to his cheekbones then to his temples, a ribbon shirt, beaded armbands, and a porcupine quill roach headdress that cascaded up from his forehead and down his back. He stood stoically. Then, upon landing, struck a triumphant pose, arms raised above his head as if to say, "I have arrived."

Castillo and other students glared at him with disbelief and contempt as the cameras rolled. But Thanksgiving belonged to no one if not everyone. Street toughs from San Francisco's Tenderloin district, down-and-outers from Warren's Bar, single-parent welfare families like Gladys Ellenwood and her children, and just plain Indian folks joined the scraggly students and photogenic old people. The food kept coming, the drums kept a steady beat, and everything seemed just right. Even the weather was less harsh than usual. Later in the day, a boat pulled up with a band on it playing rock and roll. They powered their amps with car batteries. As the sun went down, Bay Area Indians knew they were part of something big. And so did their friends from reservations and urban areas from around the country who were following the Alcatraz story in the media or who were piling into cars and heading west.

With the occupation receiving so much attention, Richard Oakes had become a celebrity. His picture was flashed around the world and he was often the focus of news stories. Writers said he looked like Victor Mature. A young woman answering phones for the occupation at the temporary San Francisco Indian Center tearfully said he was the greatest Indian since Tecumseh. All things considered, Oakes seemed to be handling it all amazingly well.

Three weeks into the occupation, wearing a button that said "We won't move," he embraced his wife Anne against the endless cold and wind. They huddled in front of the warden's residence. In a conversation with a reporter, surrounded by Anne and their five children, he called the prison a symbol of hope, a monument for the living. "We're only young people concerned about our future," he said. "These are the future leaders of most of these tribes." And, "we might—might—just wake up the conscience of America."

Oakes spoke of planned facilities for the island once Indians of All Tribes received free and clear title to it from the federal government: the Center for Native American Studies, the American Indian Spiritual Center, the Indian Center of Ecology, the Indian Training School, and the American Indian Museum.

A sailboat drifted by, and gawking spectators shouted "woo, woo, woo!" The young leader was nonchalant. "It's hard to say whether they're friend or foe. We get quite a bit of harassment from sailboats and cabin cruisers. But I'll wave at them anyway." He had harsh words for no one and only one complaint. "Our biggest problems are freelance photographers and the hippies. They stay and eat up our stores, then leave. Then we have to clean up after them."

What about the problems of governing the new nation that had opened its doors to all Indians? Oakes answered this way: "We have the ultimate punishment for any Indian on our island. We ask him to leave." Those words would come back to haunt him.

"There's a sad neglect of all the different tribal cultures," he said in another interview. "Ten years from now, there may not be anybody out on the reservation to retain our culture and to be able to relate it. So, this is actually a move, not so much to liberate the island, but to liberate ourselves for the sake of cultural survival."

"The sad fact about the non-Indian world is that most of it is not based on the truth," he said. And, as if he were using the island as a prop, he continued, "that's why it's going to fall, to crumble. It's crumbling now, it's falling apart..."

"I speak as a youth, and I speak as a spokesman for the people on the island here," he concluded, "and we are ready to start listening to the old people. Leave the land that has caused so much trouble and heartbreak, and come to a neutral area; and leave with us the knowledge so we can teach your children."

Though Oakes and other occupiers clung to ambitious dreams of altering the consciousness of Indian children everywhere, they may have had little notion of the hundreds of small ways in which they would stir the hearts of many of their Indian contemporaries. One day at work arranging displays at Design Research, a home furnishings store, one Seneca was startled into a silent reverence for the occupiers when he least expected it. Pete Jemison looked out from his workplace to see, across the Bay, a splash of red among the rocks that rivaled the boldness of the colorful Marimekko fabrics he arranged to catch the eyes of wealthy customers. Jemison realized that the occupiers had painted the entire side of a building on the island, and the fiery hue spoke to him in a way that none of Oakes's or his companions' defiant rhetoric ever could.

The potency of their message wasn't limited to the Bay Area. In early December, San Francisco mayor Joseph Alioto returned from a trip to Europe and held a news conference. He told reporters they had no idea how much publicity the occupation received there. "Everywhere I went I was asked about Alcatraz and the Indians."

By three weeks in, the occupation had become a freewheeling event that no spokesperson, coordinating council, or reporter could keep track of. Among the new recruits were people who brought valuable expertise to the island. In their daily updates of activity on the island, newspapers reported a generator was hooked up and running, thirty-five toilets repaired, a fishing spot located and a mess of red snapper caught, and a film company donated twenty-eight tepees. The rock band Creedence Clearwater Revival paid for a boat, and the occupiers named it the *Clearwater.*

Meanwhile, the council set about trying to plan and coordinate storage and distribution of food and clothing, planning a conference for later in the month, seeking support from tribal governments and Indian organizations around the country, and producing documents that explained the goals and purposes of the occupation. They also had to keep track of several benefit concerts to raise money and visibility. One concert took place at Stanford University on December 18, and featured Cree folksinger Buffy Sainte-Marie.

The opulence of the Stanford Memorial Church stood in stark contrast to the deteriorating Rock. Driving up the Palm Drive onto campus, the church is the focal point of the view. The ornate church's towering facade, featuring colorful gilt-framed mosaics of Faith,

Hope, Charity, and Love, intricate Spanish Revival masonry, and stained-glass windows that were covered in mesh to protect them from rock-throwing student protestors, welcomed the occupiers and their supporters that night.

There, in a church dedicated to the memory of one of Northern California's robber barons, Alcatraz would show its public face, a face that could stare defiantly into the eyes of America and proclaim Indians as not vanished, not quiet, and not about to allow ignorance, paternalism, or a hundred other protests and actions to keep their handful of scraggly protesters in the shadows.

Inside the church, among hardwood pews, marble pulpits, vaulted ceilings, and Old World sculptures, Adam Nordwall was master of ceremonies. Some on the island considered him an opportunistic publicityhound, taking credit for the occupation without enduring the hardships of island life, but on this night the smooth-talking businessman was in his element. In front of an anticipatory audience of hundreds, his comfortable, soothing baritone provided a counterpoint to the hard-edged words and voices of the occupation.

"I would like to invite to the stage a young lady who has been on the Rock quite a bit," Nordwall said in introducing Shirley Keith. "Come on, ladies and gentlemen."

Keith approached the mike and spoke without the stage presence of Nordwall, but with passion and commitment. "Uh, I am going to tell you why we are not leaving the Rock and why it's ours," she began. "I am going to be very brief about this.

"We call ourselves out there the Indians of All Tribes. That is pretty significant. This is one of the first political pan-Indian movements in this country." Perhaps other things had united Indians across tribal lines in the past, Keith argued, but to her those had almost always been about powwows and Indian centers. Alcatraz was about that and more—it was politics. Alcatraz was about creating a space not just for dancing, but for building an Indian future.

She offered a promise. "This is going to become even more evident on December 23 when we have a confederation of American Indian nations, from every tribe, nation, and band on Alcatraz. We are giving our pan-Indianism a political definition."

Chances are, most people in the audience that night had no frame of reference for Keith's remarks. A few applauded when she said, "Let me tell you first of all that you can take the credit for us being on Alcatraz because you and your government forced our backs against the wall." They had heard that kind of anger before. But as she spoke of the occupation's objectives more specifically, Keith began losing her audience. "We're out there to create a starting point for basic changes in Indian-white relations. We reject the alternatives of the federal Indian policy. We reject either extermination of our cultures, which we refuse to have end up on museum walls for the pleasure of non-Indians. We reject the chronic and cyclical poverty of reservations and the relocation transfer of that poverty into Red Ghettoes in the cities. We reject these alternatives. This is why there's no more end of the trail for us. We're on a new trail. We're creating our own alternatives!"

Keith spoke of treaties, relocation, and federal policy, but the audience reacted with most fervor to her parallels and symbolism: The Indian situation is comparable to Vietnam, or to the Holocaust. The occupiers of Alcatraz had gained unprecedented visibility, but how much was the price of that visibility living life as a metaphor?

"We reject the fact that your government thinks it can legislate us out of existence," said Keith that night, "that it can legislate what it wants, when it wants, and how it wants, with the complete disregard for the Indian people's treaty rights, tribal rights, human rights, civil rights, and any other rights—not privileges, rights—and that is why we are staying and we are not moving." With that, and a soft thank you over the ensuing applause, Keith made way for the entertainment portion of the program.

The opening act was Malvina Reynolds, a folk singer best known for her protest song against the endless replication of suburban life, "Little Boxes." In honor of Alcatraz, she had written a new song, full of shallow references to Indian spiritualism and a refrain that took a shot at Lamar Hunt, the Houston oilman with big plans for the island. As Reynolds said, what the island needed was a return to an earlier time: "When the Indians had their day / Who needs an Astrodome in San Francisco Bay?"

The evening's eagerly awaited headliner was Buffy Sainte-Marie, a Cree folksinger with broad appeal, whose music cut to the heart of the modern Indian dilemma. Her songs "Now That the Buffalo's Gone" and "My Country 'Tis of Thy People are Dying" were stirring indictments of a society that had yet to confront its mythologies of Indians being artifacts of the past rather than people with a present and a future.

As Buffy ended her set, the crowd applauded appreciatively. They had seen the heroes of Alcatraz. They had heard from Indians on the front line, and songs from a star of the folk world. Then, from the wings came a man bearing flowers for Buffy. They exchanged words as Nordwall came to the mike.

"Ladies and gentlemen," he said, "I am sure this is an occasion in which all of us are thankful that Malvina and Buffy could be here. By the way, the young man that presented Buffy with the flowers, I'd like to ask him out. I'm sure that many of you did not recognize who he was, but I'd like to have you all meet Richard Oakes of Alcatraz."

Here in the flesh was the biggest star of Alcatraz. The audience settled back to hear what he had to say. Surely it would be a lot.

"Thank you," Oakes began. "Thank you people for giving us the chance, the opportunity to express ourselves; the young people. And we thank very much the people of Alcatraz. Thanks very much. Thank you." He paused, and with his voice trailing off, "That's all I can say."

Nordwall would take care of filling the room with words. He saved his biggest laughs for last and before the evening was over, made Alcatraz the turning point in Indian history.

He read the Alcatraz Proclamation:

Proclamation:

We, the Native Americans, reclaim the land known as Alcatraz Island in the name of all American Indians by right of discovery.

We wish to be fair and honorable in our dealings with the Caucasian inhabitants of this land, and hereby offer the following treaty:

We will purchase said Alcatraz Island for twenty-four dollars (24) in glass beads and red cloth, a precedent set by the white man's purchase of a similar island about 300 years ago.

We will give to the inhabitants of this island a portion of the land for their own to be held in trust by the American Indian Government and by the Bureau of Caucasian Affairs to hold in perpetuity—for as long as the sun shall rise and the rivers go down to the sea. We will further guide the inhabitants in the proper way of living. We will offer them our religion, our education, our life-ways, in order to help them achieve our level of civilization and thus raise them and all their white brothers up from their savage and unhappy state.

We feel that this so-called Alcatraz Island is more than suitable for an Indian reservation, as determined by the white man's own standards. By this we mean that this place resembles most Indian reservations in that:

It is isolated from modern facilities, and without adequate means of transportation.

It has no fresh running water.

It has inadequate sanitation facilities.

There are no oil or mineral rights.

There is no industry and so unemployment is very great.

There are no health care facilities.

The soil is rocky and nonproductive; and the land does not support game.

There are no educational facilities.

The population has always exceeded the land base.

The population has always been held as prisoners and kept dependent upon others.

Further, it would be fitting and symbolic that ships from all over the world, entering the Golden Gate, would first see Indian land, and thus be reminded of the true history of this nation. This tiny island would be a symbol of the great lands once ruled by free and noble Indians.

After showing why Alcatraz was similar to an Indian reservation, the proclamation said five institutions would rise on the site. A Center for Native American Studies would include traveling universities. The American Indian Spiritual Center would allow the practice of "ancient tribal religious and sacred healing ceremonies." The Indian Center of Ecology would carry out scientific research, depollute the water and air, and establish "facilities to desalt sea water for human benefit." The island's Great Indian Training School would operate a restaurant, offer job training, and sell Indian arts and crafts. Finally, the proclamation said part of Alcatraz would remain as it is, a fitting place to remember Indian captives and to teach "the noble and tragic events of Indian history, including the Trail of Tears, and the Massacre of Wounded Knee."

Nordwall reveled in the humor and heavy irony of the text. Nobody could emcee an event like he could.

The parallels to reservation life that the occupiers made so often were accurate in regard to the kinds of donations they increasingly received. Church groups and other compassionate citizens around the nation sent off their second-hand clothes and junk to reservation communities and considered doing so a primary good work. Sometimes by the truckload, rummage from Denver or Indianapolis arrived at a Sioux reservation in North Dakota or Navajo country. Some of that traffic began arriving at Alcatraz. So much arrived that most of it ended up at the San Francisco Indian Center, where local Indian people could avail themselves of it. On the island, piles of it remained dockside, waiting for takers.

Richard Oakes said "It felt like the monthly commodities coming in for the Indians. You know, surplus food for the Indians. 'Here it comes, fellas.' We were sent a whole load of cans and goods containing cyclamate. I remember unloading it. I told them to take it back, and they did. Some of the cans that were given us were spoiled, leaking, and probably poisonous."

But by then, a month into the occupation, the mood on the island had changed. Richard Oakes seemed not to be around very much in the weeks following Thanksgiving. The closest contact most of the occupiers had with their spokesperson was through the newspapers that would make it across from people shuttling back and forth to the mainland or which supportive reporters dropped from the traffic helicopters that passed overhead each morning. And they heard little about all the planning and strategizing that was going down. When they read the stories or caught word of the newsletters, conferences, colleges, community centers, and other big plans, a lot of them must have chuckled.

"It's hard to live a lie," Richard Oakes had once told a reporter, but after a few weeks into the occupation of Alcatraz Island he continued to speak of the marvels of the island in spite of deteriorating conditions. Blame sheer boredom, exuberant anarchism run amok, or a youthful commitment to hard partying—fights and accidents became more and more common, as did a general lack of cohesion and purpose among those who weren't part of the leadership. And, along with the plumbers and electricians who made their way over after Thanksgiving, criminals and others from the underside of the Indian world began to arrive.

Street punks and winos from the Mission who had seen the layout on Thanksgiving came back to set up housekeeping. No police, no social workers, no hassles. Most of them didn't want to cause problems for the glorious occupation. They just wanted freedom. They could party in the cellblocks until the early hours of the morning without disturbing the families who lived in the guards' apartments. Some thought of the unruly newcomers as the root of the growing problems, but others among the November 20 occupation force were more than happy to join in the messy reveling.

For more than a month Ed Castillo held out as conditions worsened. Like others who had been there from the first, he believed those who were holding the Rock ought to stay there and not leave unless absolutely necessary. It was, for them, a political line in the sand, not some form of temporary entertainment. And, in spite of the growing problems, Castillo managed to pass his time pleasantly enough.

Mainly, he sat reading the several books he had brought with him, most of them about the history of California Indians. He would chat with non-California Indians about the state's tribal groups, mostly small tribes who had survived a bloody history under the Spanish, then the Americans. When the occupation's fame prompted visits from celebrities for tours of the island, Castillo hung back from the flurry of excitement. Embarrassed, he watched fellow citizens go running to stand in the wake of Anthony Quinn or Jonathan Winters. He considered the people who did this nothing more than fawning sycophants.

In Castillo's corner of the island, he and his friends could continue doing what they had been doing since they arrived. They sang, fixed up places to live, fell in love, talked into the night, and dreamed as they gazed into the bay. They even did their share of partying, but tried not to let things get too far out of control. What they refrained from doing, though, was ask questions about all the money they kept hearing was coming in hand over fist. Doing so was sure to bring a crew from the "security" contingent down on them and fast, intimidating them and telling them that they didn't need to worry about finances.

But five weeks in, Castillo finally broke. He had to get off of the island, if only for one night. The unraveling of the occupation was getting to him, as was his own body odor. Since his only option for bathing was washing off at a tub of tepid or cold water with no towel to dry off with, he hadn't bathed or changed his clothes since he arrived. So, he gathered up his latest girlfriend and headed for the dock. They each received nine dollars for their shore leave excursion.

Since Castillo was on payroll at UCLA as a lecturer in the new Native American Studies program rather than on scholarship like most of the other student occupiers, he had some access to money. He used credit cards to buy some new clothes and a few magazines. He and his friend used their pooled eighteen dollars for a hamburger dinner, then found a motel near the wharf where they took baths and reveled in their own beautiful Indianness. For one night, at least, Castillo would forget about the drunks, the security patrol, and the dreams of glory which were rapidly beginning to slip away.

Christmas on Alcatraz was an awkward affair. A Girl Scout troop held a party for the children on the Rock, and for Hanukkah, the American Jewish Congress delivered food and blankets. Mattel sent thousands of brand new toys. Luwana Quitiquit kept them in a vault and made sure they went to the island's kids. There were a few wrapped presents, but most people shied away from any overt holiday observances.

A visitor noted only one Christmas decoration. "In the hall far below," she recalled from her walk through the main cellblock, "the Christmas tree was a limb of driftwood, its forked branches ornamented with the tops of tin cans hung on threads. They moved in the cold air, taking the light, the names of tribes painted on them, and on some, the single word, 'Genocide.'"

In the midst of the Christmas season, on December 23, an ambitious pan-Indian conference that spokespeople—like Shirley Keith, who had talked of a meeting of "every tribe, nation, and band" in her remarks at the benefit at Stanford—had been touting for weeks, fizzled. Less than one hundred people attended, and the sessions featured issues so removed from the gritty reality of the island the participants might as well have been discussing quantum physics. The conferees met in the main dining room, a cold and dark place surrounded by prison cells, and discussed admission policies for the proposed Thunderbird University, the merits of a paid staff versus a volunteer staff, and architectural themes. Despite the disappointing turnout—from the hype, organizers seemed to expect thousands—Indians of All Tribes issued a press release calling the modest event "the most important conference since the days of the Ghost Dance."

Fourteen-year-old Colin Wesaw knew none of this as he drove from Chicago in a borrowed green and white Volkswagen bus featuring a giant Band-Aid sticker (to comment on its mechanical fragility) and the painted slogan "Alcatraz or Bust." Wesaw traveled with his sister, a cousin, and two others. In Sante Fe more prospective occupiers joined them and they made a beeline for San Francisco. At Fisherman's Wharf, as they wondered how to get to the island, they noticed a group of Indians in a heated argument that was turning into a brawl. A large, striking Indian was keeping several obviously drunk Indians from joining him in his boat to the island. He didn't want them there if they were drunk.

The drunks finally gave up and left. Wesaw and the others approached the man and learned he was Richard Oakes. Wesaw's cousin remembered his name from news accounts. Oakes found out they had come all the way from Chicago and immediately offered them a ride across the Bay to Alcatraz. It was Christmas Eve.

To Wesaw, Oakes seemed kind and generous, with a good heart for his people. Oakes, tickled to have visitors from Chicago, talked to them about his plans for Alcatraz as they motored toward the island.

When they arrived, Oakes showed them around. As they walked

through the cellblock, Wesaw was struck with how dark and eerie the place felt. The gale force of the wind felt as though it would pick them up and carry them away. In the background, Wesaw could hear drums—his group followed the music. That night, they found places to sleep, and awoke Christmas morning a thousand miles from home in the middle of San Francisco Bay.

Lacking money for their own needs or to put into the communal pot on the island, they returned to the mainland. While in line at the Western Union office, a woman asked them if they were part of Alcatraz. She appeared to be African-American, but she said she was also Indian. She invited them to her house for a Christmas meal. They agreed. She served turkey, chicken, soup, cakes, and pastry. She explained that this is how her people do it. She cried when they left.

Back on the island, they joined in the Christmas celebrations. A powwow was going strong, and if there was drinking it seemed to be mostly out of sight. After a few more days, a new semester of school beckoned them back onto the road. If nothing else, Wesaw felt thankful they were able to show their support for a few days.

Other holiday visitors brought relatives and friends of the occupiers to the island. "They would come to the island and see for themselves," said Quitiquit. "My mother would come when she could. My brother, who was in Vietnam at the time, was home on leave and he came to the island, which surprised me. Here he was fighting for America. To come home and support us! It was kind of strange to see him there."

The island had become a truly wild place, a strange combination of a constant powwow and a street fight. Young radical idealists, community people, folks in search of weekend diversion, and down-and-out denizens of the underworld lined up to stake their claim to a piece of the dream. Indians held a brilliant, astonishing metaphor— a defiant, isolated Rock surrounded by foreboding seas, a reservationlike piece of real estate with stark conditions, and a prison that represented the incarcerated spirit of Indian people everywhere.

Alcatraz was a perfect symbol but a dangerous place to live. The citizens of the island nation occupied a surprisingly vast area, and the hundred or so people who lived there (by some accounts an optimistic estimate) used hardly any of the available space. Given the amount of space and the number of nooks in it, enforcing any kind of real security on the island was impossible. How could anyone hope to stop a drug dealer from blending into the general population while maintaining a cache in some dark basement closet? Who could hope to deter out-of-hand parties when the revelers always had somewhere else to go? The abandoned prison offered a thousand places to hide, and a million ways to get in trouble.

Alcatraz belonged to Indians of All Tribes, and that was exactly the problem. No one had imagined how much goodwill, attention, and fame or how much disunity, discord, and heartbreak would come on the heels of the late-night crossing in November. Richard Oakes, the ironworker turned bartender turned revolutionary who was responsible for somehow keeping it all together, ended the year using his fists against drunks who wanted to join his occupation. The press called him the Mayor of Alcatraz, but this city was like no other.

Those same press stories and many of the occupiers would mistakenly designate Alcatraz as the beginning point of modern Indian radicalism. But Oakes was, in fact, inheriting a mantle of leadership that had likewise frustrated other charismatic young Indian leaders.

The Rock.

Richard Oakes, a Mohawk from New York, inspired Indians across the country but lost the support of the occupiers.

Alcatraz activist LaNada Means.

Clyde Warrior, leader of the National Indian Youth Council, shocked the Indian establishment in the years before Alcatraz.

Alcatraz Quarters.

Enjoying a sunny moment at Alcatraz.

Alcatraz press conference on the eve of the May, 1970 evacuation deadline.

John Trudell at Alcatraz.

Chapter 3

Fancydance Revolution

he remarkable—if perplexing—story of Alcatraz was hardly the first moment of mid- to late-twentieth century Indian radicalism. The press missed the point, but nearly everything that was happening in the Bay begged for context about what had happened between the end of the Indian wars in the nineteenth century and the emergence of raggedy Indian students on a decrepit island prison in 1969.

In one way, in fact, the only new thing about Alcatraz *was* the press attention. The Bay Area, after all, had an organized Indian community before the takeover, even if Oakes and others on the island disagreed with the politics of its leaders. Island leaders appealed for support from established national Indian political organizations that could draw several times as many people to their meetings than the failed Christmas meeting on Alcatraz had, even if most Indian people didn't have a clue as to what those groups were doing. And some of the strongest supporters of the occupation were leaders of urban radical Indian groups that were publishing newsletters and attending national conferences years before the island became a matter of national concern.

The occupation was a fulcrum, a turning point, but it wasn't the genesis or ground zero. And what had gone on in the years previous to Alcatraz and the forty-two months of intense activism that followed is at least as important as what happened during or after—especially since a number of people had predicted that the Indian world was going to erupt in almost exactly the way in which it did.

Clyde Warrior was one of those who had seen it coming.

"What it amounts to," Warrior said in 1966, "is that the Indians are getting fed up. It's just a question of how long the Indians are going to put up with being took every day." In a moment of prescience, he spoke of the situation Indian people found themselves in vis à vis American society, "How long will Indians tolerate this? Negroes, Mexican Americans, and Puerto Ricans could only take colonialism, exploitation, and abuse for so long; then they did something about it. Will American Indians wait until their reservations and lands are eroded away, and they are forced into urban ghettoes, before they start raising hell with their oppressors?"

People like Warrior had seen the wave coming in spite of the fact that among national Indian organizations the idea was still current that Indian people distinguished themselves from other 1960s groups by patience as opposed to unrest, level-headedness as opposed to riotousness. Outsiders might see Indians as passive in the midst of societal upheaval. But many within groups like the National Congress of American Indians (NCAI), the oldest and most established of Indian advocacy groups, wore their steadiness as a badge of pride, a symbol of moral fortitude in the midst of anti-Vietnam rallies and race riots that increasingly seemed to them protest for protest's sake. Indeed, as late as 1967 the National Congress flew a large banner proclaiming "Indians Don't Demonstrate."

But to those who had a finger on the pulse of Indian country, that was wishful thinking. Since the late 1950s, student groups had been working on campuses and in communities, producing cohorts of college-educated tribal officials and admininstrators. At the same time, traditional people and local poor and working-class people had been getting to know each other around the country and staging courageous, if often ignored, protests. Indians in the cities were organizing themselves into impressive organizations that could swing deals with city halls. War on Poverty money was making new programs possible on reservations.

Threatened by federal policymakers—like 1950s BIA Commissioner Dillon Myer, who wanted to terminate the relationship between American Indians and the United States—national Indian organizations went through purges that opened up space for new leaders and fresh ideas. The United States itself was shifting under the pressure of students, minority groups, women, and others, to make the U.S. a fundamentally different place to live.

The changes were anything but subtle, but the broad base of Indian people saw evidence of them in the presence of new offices in their communities, more young people from their families having educational opportunities, and increased energy among some people for community organizing. When the press painted Alcatraz as the story of the Indian world suddenly and unexpectedly waking up, joining the rest of the armies of the discontented in protest politics, they chose flashier copy over a reasoned recitation of just how much struggle, how much sacrifice, and how much rock-hard tenacity had gone into trying to make things better for Indian people long before Indians of All Tribes set foot on Alcatraz.

Many could lay claim to their stake in being part of the process of change. Various individuals had transformed national organizations, turning them from groups concerned only about the bottom lines of federal budgets into groups whose leaders grappled with fundamental questions of the future of Indian communities. Others could point out how their administration of federal programs created new opportunities for Indian people to access funds for community-based education and economic development. Still others could display the physical scars from standing against racist thuggery in local protests that most people never heard of.

New energy among Indian young people cut across all the developments. The story of Ponca activist Clyde Warrior, with little doubt the most compelling and important leader of this emerging youth movement, qualifies as the top story the press missed in the years leading up to Alcatraz and demonstrates that press attention and significance are not always the same thing.

As a teenager in the late 1950s, Clyde Warrior posed for a souvenir postcard that featured him and another young Indian man in
their powwow clothes. In the colorized black-and-white postcard,
the slim, slightly smiling Warrior is standing on small boulders on
the Oklahoma prairie. He is wearing an eagle feather bustle, an in-
tricately beaded belt, beaded armbands and wristbands, a blue
broadcloth breechclout with colorful flower embroidery, a bone
chestpiece, and bells around his calves. On his head he has a beaver
quill roach with an eagle feather standing atop it. In his left hand he
carries a long, beaded dance stick; in his right, an eagle feather fan.

At powwows and tribal dances, he had earned the right to wear it
all. Often he found himself in the middle of victory photos as the
fancydance champion. One photo shows him downing a Nehi as he
struts about the powwow arena in full dress. By many accounts of
those who saw him dance in his prime, he could be a formidable fancydancing presence, one of the rare people who could swing his
dance sticks, his bustle, and the rest of himself in fluid motion, spin-
ning himself into a blur of light-stepping color.

He would later work at Disneyland as a costumed Indian character paddling a canoe, but his background and upbringing were at
odds with the simulated consumerism of the happiest place on earth.
As the sixties wore on and he heard leaders talk of alienation, cultural revival, and renewed pride in Indianness, Warrior would bristle
at such language. How, he asked, can you revive something that is
living and breathing? Indian people, perhaps even most of them,
needed renewal, but Indian culture?

Born in 1939 near Ponca City, Oklahoma, his grandparents had
raised him in the bosom of Ponca language and culture. A relatively
small group living in north-central Oklahoma, many Poncas have
clung tenaciously to their way of life—elaborate dances and ceremonies, a complex system of clans and extended families, and
ancient values, such as "visiting" relatives and people from other
tribes for days on end. In the nineteenth century the Poncas had been
batted around the Plains by a pernicious U.S. government and their
struggle for justice was, for a brief time, a *cause celebre* among the
literati and genteel liberals of Boston and Philadelphia.

In spite of their relatively small numbers and endemic economic poverty (or maybe because of them), Poncas have produced some of the best fancydancers and southern Plains drum singers. Various Buffaloheads, Rough Faces, Warriors, and Camps have sung and danced their way into the histories and legends of powwows and ceremonies around the country. Clyde Warrior was among the leading singers and dancers of his generation.

Typical of Ponca people, he was comfortable and respectful no matter what tribal tradition he found himself in as he wandered the country, first as a powwow dancer, then a political organizer. Without passing judgment, he learned the protocol of ceremonies, the words and music of songs, the meaning of symbols. And unlike an invasive anthropologist, he wasn't in the business of collecting anyone's tribal secrets. But whatever people were free to share, he loved. He was an always-growing walking library of intertribal songs and stories.

Given his profile, Clyde Warrior's path should have been college, a job as a tribal administrator, then later a career as an elected tribal official and high-level government employee. Instead, like many of his generation, he began questioning the assumptions behind that appointed path.

Central to the emergence of this new generation was a summer program that brought students from around the country to the University of Colorado at Boulder to learn about the state of Indian affairs. For three weeks in the summer, the young Indian students lived in dorms and attended classes taught by anthropologists, BIA administrators, and others who knew the inside story of the way the United States conducted its business with Indians. At night and on the weekends, they would head off to one of the canyons near Boulder and "49," the term for backroads parties where young people sang social songs like "You know that I love you sweetheart, but every time I turn around I see you with another one. You know god-damn well that I love you. Way yah he, way yah he." The unwritten rule at the workshops was, stay out as late as you want. Just don't miss class.

Since Warrior traveled to powwows in faraway states, he had seen a lot of the Indian world. But it wasn't until the workshops and his involvement with the Southwest Regional Indian Youth Council—a group that started in New Mexico in 1955 with the purpose of drawing young people from various tribes together for educational activities, that he started talking much about that world in terms of where it was headed socially, politically, and economically.

One of his earliest existing writings is an essay titled, "What I Would Like My Community to Look Like in Ten Years." His first priority was in the area of Indian-white relationships at the local level, where "the white man tends to rate the Indian as being lazy and worthless." Stemming from that, according to the young Warrior, was the root problem. "The Indian," he writes, "seems to make it a point to act and be exactly as he's rated." Yes, Warrior argued in this essay and other forums, Indian people needed economic development programs, educational opportunities, and technical assistance, but not until Indian people changed their view of themselves and took pride in who they were would any form of assistance make any real difference.

When Warrior made statements about Indian pride around other students, many of them started getting uncomfortable. They had been bombarded with the opposite message their entire lives; being Indian was a problem, life in Indian communities was backward, copying whites as closely as possible was the only way out of poverty. For this handsome, articulate, twenty-year-old Ponca to stand up and say something different was nothing short of revolutionary for many of them. Some considered him an arrogant blowhard. Others secretly agreed with Warrior and admired his boldness. Still others whispered in horror that Warrior and his kind were taking Indian people in the direction of those southern Negro agitators. Most importantly, though, Warrior found people, including Mel Thom, and Bruce Wilkie, who shared many of his opinions, even if their styles were less confrontational.

As Browning Pipestem, an Osage and Oto who became friends with Warrior at the workshops, says, Warrior exploded the notion that "Indian people must change." That notion and its expression in political ideologies and government policies had been around for centuries. The effect on the self-image of many, perhaps nearly all, Indian people, was that, in Pipestem's words, "People had made peace with a lot of untruths and plugged the gaps with half-truths." What Warrior did was to "take that negative image of Indians and shove it down people's throats."

One example of that comes from Warrior's bid to become president of the Southwest Regional Indian Youth Council in 1960. His opponent's campaign speech stressed the standard lines of the day—the need for education and professionalism. Warrior mounted the podium, pushed his cowboy hat back on his head, and rolled up his sleeves. Pointing to his bare arms, his speech consisted of two lines: "This is all I have to offer. The sewage of Europe does not flow through these veins."

Warrior won the election that day in a landslide, but making significant inroads into the scarred psyche of Indian youth over the long haul would prove to be more difficult. "It's painful," as Pipestem put it, "to have to admit you'd given yourself over to self-hatred." Plenty of Indian people, especially those most invested in the status quo, rejected the message and the messenger. "They hated him," says Pipestem, "because they knew he was right."

But no amount of rejection deterred Warrior. Frustrating as it may have been, he loved Indian people too much to turn his back on them. That love was as much for the most down-and-out, denigrated Indians who lived on the edges of society as it was for the most honorable traditional people. Within his own family and community, he intimately knew the full range. For the many young people who had nagging doubts and insecurites, Warrior's embrace of them, as they were, made all the difference.

By the end of the summer of 1961, the growing group of vocal discontents was in the middle of a whirlwind that was heading far beyond the confines of student workshops. That summer, students from Boulder participated in a national conference on Indian affairs in Chicago. Later in the summer, in Gallup, New Mexico, they met again and formed the National Indian Youth Council. Clyde emerged as one of the leaders of the small group.

After the meeting was over, Mel Thom, another student leader from the workshops who would later earn the nickname Mao-Tse Thom, wrote a statement of purpose. In it, he says, "With the belief that we can serve a realistic need, the National Indian Youth Council dedicated its activities and projects to attaining a greater future for our Indian people. We believe in a future with high principles derived from the values and beliefs of our ancestors." It sounds innocent enough—an organization of young people concerned for their own future.

It represented, though, a major change. For two decades, only one viable national Indian-run organization, the National Congress of American Indians (NCAI), had existed. Founded in Denver in 1944 by tribal leaders and former employees of the BIA, the NCAI became the sole intertribal rallying point from which Indians could engage Congress and the federal bureaucracy on an ongoing basis. In starting the Youth Council, Thom, Warrior, and the others were breaking ranks with the way things were done. And at a time when young people of all sorts outside the Indian world were making their voices heard, the creation of the NIYC was a major event for those in the world of Indian affairs. Suddenly, a loose cannon had appeared. What would it do?

For its first two years, the answer was, attend more meetings and workshops. Warrior and Thom, whose more deliberate, consensus-centered approach to leadership complemented the Ponca leader's abrasiveness, started sitting on the boards of groups like the United Scholarship Service, a group in Denver that provided scholarships to Indian and Mexican American college students. But the steady flow of meetings and conferences was not exactly the earthmoving stuff of revolutionaries.

If they didn't immediately make fundamental changes in the Indian establishment, they did commit themselves to doing things differently in their own fledgling organization. For instance, the Youth Council decided to hold its annual meetings on Indian reservations rather than in convention hotels in major cities, as was the custom of the NCAI. And they ended every meeting by gathering around a drum and sharing tribal songs. The leader of those songs was often Clyde Warrior, who astonished many in the NIYC with his memory for songs from all over.

By the time the group met for its annual summer meeting at Fort Duchesne, Utah, in 1963, Warrior was ready for the NIYC to do more than attend board meetings. He brought actor and civil rights activist Marlon Brando to the meeting. Fresh from Martin Luther King, Jr.'s March on Washington, Brando advocated the Youth Council's involvement in civil rights protests. Not many people thought doing so was such a good idea. What was the use, after all, of becoming a small part of an established movement? Negro causes carried little credibility in most Indian communities. Still, some people liked the idea of public protest.

Clyde Warrior was the loudest advocate for moving away from educational and organizational initiatives to direct, local action. Mel Thom preferred a more measured, waiting-for-a-consensus approach, and many in the NIYC agreed with him. The group never moved without consensus, so they tabled the idea of taking up direct action.

But at the group's winter meeting, those who were timid stayed away and Clyde Warrior won the day. Hank Adams, a young Sioux/Assiniboine who had grown up on the Quinalt Reservation in Washington, was also enthusiastic about direct action, and headed home with Bruce Wilkie, one of the original members of the NIYC, to help organize a protest.

The issue they targeted for their protest was a straightforward one, as was the plan. For a century, fishing tribes along rivers in the Pacific Northwest had battled Washington state and Oregon over their rights to fish, in the words of treaties they had signed in the nineteenth century, in "usual and accustomed" places. In spite of the treaties, Indians who fished found themselves harassed, often arrested, for dropping their nets and catching fish.

Hank Adams, who would carry the NIYC's organizing torch at the fishing protests was, at nineteen years of age, already a seasoned and in some ways disillusioned activist. At age fourteen in 1958, he had watched the state government in Washington and the federal government in Washington, D.C. foist Public Law 280 on the Quinalt Reservation. The law, which Congress passed in 1953 as a companion to its termination legislation, made it possible for states to assume jurisdiction on Indian land. Before the new law, Indian groups were by and large responsible for policing their own people on their own lands, which gave them a measure of protection against racist police and policies in the states surrounding them. Adam lived with his mother and his Quinalt stepfather in one of the communities the law affected.

Adams, like others, was outraged when the state imposed itself and its rules on a community that had been successfully dealing with its own problems. The arbitrary enactment of the statute—over the strenuous, near unanimous objection of the Quinalts—saw the county, where alcohol had been legally prohibited under tribal jurisdiction, inundated with alcohol readily available to young people. Soon the communities on the reservation were in a form of communal chaos and had only limited means by which to intervene in their mounting social problems. Suicide among the growing group of alcoholic youth became epidemic.

Though still a teenager, Adams was one of those who sought to intervene. He was part of press conferences and lobbying efforts. Regional and national Indian leaders, impressed with his work, began grooming him for leadership.

By 1963, though, he had vast doubts about any approach to changing the Indian situation centered in the established Indian organizations. He attended his first meeting of the National Indian Youth Council that summer and sided with Clyde Warrior and those who favored more radical tactics. In the fall, as a sophomore at the University of Washington, he decided to give up on the standard approach of going to school, gaining skills, and returning to his home community to help build something. He wanted something different, and dropped out of college the same month John F. Kennedy was assassinated in Dallas.

These events were propelling him into working with the Youth Council. After the December meeting in Denver, he worked as a liaison between the Youth Council, the local people, and Marlon Brando in early 1964 as they sought to shine the light of national attention on Indians who fished the rivers of the Pacific Northwest under treaty rights from a century before.

The Youth Council and Brando arrived in the Pacific Northwest in March of 1964. The plan was for Brando to get into an Indian fishing boat in full view of state fishing wardens and national media and commence fishing. In spite of complications, the protest, which the media dubbed a "fish-in," went well. Although wardens apprehended Brando, but they soon released him, fearing his celebrity would add to the media tide rising higher for the Indian cause, the action surpassed the organizers' expectations.

More fish-ins happened over the years, though the national

media usually showed up only when a star like African-American comedian and activist Dick Gregory or Jane Fonda joined in. Some local people were dissatisfied with the Youth Council's involvement from the start, accusing NIYC of being college kids in sports jackets who showed up merely to make themselves look good. The presence of the charismatic, media-savvy Youth Council had certainly ruffled the feathers of some local activist leaders. But Clyde Warrior's vision—supported by a growing cast of like-minded people such as Hank Adams—of a Youth Council engaged in actions in the same vein looked to be the shape of things to come.

Though the National Indian Youth Council was the cutting edge of national Indian politics in the mid-1960s, plenty of other factors were coming into play as well. At about the same time as the fish-ins, for instance, the federal government was deciding where Indians fit into the Office for Economic Opportunity (OEO), the bureaucracy set up to administer the Johnson Administration's War on Poverty programs. National Indian advocacy groups that feared Indian communities would be overlooked as state agencies divvied up the new monies succeeded in getting the bureaucracy to set aside a portion of the program specifically for Indians.

Almost overnight, the increasing numbers of educated young Indian people emerging from American colleges had opportunities to return to their communities as directors of OEO programs. Within a few years, new educational, social, and health programs began popping up with regularity in Indian communities.

The National Congress of American Indians, the major national Indian organization, was also undergoing wholesale changes. Always understaffed and underfunded, NCAI's effectiveness varied based on the enthusiasm and purse strings of its member tribes. In 1964, the group swept out an older generation of leaders in favor of younger people. Its membership chose Vine Deloria, Jr., a thirty-year-old Standing Rock Sioux as NCAI's new executive director.

Deloria, who had grown up the son of a Sioux missionary on the Pine Ridge Reservation in South Dakota, had attended prep school, college, and seminary. Foregoing a career in the ministry, he worked in the early sixties at the United Scholarship Service, a group in

Denver that supported American Indian and Mexican American college students. Before leaving for the NCAI, Deloria had developed a program through which Indian students attended east coast prep schools like the one he had graduated from. Like Warrior, Thom, and Adams, he added a particularly intellectual bent to a milieu dominated by organizational types up to that point.

While the world of Indian organizations was changing, impressive numbers of younger people were running for and winning election as tribal officials, replacing older, more conservative leaders. In a 1966 interview, Deloria was able to list over a dozen talented young people who had recently assumed leadership positions in their tribes. The youth movement in Indian affairs effected changes that would alter the Indian world for decades to come.

Beyond the youth movement, in the harder-to-find nooks and crannies of the Indian world, local people like the ones in the Pacific Northwest were coming together and making a network of their own outside the official channels of the BIA, NCAI, or NIYC. They stayed in touch through mimeographed newsletters, often providing more support for one another across hundreds of miles than the bureaucrats in the BIA offices did just steps from their homes. The reform-minded Deloria, when he discovered this network of people in the mid-1960s, encouraged them to become part of the NCAI and mix things up among the more conservative elements in the organization.

Reaves and Clydia Nahwooksy predated the youth movement by a few years, but their lives are an example of how the once constricted and insular bureaucracy affecting Indians changed over the course of the decade, offering new possibilities for activists determined to force change on seemingly immovable agencies. They had arrived in Washington, D.C. from Oklahoma in 1961, feeling something like their ancestors before them. "You meet the Great White Father on his own ground," Clydia had thought as they considered the move, "and maybe . . . you'd change things."

In certain ways they were old-fashioned. Reaves, Comanche and Kiowa, grew up speaking Comanche near Lawton, Oklahoma. Clydia's Cherokee folks were people who isolated themselves from

modern tribal governments and federal programs in eastern Oklahoma. But the Nahwooksys hadn't come to Washington decked out
in tribal vestmests ready to deliver impassioned pleas for justice in
the manner of a nineteenth-century tribal delegation. They were, instead, a highly modern couple. Reaves's Baptist parents had expected
both he and his sister to go to college and worked hard to make that
possible. He had done a tour of duty in Korea, so had seen something
of the world outside of rural Oklahoma.

They met each other as students at the University of Oklahoma
in 1952, after Reaves returned from the service. Within three months,
they were married. Reaves graduated in 1955 and they went to Fort
Sill, near where Reaves had grown up, so he could work in the Indian
school there as a teacher and athletics coach. By returning home to
work with Indian kids, they hoped to change some of the experiences
they had had growing up.

Many were the times, for instance, when as a young man Reaves
would accompany his grandparents to the BIA agency, where he
would translate for them from Comanche as they were put into the
position of having to virtually beg for their own money. That process
of Indian people being able to access more than a few hundred dollars of their own money was often a long-drawn-out nightmare of
red tape in which the local agency superintendent, the Secretary of
the Interior, and every bureaucrat in the chain of command between
them would have to sign off.

Reaves had also watched as his father worked hard to farm 320
acres on two tracts of land. He had to take out a large loan to get the
operation running. In spite of being "very frugal," the family struggled. Then, in the early 1940s, they were blessed with a bumper crop.
Reaves's father came home one evening bubbling with excitement. In
one swoop, he could pay off the loan. "Tomorrow," he said, "we will
go up there and slap this [money] down and tear our note up."

The next morning, though, before they could get to the agency, a
car pulled up to the house. Bureaucrats—including some of their Indian relatives—piled out of the car, came to the door, and conde-
scendingly said they knew that things weren't going well and the
family was struggling, but that the Nahwooksys were going to have
to pay off the loan anyway and they were there to work out arrange-

ments. They didn't stop to ask how things were going. They didn't entertain the possibility that maybe Reaves's father was taking care of the problem himself. They just barged in and assumed control.

Reaves's father told them, "I will pay it when I good and well please! It's not due yet," and soon asked them to leave. The next day, he paid off the note on his own terms.

Clydia's family stayed away from that kind of involvement with the local, federal machinery that attempted to run the lives of Indians. But she had still seen her share of bureaucratic indifference. Late one night, she went to an Indian hospital with a sick child, only to find the hospital waiting room full of sick children. A doctor was in attendance, but he looked at the room full of sick children and said, "Well I don't have time to fool with these people right now. I have to go home and eat dinner." He walked right out through the waiting room.

These and a thousand other incidents drove the young couple to ask themselves, "How can this change? How can we have some, or how could anyone have some effect on what's going on?" When the opportunity arose for Reaves to enter a federal management training program in D.C. in 1961, they decided to seek answers to their questions at the source of U.S. government power. Over the next ten years, they would be a part of a process of significant change in the way that Washington, D.C. conducted its business with Indians.

Not long after his management training program was over, Reaves used some of his new connections to get a federal position working with the Shoshone and Bannock tribes at Fort Hall, Idaho. For four years, he and Clydia worked at Fort Hall to make things better from within the BIA. But they increasingly believed that changing things was not simply a matter of better people doing a better job. The Bureau, most people agreed, was an institution gone terribly awry. Instead of managing forests or regulating the railroads, Bureau employees micromanaged the lives of Indians. Reports on the endemic structural failings of the Bureau had issued forth in a steady stream since before the Great Depression. The findings were consistent across decades: The treatment of Indian people at the hands of the federal bureaucracy was a moral outrage that could only be addressed by the most drastic of means. But perhaps the biggest

problem with the exposés and the attempted reforms that came from
them was that, finally, the Bureau was holding no smoking gun. No
reformer could point to a single straightforward fact, or small set of
facts, that they could change.

The problems were more endemic; the Bureau was at its roots a
federal agency. Those employees who weren't political appointees
were civil servants and, as such, couldn't be gotten rid of. Outrage
over the system occasionally would register with members of Congress, other Washington politicos, members of various Indian reform
organizations, and sometimes even with the national public. But the
outrage never lasted long enough. The numerous commission and
task force reports gathered dust on shelves.

Meanwhile, it was always the hundreds upon hundreds of stories
of neglect and humiliation that revealed how real people in real time
experienced the Bureau and its agencies. The major crimes of the
Bureau, in fact, were small potatoes in comparison to the cumulative
effect on Indian communities of the message from the U.S. government that said they couldn't manage their own affairs without the
bungled and inept assistance of federal bureaucrats.

Some Indian people implicitly concurred with that sentiment,
preferring a system that didn't work to the possibility of shutting
down the Bureau and ushering in termination of their relationship to
the federal government. As the disastrous effects of the termination
policy set out by Congress in the 1950s were playing themselves out
in select locations around Indian country, few were willing to undo
the Bureau without having something concrete to put in its place.
Whatever else the system was, Indian people could figure out who
was in charge, and navigate the red tape.

Given the Bureau's shortcomings, in 1967, when Reaves Nahwooksy was offered a position back in Washington with a civil rights
project of the Public Health Service—a government office outside
the BIA—he got out of the Bureau for good. The Nahwooksys
wouldn't work within the system, but they wouldn't work completely
outside of it either.

The Washington scene the couple returned to was changing from
what it had been in 1964 when they had left for Idaho. For one thing,
more and more Indian people were working in the capital due to the

proliferation of War on Poverty programs targeting Indians. Clydia, in spite of still shouldering the majority of the responsibilities to her family after their return to D.C., took a position with the Smithsonian, hoping to find out what she could of the institution's resources and how she might make them available to Indian people. Reaves, not long after taking his new position in the Public Health Service, was detailed to Vice President Humphrey's National Council on Indian Opportunity (NCIO), which started not long after the Nahwooksys returned to Washington. The Council was to coordinate an administration response to the now burgeoning activity in Indian communities.

One of Reaves's first responsibilities was to help make arrangements for a series of hearings the NCIO planned in order to hear about the problems and concerns of Indian people living in cities. By that time, nearly half of American Indians were living in the cities. While some were recent arrivals from the Bureau's relocation programs, others had been around for generations.

As Reaves met the urban leaders in setting up the hearings, he noticed that "These guys were really confronters and they were hurting and searching for ways to become effective." He met them officially and unofficially in the process and was impressed, since, "You began to see what was going to form and the people were mad! They had to be responded to."

When Republicans came to power in January, 1969, Reaves was out of a job with the National Council on Indian Opportunity. He returned to the Public Health Service, surveyed the landscape, and decided to throw his lot with the Department of Housing and Urban Development (HUD). As colleagues in other agencies in the capital were doing, he worked to establish an "Indian Desk" at the department, a central place within the bureaucracy from which to coordinate federal housing programs for Indians. Though he didn't have the same amount of clout as the Commissioner for Indian Affairs, he did have access to people in high places.

Old-liners in the BIA normally fought against such separate offices as the emerging "Indian Desks," arguing that non-Bureau programs would siphon money away from the BIA's budget. In fact, though, the Indian desks prompted new inititiatives and new sources for funding without making an appreciable impact on the Bureau's budget.

The Indian desks were a small, mostly unnoticed change in the larger scheme of things. But they made a difference. With people like Reaves and Clydia Nahwooksy in key positions, Indian people could enjoy the same informal back-and-forth that others who dealt with the federal bureaucracy enjoyed. For once, when Indians testified before representatives of a federal agency, an Indian face looked back at them. And afterwards, in the more informal setting of a hotel corridor, they could communicate with another Indian about what the people they represented really needed.

The Nahwooksy home in suburban Virginia was a place where tribal and organizational leaders could stay while they visited the capital. Often strapped for cash, elected tribal officials could find a little slice of home as they confronted whatever bureaucrats they were in town to see. Reaves and Clydia gleaned from their guests a sense of what was happening at the local level. And Clydia, in her position at the Smithsonian, would sometimes escort her guests to the vaults of the museum, standing by as older people wept openly as they saw sacred objects and artifacts that had been gone from the lives of their communities for over a century.

A few years later, in the firestorm of activism that was jump-started by Alcatraz, the Nahwooksys and other Indians in the capital would play host to a much larger, much angrier crowd.

Meanwhile, half a continent away from D.C., Clyde Warrior watched as his fame and constituency grew, especially among American Indian college students. In December of 1964, he published an essay in the NIYC's newsletter called "Which One Are You?: Five Types of Young Indians" that laid out much of his ideology.

Those types were, according to Warrior: the Slob or Hood (the young person who lives up to their problematic status as defined by society); the Joker (the young person who makes a fool of him or herself in front of non-Indians in hopes of gaining acceptance from them); Redskin "White Noser" or Sell-Out (someone who ingratiates him or herself to non-Indians and accepts the values of non-Indian society); the Ultra-Pseudo Indian (one who is proud in a general way

of being an Indian person, but who doesn't have a knowledge or experiential base in Indian community life, so tries to copy popular and
academic images of Indianness); and the Angry Young Nationalist
(one who rejects American society, but is too ideological and abstract
to have an impact among local Indian people).

The fifth group, according to Warrior's essay, comes closest to
being "the ideal Indian," but he argues that something to connect
young Indian anger to people in local communities was necessary for
real social change to occur. "It appears that what is needed," he says,
"is genuine, contemporary, creative thinking, democratic leadership
to set guidelines, cues, and goals for the average Indian. The guidelines and cues have to be *based on true Indian philosophy geared to modern
times.*"

That, in a nutshell, was the challenge. Warrior could give voice
to it. He could embody it. After all, here was a man with a rare gift
and passion for being a culture-bearer who kept track of what was
happening in the decolonizing world of Africa and Asia. His first language was Ponca and he was an avid reader of *Time, Newsweek,* and
his favorite, *The New Republic.* What would be for most people vivid
contradictions were for Clyde Warrior just a day in the life of what
he believed the shape of the future must be.

But over the next two years, he would find his ideas pushed increasingly to the margins. He remained a central figure in national
Indian politics, but by 1966 it was clear that attention-grabbing protests like the ones in the Pacific Northwest were not going to happen
on a broad scale anytime soon. His role became that of being the outrageous alternative that set the table for more moderate, pragmatic
proposals. Increasingly, Warrior, Hank Adams, and Mel Thom were
among the few who remained committed to a political program that
called into question fundamental realities in Indian-white relations.
People would still talk about radical ideas, but when it came to action, the vast majority were content to steer a moderate course.

By then, Warrior was a different man than the slim twenty-year-
old who had shocked the sensibilities of other students at the Boulder workshops. In 1965 he married Della Hopper, an Oto-Missouria
woman he had gone to college with. They had one daughter and
would soon add another. They took up residence in Tahlequah, Ok-

lahoma, the capital of the Cherokees, where Clyde worked as a field researcher for Murray Wax, a white anthropologist from the University of Kansas who had spent his career working in Indian programs like the Boulder workshops.

Warrior's weight had increased dramatically since his slender workshop days. The culprit, most people agreed, was alcohol. He was a drinker of legendary proportions among a group of people in Indian affairs—both Indians and whites—for whom drinking was a constant theme. Stories abound of board meetings where board members would close down bars then begin work the next morning through the hazy eyes of hangovers. Warrior's Tahlequah house, as well, was a place where young people gravitated to party late into the night as their host threw back I. W. Harper or Jim Beam while expounding on his latest ideas. The physical toll was immense. Warrior's face grew rounder and puffy. His increased girth and increased family responsibilities led him to hang up his fancydance clothes and put on the outfit for the straight dance, a slower event.

His life remained a steady flow of board meetings, conferences, and college speeches, but the possibility that the NIYC would be a major agent of change became more and more remote. In an interview in 1966, Warrior commented on the irony of how the NIYC had been such a force when it was founded five years before, but was increasingly little more than a training ground for jobs in the status quo National Congress of American Indians, the Bureau of Indian Affairs, and Office of Economic Opportunity programs.

Still, he predicted that the growing instability of mainstream America would continue to foster unrest. And, Warrior predicted new groups would pick up the mantle of radicalism from NIYC. As he told a predominantly white college audience in 1966, "I . . . see an alliance between these young educated nationalists with the old traditionalists who are still very nationalistic in their own thinking. And when this alliance comes about," he warned, "there are several towns . . . in this country that better look out, . . . because it is liable to make the mau-mau of Africa look like a Sunday school meeting."

When he resigned from the NIYC, the group offered him its presidency, a position that various of the founders had filled over the years. Warrior relented, but he could do little to change the group's direction. Testifying for the group before a presidential advisory commission in February of 1967, he presented perhaps his most mature articulation of the challenges Indian people faced in confronting the future. The basic problem, he pointed out, was that Indian people "are not free. We do not make choices. . . . Choices and decisions are made by federal administrators, bureaucrats, and their 'yes men,' euphemistically called tribal governments."

He dismissed the efforts of the War on Poverty programs that were springing up in Indian communites. "We know that no one is arguing that the dispossessed, the poor, be given any control over their own destiny." To him, those programs Washington bureaucrats considered to be working the best were those that created the least "static," when what was really needed were programs that inspired local people to forcefully and even clumsily take control of their own futures.

That, in the end, was the nub for Clyde Warrior—Indian people helping themselves and, perhaps most importantly, learning from their own mistakes. "We must be free in the most literal sense of the word," he told the commission, "not sold or coerced into accepting programs for our own good, not of our own making or choice. Too much of what passes for 'grassroots democracy' on the American scene is really a slick job of salesmanship. It is not hard for sophisticated administrators to sell tinsel and glitter to simple people—programs which are not theirs, which they do not understand and which cannot but ultimately fail and contribute to already strong feelings of inadequacy."

Warrior's solution was much the same as he had proposed in his "What I Would Like My Community to Look Like in Ten Years" essay from years before. Indian people must, at whatever slow speed necessary, move from underneath the cloud of dependency and learn to take care of their own affairs. Only in that act of imagining themselves the authors of their own futures, Warrior argued, could Indian people assume the mantle of responsibility for themselves, their children, and their grandchildren. "Programs," he said, "must be Indian creations, Indian choices, Indian experiences. Even the failures must be Indian experiences because only then will Indians understand why a program failed and not blame themselves for some personal inadequacy."

Frustratingly to him, even his own comrades in the NIYC were less and less willing to listen to his solutions as various governmental War on Poverty programs expanded. But Warrior, who returned to the Boulder workshop each year as an instructor, could look to the new groups of young people coming up and hope that they would gain from the collective wisdom of his generation.

In spite of the setbacks, he held on to a hope for change. His passion for politics and his abiding love for Ponca and other Indian culture were seamlessly woven into his personality. And as a father, he did what he could to raise his daughters with the same sort of Ponca traditions that he had had. He "paid" for both of his daughters (initiated them into the traditional ways of the Poncas) when they were both young. The youngest, in fact, was still on her infant's cradleboard when she went through the ceremony.

Murray Wax, the anthropologist who hired Clyde Warrior to work in Tahlequah, hadn't crossed paths with his field-worker for several months when he saw him in the fall of 1967. Warrior's work on the project in Tahlequah had been a disappointment to the academic. Wax chalked up Warrior's lack of productivity to his packed schedule and his drinking. In October of 1967, though, Wax saw a much different Clyde Warrior. Through the ministrations of Tillie Walker, a Mandan woman who had been sort of a big sister to the NIYC, and others, Clyde had entered an alcohol rehab center in Los Angeles. It was one of two attempts at sobering up, the other being at a program in Colorado.

The program in Los Angeles used techniques such as berating the families of its clients and shouting them down into submission; methods that were so against the fabric of Warrior's being that he didn't last long. But he resolved to quit drinking in spite of the bad experience. As Wax said in a letter to Walker, "Clyde is back, looking chipper and healthy. . . . For the time being he is off liquor and making a genuine try at graduate studies." And, he added, "the man is indestructible."

That's what many of his friends and admirers had thought, too. But over the course of the next eight months, Clyde Warrior would prove them wrong, as whatever resolve he had had melted away at conferences and board meetings. He fell off the wagon, and he fell hard. He continued to balloon as his liver failed. His doctor warned him that his next drink might be his last.

In the spring of 1968, Clyde's mother, Anita Collins, died in Oklahoma and the family moved back to Ponca City to be with his grandparents. When Browning Pipestem arrived to pay his respects, Clyde, who had adored his mother, told him, "I hurt all over."

That summer, Della was to run a six-week OEO kindergarten program on the Navajo Reservation. After arriving there, Clyde took seriously ill. They headed back to Oklahoma. In Enid, Oklahoma, where Della's folks were living, Clyde's liver failed. Though he was not in pain, he was failing fast. Della took him to a hospital, where in just a few days, he died. He was a month shy of turning twenty-nine.

For four days before his funeral, the haunting, mourning voices of Ponca singers singing tribal family songs to the steady beat of a drum rose in the Oklahoma summer night. The mourners ate and sang together at breakfast, dinner, supper, and a late lunch after the songs at night. A local couple the family had called on cooked for everyone who showed up. The funeral took place in the heat of July, south of Ponca City at Warrior's grandparents' place.

The fourth day, Della dressed their two daughters and put on the white blouse and blue suit that her mother had brought over from Enid. In a daze, she received the several hundred people from around the state and around the country who had come to pay their respects. She reminded some of Jackie Kennedy and Coretta Scott King.

Area Indian people who had known Clyde Warrior as a powwow dancer and singer of tribal songs joined in with those who had known him as a political leader, in finding places to sit for dinner under cottonwood trees or in a plowed field at his grandparents' house. Many of the Poncas and other locals, accustomed to such feasts, brought their own folding chairs, utensils, and TV trays. Warrior's male relatives served the food to the gathering. They served corn soup, pork and hominy, chicken, fry bread, coffee, Kool-Aid, cakes, pies, canned peaches, apples, and oranges.

After they ate, Della got up and did a giveaway to honor those who had helped her and supported her during the first days of mourning. Many had reached out to her, including many who could not be there that day but who had sent telegrams. To those who did make it, she gave away basket after basket of shawls and blankets. Finally, they moved to the nearby Ponca cemetery for a final service, where Clyde was buried next to the still fresh grave of his mother. The headstone that would later mark his grave has NIYC logo at the top and the epitaph, "A Fresh Air of New Indian Idealism."

Around the time of Clyde's death, Stan Steiner's book *The New Indians* appeared and Clyde was a major character. The book billed itself as "The first report on the growing Red Power Movement" and named Clyde Warrior the "prophet of Red Power." In one place, Steiner has Clyde at the house in Tahlequah, defying stereotypes of Indians in buckskin, beads, and feathers by appearing in a loud Hawaiian shirt and bermuda shorts. Steiner quotes Warrior as saying, "And, as I see it, before we change, things are going to get worse. There are going to be more riots. And if it doesn't change, then the students and the Indians might just smash it, and change it themselves. These people are going to get so angry, so mad, that they're going to destroy the American society, without any thought of what to replace it with."

Until his death at the age of twenty-eight, Clyde Warrior had been the epic example of the struggle his still young generation faced. The gorgeous fancydancing, the near constant joking and laughing, the assault upon worn-out structures and tired ideas, and the willingness to stop pulling punches made him a symbol of what was possible. He and people like Mel Thom and Hank Adams had convinced themselves and lots of others that Indians deserved not only more, but the best. They envisioned a world in which the necessities of modern culture could exist alongside elaborate, old-fashioned, community and family-centered feasts and ceremonies. But the decade was coming to a close, and the prophet of Red Power wasn't around to see what would become of his prophecies.

Warrior, in fact, was standing on the tip of an iceberg. Plenty of Indian people, in spite of their stated values to the contrary, had seen over a decade of the Civil Rights then Black Power movements and felt a yearning for the same kind of attention. They had watched nations in Africa and Asia assert and fight for their independence and freedom and wished something of the same for themselves. They had supported their sons, cousins, brothers, and uncles as they headed out for Vietnam but at the same time were gnawed in their consciences by a war against brown people twelve thousand miles away, a war whose frontiers military brass still called "Indian country."

Hank Adams had watched all the twists and turns. Though he had parted ways with the Youth Council in 1966 in a disagreement over what he saw as the group's lack of commitment to the fishing rights struggle in the Pacific Northwest, he kept in touch with Clyde Warrior all the way until Warrior's death. Together, they had worked on the Indian involvement in Martin Luther King's Poor People's Campaign. Clyde Warrior's death came just a few months later, while the Poor People's Campaign was going on in Washington, D.C. Adams and others arranged for a press release in honor of Warrior's contribution to the struggle for justice.

As the NIYC became more and more centrist, Adams remained committed to Frank's Landing and the national fishing rights protests that had begun there over five years before. New radical leaders were emerging on the scene. Some of them, like Richard Oakes, would make a deep impression on Adams, the still young veteran of Indian affairs. But no one, according to Adams, came close to the sheer vision, analytic capacity, and willingness to confront established bases of power as did Mel Thom and Clyde Warrior. As Adams has said of Warrior, capturing in one phrase the complexities of his political acumen, his love for Indian people, and the way in which he could never resist the beat of a drum, "his life was in the song."

Chapter 4

Life As a Metaphor

n January, 1970, a year and a half after their mutual friend Clyde Warrior died, Hank Adams and Browning Pipestem found themselves sharing a boat to Alcatraz. Pipestem was by then working as an attorney at the prestigious Washington, D.C. firm of Arnold and Porter. When Indians of All Tribes occupied the island in November, 1969, Pipestem agreed to do pro bono legal work for them. Adams was still living in the Pacific Northwest, organizing and lobbying regarding the fishing rights struggle there. He had used his connections with the Episcopal Church headquarters in New York to arrange a $10,000 grant for Indians of All Tribes and was headed to the island to get signatures on the paperwork.

For both Adams and Pipestem, the occupation was a completely different scene than the one they had been a part of with the National Indian Youth Council. For the most part, the Youth Council had been comprised of clean-cut young people from tribal communities. And the leaders had been intellectuals as much as they were activists.

Though not all that far apart in terms of age, the young people of Alcatraz were, in comparison, messy. To Adams, the majority seemed to be people who had come to the island to figure out what being Indian was all about. And to him they seemed to be taking many of their cues—in an odd twist of reverse assimilation—from the hippies of San Francisco's Haight-Ashbury district, who were dressing in Native American inspired beads, headbands, and feathers.

Richard Oakes and some of the other leaders who would emerge during the occupation had spent time immersed in the daily life of tribal communities and could speak quite eloquently about horrid boarding school experiences or the crimes of the Bureau of Indian Affairs. But most of the island's population were college students who were the second-generation product of relocation and urbanization and simply didn't have an experiential base about those things. That they came across as politically and culturally inexperienced to Adams, Pipestem, and other veterans of Indian affairs comes as no surprise.

The Indian attorney and the seasoned Indian activist also noted a lack of organization and coherence. Furthermore, people on the island seemed not all that interested in the assistance Adams and Pipestem offered them in addressing some of their problems. With the tide of goodwill still running high for the occupation, islanders apparently didn't perceive a need for help from anyone.

But no amount of goodwill was going to solve the mounting problems at Alcatraz, and the organizational void was particularly noticeable as late December turned into January and a new decade. Winter's arrival added to the gloom of life in the ruins of the abandoned federal prison. The nights seemed to last forever, and with only a precious few generators providing light, fires were the main weapon against the darkness and the cold. When rain fell in sheets, sometimes all day and all night, the fires were useless. And when the fog settled in and the lights of the city disappeared, Alcatraz could feel like some distant, dark planet.

Alcatraz had become an increasingly dangerous place. Anthony Garcia, the Apache Vietnam vet, early on had put his medical school ambitions to the test and helped organize a clinic. Residents called him "The Doctor," and he stayed busy, dispensing bandages for the many scrapes and bruises the concrete wreckage inflicted. But the clinic couldn't treat more serious cases. And those began occurring with alarming frequency. One of the island's cooks fell from a tier in the main prison cellblock and fractured his skull. An older man suffered a heart attack. One child had a severe ankle injury, another suffered from pneumonia.

Just six weeks earlier, in the first few days, intrepid bands of students had defied the U.S. Coast Guard from landing on their liberated territory. Now, a Coast Guard clipper had become the island's ambulance service, and it became a familiar sight as it ferried injured occupiers to San Francisco area hospitals.

For those on the island, the hardship of life on the Rock became a badge of political courage. Almost everyone in the Bay Area Indian community supported the occupation, at least publicly. But who had the guts, the revolutionary commitment to live there amid the decaying, postindustrial ruins? And, more importantly, who should make decisions for Indians of All Tribes, the ones supporting the occupation from behind their desks on the mainland, or those braving the elements and enduring the severe conditions on the island?

That became the dividing line. The hard work of Adam Nordwall and others in the Bay Area Indian establishment was as crucial to the success of the occupation as the efforts of Richard Oakes and his fellow students. For weeks, a coordinating office in San Francisco organized by older members of the community had played an important role in collecting funds, handling press calls, and arranging visits to the island. With no telephone service and irregular ferry service, the occupiers could not have managed these tasks on their own.

The occupiers spoke constantly of unity. Unity between tribes, from those native to California to those from the Dakotas, New England, and North Carolina. Unity between the hard-luck survivors of mean streets and reservation dirt roads and those who lived the American dream but refused to turn their backs on their less fortunate brothers and sisters. Unity between urban and reservation people, from those who spent their entire lives in Oakland to those who came to the city only to see with their own eyes this prison turned liberation headquarters.

Richard Oakes himself embodied these varying experiences to a remarkable degree. He was born on a reservation, but spent much of his life in cities. A Mohawk from the east, he now led a rebellion in the west. A skilled blue-collar worker, he was an enrolled college student. Considered a reflective, thoughtful man by his friends, described by some as an intellectual, he had nonetheless spent far more hours in bars than libraries. Even his choice of a wife—a Pomo from California—seemed to complete a perfect resume for a leader who could find something in common with almost any Indian.

Yet none of that would be enough. Resentment of him had been building from the first days of the occupation, fueled more by jealousy than specific ideological differences. Suspicion and distrust of authority ran deep, and some had only reluctantly agreed on the provisional designation of Oakes as spokesperson. And Oakes clearly had become more than just a spokesperson. The fact that in recent weeks he spent more and more of his time on the mainland, dining out with important people and organizing support, made him a vulnerable target. It was possible to spend days, even weeks, on the island without a sighting of Richard.

His enemies had no trouble spreading damaging rumors. (Where is our leader? Oh, he's too busy partying with celebrities and reading his press clippings to bother with actually showing up here anymore.) His opponents on the council searched for a smoking gun, and they didn't have to look far. The issue of money—who got it, who decided how it would be spent—had been simmering from the earliest days. If movie stars and reporters from around the world flocked to Alcatraz, it stood to reason that a blizzard of financial contributions followed in their wake. When a donor in San Francisco announced his intention to donate stocks worth $16,000, a dispute broke out between those in the office on the mainland and those on the island, about who should receive and manage the funds.

In a tension-filled meeting with the council, Luwana Quitiquit said she had very specific instructions from Richard Oakes on the sorting of mail. Letters addressed to Indians of All Tribes were opened, the checks collected and deposited. But letters addressed to Richard Oakes, or Richard Oakes, Indians of All Tribes, went straight to Richard, unopened. He insisted on this, she told them, and he came to pick them up personally. She told the council that she believed every piece of mail had a check in it.

Oakes effectively lost whatever credibility he had retained

through the weeks of rumors. To Quitiquit and others, it was obvious that the money was not the real issue. "They were looking for
anything," she said. No one knew if Oakes took those letters and deposited all the money in the communal bank account or if he used
the money to cover the legitimate expenses of being Richard Oakes.
And that finally was what he was accused, tried, and convicted of—
being Richard Oakes.

Reined in and disgraced but still the single enduring public face
of the occupation, he was allowed to remain on the council. Although he spent even more time away from the island, Oakes still
maintained an apartment on Alcatraz with his wife and five children.

In spite of problems like the ouster of Oakes, the island still
offered its own special magic. Indians continued to arrive from
around the country, seemingly from every place where Indians lived.
In early January, there were still warm afternoons when you could
toss a Frisbee on the parade ground, or fish off the dock and listen to
rock tunes on the radio. The rich still floated by in yachts, offering
power salutes and champagne toasts. Lovers still held each other at
twilight as the lights of the Bay Bridge ignited, one by one. New
friends huddled around fires late into the night in quiet conversation,
sharing the common pain of those who understood, really understood, what it meant to spend your life ignored and invisible, a walking museum piece, a joke.

Alcatraz had blown away that fog of invisibility like nothing that
had occurred in the previous decade. Indians of All Tribes was more
than any one person, it was a living thing inventing itself by the hour.
They faced problems, sure, but the Rock was to them still ground
zero of this messy, beautiful, disorganized movement.

They took comfort from the stubborn perseverance of a tepee
the occupiers had erected, which greeted those entering the Bay as
they passed underneath the Golden Gate. During winter storms,
wind ripped through the place with such ferocity you could practically hear the concrete being ripped from iron foundations. But
when the storm passed, impossibly, there it was: defiant, hanging
tough, and standing tall. That tepee never blew over, not once. The
occupation was like the tepee—it might bend but it would never
break. They would survive the storms.

But then, on January 3, a tragedy struck the island that threatened to rip that perseverance to shreds. On that Saturday morning, a child fell three stories down a stairwell. Her limp body, barely clinging to life, was whisked off the island to an Oakland hospital by a Coast Guard cutter. Yvonne Oakes, daughter of Richard and Anne, was twelve years of age.

The accident never quite made sense and rumors began almost immediately that it was not an accident at all. It happened in one of the safest buildings on the island. The brick apartment building where the Oakeses lived, and Yvonne fell from, had been home to the prison's guards, and more recently the island's caretaker. It was one of the few structures to have undergone renovations in decades. Apparently, Yvonne had been playing on the third floor landing, her arms draped over the railing, when she somehow slipped.

The whispered speculation was that someone had pushed her in order to send a message to Oakes. It seemed unbelievable, yet some were convinced, and many others were willing to entertain the possibility. Ed Castillo, the young professor from UCLA, did not know if Yvonne had been pushed or not, but he said "there were some crazy people on that island. There are some people who would have been capable of it." Indeed, another young person had been seriously beaten not long before Yvonne's fall. But attempted murder? Anthony Garcia, who ran the island's clinic, found the rumors outrageous and completely without merit.

Others blamed Richard and Anne for the tragedy, charging that during their visits to the mainland they often left their children alone. Luwana Quitiquit, Oakes's secretary who lived in the same set of apartments where Yvonne fell, regarded the Oakes children as out of control. She heard disturbing reports from her own children about the scene at the Oakes's apartment when the parents were gone: "Kids could go in and do whatever they wanted. The word was out that these kids were sniffing glue and that she was playing on the rail up there, which was nothing but an iron rail. Straight down, just cement. She was at the top playing, and she easily could have slipped, and if she was stoned, it would have been easier wouldn't it?

"When it happened, no one said anything about sniffing glue, about these kids being unsupervised. It was all these glorious dedications to Richard Oakes's daughter and all this stuff and how horrible it was. Nobody said a word about all this stuff. I'm sure they knew. They didn't say anything about her having any problems with drugs or access to them."

For five days Yvonne lay near death at the Public Health Service Hospital. Flowers, phone calls, and other expressions of sympathy poured in as Richard and Anne kept a vigil.

She finally succumbed to massive head injuries on Thursday, January 8. That morning, the *San Francisco Chronicle* ran the second of a devastating two-part series on the occupation. The timing was coincidental—the series had been in the works for some time—but eerily appropriate. It read like an obituary.

The island, the articles said, had turned into something out of William Golding's nightmarish novel *Lord of the Flies,* in which children, away from adults and civilization, establish their own brutal society. Drunkenness was rampant, mindless vandalism widespread. In the Alcatraz proclamation, the proposed security force, playfully named the Bureau of Caucasian Affairs, was merely an amusing rhetorical jab at the Bureau of Indian Affairs. But the BCA had become frighteningly real. Young toughs, outfitted with special jackets and now calling themselves the Thunderbirds, roamed the island, threatening and beating residents. They were demanding their own building, for "training," and no one seemed to know what kind of training they had in mind. What had been for a moment a dreamy, idealistic place with real but workable problems, was coming to resemble its own prison setting. And the prisoners were in charge.

The author of the series was Tim Findley, the very person who brought Richard Oakes and Adam Nordwall together at the Halloween party at his home. Findley had written sympathetically on Indian issues in the Bay Area for years, which made his portrait of the occupation as a disaster even more painful and that much harder to dismiss. The *Chronicle* never reported any of the rumors about Yvonne's death. But the series, seven weeks after Alcatraz had begun so auspiciously, marked a turning point in how the occupation was perceived in the Bay Area.

As Yvonne slipped away and the *Chronicle* series demolished much of the occupation's credibility, Alcatraz itself was marooned by bad weather and severed telephone lines. Reporters seeking re-action on the girl's death were told by the mainland office that be-cause of stormy waters in the Bay, the occupation's boats had been grounded, and therefore the island's current leadership was unavail-able for comment.

When the weather cleared, most of the remaining students who had been in the invasion force in November slipped off the island, just in time to enroll in a new term at the campuses from which they had come. They finally admitted to themselves that the heady days of idealism had given way to criminality, petty infighting, and vicious rumormongering—many of the problems Findlay had writ-ten about.

Yvonne was buried on the Kashia Indian Reservation in Mendo-cino County, a few hours to the north. Indians of All Tribes offered to pay for her shroud. Richard Oakes returned to Alcatraz only to pick up his belongings.

From a law-enforcement point of view, the dozens of college students who invaded Alcatraz on November 20, were guilty of nu-merous criminal offenses, including trespassing, interfering with navigation, and destruction of government property. Responsibility for the protection and upkeep of Alcatraz had passed to the General Services Administration (GSA)—the government agency responsi-ble for maintaining transitional federal properties—after the prison had closed its doors in 1963. When the occupation began on Thurs-day, November 20, GSA boss Robert Kunzig decided to give the Indians until Friday at noon to vacate the island. After that, U.S. mar-shals would remove them, at gunpoint if necessary. Marshals began preparing for a full, frontal assault.

In San Francisco, the task of implementing Kunzig's decision fell to Tom Hannon, the GSA's West Coast regional administrator. By Friday morning, the excited press reports made it obvious that the Indians were not going to leave Alcatraz on their own. This made the briefing by Frank Klein, the director of the marshal service, even more alarming. Hannon listened as Klein detailed the kinds of weaponry and ammunition the operation required. It seemed to Hannon that the marshals would be packing an awful lot of firepower against a bunch of kids. Kids who, as far as anyone knew, were unarmed. The whole thing looked like a college prank, but Klein seemed ready for Vietnam.

Hannon suggested that perhaps other methods could be used to apprehend the trespassers. The marshal angrily replied that he would not be dictated to regarding proper tactics. Klein's vociferous response to Hannon's doubts about a military response prompted, for Hannon, frightening visions of a possible bloodbath. He brusquely ended the meeting and told Klein his services would not be needed.

Hannon returned to his office and agonized over the implications of what he had just done. His actions seemed foolish at best, career-ending at worst. He had no authority to reverse specific instructions of his agency's director.

The clock was ticking. It was eleven A.M., one hour before the deadline. The phone rang. It was Kunzig. Hannon braced himself, but before he could explain anything, his boss, seething with anger, said that the GSA had been relieved of responsibility for Alcatraz. The White House had taken over the management of the crisis. Kunzig, his rage palpable at having been dismissed, said that Hannon would be reporting directly to the White House, specifically to two men named Garment and Patterson.

Unlike many who worked for Richard Nixon, Leonard Garment was actually a friend of the President. They had been partners at the same New York law firm when Nixon, still in the political wilderness, had first started planning his famous comeback. Garment helped run the successful 1968 campaign, and had been rewarded with a White House position.

Also unlike many at the White House, who often saw political opponents as implacable enemies, Garment had an open, cosmopolitan outlook. He attended parties at Ethel Kennedy's house, and in Washington he developed a reputation as a kind of unofficial ambassador to Democrats and the discontented. Garment, with his assistant Brad Patterson, became known as "Nixon's house liberals."

Garment knew that in Alcatraz lay the seeds of disaster. Massive antiwar demonstrations had already taken place in Washington on October fifteenth and November fifteenth. If not properly managed, a confrontation with Indian activists could be deadly. He contemplated the prospect of federal officers in an armed confrontation with young Indian protesters, in San Francisco of all places, the most liberal big city in the country. The cost to the administration of such a catastrophe would be enormous.

His first action was to phone Kunzig at the GSA. His second was to set into motion a federal response to Alcatraz that in the following weeks would see the establishment of a full-blown federal task force, with representatives from half the cabinet, exclusively devoted to Alcatraz. Instead of a minor trespass handled by law enforcement, the occupation became a crisis managed at senior levels of the White House.

The invasion was a spontaneous affair, and many of the students hadn't even remembered to bring the right clothes or pack enough sandwiches, but within two days they were, quite literally, a matter of state.

Garment and his allies saw opportunity in the occupation. They already believed that Indians could be a showcase minority for the administration, and knew that very little had been done in the way of programs for Indians living in urban poverty. With Alcatraz, Garment and his crew had a chance not only to avert needless bloodshed but to pioneer constructive solutions to this new, vexing problem of Indians in America's cities. They also had a remarkable degree of latitude to act.

Nixon, with roots in the Quaker church—a denomination with a long history of opposing government Indian policies— had a soft spot for Indians. At Whittier College, a Quaker school, Nixon was a not very good football player who made the team only through sheer determination. His coach was an Indian man named Wallace "Chief" Newman. Nixon revered his coach in college and throughout his political career. Newman was an enthusiastic supporter of his former player, and Nixon showcased him at fundraisers, at political picnics, and in electoral victory parades through the town of Whittier.

Another reason Nixon was open to changes in Indian policy was his relative indifference to domestic affairs. He had learned under Eisenhower how much power chief executives enjoyed in foreign affairs, compared with the arcane battles with Congress over the less imperial questions of agriculture and transportation and crime. He entered the White House with an ambitious foreign policy agenda and an interest in domestic policy that did not appear to extend much beyond how those issues would affect his reelection. He trusted Ehrlichman, his domestic policy advisor, who trusted Garment. On issues like Indian affairs, if they didn't embarrass the President, Garment and Patterson could do pretty much anything they wanted.

Garment kept in close touch with the GSA's Hannon—who visited the island numerous times, bearing cigarettes and candy—and was gradually getting to know some of the Indians. Occasionally Garment would personally intervene. Learning of Yvonne Oakes's fall, he instructed Hannon to go to the hospital at once. Garment also sent Richard Oakes a personal note of condolence.

The federal task force met in December in Washington to consider the issue not only of Alcatraz but urban Indians in general. There were nearly as many people on the task force as lived on the island. There were officials from the Departments of Labor; Health, Education and Welfare; Interior; Housing and Urban Development; as well as the Office of Economic Opportunity and the Bureau of the Budget.

One organization represented on the task force was the National Council on Indian Opportunity (NCIO). Created during the Johnson administration, the NCIO functioned as a voice for Indian policy initiatives in the executive branch, a partisan tool, or both, depending on one's point of view. It was under the jurisdiction of the vice president, and its executive director was a Republican political operative from Nevada named Robert Robertson. The NCIO took a leading role in the task force deliberations, and when the time came to choose a member of the task force to negotiate with Indians of All Tribes, the group decided to send Robertson.

On Alcatraz people had been meeting as well. New elections were held for the island's government, a seven-member council with ninety-day terms. With Oakes gone, three very different people emerged to play leading roles.

The most controversial was Stella Leach, a registered nurse who worked in a well-baby clinic in Oakland. Abrasive, sharp-tongued, and, at fifty, older than most of the occupiers, she had been an out-spoken member of the Bay Area Indian community for years. She made no secret, for instance, of the anger and resentment fostered during her childhood years in a terrible BIA boarding school. She had two sons, one a Vietnam vet who lived on the island.

To some, she seemed exactly like the authority figure that the young people on Alcatraz needed. For others, the Leaches were an intimidating presence and a major force behind much of the recent turmoil. They considered Stella power-mad and dangerously un-stable; and in reference to the feared "security" detail, they pointed to her sons, David and Michael, as Exhibits A and B.

If conflict and sharp edges defined Stella Leach, John Trudell, a twenty-three-year-old Sioux, seemed her opposite: likable and easy-going. In December the KPFA-FM radio station in Berkeley offered Indians of All Tribes a half-hour of radio time five days a week. Trudell hosted the show, which never came close to broadcasting daily with any consistency. WBAI-FM in New York and KPFK-FM in Los Angeles, stations with similar leftist politics as KPFA, also car-ried the program, popularly called "Radio Free Alcatraz."

Trudell interviewed residents and visitors to the island, read from dated books like Mari Sandoz's *Cheyenne Autumn*, and, more in sorrow than in anger, lamented the government's response to the takeover. Calm, articulate, and quietly intense, through Radio Free Alcatraz he became the island's public face. Few hated John Trudell, but few lionized him either. If Oakes's charisma was to some remi-niscent of Tecumseh or Crazy Horse, Trudell was more likely to re-mind them of their favorite disc jockey.

A third key figure was LaNada Means, a Shoshone-Bannock. She had spent a tough childhood on the Fort Hall Reservation in Idaho, then got shipped off to a miserable BIA boarding school in Oklahoma before going to the Bay Area on the relocation program. In 1969 she enrolled at Berkeley, and, with Lehman Brightman—an older Sioux and Creek man from Oklahoma who was a Native American Studies instructor at the university—cofounded an organization called United Native Americans. Their symbol was an Indian on horseback, proud and imposing, a deliberate reversal of the iconic "End of the Trail" sculpture that featured a sad, defeated, hopeless Indian.

Means and the mostly female student group at Berkeley met up with the mostly male San Francisco State Indians and others. They participated in the struggles for People's Park, the antiwar demonstrations, and yearned for a movement of their own. Or at the very least, a place of their own, to talk and drum and sing. Often they gathered in the Berkeley hills, or bars, until the police were called. For Means, a young woman of increasingly limited patience, it was intolerable: How dare they tell us when and where we can sing in our own country!

She had been on the island from the beginning, and had a young son, Deynon, who became known as the Alcatraz Kid. Tireless, politically experienced, and possessed of raven hair and great presence, she was equally comfortable briefing reporters on how reservations operated—her father had been active in tribal politics—or directing clean-up efforts on the island. LaNada knew her stuff. And she knew how to go in only one direction: forward.

After Richard Oakes's inauspicious exit from Alcatraz, LaNada Means, John Trudell, and Stella Leach faced the daunting task of rebuilding the island's shattered reputation in the wake of tragedy and a torrent of bad press. January had been cruel to the island almost beyond belief, and the month was not even half over. Perhaps, with some breathing room, they could turn things around. The occupation desperately needed a break, a hiatus; time for healing and reflection. Only a few days after Tim Findley's damning series in the *Chronicle*, on January 10, the White House emissary arrived.

Bob Robertson had a disarming way of admitting he was no expert on Indians. His life had been in Republican politics, most recently with Nevada Governor Paul Laxalt. Robertson contacted some of Nixon's campaign people after the election and said he might be interested in a job with the new administration. The response was encouraging. The new vice president, Spiro Agnew, would inherit four statutory commissions: the Presidential Commission on Space, the Presidential Council on Youth Opportunity, and another one on Marine Sciences. The newest, just created in March of 1968, was the National Council on Indian Opportunity. In Nevada, Robertson had handled requests to the governor from the state's tribes, and landed the NCIO job on the strength of that experience.

A year later he found himself picking his way carefully through Alcatraz, where there were few, if any, Republicans. There were, however, jail cells carefully branded with the names of Vice President Agnew—Robertson's boss—Governor Ronald Reagan, Attorney General John Mitchell, President Nixon, Interior Secretary Walter Hickel, and other GOP officials.

The island seemed to be in shambles. A week earlier Yvonne Oakes had fallen to her death, and everything Robertson saw convinced him more deaths were inevitable; he watched, for instance, a toddler crawling at the edge of an eight-story drop and saw people wandering past disintegrating retaining walls and beneath crumbling stairways. The Coast Guard told him that the water barge was falling apart and good for only a few more trips.

With John Hart, the caretaker who had lived on Alcatraz with his wife for the past seven years, he inspected vandalism that had taken place since the student landing eight weeks earlier. Windows in the old power plant had been smashed and fires had been set on the wood floors of several buildings. Indians, it appeared, had taken a condemned, decaying prison and made it noticeably worse. He summed up his impressions this way: "One would have to search hard to find a more inhospitable location for human habitation."

The next day, Robertson returned with Tom Hannon and Sydney Smith of the General Services Administration to begin negotiations. The session was held in the dining room of the main cellblock. They expected only members of the Indian Council. Instead they found sixty-five people waiting. The visitors learned that the council could only operate in emergencies, and the entire group, not just a few representatives, would make decisions. This included both the "permanent" residents and visitors. Also, they would hold no secret meetings, and the council had no chairperson, because those on Alcatraz practiced pure democracy.

Grace Thorpe, daughter of Olympic track-and-field legend Jim Thorpe and public relations director for the island, had come to Alcatraz from Phoenix in December. She served as moderator. Robertson found it interesting that of the Indians present, ten were children, ten were men, and the rest, forty, were women. Also in attendance were a white doctor and four white lawyers, including

Aubrey Grossman, the radical attorney who had advised the occupiers before the occupation. Reporters were excluded.

The Indians wanted to talk about receiving title to the island, but the government representatives had already made it clear they would only discuss health and safety issues. After Robertson explained this, the doctor presented a list of medical supplies needed on the island. Stella Leach added to the shopping list, saying that a new generator was needed because they were moving the kitchen to a safer location.

Robertson felt as though the Indians expected him to start writing checks right there. Exasperated, he turned the meeting over to Tom Hannon, who told them the water barge would be sinking into San Francisco Bay any time now, and how the needed improvements to render Alcatraz livable would cost something like $8 million. The expense of the new university/cultural center/environmental center was in addition to this sum. The Indians dismissed Robertson's assertions. He summarized their position: "If we can render foreign aid, fight a war, etc., etc., we can give them everything they want."

When the government men tried to turn the meeting back to safety issues, Grossman said Indians knew the hazards on Alcatraz and were staying despite them. Robertson used that opening to express his sorrow at the death of Yvonne Oakes, and said he believed it was only a matter of time before another tragedy occurred. Stella Leach, as usual not mincing any words, shot back that Yvonne "died for the cause and others would too."

Robertson had a proposal: that all women and children leave the island, and a small group of up to fifteen men could remain as a "symbolic demonstration" force. Women responded to this by saying they would never leave, and that they would have to be carried off dead.

Not leaving well enough alone, Robertson said the government would be willing to pay the men who stayed on as caretakers. This suggestion brought cries that he was trying to buy them off. The two parties, Robertson realized, were talking past each other. The meeting ended with nothing accomplished.

Pure democracy had its limitations. That evening, LaNada Means insisted that Robertson join her for dinner. After refusing at first, saying that he didn't want to be accused of operating behind the backs of the others, he finally relented and met her and three white attorneys. They asked for improvements that would cost, everyone agreed, about $500,000, plus a planning grant. In return LaNada said they would stay in the habitable areas and keep others away from danger. Robertson turned them down. The next day, only Stella and David Leach from the Indian Council bothered to show up for the scheduled meeting.

Robertson returned to Washington discouraged. He reported to Vice President Spiro Agnew and Leonard Garment that "reason is a commodity they want nothing to do with—they are emotionally charged, naive and not used to responsibility. All they want is the island and an unending flow of money to do what they want, whether what they want has any chance of success or not. Their attorneys are good only for throwing fuel on the fire of unreasonableness."

Robertson stayed in close touch with Tom Hannon, the GSA official who had refused to send in the marshals. The two became friends, sharing the frustration and absurdity of their role as flak-catchers to Indian revolutionaries. For them, the situation was quite strange. Most of the time they were anonymous, mid-level government employees, but when they rode the Coast Guard cutter to the island they became representatives of genocide and imperialism.

When Hannon returned on January 26, he reported "that the only real change in this situation is that conditions . . . have deteriorated to a very sad point." He had taken a photographer along who documented in vivid detail the amount of filth that was accumulating as the unflushable toilets were overflowing and garbage piles were mounting. Worst of all, Hannon said, he didn't "know who the leaders are anymore, that it is becoming increasingly difficult to contact the supposed ones."

A few days later, though, he returned and later told Robertson's office it seemed that perhaps the occupiers were doing something about the mess. Everyone had moved out of the cellblock, the lighthouse, and other hazardous areas. He still couldn't find any leaders, but he noted that at least some planning seemed to be going on somewhere.

Alcatraz had become a place where different people carried out different agendas. For some in the Thunderbird security force, the agenda was bootlegging liquor and thrashing residents who criticized the leadership or who asked too many questions about finances. For others—at the same time on another corner of the same tiny piece of real estate—the agenda was running a health clinic or a school.

Though the drinkers, the drug dealers, and other agitators were still around, some people were making constructive progress. Some of them, for instance, fulfilled jobs such as cutting hair, or finding a way to get donated vehicles to the island. When Hannon would visit during the weekdays, it was no wonder he couldn't find anyone. Often, people who were trying to make something happen were on the mainland, squirreled away in an office pounding out copy for the newsletter or sending thank-you letters to the people who sent in their two dollar or ten dollar contribution.

LaNada Means worked on a proposal for a cultural center to give to Robertson. She was translating the rhetoric and demands for the cultural center into real numbers. Her early estimate said it was going to cost at least $170,000 just to get it off the ground.

The occupation had another strong asset. Robertson's NCIO had given a $50,000 planning grant to an ad hoc organization of Indian leaders in the Bay Area to study ways to improve the delivery of social services. And those mainland leaders, whatever their personal misgivings, remained committed, at least for now, to the occupiers. They made it part of their negotiations with Robertson that no matter what happened for the Bay Area, NCIO would first have to deal with Alcatraz.

In spite of Hannon's perception that no one was in charge anymore, the new council met and took up the full range of issues confronting the occupation. One meeting considered proposals from two Hollywood studios that wanted to explore the possibility of premiering their new Indian movies on the island. The next item was the now chronic issue of public drunkenness. Someone suggested making everyone take an oath of "I will not drink." Someone else thought that having someone in uniform would do the trick. Still another person advocated a strong warning issued to the troublemakers. That motion passed.

On February 23, LaNada Means finished her proposal and presented it to Robertson. The total amount she was seeking was $299,424. They would have Indian consultants, Indian teachers, Indian librarians, and a full-time Indian staff leading people around the center, telling the story of Indians of All Tribes. Robertson said he would study the whole thing and would get back to them in three weeks.

Even as the occupiers were becoming more coherent and organized, public support in the Bay Area dropped off sharply. Both the bad press and the tediousness of the occupation ushered in a precipitous decline in local good feelings toward those on the island. In its early days, the event offered daring, courage, and a bold leader; more, it educated non-Indians about the existence of this ignored community. But the story became repetitive and tiresome. When the upbeat coverage changed tone and the problems of the occupation became more public, the leadership responded defensively and banned reporters from the island unless they promised favorable coverage.

While the local press was growing tired of the story, the national press was just getting around to it. And the operative equation seemed to be that the farther away from California, the better the coverage. A flattering spread in *Look* featured the young Indians gazing through the bars of the main cellblock ("The Uprising That Worked"), and talk show host Merv Griffin flew out to tape a show.

The continued attention validated the efforts of those determined to keep it going. Movie stars and the world's press still showed up, even if they were no longer exactly beating a path to Pier 39. The vice president sent his personal emissary. And most important, Indians still arrived regularly. Maybe those who were sticking it out after the first wave had left didn't have all the answers to every problem the occupation presented to them. But, as they entertained celebrities and totaled up each day's contributions, dismissing the criticisms wasn't all that hard to do.

Upon returning to D.C. after his meetings in early January, Bob Robertson told his superiors at the White House that, in spite of his own exasperating experience trying to negotiate with the occupiers, he believed he could work out a solution. He asked for more time; they gave him more. For two more months, Robertson virtually commuted to San Francisco from Washington. He met with the "responsible" Indian leadership in the Bay Area, the occupiers, the Coast

Guard, and the Navy; commiserated and strategized with Hannon; and tried to find an approach that could bridge the enormous gulf between the two sides and finally resolve the crisis.

When Robertson returned in March, he brought a new proposal. It would be the government's last, best offer. This time he met with some forty Indians in the lunch room on the fifth floor of one of the apartment buildings. Wary but hopeful, Robertson outlined the proposal. The plan called for demolishing seven buildings and replacing them with an Indian museum and cultural center. Hovercraft would zip visitors from the Embarcadero in San Francisco, Sausalito, and other locations to Alcatraz. Operated as a business, proceeds from the state-of-the-art transportation system would be plowed back into the museum and cultural center. Statues of Indian historical figures would adorn the island.

This operation would be run by the U.S. Park Service, staffed largely by Indians, and overseen by a board of directors made up of elected tribal officials from around the country. To develop the project, a joint planning committee would be created to "protect the symbolic value which has been effected on Alcatraz over the past months, and to insure that the park plan will have a maximal Indian quality."

As far as a university, the plan offered no position but agreed to study the question. This was a diplomatic concession rather than a change in point of view. Robertson made clear he still doubted the practicality of building a university on the island because of the problems of accessibility, water, sewage, and heating.

The federal government agreed to spend millions building institutions on the island for and about Indian people, with the occupiers directly involved. Granted, they would not have title, nor operational control. But the proposal, at the very least, seemed to answer nearly all of the Indians' demands. If the Indians accepted, wouldn't most people—Indians and others—consider the occupation an astonishing success? On November 20th, could anyone from the midnight crossing really have imagined that in just four months they would be entertaining such a grand proposition from an official representative of the President of the United States?

One problem, from the point of view of the Indians, was that the proposal was largely crafted before the occupation in November. Developed by the U.S. Park Service, ironically, it called for an Indian theme park, with a Native American name. All Robertson did was add some bells and whistles—some of which, like the hydrofoil system, had no financing in place and thus were little more than interesting suggestions—to something the U.S. Park Service already wanted.

What the Indians demanded was title. Free and clear. Nothing less. They did not want to give Alcatraz to "elected tribal officials." They had come too far, sacrificed too much, to hand it over to a bunch of sell-out, Nixon-supporting, crew-cut Republican buddies of Bob Robertson.

Even more than the title, the Indians who still occupied the island in the spring of 1970 really wanted to continue the occupation on the symbolic terms that had been its hallmark. On Radio Free Alcatraz, John Trudell expressed it this way: The island had become a symbol, and you can't trade away the symbol.

This had become the governing ideology. It wasn't really pan-Indianism or revolution or cultural revival. Struggling on those terms would have been an attempt to win more tangible victories. Alcatraz was only tangentially about winning a new health center or job training to improve the hard lives of Indians in the cities.

For increasing numbers of people on the island, the point of the occupation was to occupy Alcatraz. For Trudell and the others who remained, a tangible victory could only mean certain defeat. This political philosophy—call it symbolism—rendered the details of a settlement meaningless. They were a rejectionist front with no back; hard-liners of uncut diamond. The occupation had become its own purpose. They were, as one writer put it, "symbols of arrival, . . . like flags on the moon."

A solution, in fact, would be a nightmare. There would be no more radio show, no more rallies with radical actress Jane Fonda or Irish revolutionary Bernadette Devlin or television interviews in Japan or fourteen-year-olds from Chicago driving three days across the country on a wing and a prayer just to be a part of something that crazy, that wonderful, that inspired.

Instead, there would be tour guides in green uniforms and

Smokey the Bear hats, tourists snapping pictures, bureaucrats sitting in offices supposedly helping Indians to find work or stop drinking, and a museum where everyone whispered.

Robertson felt bitter disappointment. Garment and others had gone out on a limb to endorse the latest proposal, and he knew there would never be another one as generous. This was it. He explained again to the occupiers that obtaining title was out of the question. It would never happen. Title would be tantamount to creating a reservation in the middle of San Francisco Bay.

The meeting ended badly, twice. First when it became clear that there would be no breakthrough and the government proposal would be rejected. Second, during dessert.

Coffee, Jell-O, and cake were served. In a written statement made three days later, a Coast Guard's observer described what happened next. "I noticed one man (later identified to me from a photograph as David Leach) who already had a cup of coffee, asking the man passing out the cups for an empty cup. I noted that the cup (white with blue stripes) was different from the other cup. Mr. Leach removed something from his pocket and showed it to those sitting in his immediate area. He then broke or crushed the object over the cup. I did not see him drop the object into the cup, but it appeared to be about a half-inch in diameter. I could not ascertain its color or shape, but did see a reflection from its service. Those sitting near Mr. Leach laughed as he was doing this. In a short while the same cup with blue stripes appeared, full of coffee, in front of Mr. Robertson. Since Jake Ours was sitting between me and Mr. Robertson, I asked Jake to pass the word not to drink the coffee. He did—and Mr. Robertson did not consume the coffee."

Donald Carroll, who had taken over for the retiring caretaker John Hart earlier in the year, told government investigators that he heard three Indians discussing the incident the next morning, April 1. They identified David Leach as the one behind the act, and the drug involved as mescaline. One of the three, a woman he knew as Marilyn Miracle, said it was a stupid thing to do. Another said that he was glad that Leach had made the attempt, since Robertson was "part of the bureaucratic system, that he was now lying to them, and that this whole thing was going to be another long, drawn-out hassle."

Robertson went directly from that meeting to talk with waiting reporters. The results, without the observer's sharp eyes, might have been truly newsworthy.

Three days later Indians of All Tribes issued a scathing response to Robertson's offer:

> The government's proposal is nothing more than the formation of another park, whether it is state or federally owned; unneeded, undesired, and actually an attempt to end the Alcatraz movement. A movement which is the hope of Indian people to advance themselves culturally and spiritually; a true belief of our own ideals. Mr. Robertson, in his press conference concerning our meeting of March 31st, presented such a pretty picture for the public of an open air park with lovely Indian statues secluded here and there among the Indian Cultural Center and Museum, with Indian guides strolling around showing people where all the birdbaths are. We will no longer be museum pieces, tourist attractions, and politician's playthings. We do not need statues to our dead because our dead never die. They are always here with us. We remember the deeds that our people do in our hearts, and this is where heroes should be remembered. The public thinks this is really going to be a tribute to the American Indian, but this proposal of the government's provides for a park, which will have some supervision by hand-picked Indians subjected to governmental control and then from then on Alcatraz will become just another government park. Thus, we feel it our obligation as Indians of All Tribes Inc. for Indian people to ask the government to submit a counter-proposal to the proposal that we gave them. We will give them until May 31 to do this. We are willing to negotiate on money and the time and the day that they will turn over the deed to this island. That is all that is negotiable.

In April, Vine Deloria, Jr., the nation's leading Indian intellectual and author of a sharp, entertaining bestseller, *Custer Died For Your*

Sins: An American Indian Manifesto, visited San Francisco. He had visited the island in the early days of the takeover, and was impressed with the energy and boldness of Alcatraz but felt the activists' inexperience severely limited their effectiveness. During his April visit, he told reporters that "only ten Indians in the country are qualified to negotiate with the federal government." His obvious sense that none of them were affiliated with Indians of All Tribes was not lost on island residents, and on May 7 the council voted to send a letter in response.

The council, which normally responded to criticism with extreme defensiveness, basically seemed to agree with Deloria. The minutes record that "Al Miller made a motion to send a letter to Vine Deloria, Jr. about the statement which he gave to the white news media on April 3, 1970, of there being only ten Indians able to deal with this government. This will be sent to him because of our 'dire need for consultation.' Motion passed."

But by that point, veterans of Indian affairs who might have been willing to reach out to the occupiers had, like so many others, lost interest. All that Indians of All Tribes could do was wait. But as the weeks dragged on, the obvious message was that neither the government nor anyone else had anything to say to them.

In May, the feds began proceedings to transfer the property to the Department of the Interior and the National Park System. On the island, this prompted new, frenzied activity. Caretaker Don Carroll reported an increase in both the numbers and the militancy of the new arrivals. Knowing he was a conduit to the feds of information, bad interpretations, and rumors, people on the island no doubt told him things they wanted to get to Hannon. His reports from the month of May are replete with the sense that something big was going down, fueled not in small part by the fact that members of the Indian liberation force had beaten his dog, which Carroll had to put to sleep. The caretaker heard that one thousand people would come Memorial Day weekend and "take over the island completely." Also, the lighthouse would be blown up.

Richard Oakes came to the island on May 3 with fifteen friends to make one last visit. They were, according to Carroll's report, "extremely abusive and attempted to break in[to] the lighthouse." As the month wore on, he reported the presence of about fifty firearms (though no automatic weapons), and a general cleanup of the cellblock. He heard rumors of stockpiles of sleeping bags and canteens and that ten men on the island had guerrilla warfare training and were hiding automatic weapons. Some of the residents told Carroll they expected President Nixon to make them important again with a live, televised speech regarding the island.

As Memorial Day weekend approached, Carroll planned on sending his employees off the island. He checked the emergency radio system he was to use in case his life was in danger.

The occupiers gathered their supporters and their friends from the media for a press conference on the island over the holiday weekend, but the number of people there fell far short of a thousand. Trudell, Stella Leach, and the others who spoke proved once again that they could put on a good show. A drum group performed tribal songs. A tribal elder spoke of spirituality and unity. They vowed never to leave, never to surrender. Their tone was anxious, fearful. If the government tried to remove them, Stella Leach promised they would have another Wounded Knee on their hands, raising the specter of the 1890 massacre.

For all of the activity, the posturing, and redoubled efforts to make the occupation work, the message from Washington's silence as the deadline for a counterproposal came and went was clear. The government was acting as if they didn't exist.

Part Two

The Native American Embassy

Chapter 5

The Monument Tour

long with problems of logistics, leadership, media, and the federal government, the rebellious youth on Alcatraz and around the country had to deal with those in Indian communities who weren't sympathetic to the growing tide of radical rhetoric. Some California Indians charged those on Alcatraz with being little more than colonizers themselves, since they had not sought permission from the descendants of the people who originally lived in the area. Those California Indians argued Alcatraz did not belong to American Indians in general but to them specifically, and there were few California Indians involved in the occupation.

Others found it a baffling exercise carried out by privileged, misguided youth. From Los Angeles, a Comanche named Howard Yackitonipah offered this opinion: "I believe the Indians back home in Oklahoma don't understand why Indians are taking over Alcatraz. What do they want Alcatraz for? It's gonna cost, and if the federal government can't keep Alcatraz going with all the money that the government's got, what's the Indian going to do? Sure, people are donating this and donating that, but you gotta keep that thing in water, you gotta keep toilet service, you gotta keep electricity, and all they think about is just the island and the land. They're not thinking about what keeps it going."

Lois Knifechief agreed. "If those Indians on Alcatraz would have found a place worth having, I would be the one to say, why yes, we'd like to have it, but why Alcatraz, pray tell me. What do they want out there on that stupid rock? There's nothing but junk!"

John Knifechief thought the occupiers were spoiled. "They have no reason whatsoever to be militant or be demanding of anything, because they have everything. They can do whatever they want to do. The thing is, the biggest part of them kids don't know anything about reservation life. I really don't understand what they are demanding because they have educational opportunities that we didn't have. There's grants that Indian students can get. They can better themselves if they want to. I can't see what these young people are demanding." No amount of pronouncements from Indians of All Tribes about pan-Indianism, unity, and the national significance of their occupation could disguise the fact that plenty of people in the Indian world had no intention of being led to revolution by a bunch of student radicals.

But to others, who saw plenty of reason to be militant, Alcatraz and, more importantly, the idea of public protest made perfect sense. Indian protestors had plenty of people to take their cues from. Armed battalions of the New Left bombed computer centers and carefully chosen government installations. African Americans set fire to entire city blocks and asked the nation to consider the implications of National Guardsmen in jeeps quelling a rebellion only blocks from the White House. Others operated as commandos and robbed banks to fund a people's guerrilla army.

The targets of Indian protest were invariably government installations or historical sites of deep, double-edged meaning. Indians in New York attempted to liberate Ellis Island. Mount Rushmore, where Washington, Lincoln, Jefferson, and Roosevelt stared into the sacred Black Hills, was briefly occupied by Lakota and Chippewa militants. On Thanksgiving, a group of Indians led a protest at Plymouth Rock. And numerous demonstrations occurred at local offices of the Bureau of Indian Affairs in Denver, Minneapolis, Oakland, and other locales.

Behind the wave of protests were numerous organizations, nearly all of them from the cities. As had happened in the Bay Area, urban communities of Indians in Minneapolis, Chicago, Los Angeles, Cleveland, Denver, and other cities had transformed themselves over the course of the previous decade, shifting their main focus from Indian culture to an increased engagement in politics. Everywhere the government's relocation program had sent Indians, groups emerged to boisterously and aggressively complain about the conditions they found themselves living in.

The local groups that exploded onto the scene in 1970, were a scattered collection. No central committee met and planned their various operations. At most, the leaders met at conferences, sometimes bandying about the idea of creating an umbrella group under which they could all fit. For the time being, though, they had to settle for finding ways of outdoing each other on the evening news.

One of the groups directly inspired to action by Alcatraz was the Seattle Indian community. When Bernie White Bear, a leader in the community, learned of the events in San Francisco, he and others around the city took notice. Then, they sent word to the island. They were going to have an Alcatraz of their own, and would include in their liberation force a contingent of present and former occupiers of the island.

Their target was Fort Lawton, an abandoned military installation on the coast near Seattle. The site, which they planned to occupy, was surrounded by high fences on one side, while the other side featured precarious, dangerous cliffs. In early March of 1970, and again a week later, White Bear and about a dozen others arrived at the site and were arrested for trespassing.

Two weeks later, White Bear and the others in Seattle tried again. This time, Jane Fonda joined them, assuring them a place on the evening news. Then, on the day that those arrested in the first actions were to go to court, White Bear and his occupation force made their way one more time to Fort Lawton. Again, they were arrested. Among those there to support the action was Richard Oakes. As they stood and sat in the crowded brig of the abandoned post, Oakes used his gift for oratory to encourage and inspire the activists.

In laying claim to Fort Lawton, they initially used the same questionable 1868 treaty logic that the occupiers of Alcatraz were using. Eventually, though, they applied for a portion of the land through a federal project, outlining their plans for a cultural center. In doing so, they shifted their focus from dramatic direct action to the vagaries of bureaucracy and red tape. But a year and a half later, bureaucrats approved their application and the land was theirs.

Other attempts were not as successful. Bruce Oakes, who knew his cousin Richard only slightly while growing up in New York, was one of the leaders in the attempt to seize Ellis Island.

In the summer of 1969, while his older cousin was organizing in California, Bruce signed on with an internship program of the United Scholarship Service (USS), which had grown from an understaffed program that provided small grants to Indian and Mexican American college students to a wide-ranging foundation assisting in the placement of secondary students in East Coast preparatory schools, undergraduate and graduate school scholarships, and summer internship programs in local Indian communities and in Washington, D.C.

Oakes had recently graduated from The Pomfret School in Connecticut. USS sent him to the small town of Havre, Montana, near the Rocky Boy and Fort Belknap Reservations, where juvenile delinquency among Indian youth was a chronic and growing problem. In his program proposal to the USS he stated, "What I'd very much like to do is deal with the younger people and seek out their problems and perhaps offer a possible solution to these problems . . . I will document cases [that] . . . Indian 'militants' can use to fight for Indian rights and needs. I will also try to give the youth I meet a chance to organize and think as a group."

Once on the ground in Havre, however, the young Oakes found himself feeling a little like a delinquent himself. "Without transportation," he wrote to the USS soon after arriving, "I've found myself bored and useless. If this has happened to me in a week, picture what an Indian kid raised here must go through. This is where the delinquency problem comes into view. There is a place called 'the Scene' that Community Action [a War on Poverty program] has made but I see this isn't going to cure the problem. The Indian kids in this town aren't going to find themselves satisfied in a little recreation room. They want excitement. They want something to look forward to such as breaking [into] a store or boozing in a car."

Oakes placed the blame for delinquency square at the feet of the Bureau of Indian Affairs and the Office of Economic Opportunity (OEO). Those, after all, were the agencies that were supposed to be responding to the real needs of local Indian people. His superiors suggested that he document specific cases of BIA and OEO negligence and help the young people initiate legal action. Instead, he and some of his new friends established a psychedelic coffeehouse in the basement of the Community Action Program office.

Two weeks before the internship was to end, Bruce Oakes packed his bags and headed home for Syracuse, New York. Though he had a glitzy prep school diploma in hand and could have been on the fast track, a summer fighting the War on Poverty with the youth of Havre convinced him to wait a while before going to college.

He saw the news of Alcatraz on television while living in Syracuse. When he realized his cousin Richard was one of the leaders at Alcatraz, Bruce felt immense pride. Student friends asked him to come to New York to help organize support for Indians of All Tribes, and he readily agreed.

Although only eighteen, he found himself living in a storefront without windows or even a bathroom, in a rough neighborhood in Brooklyn. With other Alcatraz supporters in New York, he worked on staging events in support of the occupation, and frequently spoke on the phone with those on the island, including his cousin.

Soon after arriving, he learned that people were already planning an East Coast equivalent of Alcatraz: an occupation of Ellis Island. Bruce, along with David Leach and LaNada Means, two leaders from Alcatraz who were in New York to raise money and speak about their island occupation, became involved in the planned seizure of another landmark.

Organizers lined up boats and the needed supplies. The appointed day, bitterly cold, arrived. Oakes and his comrades went ahead with the plan despite the temperature, and drove to New Jersey where the boats waited. They struggled for an hour before realizing the fuel lines were hopelessly frozen, and decided they would try again the next night.

Bruce returned to the car and then heard on the radio an excited voice announcing that Indians were landing on Ellis Island. Bruce and David couldn't believe it. Despite their careful planning, one of their number must have telephoned the news media before confirming the operation had succeeded.

David went nuts, saying now they had to get to the island no matter what, even if it meant swimming there. Bruce knew that was impossible, that however cold the water got in chilly San Francisco, the weather there was nothing compared to winter in New York. Helicopters with searchlights flew overhead and police cars arrived soon after that, and the Indian invasion force found themselves with a police escort back to Brooklyn.

They weren't arrested, since no one had actually landed. David and Bruce vowed revenge on the person responsible for this fiasco, an Indian from Maine who only joined the group that very evening. He had apparently decided on his own to notify the press, even though there was a carefully worked out plan to release the news only after the island had been taken.

Fury and humiliation dogged them until sunup, when David insisted that he and Bruce go to Manhattan, where David knew important people. Bruce followed David as they stormed into talk show host Merv Griffin's office. Griffin had recently done a show on Alcatraz, the single biggest media prize yet. Bruce's eyes widened as they walked past champion ice-skater Peggy Fleming and British celebrity Arthur Treacher. "Tell Merv Griffin, David Leach from Alcatraz Island is here to see him!"

Bruce and David still wore their muddy clothes from the failed landing the night before, and Griffin took one look at them and said, "Boys, go get something to eat." He gave David a crisp one hundred dollar bill.

David felt that Griffin could arrange transportation for them to Ellis Island. Griffin rejected the idea, arguing that the place was too hot, that nobody could take it over now. After a few more days, David and LaNada went back to the West Coast. Plans for an island occupation in New York Harbor never panned out.

However disappointing or temporary actions like the one at Ellis Island were, one thing was clear—the season of protest Clyde Warrior and others had foreseen had come upon the Indian world with a vengeance as dozens of actions erupted around the country. Pent-up rage—especially among impoverished, underserved Indians in the cities—found an outlet. And if pragmatic concerns of people in Indian affairs for programs, budgets, and policies seemed to have next to no place in the rhetoric and demands of those taking over monuments and government offices, something deeper—the desire of people to take charge of their own destiny—was finding its voice.

Back on Alcatraz, June was a month of fire and anguish, adversity and defiance, with a couple of miracles thrown in for good measure. Fire had been a nearly constant presence in the drama from the beginning. The fire that destroyed San Francisco's Indian Center in October helped instigate the takeover in November. And fire had been the primary source of heat and light for the occupiers, and sometimes the fires burned out of control. The damage, so far, had been limited, but the near constant shortage of water raised frightening possibilities.

Those possibilities were realized on June 1, 1970. A spectacular inferno swept through Alcatraz, and from San Francisco it looked like the entire island was on fire. It raged for several hours, as helpless island residents could only watch. The next morning, reporters found out that four of the historical buildings on the island had gone up in flames. The buildings were so far apart from one another that the only conclusion possible was that someone had set the fires deliberately. John Trudell took to the airwaves and claimed that someone had sneaked onto the island in the middle of the night and set the fires to make the occupiers look bad, but few believed him. The fire did not end the occupation.

LaNada Means survived several fires on Alcatraz. One incident, however, she would never forget. Fast asleep in her room, she woke up suddenly to see the curtains on fire. She reacted swiftly, thinking only of protecting her son, Deynon, and tried to put out the flames with her bare hands. Dazed, she picked up her child and walked to the dining hall, as smoke from the blaze followed her.

People looked up from their coffee and rushed to LaNada. She handed Deynon to someone and then fell over. As some of the neighbors rushed to investigate the fire, others attended to LaNada. She had gone into shock. There was no water, so they put her hands in cold milk and carried her to a bed near the kitchen. She felt no pain, and was happy to see people working together.

Stella Leach covered her in a Pendleton blanket and stayed with her all night. People she could trust stood guard by her door. LaNada's eyes were closed, but somehow she could see everything around her. LaNada remembered her mother's guidance on receiving spiritual direction through prayers at sunrise. She described what happened next. "I gathered my blanket around me and slipped out of the kitchen into the yard and over to the edge of the island. I lifted my hands to the sun and prayed as it rose out of the bay over the Bay Bridge from the east. I knew I would be all right as I experienced a deep knowledge inside of me."

A few hours later, she was in Oakland. A doctor examined her hands, black and charred; looking, she thought, like boiled wieners. The damage was severe: first- to third-degree burns on both hands, down to her tendons. He insisted she get treatment at a hospital. LaNada declined, and left his office in bandages, with his prognosis ringing in her ears: Her fingers might never fully recover, and it would be six months to a year before she could use her hands again.

LaNada returned to the island. Six weeks later, her hands had fully recovered, fingers too, with hardly any trace of scarring. It was, she said, her first spiritual experience. LaNada seemed to lead a charmed life in other ways. *Ramparts*, a leftist magazine, had placed her on one of its covers which proclaimed "Better Red Than Dead." Jane Fonda saw it, arranged to meet Means, and the two became fast friends. The actress visited not only the island, but also traveled to Idaho to meet LaNada's family.

Less than two weeks after the huge fire of June 1, Richard Oakes, a nearly forgotten figure from the early days—all of seven months before—made the news again. It happened at Warren's, the "Indian bar" in the Mission District. Warren's had been a constant in all of

Oakes's incarnations in the Bay Area. As a new arrival seeking work, it was a place of employment. As a community activist and student leader, it was a place from which he organized. On this particular night, the evening of June 10, he was a customer. A fight erupted between Oakes and a group of Samoans, and one of the Samoans broke a pool cue over his head.

His cousin Bruce heard the news in South Dakota. He was already on his way to Alcatraz, to see for himself the island that had dominated his life for the past several months. He and some friends set out for California in a typical Indian car, festooned with all the usual bumper stickers and powered by the kind of engine that burned more oil than gas. After a few states the hood had a permanent bulge from the oil cap bouncing against it. In Cannonball, North Dakota, they ran out of money and had to cut grass to earn a few dollars. When they noticed people laughing at them, they realized that hiding in the grass were rattlesnakes and copperheads.

In Rapid City, they stayed at the house of an Oglala who had studied at Harvard. The phone rang during their stay and Bruce got the terrible news: Richard had been severely beaten in a bar in San Francisco. He might not live. Bruce and his traveling companions headed to California immediately, arriving a few days later. Richard was in a coma, and many felt he would not make it. Bruce met Anne, Richard's wife, for the first time.

Bruce took the Clearwater across the Bay to the island, anxious to finally set foot on Alcatraz. As the boat pulled closer, he could see LaNada waving to him. Once on land, however, the mood changed sharply, as he saw LaNada Means and Stella Leach in a wild argument. He felt bad vibes the second he stepped on land. During the several weeks he spent in the Bay Area, he went back to the island only three or four times.

When he returned to the hospital, his cousin was still in a coma, though sometimes Richard would squeeze Bruce's hand, and his eyes would seem to move rapidly even though they were closed. Bruce felt he was thinking, struggling, and fighting.

A Tuscarora leader named Mad Bear Anderson and a medicine man named Peter Mitten visited Richard's room and performed healing ceremonies. Richard emerged from his coma a few days later, stunning his nurses and doctors. But Richard, now dependent on crutches, was not the same. He would not talk to Bruce about Yvonne, or about events on the island.

Richard moved up north, to the place where Anne grew up. Bruce headed back east and that fall started college at Dartmouth.

By midsummer, newspapers continued to chronicle the decline and fall of the Alcatraz occupation. In July, the *Los Angeles Herald Examiner* wrote a "The Dream is Over"–type article that exposed the leadership, organizational, and crime problems that plagued the island. John Trudell's wife, Lou, fired back a response. She noted the newsletter was still being printed, the radio program was still being aired, school was about to begin after a summer break, and the medical and dental clinics were doing just fine. "You stated tragedy has come to Alcatraz," she wrote.

> Yes, the warden's "mansion" burned and so did two other structures near it, but that was on the upper level where no one resided and, Mr. Schultz [the author of the article], that was not a tragedy.
>
> The death in January of the young girl was tragic as is the hospitalization of Richard Oakes. . . . The Indian has had a tragic past, Mr. Schultz, needless to say a tragic present but we are here on Alcatraz and on Rattlesnake Island and in Pit River to prevent a tragic future.
>
> There is definitely no one leader or president here Mr. Schultz, nor has there ever been. We have a seven man council but none are so-called leaders or chiefs. The leaders are the whole body, the whole population on Alcatraz for without them there would be no Alcatraz and there would be no hope.
>
> Incidentally, Mr. Schultz, the young Indian rumored to have committed suicide did not, and is alive and well, and the day after your article was printed I gave birth to a beautiful boy here on Alcatraz. That, Mr. Schultz, is hope.

John and Lou Trudell named the baby Wovoka, after the Paiute visionary who inspired the Ghost Dance movement in the 1880s. That movement, which offered reunions with dead loved ones and visions of a new continent rolling out on top of this one, spread quickly from Nevada to the Dakotas, fueling government fear and yellow journalistic fervor. The movement all but ended when that fear and fervor prompted the Wounded Knee massacre of 1890, when the Seventh Cavalry gunned down over three hundred Minneconjou Sioux as they sought safe haven from Army harassment.

At the White House in August, Garment and Patterson made less dramatic plans for ending the Alcatraz occupation. They decided to send in armed federal agents and track down the occupiers one by one. Hopefully, there would be little or no violence. Unfortunately for them, the *San Francisco Chronicle*'s Herb Caen learned of the plan and wrote about it in his popular column. For the time being, Garment and Patterson would have to wait.

Some Alcatraz leaders insisted from the start that the island occupation was a "movement." Its end, they contended, would signify the demise of the Indian revolution that was sweeping the country. Nothing, though, could be further from the truth. Seizing the Rock had been a stunning turning point in the history of Indian protest. But it hadn't created the conditions that Indian people protested against. If, as some people in Indian affairs wished, the occupation had lasted just a few weeks, its place in history would have been assured. And if it had never happened, some other event would have provided the fulcrum for the new season of Indian occupations and direct actions.

As always, what Alcatraz offered most was its symbolic value. Few people came to the island seeking leaders for their own protests. A group might invite people from the island to be part of their protest, as the National Indian Youth Council did in 1970 when they were protesting at the Gallup Ceremonial, an annual event in New Mexico that many people thought exploited Indian people. But few people thought of the occupiers as being somehow in charge of—or even central to—what was happening in their own communities.

People with a longer view could see that what was happening around the Indian world was much deeper than any one event or any single organization. One such person was Hank Adams, the Assiniboine-Sioux activist who had been involved in protests since even before the establishment of the National Indian Youth Council. While most others from the NIYC were gone from the scene or had taken jobs in the system, Adams remained committed to the local fishing protests at Frank's Landing that had begun over five years before. He made as many enemies as anyone involved in politics, but even those who disagreed with him would not begrudge him his keen intellect and searing analytical skills.

Still, he was a walking contradiction—a community organizer who had campaigned for Nixon in 1960, a college dropout who went head-to-head with cream of the crop of Ivy League grads, a staunch opponent of Vietnam who joined the Army in 1965, an activist who could do hand-to-hand combat with state police and game officials one day and hobnob at a National Congress of American Indian convention the next; someone who knew that the press coverage of the "new" activist movement in Indian country all but ignored everything that had happened previously but who also raised $10,000 for the Indians on Alcatraz.

By 1971, he had been a primary force behind Indian involvement in the Poor People's Campaign; had become a trusted political ally of the Kennedy family, Marlon Brando, Ralph Nader, and scores of other national figures; had been arrested and beaten in the various fishing rights protests in the Pacific Northwest; had run unsuccessfully for a Congressional seat; and had been mysteriously shot within inches of his life while sitting in his car in the early morning near a fishing protest site. He was as at home on the banks of the Nisqually River as he was lobbying in Washington.

Six years after being among those other Indians maligned for copying the tactics of "niggers" at the fish-ins, he was still struck at just how tame much of the new Indian political activity could be. When he met with protesting students at the BIA-run Haskell Institute in Lawrence, Kansas, in 1970, he found nothing close to the fundamental calling into question of values and authority that one might have suspected. Instead, the Haskell students were mounting a petition drive to end their ten P.M. curfew and bed checks.

Such things to Hank Adams were the real indication of where things were in America in the early 1970s. History might record the spectacular—Woodstock, the Haight, massive demonstrations against the war in Vietnam, protest actions by Indians and other minority groups—but America remained by and large a pretty tame place, where true revolution was still only a faint possibility. But more was happening and, at least, fundamental change seemed possible.

As with the Washington, D.C. scene that Adams continued to keep track of, the activist sphere was becoming more and more crowded, with nearly every region boasting of a number of groups engaging in, or threatening to engage in, direct action. Adams related differently to the new militants than he had to Clyde Warrior and Mel Thom, his closest friends in the Youth Council. He never sensed from the newer people the same level of commitment of Warrior and Thom. But neither did he summarily dismiss the newcomers.

In New York, in the summer of 1970, Hank Adams had his first long conversation with Russell Means, one of the rising stars among the militants. Adams was sharing the stage at a New York rally with John Trudell of Alcatraz and Russell Means, Dennis Banks, and Clyde Bellecourt, all three of whom were in the Big Apple to raise money and awareness for their group, the American Indian Movement (AIM).

AIM, which had started in Minneapolis in 1968 to advocate for Indian people who lived in the Twin Cities, was one of the many urban activist groups that had sprung up around the country in recent years. AIM's activity centered in Minneapolis, but groups were starting AIM chapters in Means's operating base of Cleveland, Milwaukee, and several other cities. With each new chapter, AIM was separating itself from the pack of scattered activist organizations and was closer to becoming a national organization. Like other urban activist groups, AIM had no real connection to reservation communities, but its reputation was growing among all sectors of Indian people by the early 1970s.

Over drinks in New York, Means and Adams spun out theories and strategies on cocktail napkins and placemats. Adams spelled out his growing theories on how the Indian struggle was going to have to completely abandon the idea of reforming the Bureau of Indian Affairs. Instead, he foresaw a future in which Indian people would search through their own histories and find models of education, leadership, economy, and social relations.

When Russ Means's turn came, he said that what Indians needed was either a major victory or a major defeat. The attention to militant actions was all well and good, but unless Indians could do something to make an indelible impression on the public, the struggle would be lost amid all the other things happening in American society.

For Russ, a major victory meant finding a spot to liberate, and staying there until the feds backed down or came in and killed them all. Though AIM had no constituency there yet, he talked about several places on the Pine Ridge Reservation in South Dakota as ideal spots for a military engagement. Among the four or five spots he had in mind—places that would prove difficult for U.S. forces to take back—was Wounded Knee, the scene of a bloody massacre in 1890. By the 1970s it was a small cluster of churches, houses, businesses, and a post office, about a dozen miles from the reservation's agency town. For a Lakota like Russ Means, nowhere else held as much symbolic power.

Increasingly, the various eruptions of militancy made their way to the evening news. Missile bases, public lands, national monuments, and BIA regional offices were all fair game as the seventies unfolded. But the ragtag bands of Indian militants who were making names for themselves had not appeared magically out of the mists of time nor were they the newly arrived shock troops who would finally get something going in Indian affairs.

Many of those labeled simply "militants" were, in fact, students enrolled in the kinds of equal opportunity programs the National Indian Youth Council had lobbied for, and who could drop out of school for a semester or even just miss a few weeks of classes while occupying surplus federal land. Many of them still drew scholarship money while doing so. Others worked in dead-end jobs in the cities not yet in the purview of the national Indian organizations, making parts for icemakers or doing low-end clerical work in an insurance company.

The cast of characters in the Indian world of the early 1970s was much more complicated than the media-projected young, city-based militants versus passive reservation residents. Indian people who emerged on the public stage at the time ran their own businesses, were corporate executives, worked at newspapers, or were accountants. The relative number of organizations having nothing to do with militant protest that were sprouting up around Indian country, in fact, was staggering. American Indian educators, health professionals, journalists, artists, lawyers, artists, actors, scholars and others formed organizations and emerged onto the scene with a suddeness that was difficult even to keep track of, much less make sense of.

Even those back on the reservations were more and more often veterans of off-reservation American society. They had left to attend business school or signed on with the relocation program and learned to be truck drivers, machinists, electricians, and dozens of other professions. Some relocatees returned because they just couldn't hack it in the big city. Most, though, returned home because they preferred life there and wanted to find a way to make use of their skills there.

The reservation returnees were, in one sense, but a shade of their great-great grandparents, often lacking knowledge of tribal languages and traditions and dependent on the accoutrements of modern American life. In another sense, though, they were their grandparents' dreams—Indians who could do all those things that white government operatives did; Indians who had the skills necessary for confronting the future.

Reporters and authors finally got around to noticing the changes and produced a slew of articles and books about how the Vanishing American wasn't vanishing, but was poised to grasp at the future and didn't have much to do with his or her own past. Most of the best articles focused on the "plight" of Indians. The worst talked in terms of tragedy, with all the trajectory of what a tragedy is—something awful that cannot be undone. The media represented Indians as ancient peoples, decimated by history, rising up to reassert themselves just as the United States found itself falling apart. But, as one seasoned observer would later point out, "We weren't reborn. We were just noticed."

Entrenched stereotypes remained, such as Hollywood "Cowboys and Indians" notions of bloodthirsty savages and passive, monosyllabic nobles. So, too, did images of lazy, jobless, Indian drunks living off the public dole on prisonlike reservations out west. Along with those, several new images of who Indians were and what Indians were all about emerged into public consciousness.

The Indian militant became one more new image among others.

Hippies glorified peyote-eating, visionary Indians who existed on other planes of consciousness. Environmentalists celebrated tree-hugging, nature loving Indians who were the answer to pollution and cyclamates. Indeed, perhaps the most enduring image of Indians of the period was a Keep America Beautiful, Inc., television commercial featuring Cherokee actor "Iron Eyes" Cody pristinely bedecked in buckskin and feathers, weeping horse turd–sized tears over litter in once pristine American rivers.

Bob Robertson, the executive director of the National Council on Indian Opportunity who had put so much effort into negotiating with the occupiers of Alcatraz earlier in the year, was one of the key people in the federal government responsible for dealing with the burgeoning Indian scene of the early 1970s. In December, he organized a conference at the Airlie Center in Warrenton, Virginia to hear at length from urban Indians. The meeting was a follow-up to months of hearings on urban issues that had featured angry and confrontational testimony. The hearings had taken place during the Johnson Administration in Minneapolis, San Francisco, and other cities.

Set on three thousand acres of rolling Virginia countryside an hour from Washington, the Airlie Center seemed a perfect setting. A conference center with the feel of a resort, its brochures promised "tranquility, gentle beauty and casual sophistication." The Indians arrived for lunch on Monday, December 14, 1970. Some of the 150 participants came with the expectation that they would be meeting with the president or vice president, and were taken aback to find themselves so far from Washington. Still, everything was calm until six-thirty that evening.

At one of the center's bars, a dispute broke out between the Indians and members of a group from IBM that was also meeting at Airlie House. A little later, Indians set up a drum, and this disturbed another group meeting nearby. Complaints began pouring in to Richard Ross, the Airlie's deputy director, of "ungentlemanly behavior, rowdyism and truculence on the part of a small minority of the members of the Indian Opportunity group." He ordered the bar closed.

An Indian official from OEO, a cosponsor of the meeting, arrived on the scene and took charge. He asked that the bars be reopened, and they were. A crisis seemed to be averted, but that night some Indians trashed the International House, one of several different buildings where Robertson's group was housed. They invaded the kitchen and stole food and beverages. They ripped stuffed pheasants from the wall and destroyed them, and everything that could be vandalized, was. All attempts to quiet members of the group were fruitless. They were "truculent, pugnacious, obscene and uncooperative," Ross reported. The next day, the conference went on, seemingly with the difficulties over. In Warrenton, however, locals had sighted Indians drinking whiskey in public, then forming a human chain to block traffic on Main Street.

The real trouble began late Tuesday night. Ross got the call at 6:30 A.M. A housekeeper called him at home to say the entire place had been taken over. Guards watched every door, three members of the Airlie House staff were held hostage, and a wildly drunken group of dissident, militant Indians had proceeded to completely vandalize the place. Ross called the Virginia State Police in nearby Culpeper, and Bob Robertson in Washington.

At the Conference Center, Ross found his employees congregated, trading stories on the previous night's misadventures. One of the employees was given a reason for the mayhem; they wanted to show the white man they could take over his property as he had taken over theirs. A stunned Ross reported what he saw:

> Many of the so-called door guards were in a stupor or asleep by the doorways. All had bottles in all pockets, drapes were torn, china and glassware were broken; tables and furniture were broken, wine was spilled everywhere; carpets were burned. The Federal Room was completely vandalized, as Seals of the Government Departments were defaced and in disarray, as well as missing from the room, chairs and tables were broken; two $7,000 busts were seriously damaged; red wine was spilled all over the carpets; and, a large American flag was shredded and the pieces were used for head bands.
>
> The damage was so intense and widespread that I immediately

called for a photographer to have a photographic record of the damage. By this time, approximately 7–7:30 A.M., the vandals who were able to walk had disappeared.

Symbols fared especially badly during the night. "Two saddle blankets were stolen, as was a Navajo rug mounted on the wall, valued at $500.... Every American flag on all twenty-five outdoor lamppost was broken off and destroyed—none have reappeared. Ninety percent of the Airlie flags and the Virginia State flags were either torn down, shredded or ripped beyond repair." Robertson ended the conference a day early. As the Indians boarded buses headed back to Cleveland, Denver, Chicago, and Minneapolis, some openly wore the flags and pheasant feathers they had liberated.

The next day, Thursday, December 17, the *Washington Post* ran a four-paragraph story in the metro section; "Vandalism Mars Indian Conference" was the headline. The story described the trouble as a fairly long but nonviolent confrontation involving less than twenty Indians, and that damage amounted to perhaps $1000. The incident, unnamed Indian and government spokespersons said, illustrated a conference report that found alcoholism the number one health problem of American Indians.

Also on the same day, the NCIO called the meeting a success, and said a small group of people who had been drinking caused some property damage. That damage was being itemized by Airlie House, and no charges were being brought. The NCIO statement also quoted Dennis Banks as a leader of the American Indian Movement, the increasingly influential activist group from Minneapolis that had shared the stage in New York in the summer with Hank Adams. Banks commended NCIO's work, saying the conference had been a very successful meeting and marked the real beginning of a dialogue between the federal government and urban Indian people.

The first official meeting between the Nixon administration and urban Indian leaders had featured wild drunkenness, seemingly mindless destruction, and the seizing of hostages. But in Washington, D.C., where perception is often more important than reality, it seemed not to really have happened. In Warrenton, however, the event became part of local folklore, and decades later townspeople would still talk of the Indian uprising, and remember the way drums sounded booming through the hills.

Perhaps unconsciously, the event seemed to echo other meetings a century earlier, when the American government invited delegations of Indians to visit New York and Washington, D.C., where the Americans hoped the Indians would be awed by the power and wealth of the United States, and come to favorable terms on treaties. And at the least, the failed summit convincingly demonstrated a depth of rage among Indians that could not be written off as a phenomenon limited simply to militant college students.

Bob Robertson, the point man for the Nixon administration's efforts to understand and work with the urban Indians, was growing weary of the shrill rhetoric and explosions of inexplicable madness. Eight months earlier he had very nearly been intentionally drugged by someone who laced his coffee with mescaline. Now, a scene of destruction at a meeting sponsored by his own organization marred his attempts to reach out to Indian people in American cities. And this from the responsible elements, the so-called urban Indian *leaders*.

The GSA's Tom Hannon, Robertson's partner in making sense of Alcatraz and the urban Indian phenomenon in general, still kept in touch with his counterpart in Washington. During the previous twelve months, since the landing in San Francisco, they had shared much, and even developed a sense of humor about their work.

Hannon wrote his friend Robertson on December 28:

> Thanks for item from the *Washington Post* edition of December 17th, on the vandalism problem at the Airlie House. I was pleased no one tried to drug you at the Conference!
>
> I hope you can continue to keep your usual cool on these incidents, Bob, so that the work you are doing for Indians will continue to go forward. Best wishes for 1971.

LaNada Means, one of the leaders of Alcatraz, missed all the excitement in Warrenton, arriving on the last day of the interrupted conference. Her main agenda in Washington was to see her old adversary, Bob Robertson, and find new ways to jump-start the moribund occupation.

She had somehow managed, even with the occupation no longer a burning issue, to assemble an impressive roster of contacts. She stayed with Edgar Cahn, a prominent liberal who was coeditor of a recently published, influential critique of U.S. Indian policies called *My Brother's Keeper.* Cahn had close ties to Brad Patterson, the White House staffer who was spearheading much of the administration's Indian efforts, and another young staffer there named Bobbie Kilberg. Kilberg had experience on the Navajo reservation, assisting the tribe on legal issues, and had quickly become a key player in the developing Nixon administration Indian policy.

LaNada also relied on her new friend Ethel Kennedy, the widow of the recently assassinated New York Senator, Robert F. Kennedy. Mrs. Kennedy arranged an introduction of LaNada to Edward Bennett Williams, a celebrated and powerful lawyer who (ironically) owned the Washington Redskins football team. LaNada felt convinced Williams was exactly the person to represent the island. He was someone the government could not ignore, unlike the leftist attorneys in San Francisco.

But the connection with Ethel Kennedy boomeranged when Herb Caen, the *San Francisco Chronicle* columnist, wrote that Ethel Kennedy had set up a screen test for LaNada with a movie producer. LaNada heard about the article in a phone call from a friend in San Francisco, and though inaccurate, the story further weakened LaNada's standing with the occupiers. She had had a public quarrel with John Trudell on the dock as she left for Washington. Movie deals and lunches with Kennedys made her sound like an opportunist.

Writing from Washington in December, she reported to her colleagues back on the island on the work she had accomplished and what she believed should happen next. Things were not looking very good. Momentum had dwindled considerably. Indians of All Tribes had failed in its attempts to become a tax-exempt organization, which meant that their large individual donors were not likely to renew their contributions.

But LaNada refused to give up. "The whole action of taking the Island was symbolic of telling the American Government and American people that they are not going to continue to steal our land nor are they going to tell us what to do. We are contradicting our whole move of liberation if we just wait for the Government," she argued. "We cannot let Alcatraz die because just as it was symbolic in reawakening Indian consciousness and bringing attention to Indian people, it will be symbolic of our death if it should die."

She made her case for wanting to hire high-profile attorney Williams to make the legal claim to the 1868 Fort Laramie Treaty. "He has taken cases such as the Jimmy Hoffa case and other well-known cases. He is known for being a tough fighter, a top notch lawyer, and a winner." He also "gave the color television set contribution to the Island. I have had the opportunity to meet with Mr. Williams at some length . . . and with the winning influence of Mrs. Robert Kennedy, I believe he will help us in taking the case, free of charge of course . . ."

Means waited for an answer. None came.

She returned to the island to find out why. Trudell told her that the occupation's attorneys disagreed with her approach, and the residents vetoed her proposal. Means felt Trudell was allowing white lawyers to make political decisions for the occupation, and sought an opinion from John Echohawk, the Pawnee director of the Native American Rights Fund. He visited Alcatraz and said he believed litigation could greatly increase the chances for winning possession of the island.

Her time away had cost LaNada Means severely. Trudell won the battle of the lawyers. During her return, Means was struck at the distance between herself and those who lived on the island now. She admired them; they were, she thought, down-to-earth, good people, full of sacrifice, who sometimes even went without food. But she could see they listened to Trudell, who listened to white lawyers. She felt helpless. Sadly, she realized the people she had fought for, so hard and so long, were beyond her reach.

Even in its final dark months, Alcatraz still meant a great deal to many Indians, even to some who lived there despite great hardships. One example of how young people could still find inspiration in the occupation comes from this letter home, dated April 19, 1971:

Dear Folks,

This letter is just to let you know that I am doing fine. There has been a lot of excitement around here; maybe you've already seen me on the news? Our boat sank a couple of nights ago, so we have a slight problem in getting food and water here. The channel 7 newsmen were here this morning and now a news helicopter is giving us a bad time. I spend my days cooking meals, cutting copper, and answering letters for Alcatraz. Don't get paid for it, but I am getting something a whole lot better than money out of it. It has given me a goal in life. I will be able to look back and say that I did something worthwhile. That is all that counts, right?

Alcatraz sure is a big island! Herman and I go out every day to the old workshop buildings and break apart shelves for firewood in our apartments. There is no heat, electricity or running water here, so you have to have a sleeping bag, firewood, and we have a tower containing sea water so that we can flush the toilets.

There is a flu epidemic on the island right now. But I don't seem to be catching it. I haven't been over to Hospitality house yet, since that boat sunk. Boy, what a coincidence—we rode it over to the island the last time before it was sunk. That means it could have gone down when we were on it! Well, I'm going over to the mess hall now to start dinner (hot tamales!) You can have my luggage, if you want it.

Yours Truly,

No amount of perseverance or inspiration, though, could delay what was, by the late spring of 1971, inevitable. The meeting that ended the occupation took place at the White House on June 7. The latest intelligence available to the government showed that between eleven and fifteen Indians still lived on the island. The best guess of the officials was that they were armed and not leaving the island anytime soon. They also reviewed the continuing problem of navigation in the bay without the beacon of the lighthouse burning, citing the fact that two Chevron tankers had collided in the Bay in January.

"Aside from the continuing trespass," White House officials wrote, "the intentional destruction of property and the general lawlessness of the group on the island, the lack of proper navigational aids [leaves] the federal government open to a possible negligence action should another maritime disaster occur." Alcatraz, they went on to note, "has continued to be an open wound, one that has become a symbol of different things to different people."

Now was the time to act, both because of the small number of people on the island and because during summer vacation, students might journey to Alcatraz. The government officials also took note that evicting the occupiers in June of 1971 meant "a long interval of time between now and the next election," so the public would have plenty of time to forget about the forced eviction if the scene turned ugly. The minutes read, "It was the consensus of the group that if the decision is made to forcibly evict the Indians from Alcatraz, now is the most appropriate time to do that."

The appropriate time was the afternoon of June 11. The Coast Guard sealed the perimeter of the island and approximately thirty armed federal agents landed from three boats and a helicopter. In the space of less than an hour, they located, frisked, and placed under arrest the last fifteen members of the occupation force. The agents met no resistance.

In an editorial a few days after the removal, the *San Francisco Chronicle*, once among the occupation's biggest cheerleaders, blasted the Indians:

> The long, 19 months takeover of Alcatraz had to end sometime, because the colonizing of the island as a permanent Indian home made no sense—even if the squatters had had any demonstrable talent for it. That they had none is clear from the accounts of reporters who have witnessed the scene of squalor, vandalism, filth and degradation which the trespassers left behind upon their removal from Alcatraz last Friday.
>
> This does little to create sympathy for the Indians' claim. No culture worthy of the name could be expected to spring from such litter, and in any case the bleak, cold isolation of Alcatraz would deter and discourage the most determined of colonizers.
>
> It is thus appropriate that the Federal Government, after nearly two years of exemplary restraint in dealing with the problem, ended the Indian trespass.
>
> The relighting of the Alcatraz light, which was shining again

yesterday, is, literally, the brightest event in this dismal affair. Seeing it come on again in its steady rhythm will be welcomed by all San Franciscans, and most by mariners, to whom for more than a century it has been an important safety beacon.

The symbol had become an embarrassment, a tasteless, even lethal joke and an insult to the lofty dreams of the early days. By the time the fifteen who remained were dragged off, few voices in the Indian world were raised in protest. Ed Castillo, who had been in the invasion force in November, 1969 and who had moved to Berkeley to be a teacher and graduate student there, watched a report of the end of the occupation on the evening news, still wondering what might have been.

Could things have been different?

For established community activists like Adam Nordwall, the answer was clearly yes. They saw more attention lavished on their community in the first few weeks of the occupation than had ever occurred in their lifetimes, and knew that attention could be parlayed into something—a new community center, job training, commissions, and more. Mainland organizers, in time, got most of those things for the local community, but with precious little help from the hard-core people on the island. In some ways, the occupier's single-minded goal of obtaining title to the island from the federal government let the city of San Francisco and other Bay Area communities off the hook.

But even if the federal government had poured in the massive dollars to create Thunderbird University, how many of the lost young people of Alcatraz would have found jobs there or been successful students? The jobs would have gone to Indians who had made it in school or already had jobs administering Indian Studies, health clinics, Community Action Programs, or nonprofit programs. It is as if the hard-core members of the Alcatraz nation understood very well that their only victory was symbolic.

The people at Alcatraz and the leaders of other Indian protests had not yet addressed successfully a further issue: how what they were doing related to the people and politics on reservations. In the National Congress of American Indians, the issues of Indians living in cities were an annoyance at best, dangerous diversions from the political program for reservations at worst. Many tribal leaders, in fact, dismissed the protests coming from the cities out of hand as the work of criminals and malcontents.

But whatever else they may or may not have accomplished at Alcatraz, the seventy-eight people who landed on the rocky island in November, 1969 learned a fateful lesson, which was that sympathetic media and guerrilla theater could generate instant attention, and place Indian issues hardly anyone in the press had ever cared about before on the front pages of major newspapers around the country and around the world. Others had learned the lesson before, and some among the occupiers would take too much credit for beginning an Indian revolution, especially as time passed and the occupation became more legend than fact. But not until Alcatraz had anyone tapped the potential of media-fueled, spectacular protest on such a grand scale.

The future of Indian activism would belong to people far angrier than the student brigades of Alcatraz. Urban Indians who managed a life beyond the bottles of cheap wine cruelly named Thunderbird would continue down the protest road. And, more importantly, the invisible reservation people whose tribal leaders were so uncomfortable with the wave of direct action that was continuing to grow, and who had yet to weigh in with their opinion of where the Indian world was headed, were about to add themselves to the mix.

Dennis Banks left a successful job at Honeywell Corporation to join AIM.

No one in AIM was loved or hated as passionately as Russell Means.

Dennis Banks helps escort women and children from building in anticipation of police attack.

The Trail of Broken Treaties waits for possible police attack.

After declaring BIA headquarters the Native American Embassy, occupiers erected a tepee on the lawn.

AIM founder Clyde Bellecourt. Clyde, with his brother Vernon and Dennis Banks, put together the coalition of liberals, churches, and progressive lawyers that made the organization a local power in Minneapolis/St. Paul.

Graffiti lines hallway of BIA building after a week of occupation
by the Trail of Broken Treaties caravan.

Nixon aide Leonard Garment opened negotiations with the rebels
at Alcatraz, bargained with the Trail of Broken Treaties during the
BIA takeover, and offered Indian activists unparalleled access to the
White House.

Hank Adams worked with the Red Muslims of the National
Indian Youth Council in the early 1960s and the American Indian
Movement during the Trail of Broken Treaties and Wounded Knee dur-
ing the 1970s.

Chapter 6

Yellow Thunder

he police found him in the cold of February in 1972, slumped over the wheel of his pickup truck. The truck was parked in a used-car lot in the border town of Gordon, Nebraska, just across the state line from the Pine Ridge Reservation. Police estimated that Raymond Yellow Thunder, an Oglala from the nearby reservation, had been dead for about five days.

Sadly, in a reservation border town like Gordon, the discovery of a dead Indian man in a pickup truck was hardly big news. The only thing cheaper than Indian lives in places like Gordon was the fortified wine that was at the center of a border town's character and identity.

But Raymond Yellow Thunder's death would be different. In the space of just a few days, Indian residents of Gordon and Pine Ridge would rise up in an unprecedented demand for justice. And the American Indian Movement, which the people of Pine Ridge would call upon to support their efforts, would emerge as the single most influential Indian organization in the country—not just in the cities, where their message had already been gaining a place of prominence, but among reservation people as well.

Yellow Thunder, the Oglala whose death was to be at the center of the firestorm to come, was a fifty-one-year-old cowboy. He had been living in Gordon for the past several years, and worked at various ranches in the area. Yellow Thunder had never moved very far away from the small community of Porcupine at Pine Ridge where his family was from. He returned home on weekends, looking forward to catching up on the latest news with his friends and family and playing with the kids. He was a good cook and a willing baby-sitter, usually arriving with a bag of groceries. Those visits, his relatives said, were like clockwork.

When he missed one of his usual appearances, the family grew worried and looked around the frozen streets of the border town for some sign of him. For nearly a week they traveled the thirty miles to Gordon each day with no success.

They had reason to worry. The Nebraska town had a bad reputation on the Pine Ridge Reservation. Many Indians could tell stories of being cheated, harassed, disrespected, and worse by the town's two thousand white citizens, whose livelihoods in large part depended on commerce from the reservation. To cash a check, buy hardware, see a movie, or buy liquor one had to go to a border town, as the sprawling reservation offered none of these services. For many Oglalas, those drives to Gordon, Rushville, or Scottsbluff, Nebraska—where they were waited on by rednecks who hated Indians and who probably hated themselves because they made their living from the very Indians they despised—were infuriating experiences.

On February 20, the Yellow Thunder family realized their darkest fears with the discovery in the used-car lot. Yellow Thunder died, the coroner reported, of exposure and head injuries. The family asked to see him. They would get a chance to view the body, the authorities said, but only after morticians had prepared his body for burial. In the meantime, the family could do nothing but wait and wonder how Raymond Yellow Thunder had spent his final hours. As they waited, details of his brutal death emerged with agonizing slowness.

Those details were as follows: Raymond Yellow Thunder had

been standing in front of a bar when a group of four whites—brothers Melvin and Leslie Hare, Bernard Ludder, and Robert Bayless—seized the Oglala, stripped him of some of his clothes, and beat him. The four threw Yellow Thunder into the trunk of their car and drove around town for a while, ending up back at American Legion Post No. 34, where a dance was underway. They shoved Yellow Thunder into the hall, where his tormentors encouraged the "drunken Indian" to dance.

His harassers then threw him out into the cold night. Some of the whites who had witnessed the scene in the hall came to help him, but he sent them away, claiming he was all right. Later that night, Ludder, Bayless, and the Hares ran into him again and he seemed to be okay. But he wasn't. Sometime later, his wounds and the weather caught up to him, and he died in his pickup.

As the news spread of Yellow Thunder's death at the hands of white racists, so did angry rumors about why the coroner was denying his family permission to view the body. Some speculated that his tormentors had beaten him so severely that morticians were hiding the body in order to prevent a riot. Others imagined even more terrible scenarios—he had been castrated, or his skull was crushed, or his body was covered with cigarette burns.

Dissatisfied with the Gordon authorities, the family sought assistance from everyone they could think of, including the Oglala Sioux Tribe, the Bureau of Indian Affairs, and private attorneys. No one was much help. They ran into one brick wall after another.

At Porcupine, Severt Young Bear, one of Yellow Thunder's nephews, had returned home from work and was watching television when three of his aunts drove up. They entered his house weeping. "Sonny, we don't have no place to turn. So we came over—maybe you can help us. You have some friends that are with AIM. I wonder if you could go to them, ask them that we want something to be done to the people that killed our brother, and we want a full investigation."

AIM was becoming the brightest star among the many Indian activist groups that had sprung up in the cities over the previous decade. Several Chippewa people had founded the group in Minneapolis in the summer of 1968, mainly out of concern for the way police were treating Indian people in the Franklin Avenue neighborhood of the city. By the time Raymond Yellow Thunder died in 1972, the group had established a reputation for being able to generate headlines and to be an effective advocate for Indian people in various protests around the country.

But the people from Porcupine—who spoke to each other in Lakota, practiced ancient traditions, and maintained a steady resistance against the encroaching influences of American society on their political, social, and spiritual lives—needed more than AIM's growing reputation for them to ask the radicals for assistance. That something more was Russell Means, one of the leaders of AIM, whose Oglala family came from the same community as Raymond Yellow Thunder. His mother, Theodora, had lived there, a fact which gave the urban-based radicals a level of credibility with people there that they would have had to fight hard to establish otherwise.

So, when Young Bear's aunts asked him to approach AIM, which he knew was meeting with other activist Indian organizations not far from Pine Ridge in Omaha, Nebraska, he agreed. He got a storekeeper to donate the gas, packed, and drove straight through, arriving sometime after three in the morning. Young Bear spoke to the AIM people and others that night about Yellow Thunder's violent death, and the next day the conference passed a resolution condemning racist violence. They also promised to send people to Gordon to demand justice for Raymond Yellow Thunder.

Young Bear returned to the reservation. He told people that AIM would be arriving, and they prepared the Billy Mills Hall in the agency town called Pine Ridge Village, for a rally. Three days after his midnight run to Omaha, AIM kept its promise. Hundreds of AIM members and residents of Pine Ridge drove in a caravan south to the Nebraska town. Others came on their own. Before the week was out, fourteen hundred Indians from over eighty tribes would arrive to wake up Gordon.

For three days the streets of the whiskey town were filled with angry Indians who convened a peoples' grand jury, organized economic boycotts, and engaged in near constant demonstrations. The whites of Gordon made themselves scarce, and most merchants shuttered their doors. Gerald One Feather, Oglala Sioux tribal president, quickly began arranging for the transfer of over $1 million in tribal program monies kept in Gordon banks to other nearby localities. In a flash, an act of injustice that would have gone by the boards just a few years before had brought the border town to its economic and political knees.

As a result of the protests, town officials agreed to create a human rights commission, and suspended a police officer accused of mistreating Indian prisoners in the city jail. The state legislature in Lincoln ordered the attorney general to conduct a thorough investigation into Yellow Thunder's death, and the governor sent a personal representative to meet with the protesters. In Washington, Interior Secretary Rogers Morton said his agency would also investigate Yellow Thunder's death and had asked the Justice Department to determine if federal laws had been violated.

Sheridan County Attorney Michael Smith charged the five locals with manslaughter and false imprisonment, and released them on bonds of $6,250 each. Smith called the incident a "cruel practical joke" carried out by "pranksters." The Indians were angered by the charges and the low bail, and when the results of the autopsy showed no evidence of torture, they insisted a second autopsy be conducted. When a lawyer with the Native American Rights Fund, brought in to represent the family, announced that the second autopsy confirmed the first, tension eased. At least the frightening stories of torture were not true.

"It wasn't as bad as they made it out to be," said one white resident with obvious relief. "Oh," answered an Indian woman, "is he then still alive?"

As the demonstrations came to a close, people from AIM and people from Pine Ridge Indian Reservation sat on the floor of the Town Hall and smoked a Lakota pipe. They invited no city officials to join them.

When the demonstrators left town, they left behind a community in shock from the days of rage. A white woman whose husband ran a drugstore said "The spell has been broken and life in Gordon will never be the same again." An Indian father spoke with obvious satisfaction, "I think people around here now know that we're not just a bunch of little Indians." A thirty-two-year-old Lakota woman said,

"Yellow Thunder wasn't the first of us to be mistreated, but he'd better be the last. We're tired of being cursed on the streets, tired of being beaten in alleys. And we're tired of doing the white man's dirty work."

It was a tremendous and unexpected response to the death of a rather ordinary man. Raymond Yellow Thunder's story reached out to every Indian person who could see in him not just another Indian drunk, but a brother, a father, an uncle, or a cousin.

In the aftermath of the successful campaign in Nebraska, the American Indian Movement, in an overly ambitious moment, announced to the press that ten to thirty thousand Indians from around the country would arrive in a few days to carry out similar consciousness-raising in the nearby border towns of Winner and Martin in South Dakota, and Scottsbluff and Valentine in Nebraska, all of which had reputations for racism similar to Gordon. AIM invited the U.S. presidential candidates, the BIA commissioner, and the secretary of the interior to attend. They advised presidential candidates, in particular, to show up if they expected to win Indian votes in November. The candidates, secretaries, and commissioners never arrived.

Neither did the Indians, and the big events AIM leaders promised didn't materialize. The Gordon operation had taken everything the activists on Pine Ridge and in AIM had in the way of resources and people, and to imagine they could have immediately continued and expanded such an intensive effort was unrealistic. But those days in the border town had shown local reservation people—who were hardly ever followers, much less leaders, of organizations like AIM—that they could stand up against the injustices they had swallowed through clenched teeth all of their lives.

And Gordon had shown the young radicals who made up the rank and file of AIM—most of them from the cities where conditions were much different than on Pine Ridge—that they could do more than lay claim to national monuments and abandoned military bases and prisons like the Mayflower II, Mount Rushmore, Fort Lawton, and Alcatraz. At Gordon, Indian people saw that they could stand with each other, look straight into the eyes of once-disdainful waitresses, once-dangerous young toughs, and once-sneering business-people, and see fear.

As a group of them did on March 9, when, filled with anger and exhilaration from their days in Gordon, three hundred of those exhilarated Indians took a detour on the road back to Pine Ridge and stopped by the Wounded Knee Trading Post and Museum, ironically just steps from where history books claimed hostilities between Indians and whites had ended in massacre over eighty years before.

Lakotas hated few places on their reservation the way they hated the strange complex of buildings that made up the trading post. Huge billboards invited tourists to VISIT THE MASS GRAVE and to SEE THE WOUNDED KNEE MASSACRE SITE. The owners, Mr. and Mrs. Clive Gildersleeve and Mr. and Mrs. James Czwczynski, sold Indian jewelry, western clothing, groceries, and gas. One could also buy postcards with the grotesque images of massacred Indians from Big Foot's band, frozen stiff.

The trading post stood accused of loaning money at exorbitant interest rates, buying crafts at a fraction of their real value to sell to tourists, and other exploitative business practices. On this Thursday afternoon, still raging from Raymond Yellow Thunder's death and upset over reports that owner James Czwczynski had choked a fourteen-year-old Indian boy the previous day, the group stormed the trading post, ripped off merchandise, and threatened the Czwczynskis. "It was terrible, terrible," Mrs. Czwczynski said. "They took my husband outside, got him in the middle of a large group, called him a 'honkey,' and told him they would like to do something to him 'like the white men did to Yellow Thunder.'" Her husband added that he recognized only a few of the Indians, and theorized that most of the participants were not from Pine Ridge, but from somewhere else. As proof, he said "honkey" was an expression not normally heard on Pine Ridge.

The owners estimated their loss at $50,000, a figure that would provoke much laughter among Indians in the following days. Mrs. Czwczynski said moccasins and beaded outfits were stolen, and pottery smashed. She denied that her husband had choked the Indian boy. The boy had become abusive, she said, after being asked to leave, and was escorted out by the arm. As a possible crime on a federal reservation, the incident was turned over to the Federal Bureau of Investigation. The local sheriff, John D. Manke, offered his opinion. "It's just like the rest of these demonstrations. All it is, is an excuse to loot and destroy."

The scuffle at the trading post was but a skirmish in the new round of hostilities that had opened in Gordon. But it was a harbinger of things to come. And Wounded Knee, a holy place of bitter memories and trashy souvenirs, had already become a battleground.

Gordon had the look of a classic civil rights struggle. People rose up against a particularly gruesome example of racist thuggery. They boycotted, marched, and even won favorable coverage in the *New York Times*. But the action exposed another wedge besides the one between Indians and whites. For many who lived on Pine Ridge, the action in Gordon was a case of disenfranchised Lakotas holding their own tribal government responsible for not protecting Raymond Yellow Thunder, and, by implication, for other incidents of racism and humiliation people on the reservation routinely suffered.

Writing for the American Indian Press Association, Yakima journalist Richard La Course called the events surrounding Yellow Thunder's death "a signal turning point in the history of contemporary American Indians." He praised AIM for turning a tragic situation "into one of great promise. AIM's ability to capture the imagination and loyalty of reservation citizens—from the very young to the very old—was proven to an unanticipated degree."

La Course also noted another less obvious consequence of the Gordon actions, which had arisen in the AIM-organized peoples' grand juries. These gave reservation residents a forum for airing their grievances against racism in border towns and against their own tribal governments. La Course writes:

> The central AIM effort was to encourage local residents to candidly address the agonies and horrors they faced before grand juries consisting of Indian people. Often the grievances expressed by local Indian citizens had some direct relation to the current ineffectiveness of local tribal government.
>
> When grievances are expressed against tribal government,

there is the lurking danger that the reservation citizenry may become pitted against that government if the government does not swiftly and immediately respond. The ultimate question thus raised is the legitimacy of the existing government itself, and at least its responsiveness to its constituent tribal members.

The grand juries gave voice to a deep-seated resentment that many people on Pine Ridge shared toward the conditions under which they lived. And however much tribal officials wanted to believe that the spirit of protest was an aberration from the cities, the testimony of those who lived on reservations and in border towns in Nebraska and South Dakota confirmed that those officials were wrong.

Indeed, in the eyes of people in the traditional districts like Porcupine and Medicine Root, the government in Pine Ridge Village had never truly represented them in the first place. They believed the tribal government to be a 1930s imposition by the Bureau of Indian Affairs against the clear sentiment of most Lakotas on the reservation. It brought foreign concepts of election campaigns and parliamentary procedure to a community where traditional forms of government were still viable. They didn't simply object to the individuals who held office, but to the system itself.

As with other Plains Indians, such as the Omahas, the Osages, and the Pawnees, the dividing line between the two points of view of those on Pine Ridge had developed in the nineteenth century. Most Indians willing to cooperate with the United States (though certainly not all) had parents or ancestors who were French traders who had come to the Plains seeking fortune and married Indian women. The children of those unions produced a new class of people in the tribes on the Plains (and elsewhere in other periods of history as well), a class that lived among the tribe but took up the accoutrements of white culture much more quickly and with more enthusiasm than their more defiant tribespeople, who usually had unbroken tribal lineages.

Conflict between the groups was built-in, but the U.S. government egged it on through divide-and-conquer tactics such as rewarding the more pliable group with more rations or, later, educational opportunities, political clout, and jobs. The designations of these groups—full bloods versus mixed-bloods or traditionals versus nontraditionals—have often been taken as ironclad, biological distinctions, when in fact they are shorthand for a complex set of political, social, religious, and economic differences that have not always held true. How that has worked itself out in the political realities on Pine Ridge for the past century is that most people from the outlying districts—like those who had demonstrated in Gordon, most of whom fall into the traditional, full-blood categories—have been staunch and disenfranchised opponents of the government that was supposed to represent them.

In national Indian politics, this issue of the extent to which tribal government truly spoke for reservation people had usually been submerged. For a decade, Indian critics of tribal governments spoke of apples (sell-outs who were red on the outside and white on the inside) and Uncle Tomahawks, but the question of the legitimacy of reservation governments had never really been addressed, except in a rhetorical sense by activists who usually practiced their activism off reservations.

In fact, the basic thrust of Indian organizations like the NCAI had been to strengthen the tribal governments, to increase their power, funding, and expertise. The struggle in Washington was to convince Congress that the tribes were responsible enough to handle their own affairs, and that the era of the BIA controlling the lives of Indian people should end. Leaders of Indian organizations like the National Congress of American Indians would complain bitterly about incompetent or corrupt tribal officials, but mostly in private. If problems existed with the quality of leadership in some tribal governments—and how could there not be, given a century of BIA paternalism—then the solution was less federal interference, even if that meant a system that was flawed and that people like those who had taken to the streets in Gordon increasingly rejected out of hand.

For the established Indian organizations, the scenario that Gordon presented—reservation people publicly questioning the legitimacy of their tribal governments—was a troubling, even alarming one. But it was a logical step in the process of change that had been going on for a decade, a new challenge to an Indian political world already experiencing rapid change.

Ten years earlier, Clyde Warrior, Mel Thom, and others from the

National Indian Youth Council had challenged the NCAI, setting their young faces against an establishment they saw as deeply in need of reform. By the time of his untimely death in 1968, Warrior had been exaperated at the slow pace of reform and had predicted that the patience of the masses of Indian people was running out and that revolution was just around the corner. Even as Warrior was making his prediction, disenfranchised Indian people from the cities and on college campuses were organizing themselves, and over the next three years grabbed headlines in protests and occupations from Alcatraz to Plymouth Rock.

Until Gordon, tribal officials and Washington bureaucrats could take solace in the fact that reservation people, especially those who lived on the larger ones like Pine Ridge, had by and large not joined the students and the urbanites. The Indian establishment could dismiss the activists as hotheads who weren't really tuned into the authentic Indian world. In the activities that followed the death of Raymond Yellow Thunder, activities in which reservation people and the people from the cities worked together, all that changed.

Vine Deloria, Jr., the most prolific Indian writer who was analyzing the burgeoning scene and a consummate Indian affairs establishment insider (he, for instance, had directed the NCAI from 1964–68), had attempted to intervene in the growing antagonisms for years. In his 1969 best-seller *Custer Died for Your Sins: An American Indian Manifesto*, he contended that "urban Indians have become the cutting edge of the new nationalism" and that federal bureaucrats and tribal officials ignored the activists from the cities at their own peril. When that book came out, it became required reading among Indian student radicals.

In another publication, this one from 1971, Deloria castigated his peers on the inside of Indian affairs for missing the boat on the activism that had emerged since Alcatraz. As he says there:

> By late 1970 the tribal leaders were cringing in fear that the activists would totally control Indian affairs. . . . But it was the tribal leaders' own fault that the activists had parlayed Alcatraz into a national phenomenon. For decades the NCAI and other national groups had cast aside young people and urban Indians in favor of local reservation citizens.

He goes on to argue that tribal leaders could have supported the wave of protests, thereby grounding the activists—whom Deloria saw as inexperienced in the details of reservation issues—in the "real needs of reservations . . ." Their failure to do so, however, "doomed them thereafter from raising their issues in a context in which they could have gained public support."

Deloria saw both dangers and opportunities in the current political environment. The recent wave of activism had demonstrated that widespread non-Indian support existed for Indians. Just as important, the Nixon administration had shown encouraging signs. In July of 1970, the President himself surprised many Indian leaders by embracing policies of self-determination for Indian nations and specifically calling for an end to the termination policies that people in Indian affairs had been fighting against for nearly two decades. Though the legislation that would bring about promised reforms was coming out at a snail's pace, the number of bureaucratic and policy successes was growing into a litany that Deloria argued was a testament to the hard, patient work of a generation. Such a wide opening to win major reforms from Washington hadn't existed in forty years. Yet, the increasing signs of fracture among Indians themselves were crystallizing in a way that threatened any chance for such a victory.

At the NCAI's national convention in November, 1971, Deloria offered another warning, this time in the form of a proposal called Resolution 26. In it, Deloria proposed that NCAI work in coalition with three other Indian organizations: the National Indian Youth Council (NIYC), the National Tribal Chairmen's Association (NTCA), and AIM.

Until the Youth Council emerged in the early 1960s, cooperation among national Indian groups was unnecessary since for almost two decades only one organization—the NCAI—had had a national, intertribal constituency. Operating from a Washington office with only a modest budget and a small staff, NCAI devoted most of its energies to lobbying Congress.

NIYC, the group founded by Clyde Warrior, Mel Thom, and others a decade earlier, had lost the cachet it previously enjoyed as Red Power's vanguard when it was lambasting the state of Indian affairs and organizing campus chapters. Even the term Red Power had passed out of fashion, and the Youth Council had little national presence. Some of their leaders were dead or out of action, while others now worked for the BIA, trying to reform the institution from the inside. Even with their waning profile, however, NIYC still had an active, mostly student, membership.

NTCA, the group composed of tribal chairmen, was barely a year old. Its existence was an implicit vote of no confidence in the NCAI. William Youpee, the chairman of the Fort Peck Reservation in Montana and president of the NTCA, said their group had become a necessity because of a recent, though hardly unusual, NCAI financial crisis, and because of "the great concern of elected tribal chairmen over the state of Indian affairs." At NTCA's founding meeting, in February 1971, he made clear that part of what he disliked about the current state of Indian affairs was the increasing attention to Indians who lived in cities. "We sympathize with their causes," Youpee said, but tribal leaders "have an obligation to the reservation people, and we intend to uphold this responsibility." In NTCA's view, programs for Indians in cities would necessarily come at the expense of reservations. And as for this newfangled bunch of hotheads who took over national monuments, prisons, and BIA offices—they were being taken too seriously by the news media, and even by the NCAI.

Former BIA commissioner Robert Bennett Oneicla was more direct. "It appears that the federal government is dealing more with individual Indians and self-styled Indian leaders who, because of the availability of the mass media in urban centers, are receiving more than their share of attention. No one begrudges the help they are receiving, but when it is at the expense of the tribes . . . something must be done." Tribal governments, Bennett told the chairmen, were under attack from "eager young lawyers, financed by the government, who can't wait to get the tribal governments into court and keep them there, by pseudo-liberals who plead the cause of Indian self-determination in one breath and tell tribes what to do in the next."

AIM was the wild card of the four: new, urban, and playing by its own rules. For some in the NCAI, they were an important bridge to people in cities and on reservations who felt left out and needed to be included, and for others they were irresponsible amateurs who knew little about Indian policy.

Deloria made his case for the proposed coalition in an article, "Toward a Common Indian Front," which the National Indian Press Association News Service published in December, 1970. He observed that "NCAI is not the only organization in the field now. It has many competitors. Other organizations are doing some of the same things that NCAI used to do. And they are doing them better." These four organizations, Deloria wrote, working together in concert, would make an excellent team. NCAI would focus on lobbying Congress. NTCA would deal with the Bureau on issues affecting the reservations. NIYC would "organize Indian youth and get them into the various programs available to Indian people. The other organizations will not have to have youth programs with NIYC around. They can concentrate on doing their jobs without having to stop and develop other programs that do not relate to what they are doing." As for AIM, they would provide "the activist punch that any solid movement needs. At times the bureaucracy needs a swift kick in the you-guessed-it. AIM can provide this and NTCA and NCAI will not have to forsake their jobs to do it."

Deloria argued that the issue of NTCA's participation was the key, and addressed them directly. If the tribal chairmen refused, as most insiders expected, a number of bad things would happen. Already people suspected they were a tool of the BIA; this would be confirmed. The national Indian community would be split in the face of outside forces. The BIA "would continue to play off one Indian organization against another as it has always done." Finally, he warned, "it will be the death of the NTCA." On the other hand, "If NTCA can join with other Indian organizations to build this important coalition, 1972 can be the greatest year ever seen by Indians."

The remarkable premise of the Common Indian Front strategy was that such a coalition could be proposed among four very different groups with four very different constituencies. It conceded there were differences between the organizations, but seemed to imply they were more of attitude and style rather than substance. It rejected, or ignored, the possibility that the differences might be profound ones, grounded in ideology, class, and self-interest. An equivalent suggestion from a black activist might have imagined the NAACP, the Black Panthers, CORE, SNCC, and U.N. Ambassador Ralph Bunche plotting strategies together.

The idea ultimately failed, but its vision of unity did win the support of the NCAI convention. Wishful thinking or not, at the end of 1971 it was still possible to believe that Indians of all political stripes, backgrounds, ages, and tribes could and should stand together. They had serious arguments and differences, but every family had those. In essence, the Common Indian Front proposal said Indians are all part of the same family, and, in the end, the family would always be on the same side.

When Deloria wrote his broadside, AIM might have felt fortunate to be included on equal standing with the major players of Indian politics. In truth, they were not major players until the action in Gordon a few months later. AIM had been around since 1968, often attending (and causing a stir at) the same conferences as everyone else. Its leaders—Clyde Bellecourt, Dennis Banks, Russ Means—were a familiar sight. They, too, were family. In this family, AIM was the second cousin you knew growing up (or maybe he was you)—charming, rowdy, a bit wild, who later did three years at the state prison for stealing cars. People in the NCAI, NTCA, and NIYC were the favored ones who stayed out of trouble, entered professions, and often had college degrees instead of prison records.

If this warning of Deloria's to other insiders of Indian affairs had fallen mostly on deaf ears, so had another one that both he and Clyde Warrior had offered. Both of them believed that whoever was able to reach out effectively to the traditional people at places like Pine Ridge would be able to forge a political and spiritual alliance that could control the agenda of Indian politics.

In the early months of 1972, riding in on the cloud of fury, tragedy, and dust they had stirred up in combatting a racist murder in Gordon, Nebraska, the American Indian Movement seemed to have done exactly that.

Chapter 7

The American Indian Movement

he American Indian Movement. The name of this group that had so decisively grabbed the agenda at Gordon was perfection itself. Perfect because it sounded authoritative and inclusive. Perfect because it suggested action, purpose, and forward motion. Perfect because it was big, transcending the lesser world of committees and associations and congresses and councils. Organizations had recording secretaries and annual dinners. Movements changed history. The initials—A-I-M—underscored all of that, creating an active verb rich in power and imagery. You aimed at a target. You could aim for victory, for freedom, for justice. You could also, defiantly, never aim to please. Written vertically and stylized a bit, the acronym became an arrow.

Though the name had flair, drama, and strength, it was not the first choice of the 250 Indians from various existing organizations who met in Minneapolis in July, 1968 at the first meeting to make plans and talk about ideas for the new group. Ironically, they voted to call themselves the Concerned Indians of America. After a few weeks, the new leaders of the CIA realized the blunder, and the Concerned Indians of America became the American Indian Movement. From that point to Gordon and beyond, the blunders, spontaneous strokes of genius, and the burgeoning number of Indian people looking for exactly what AIM offered moved the group from its local beginnings to the national stage.

Minneapolis and St. Paul, unlike nearly every other major U.S. metropolitan area, had Indian populations large enough to register on the radar of city government, the press, and the public. Indians weren't the largest group in any one neighborhood, but collectively they had a presence. Subsequently, the Twin Cities had dozens of Indian organizations, though most were sponsored by churches and run by whites. AIM, in contrast, had an all-Indian board and staff.

One of the first projects of the new group was the AIM Patrol. AIM raised money to equip cars with two-way radios, cameras, and tape recorders so they could monitor arrests by the police department. When the AIM Patrol heard police dispatched to certain bars or street corners, officers would be met by Indians in red jackets carefully observing their actions. AIM also became expert at providing attorneys for those arrested. It was a tactic similar to Black Panther campaigns to monitor police in Oakland, California and other cities.

The founders and leaders of AIM were primarily Chippewas, Minnesota's largest tribal group. Some were born and raised in cities, but most were from the reservations a few hours to the north and west. For many, the trip between their reservations and the cities seemingly never ended; a cycle of returning home for weddings, funerals, ceremonies, and wild rice festivals, and in another few days or weeks or months, returning to the city for jobs or for the excitement the reservations lacked. The trip frequently included grinding poverty, hassles with police, and jail.

AIM's leaders knew the road between the reservations and the cities well. At the age of five, Dennis Banks was sent to the Pipestem Indian School, run by the Bureau of Indian Affairs, four hundred miles from his home on the Leech Lake reservation. He spent nine years there, and remembered teachers and administrators clobbering him every time he spoke Ojibway. After Pipestem he attended another school in North Dakota, and finally one more in South Dakota.

In 1953 he joined the Air Force, and spent most of his tour in Japan and Korea. He returned home to Leech Lake briefly, but soon left the reservation for Minneapolis. At home, he had seen little but unemployment, alcoholism, and slow death.

In Minneapolis things weren't much better. Before long Banks became another skid row Indian drunk, and his first arrest came in 1964; it was for burglary, and he served a year. On parole he became involved in community projects, and helped set up Little League baseball teams with his friend George Mitchell, another Chippewa. His first career in civic affairs did not last long, but it did include one curious episode in which Banks, with short hair, narrow necktie, and dark suit, walked into the office of the Indian director of the American Indian Employment Center. The center's director had organized a modest protest against a Twin Cities office of the BIA, charging that city Indians should have equal services to their reservation counterparts. Banks insisted that the picketing end. The future revolutionary, wagging his finger, said, "Demonstrations are not the Indian way."

Not long after came an arrest for forgery and a six-month sentence. When he violated parole after that stint, the authorities put him away for a year upstate at Stillwater Prison. It was 1967. His uncooperative behavior inside earned him nine months in solitary confinement. He began reading obsessively about the surging civil rights and antiwar movements, and about Indian treaties.

While Dennis spent his months in solitary at Stillwater Prison, the world outside erupted. He closely followed the progress of the student and black rebellions. "It had a tremendous impact on me, what was going on outside of prison that year," he said. "Sitting in that jail cell I began to understand there was a hell of a goddamn movement going on that I wasn't part of, the antiwar movement, the Black Panther movement, the civil rights movement, the Students for a Democratic Society. I began to see that the greatest war was going to go on right here in the United States, and I began to realize that there was a hell of a situation in this country—all these different kinds of people trying so hard to straighten this country out."

At the not-so-young age of thirty, seemingly well on the road to becoming a lost Chippewa, drifting from Minneapolis to the northern reservations to Stillwater Prison in a tedious orbit of despair and hopelessness, Banks decided that there must be a different kind of Indian politics, and that he must help build a movement to express it.

Once out of prison, ex-convict Dennis Banks found Minneapolis surprisingly kind to him. He found work with the Honeywell Corporation, recruiting Indians to make residential heating equipment. Ironically, Honeywell was a key target of the sizable antiwar movement in the liberal Twin Cities. Among its many operations, the company manufactured antipersonnel weapons. Until the war in Vietnam ended, dinner parties in certain Minneapolis neighborhoods were always at risk of being ground to a halt by guests who would produce a mock-up of the fragmentation device and patiently explain the damage it inflicts on humans.

Honeywell seemed to like both Indians in general and Dennis Banks specifically. This presented a dilemma for Banks, who enjoyed the work and ended up recruiting over four hundred Indian people for Honeywell. None of them made the horrible weapons, and the company even financially supported Banks' community organizing efforts. When he asked for a leave of absence to work with his friend George Mitchell—with whom he had previously organized Little League teams—in building a new Indian movement, they granted a leave.

But when Banks publicly stated, while on leave, that he could no longer recruit for Honeywell because of the company's defense contracts, his employment with the company ended. He observed that "organizations . . . like that are willing to give you the help you need as long as you don't step on their toes. But once you turn around and start criticizing them and biting the hand that feeds you, well, they're not going to give you anymore. That's exactly what happened to us, they decided not to feed us anymore. But it's going to be the other way around some day, you know, because it's really us that's feeding them, and pretty soon we're going to cut off their food, too."

Another of AIM's leaders, Clyde Bellecourt, had a different kind of epiphany inside the grim walls of Stillwater Prison. An amateur boxer and unsuccessful burglar who had been in and out of boarding schools and reform schools, Bellecourt despaired of ever surviving his prison sentence and refused to eat. His hunger strike would end, he said, only with his death. Another Chippewa, Eddie Benton, tossed candy bars into Bellecourt's cell each day and pleaded with him to end the hunger strike. Bellecourt refused. Benton started talking about the Ojibway religion and culture they shared, but which neither man really understood or participated in. He also left reading material on these subjects, and finally, one day, Bellecourt started reading them.

The insights gave Bellecourt a new way to regard himself and his future. He resumed eating, studied for his high-school equivalency test, and earned a license as a steam plant engineer by working in the prison's heating plant.

Clyde Bellecourt caught Banks's attention at the first AIM organizing meeting in July of 1968. Clyde spoke at length and with passion about the issues confronting Indians in Minneapolis, and on that basis was elected the first chairman of the new group. Bellecourt, Banks learned, worked for a blue-chip Minneapolis corporation, Northern States Power, as he had worked for Honeywell.

The new chairman led a group more interested in action than formal structure. A November, 1969 meeting exemplified the group's casual, direct action style. When Dennis Banks, who led the meeting, asked for new business, one of the members said that a nephew, living in small town outside the Twin Cities, had been asked to participate in a Thanksgiving play.

A copy of the play was produced, and reviewed by those in attendance. It featured a character named "Chief Smokum Pot" and other Indians who were given lines that consisted of "Ugh." People groaned as they read the play, and argued that AIM should visit the school the next day to protest the play and pressure school officials to cancel the play.

Nobody knew where the play would be staged, and the nephew's family didn't have a telephone. Clyde Bellecourt called the teacher and the school's principal, seeking information on the play. Neither would tell Bellecourt anything, or even admit that any play was to be presented.

Undeterred, Bellecourt next called the superintendent of schools, posing as a Minneapolis drama teacher interested in seeing the play "in order to get some new ideas." The superintendent gave up the time and place of the event. Bellecourt reported his progress to the crowd, and people had a good laugh at his inventive and successful efforts. They resolved to meet at a nearby cafe at six-thirty the next morning and ride over together.

Later that night, as the gathering broke up, people stayed for a while, talked, and went out for dinner, and others arranged rides to the cafe the next morning. A married couple suggested to a student who needed a ride that he spend the night at their house. The expedition proved successful, and the racist Thanksgiving play was canceled.

As a political program, it may not have been as ambitious as halting a threatened termination of an embattled tribe, or even seizing an abandoned prison, but it spoke volumes about the rootedness that AIM enjoyed in a specific place. The AIM office was a place to stop by if you needed a ride, an emergency loan, leads on jobs, or a place to live. Social services and political action were integrated. If you had been evicted and needed a lawyer, Clyde or Dennis could probably help, and if your nephew faced the humiliation of acting in what you considered a soul-scarring piece of racist garbage, they would get people together at dawn to drive over and talk some sense into a school principal.

The leaders started making their presence known at national Indian conferences. At first, they could only set up tables and pass out their materials while the delegates who represented tribes met and passed resolutions. Soon AIM demanded a seat inside. At a national conference of urban Indian leaders in San Francisco in 1969, they encountered Russell Means, who would help bring the group to national prominence.

Like the Bellecourts and Dennis Banks, Means was in his early thirties, and his checkered resume included a startling range of experiences. He was born on the Pine Ridge Reservation in South Dakota on November 10, 1939, but grew up in northern California, where his father, Hank, worked at the Mare Island Naval Shipyard.

He, his brother Dace, and his twin brothers Bill and Ted attended public schools first in Vallejo, then San Leandro. An unruly but obviously bright student, Russell often found himself in trouble. He was a stlyish dresser who ran with a rough crowd. His mother, Theodora, who had attended harsh Indian boarding schools and ruled the household with an iron hand, went so far as to send him to live with relatives on the Winnebago Reservation in Nebraska to see if he would shape up. He got in more trouble there, and eventually returned to his folks. Despite dealing drugs to his fellow students and using heroin, marijuana, and other drugs himself, Russell graduated from San Leandro High in 1958.

Soon after, he drifted down to southern California and became part of the urban Indian scene there. He left Los Angeles when authorities began tracking him down in search of child support for two children he had fathered with a Lakota woman, Twila Smith. He returned to San Francisco and, in 1964, joined his father in the first, brief Indian attempt to take over Alcatraz. From there, he lived in various places, sometimes wandering from city to city in rattletrap cars with other young Indian men, sometimes establishing himself somewhere and sending for his Hopi wife, Betty, whom he had met in San Francisco, and their two children.

By his mid-twenties, he had attended several business schools and colleges where he learned the ins and outs of accounting, worked as a dance instructor, engaged in various street scams, and built an arrest record that included petty theft, common drunkenness, assault with a weapon, and disorderly conduct. He had a knack both for the growing world of business computers and for getting into vicious, drunken barroom brawls.

In 1967 he moved to Mission, South Dakota and found work as director of the management information systems office in the Community Action Program office at the Rosebud Reservation. Means and his family left Rosebud for Cleveland, Ohio in July, 1968. There, he helped establish and became the director of the Cleveland American Indian Center. As director, he set up a credit union, established food and unemployment assistance, and launched a noisy though unsuccessful campaign to force the Cleveland Indians baseball team to change their name and their mascot, Chief Wahoo.

After meeting Means at the urban Indian conference in San Francisco in 1969, AIM leaders actively recruited him to become a part of their group. Soon, Means had established a local chapter of AIM in Cleveland, calling it CLAIM. He gave up his stylish threads and started growing his shoulder-length hair out so he could emulate others in AIM by wearing braids and ribbon shirts.

He became such an enthusiastic convert to AIM that, in 1970, he led a Thanksgiving protest at Plymouth Rock that won a moment of national attention. AIM leaders soon named Means national field coordinator, and the Chippewas who created AIM regarded him, a Sioux, as an equal. With the recruitment of Means, AIM no longer was simply an urban organization in Minneapolis with some chapters sprouting up elsewhere. Because Means was Sioux, his mere presence changed AIM from a local to a national outfit.

The Sioux held a privileged spot in the national consciousness, dating back more than a century. Apaches and Comanches were featured in many Hollywood films, and the Shawnee leader Tecumseh—who had led a confederation of Indian nations against United States expansion in the early 1800s—was arguably a more important leader than any Lakota, but no tribe had a more compelling mix of history and myth than the Sioux. Also, they had a history of drawing a national spotlight toward Indian organizations and were a source of enduring fascination for whites.

In boarding schools they frequently emerged as the leaders, though often outnumbered and despite grumbling about their arrogant manners. Though many felt that the Sioux seemed to believe that being Sioux and being Indian were the same thing, few disputed that, for better or worse, they would mix things up.

Russ Means's time on his home reservation may have been measured in months instead of years. Maybe he was more California than Pine Ridge, and even—if the myriad stories of him passing for white in his San Francisco and Los Angeles days of the early 1960s were to be believed—more Italian than Indian. But nobody really disputed that Russell Means, with the requisite tall stature and rugged good looks that Lewis and Clark recorded in their diaries and Hollywood committed to film, was stone-cold Sioux. When it came to charisma Russell Means had few peers. He made many people think of Crazy Horse, Sitting Bull, Touch the Clouds, and American Horse. Even his enemies conceded his moments of brilliance.

Without hesitation or any visible doubt, Means seized the legendary mantle of Sioux leadership. Even in their best days the Sioux were difficult to lead, and by the early 1970s they were especially divided and beaten down. Still, Means, who barely knew the Indians who lived on Pine Ridge and who spoke next to nothing of the language, was becoming the new hope of the Lakota traditionals.

In a single conversation he would boast of fistfights and of the time he worked as a dance instructor. He spoke openly of his past as a drunkard, a criminal, a junkie, and the other incarnations of his life as an urban hustler and dandy. He freely admitted to his wild days—days that were not completely over—and made Indian audiences see his experience as their own, as tragic and lost episodes of craziness born of extreme alienation.

An air of danger followed Russell Means wherever he went and everyone knew it. This was a man to watch closely, if for no other reason than to see what would happen next.

AIM leaders Dennis Banks, Clyde Bellecourt, and Russell Means were tough, seasoned, resourceful, and experienced. They knew how to talk to city officials, how to handle cops, how to alternately charm and threaten church leaders. They forged key alliances with progressive lawyers, civil rights activists, and journalists. They also understood that good news coverage was an involved and two-way process. They borrowed from the Black Panthers or other groups when necessary, and, as one member put it, "made things up as they went along."

Excellent agitators and powerful speakers, they did more than just talk. By the end of 1971, AIM had established a base, mainly in the Twin Cities, from which it won results for its constituents. AIM members served notice on police that Indians, drunk or not, were no longer without advocates. They also advised churches, educators, and antipoverty programs that had generally ignored Indians that they could no longer neglect them or take them for granted. Nationally, they had a growing set of local chapters whose members were making a name for themselves in the spate of protests that were sweeping through Indian country. They led the charge at Plymouth Rock and Mount Rushmore. And increasingly, even at protests they didn't organize or participate in, the name AIM was becoming synonymous with protests and media spectacle.

Leaders of established organizations, whether for or against public protest, could no longer dismiss them as unimportant. Clyde Bellecourt summed it up in a line that became his trademark: "We're the landlords of this country, the rent is due, and we're here to collect!"

Ironically, the first month of 1972 gave AIM a bad start to a year that would see them thrust to center stage. Only weeks before the triumphant campaign in Gordon, the ever-quotable Means found himself in a controversy that almost cost him his new leadership position. *Newsweek* ran a story at the end of January on the suit Means filed against the Cleveland Indians baseball team. Means was discussing Levi Walker Jr., a Chippewa-Ottawa who, in his role as Chief Noc-a-homa, mascot for the Atlanta Braves, emerged from a tepee and performed a war dance whenever a Brave hit a home run.

According to the article, Means said "It figures. All the Chippewas used to do was hang around the fort anyway." The quote had the ring of authenticity about it, since the Sioux had a reputation for bad-mouthing their ancient enemies, including the Chippewa. It sounded completely in character for Means, and provoked an uproar within AIM, an organization founded entirely by Chippewas. Means insisted he was misquoted. He told a reporter that he really said that Indians who help caricature their people are the modern equivalent of "hang around the fort" Indians, a reference to those Indian leaders in the nineteenth century who moved close to governmental installations and cooperated with the federal government.

The controversy became an issue of national pride for Chippewas, including many who had no involvement with AIM. One reservation group insisted Means offer a written apology, to be presented in person on Chippewa reservations. Means resigned in a letter dated January 31, 1972. He addressed it to Dennis Banks and the AIM board of directors:

> Dear D.J. and National Board Members,
>   Upon receipt of this letter I have officially resigned from the AIM National Board of Directors and from the position of National Coordinator. The reasons are clear. The Whiteman has tri-

umphed again! By deliberately restruct[ur]ing my statement concerning Chief Noc-a-homa, the Whiteman has succeeded, by using me, in dividing a major segment of the American Indian Movement. Instead of attacking the real source and thereby saying to the Whiteman and to everyone else, that we no longer are going to fall for his divide and conquer tactics, we succumb to his devious ways and let the real issues be clouded by attacking the wrong target. It is sad when AIM people permit this tried and proven method of the Whiteman's to dictate policy, create dissension and to condemn rather than support.

It is because of this lack of support that I resign. The disappointment I feel cannot be adequately expressed on paper. My only hope is the next time there is an attempt to divide Native People, AIM will provide the rallying point necessary to defeat the Whiteman and his ways. As my good friend Jerry Gambel told me, 'This is the winter part of the cycle, a time for renewal of life.' I wish each and every AIM member the strength, courage, wisdom and direction needed for the time of renewal.

In the Indian Way, Russell C. Means Executive Director, CAIC
cc: All AIM Chapters
Jerry Gambel, Akwesasne Notes
Lee Cook, President, NCAI

People in AIM rejected his resignation, saying "you can't resign from being Indian." Means would resign noisily many other times in the coming years. Each time, the uneasy marriage continued, for there was really no other organization for people like Clyde Bellecourt, Dennis Banks, and Russell Means to turn to. NCAI was hopelessly out of touch with its own reservation constituencies. NIYC was by 1972 all but a dead letter. The numerous local urban groups that shared AIM's love of protest had never been able to come close to AIM's national constituency. Only one star was ascending, and Russ Means wasn't about to let it go.

AIM survived that crisis, but AIM's major weakness continued to be its lack of solid connections to reservations. The rules of power and activism in a progressive city like Minneapolis were far different than in reservations, whose intricacies proved elusive when the movement's leaders tried to import their style of organizing. The breakthrough in Gordon that involved reservation people notwith-standing, AIM still had a long way to go if it wanted to appeal to the specific, intricate issues of the reservations.

Still, AIM—and the promise of a movement that would orga-nize and give voice to a growing chorus of the voiceless in Indian communities—exploded across reservations and cities from North Carolina to the Pacific Northwest during 1972. The national AIM leadership did everything they could to build membership, speaking and agitating tirelessly, but even without their efforts chapters would often appear overnight, absent any direct contact with the national headquarters or other AIM activists. Perhaps some knew of the AIM Patrol, or the efforts to seek justice for Raymond Yellow Thunder, or perhaps they were frustrated with the other Indian organizations, but most simply fell hard for the very mystique that established leaders scorned. If you wanted to strike fear into the hearts of whatever local power structure you were opposing in 1972, taking on the name of AIM was the way to do it.

But despite its growing reputation and membership, AIM as an organization seemed always in transition, becoming something more or something different than it had been before. In 1972 the organiza-tion was reaching out toward a traditional Indian past, becoming a warrior society of old combined with the attitude and language of third-world rebels of the 1970s. Even as some Indians in local com-munities—who saw the increasing attention lavished on the group as excessive and undeserved—began claiming that AIM stood for "Ass-holes in Moccasins," or as their critics trashed them as poseurs from the city, charlatans, felons, and freebooters of racism, AIM seized the imagination of Indian people from New York to Alaska. Particularly young people. They signed on in an instant, in Levi's and red ban-dannas and dark shades, eager to stand up for them-selves and their people. They left their homes in Montana or Syracuse or Tulsa, on Greyhound buses or wing-and-a-prayer Indian cars or via an out-stretched thumb, not bothering to promise to write or say when they would return. They were ready for action, ready for anything.

In August, AIM leaders met at Crow Dog's Paradise, the home of a young Sioux spiritual leader named Leonard Crow Dog on the Rosebud Sioux Reservation in South Dakota. Crow Dog was one of several Lakotas responsible for rehabilitating the Sioux version of the sun dance, a religious ceremony that in recent times tribal governments had cheapened and commercialized, anxious to generate income by providing amusement for tourists. AIM was, by then, advocating a return to Indian traditions and was seeking spiritual guidance from Crow Dog, a man close to their age who spoke English as a second language, and who spurned reading and writing.

At the sun dance, AIM people began strategizing about new targets for their growing constituency of activists. The University of South Dakota at Vermillion, which was one possibility, kept Indian skeletons on display. No one under the arbor seemed too excited about that. Robert Burnette, former tribal chairman at Rosebud, proposed another. He suggested a national Indian march on Washington, timed to arrive during the national elections in November. It would be, he said, a way to educate the general public, the president, and Congress. It would be a spiritual movement, without drugs or liquor—everyone would have to be on their best behavior. "This shall be," Burnette said, "our finest hour if we are successful in maintaining discipline that shall bring fruit to our hungry people."

Bob Burnette was a former tribal chairman, not an AIM radical. He was not the type of person AIM leaders trusted, and the power brokers of mainstream Indian politics didn't trust him either. But AIM was out of ideas, and this one sounded pretty good. Vernon Bellecourt, Clyde's brother, seconded the proposal, and everyone agreed that they would meet in Denver at the end of September to flesh out what were only the sketchiest of details and goals.

Burnette's notion was of a symbolic protest that would speak to a panoply of general Indian issues, but the meeting at Rosebud produced no national coordinating committee or even a single person or group to originate or execute any specific plans for the event. It frankly had the look of something that would wither at the stage of being a good idea and which would end up with a relatively small number of the usual activist suspects spouting familiar rhetoric.

Then, catapulted by a moment of tragedy, the idea of a coast-to-coast protest took on new meaning.

On September 21, a caretaker for a YMCA camp in Mendocino County, California, about an hour north of San Francisco, shot and killed Alcatraz leader Richard Oakes. Oakes and the caretaker had been arguing about Indian boys who had allegedly borrowed the camp's horses without permission. As the argument grew more heated, the caretaker shot and killed Oakes. He told police Oakes menaced him with a knife, though police found no such knife or other weapons. The caretaker told authorities it was a case of self-defense, and they freed him on $5000 bond.

In the two years since his ferocious beating at the Indian bar in San Francisco, Oakes had been living north of San Francisco, near Santa Rosa. Although partially paralyzed, with a plastic plate in his skull, he stubbornly continued to organize.

On Thanksgiving in 1970 on the Kashia Reservation, he led a group of Indians who blocked the road and imposed a toll of one dollar on all non-Indians. When a California Highway Patrolman arrived to investigate, Oakes greeted the officer with a smile, and said, "What took you so long? You can never find an officer when you need one."

The state first charged him with armed robbery, then reduced the charges to blocking a public roadway. At his trial, two motorists whom Oakes had stopped testified on his behalf. They described him as having been polite at the roadblock, and said that he had explained that the toll was a symbolic protest against land theft. The motorists said they had not minded paying the toll, and that Oakes had even given them a receipt.

Another Richard Oakes enterprise was a traveling college, housed in a converted bus, that was supposed to travel to Indian communities to share knowledge of tribal histories and cultures. A twenty-one-year-old Yakima activist named Sid Mills, who knew Oakes from Alcatraz and Fort Lawton and who admired the Mohawk leader a great deal, took part in the traveling college. Mills and his wife Suzette had painful memories of the trip, of the bus breaking down, and of Oakes becoming ill. They had had to turn back, and the traveling college became another unrealized dream.

Richard Oakes paid dearly for those dreams. In the end he lost everything. Two months after his extraordinary leap into San Francisco Bay, his daughter Yvonne was gone, dead from a terrible fall on Alcatraz. Then, he lost a vicious power struggle that mocked the occupation's rhetoric of peace and harmony. Six months later, he lost the use of his legs in a barroom brawl. From being a movement hero, he became an outcast, exiled from the community he sacrificed so much to create.

A contingent of activists and leaders from the Pacific Northwest who knew Oakes from Alcatraz and the actions at Fort Lawton traveled south for the funeral. Hank Adams, the Assiniboine-Sioux who had been an activist in Washington state since before the days of the National Indian Youth Council, issued an emotional statement. "If Richard Oakes is only to be . . . identified with Alcatraz to the public by the news media, then let the public remember that Alcatraz was instrumental in placing the needs and concerns of Indian people upon the national agenda." Alcatraz may not have succeeded, Adams acknowledged, but its example aided other pending land claims.

In any event, he wrote, "For Indians, Alcatraz was never meant for confinement of people or of purpose, nor to constrain the ideas or dreams of any. Richard Oakes' presence beyond Alcatraz and his influence upon many Indian people shall continue to live within the body and soul of Indian experience. Born to the American soil, and responding strongly to his people's struggle and suffering upon it, the living spirit of Richard Oakes could not now die nor cease to be remembered upon Indian land. Neither elegy nor eulogy can satisfy his life or death."

In the midst of the somber mourning, the subject of the as yet unorganized cross-country caravan came up. Fueled by outrage and sorrow over Oakes's death, fresh ideas for the caravan began to emerge. Meanwhile, halfway across the country, in Minneapolis, AIM organizers also stepped up their efforts at the news of Oakes's killing. The idea of a coast-to-coast caravan, which had been floundering and disorganized, suddenly took on new intensity and significance. It was Richard Oakes's final gift to his people.

Until the organizational meeting in Denver on September 30, the various players—Burnette, AIM leaders Banks, Means, and the Bellecourt brothers, the people from the Pacific Northwest, and others—pursued their own visions of what ought to happen in D.C. Hank Adams and the others from Washington state, who hadn't been part of the planning until Oakes's funeral, worked independently on a plan that would center on specific issues of treaty rights.

These disparate elements gathered on September 30 at the New Albany Hotel in Denver. Fifty people from organizations that included the National Indian Brotherhood from Canada, the National Indian Youth Council, AIM, the Native American Rights Fund, and the American Indian Commission on Alcohol and Drug Abuse met for three days. Others, including the United Native Americans from Berkeley, San Francisco's Native American Women's Action Council, and the Coalition of Indian Controlled School Boards could not attend but endoresed the effort. It was an interesting mix, but few of the groups had more than a small constituency. Most were advocacy organizations or locally-based activist groups.

Those who made it to the gathering voted to give the demonstration two names: the Trail of Broken Treaties Caravan and the Pan American Native Quest for Justice. Though both names would appear on letterhead and in other material, the Trail of Broken Treaties eventually became the standard moniker. The planners formed eleven committees and appointed Bob Burnette, the Rosebud Sioux who proposed the idea in August, and Reuben Snake, a Winnebago who lived in Albuquerque, as cochairs.

The plan the group came up with called for three caravans originating in Seattle, San Francisco, and Los Angeles, taking routes through most large Indian communities west of the Mississippi. They would converge in St. Paul on October 23, where the group as a whole would develop a position paper "defining Indian needs in relation to the federal government." Once in Washington, D.C., the group would present the document to the White House. Each caravan would be "led by spiritual leaders who will carry the Sacred Peace Pipe and Drum. Every drum will beat day and night reminding Americans of the treaties and every peace pipe will be smoked to remind America and history of the manner under which treaties were signed. This final effort will fulfill a prophecy destined to end the 'Trail of Broken Treaties.' Indians from every reservation, from towns and cities, whether they be living in abandoned cars, tarpaper shacks or on the streets, will join the caravans in a journey destined for what we hope will change the course of history for this country's first citizens in the Pan American Native Quest for Justice."

Organizers of the Trail, who seemingly expected word of their action to spread informally through Indian communities, took special care to exclude all persons who would "cause civil disorder, block traffic, burn flags, destroy property, or shout obscenities in the street." Burnette emphasized this policy in a statement. "We should be on our finest behavior. We must ban all alcohol and drugs, with expulsions guaranteed to violators. If we can't take all the poor and the elderly and the despairing with us, then they should be with us in our minds. Today, Indian identity is defined and refined by a quality and a special degree of suffering. The Caravan must be our finest hour." Burnette, who had lived and worked in the capital during his years with the NCAI, seemed the natural and best choice to take on the responsibility of being the advance man in Washington. He would make the crucial arrangements for housing, food, and permits.

A week after the Denver meeting ended, the caravans were on their way east. Funds were scarce, but leaders hoped to raise money in towns and cities along the way. And since the caravans would travel through places of significance to Indian history, a number of planned and spontaneous protests would take place. Sid Mills made the trip in an old panel truck, with a big green sign that read "Trail of Broken Treaties" over a map of their route to Washington. In Mankato, Minnesota, a town known for its mass hanging of thirty-eight Sioux in 1862—the largest execution in U.S. history—Mills spoke at churches about the goals of the caravan, and solicited donations. The small town seemed to be full of churches, and he found considerable support in their congregations.

Vernon Bellecourt sought assistance from leaders of the Mormon Church in Salt Lake City. His aggressive fund-raising style alarmed the Mormons, who removed the AIM leader bodily from the church. Even so, the Mormons came through with $1000 worth of gas and food.

On Columbus Day, one of the caravans paid a visit to the Custer Battlefield National Monument in Montana, leaving behind a plaque that read "In honor of our heroic warriors who fought for our lives and land against the aggressive hostile U.S. government. Donated by the Trail of Broken Treaties, Oct 12, 1972."

A significant confrontation took place in Oklahoma on October 3. Carter Camp, an up-and-coming AIM leader, led a midnight attempt to seize the Fort Sill Indian School in Lawton, a BIA–run school where tension between students and administrators had been rising. Authorities had been tipped off, and the takeover was unsuccessful. Students, however, rallied in support of the effort, and BIA Area Director Sidney Carney contacted his superiors in Washington, reporting the incident and suggesting the caravan be denied support by the Bureau.

For weeks the caravans made their way slowly toward St. Paul. There were powwows and feasts and warm receptions in some places, but often the journey was arduous, with endless meals of peanut butter sandwiches and rugged accommodations on church floors. It was a scramble each day to raise the funds for gas and food. Along the way some became ill, and the six hundred caravaners were glad to see St. Paul when they arrived October 23.

The group held sessions to solicit ideas on what the document to be presented in Washington should say, but it was drafted largely by Hank Adams. An intriguing mix of proposals that Adams and others had been mulling over for the past few years and which could not easily be labeled, the document was a serious attempt to reestablish a treaty-making relationship between Indians and the federal government. The Twenty points, as it came to be known, was partly idealism, partly a magnificent attempt to draw the United States into a new paradigm of dealing with Indian nations. With Adams' imprimatur, the Trail of Broken Treaties and Pan American Native Quest for Justice had the backing of a respected treaty expert, a movement leader with a reputation for sound judgment who was not part of AIM.

As they left St. Paul for Washington, D.C., where they would deliver the document to the White House and hopefully meet with federal officials, the effort appeared to have come a long way in the three months since the meeting at Crow Dog's Paradise. More people were joining the caravans daily, and surely more would arrive in Washington on their own. No one knew how many people would actually be there, but even a thousand Indians would make a splash during the week before national elections.

Apparently what few had considered, however, was that of all the weeks in the year to lobby Washington's politicians, the week before a national election had to be the worst possible time. With every member of the House of Representatives and one-third of the Senate up for election, the city would be a virtual ghost town. President Nixon would be off campaigning, as would his rival, South Dakota Senator George McGovern. The District of Columbia, overwhelmingly Democratic and worth only a few electoral votes, was the last place a presidential candidate would be the week before election day.

In any event, Indians were a statistical blip in national elections, and Indian policy was a nonexistent issue in this and every other campaign. If somehow a hundred thousand did march on Washington—a virtual impossibility, requiring the participation of almost one-tenth of the entire Indian population—even that would hardly rock a city used to antiwar demonstrations of a quarter million.

If the tactical aims were flawed, they were not the reason most joined the caravan anyway. People joined the caravan because their communities were in pain, and nothing of real substance was being done. At least nothing that so far had translated into widespread, visible results where Indian people lived. They were enduring the hardships of the trip not out of hope for any particular meeting in Washington, but for each other.

Dick LaGarde, an AIM member in the Twin Cities, had a nagging concern of a more practical nature. LaGarde was a logistics expert, who knew how to feed and house large crowds at a powwow or conference. AIM did it often, and in Minneapolis LaGarde was usually involved. He had attended the August meeting at Crow Dog's, and shared the general doubts about Burnette. Could he handle the complex details of taking care of the people once they arrived in Washington? LaGarde heard that arrangements had been made for everyone to camp at RFK Stadium, home of the Washington Redskins professional football team. Neither LaGarde nor anyone else from AIM had done or would do any of the advance work. Burnette was supposed to take care of all that.

Dennis Banks of AIM had written President Nixon a polite letter on October 4 requesting a meeting. A week later Leonard Garment, the senior White House aide on Indian matters, responded in kind with a letter expressing regret that President Nixon's schedule would make such a meeting impossible. He gave the matter little thought.

Brad Patterson, who worked for Garment and handled the details of implementing White House Indian policy, knew about the demonstration. He and Bob Robertson, the tireless executive director of the National Council on Indian Opportunity who had negotiated with the occupiers of Alcatraz, had attended a few meetings of government agencies involved in preparing for large events like the Trail. The two did not believe the caravan would be a spiritually oriented, peaceful attempt at dialogue with government leaders. Instead, they saw the event as an AIM publicity stunt (in spite of the fact that many non-AIM people were involved) designed to embarrass the Nixon administration and promote the media-hungry leaders of the American Indian Movement.

To Patterson, Garment, and Robertson it seemed terribly unfair. The White House had taken bold, unprecedented steps to implement new approaches to Indian affairs. President Nixon himself had issued a statement calling for self-determination of Indian tribes, formally renouncing the hated policies of termination and relocation. The Menominees of Wisconsin, a tribe terminated with tragic results, for instance, were in the process of having their status restored. Another example from the growing list of achievements was the restoration of Blue Lake to the Taos Pueblos of New Mexico. Louis Bruce, the Mohawk-Sioux BIA commissioner, had brought in a cadre of tough, idealistic young reformers, some of them practically militants themselves, and given them a mandate to clean house. Bruce's lieutenants, variously called "The New Team," or "The Katzenjammer Kids," were already getting impressive, if limited, results.

All of it happened with the full support of the president and much hard work by Garment, Patterson, Robertson and a handful of others. Often they had to battle other agencies and even cabinet members from the Department of the Interior to advance their agenda, and in most cases John Ehrlichman, Nixon's domestic policy adviser, managed to convince the president. Significant change was taking place, as far as they were concerned, and the last thing Garment's crew needed was a noisy demonstration condemning policies that had been or were being reversed.

Robertson made a prediction. He believed the militants would try to take over something. Washington, after all, was a city of monuments, and AIM's leaders had made a virtual career out of staging occupations. Probably, he thought, they would go for the Washington Monument.

Patterson and Robertson were among the very few people in Washington who gave the Trail of Broken Treaties any thought at all. The city was transfixed by the elections and by the Paris Peace Talks which many hoped would finally end the Vietnam War. Except for the bureaucrats who met with representatives of the Trail who were seeking permits for their actions, almost no one knew or cared about the Indians making their way across the country.

Harrison Loesch, a high-ranking official at the Interior Department who oversaw the BIA, did notice. On October 11, he sent off a memo instructing BIA employees to provide no assistance to the Trail. This was contrary to the normal practice of offering various courtesies to visiting Indian groups. The memo found its way to the caravan's leaders. They already viewed Loesch as an old-guard reactionary, fighting the reformers' every move, and a symbol of everything so many Indian people despised about the Interior Department and the BIA.

One group that could have lent credibility to the Trail of Broken Treaties among people like Loesch before it arrived in D.C. was the National Congress of American Indians—the largest, most established Indian organization, headquartered in Washington. The Trail leaders sent representatives to the National Congress' annual convention with the goal of winning their endorsement. The affair was the polar opposite of the scruffy Trail, a world of comfortable hotels, expense accounts, and jet travel. In 1972, as they had in past years, the NCAI invited celebrities to attend its national convention. They included Julie Nixon Eisenhower, Glenn Ford, and Burt Reynolds. And as usual, none of them could make it.

For only the second time in its twenty-eight-year history the

Congress met east of the Mississippi River, at the Sarasota Motor Hotel in Sarasota, Florida. Ada Deer, flush with victory from her successful campaign to restore federal status to the Menominee Tribe, mugged for cameras with U.S. Senator Fred Harris of Oklahoma. Carol Jean Garcia, a twenty-three-year-old Papago from Arizona, won the Miss NCAI pageant and gave interviews that endorsed miniskirts and education. Some contestants offered versions of "Amazing Grace" in their native tongue, or the Lord's Prayer in sign language. NCAI's new president, Lee Cook, a former member of the "New Team," took a hard line against the Nixon administration. He lashed out at the old-liners at the BIA. He painted a stark picture of an Indian Country besieged on all sides from virtually every institution in the United States, including Congress, local governments, and the federal education and welfare systems. "Legislation is now being used to carry on the same policies that were once carried on with guns and soldiers."

Sarasota was in the district of Jack Haley, chairman of the House Subcommittee on Indian Affairs. That was the tactical reason for choosing a place so distant from most Indians. Haley, if reelected, would likely be the chairman of Interior and Insular Affairs committee, and thus in a key position to aid NCAI objectives.

The Trail representatives were unsuccessful in convincing the NCAI, which was by then hesitant to be attached to an event that had every appearance of being AIM–sponsored and led, to join the caravans. The Trail organizers offered a statement that said "We do say that 'AIM will be prominent but not dominant' in this united effort and that there are beautiful Indian people all over this country who feel that is time for the fires to be lit everywhere and that it is time we become as one voice and seek what is truly ours." The poetic language failed to resonate with the delegates in Florida. The NCAI rejected the caravan's appeal for support without a formal debate.

Chapter 8

The Native American Embassy

n Wednesday afternoon, November 1, the Trail's buses, campers, trucks, and cars began to arrive in the capital. Washington greeted them with cold rain.

Everyone had been traveling for days, some for weeks. After so many hard floors and stale sandwiches, Indian people on the Trail of Broken Treaties eagerly anticipated reaching their destination, and with it the promise of a hot shower, home-cooked meals, and a good night's sleep. Whether they would be camping in parks or at RFK Stadium or staying in private homes or churches, it would be an obvious improvement over the rough conditions they had just endured.

Those expectations were dashed when the first arrivals disembarked at St. Stephen and the Incarnation Church, at Sixteenth and Newton Streets Northwest. The place of worship was also a place of controversy, presided over by an outspoken, radical minister named William Wendt, a friend to the oppressed and outcast. In front of the small church were mattresses, garbage, furniture, and a rough wooden cross.

A group from Des Moines AIM had arrived first, planning to cook for the later arrivals. They waited in the basement as teenagers from the neighborhood made it clear they were not particularly welcome. The Des Moines people expected to find food at the church. They didn't. Instead, they sighted rats.

AIM people thought the Trail's organizers in D.C. had arranged for Black Panthers to be on hand to greet them, but no Black Panthers were there, just local kids acting tough. Police community-relations specialists, alerted to the caravan's arrival, monitored the situation from the street. During the afternoon and evening the caravans arrived at the small church. They included infants and the elderly, some wearing tribal outfits. Most were exhausted.

During the night the demonstrators drank coffee in the church basement and wondered what had gone wrong. By now, Loesch's memo of a few weeks earlier was common knowledge among the Indians, and they became convinced that their presence in St. Stephen's was a direct result of BIA sabotage. Other churches, larger and no doubt more prosperous, had canceled their invitations to the Trail. Instead of being honored guests in Bethesda or Chevy Chase, because of Loesch they were in the basement of a ghetto church, too afraid to sleep on account of the rats.

The Loesch story, under the conditions, seemed believable. He had, after all, written an offensive, politically unwise memo that instructed federal employees not to provide assistance to the Trail. On the other hand, though, understanding how a faceless bureaucrat from the Interior Department could manage to convince area churches to withdraw their invitations based on his opinion that the people involved were trouble-makers is difficult. Why would the liberal churches of the area, proud sponsors of demonstrators for civil rights and peace, listen to some Interior Department official? The paranoid scenario bordered on the incredible. It conceded vast power to Harrison Loesch, power he most certainly did not wield.

What happened was not a political conspiracy but a logistics meltdown. Bob Burnette's advance team had assured government officials they required no assistance with food or lodging, that they were taking care of it all. Because of their pride or incompetence— or both—the caravan arrived with, essentially, nowhere to stay.

Clues to the trouble ahead could be found in a Bob Burnette press conference two days before the first caravans arrived in Washington. His title, accurately reflecting the tenuous position he held within the Trail of Broken Treaties, was "Temporary Co-Chair." He opened with a statement:

> It is time to fulfill a prophecy of old chiefs—for the nation to regain its dignity, respect, and work together in the field of brotherhood . . . we want to remain in peace, want the nation to know what kind of people we really are. Indians are not a savage, pagan, and stupid bunch of people. They are highly intelligent—have religion—have survived an onslaught of this government of destruction to save their culture. We want to show this government what their culture is all about.
>
> We have many religious ceremonies scheduled on our agenda, to show America the several tribal cultural religions we have maintained.
>
> We will also be meeting with federal officials of this capital, from the President's office to the Health Department, and the Law and Order Department, and we will have position papers on these matters.

This painful and awkward declaration, grandly invoking some vague, generic prophecy, referring to Indians in the third person, would have been understandable had it come from one of the caravaners, inexperienced at addressing the press. But Burnette was a former tribal chairman from one of the larger reservations and former president of the National Congress of American Indians, who had lived and worked in Washington. His role on the Trail of Broken Treaties was in large part to contribute expertise and sophistication. This he failed to deliver. And he made things worse when he attempted to impress reporters—who in the last two years had seen frequent, massive antiwar demonstrations—with promises of an assembly that would be far smaller. "We have already sixty-five Indians from out of town who are here," he told those gathered at the press conference.

He went on to outline activites the Trail had planned, which included the construction of symbolic tepees and sweat lodges in West Potomac Park, evening sessions of entertainment at the Sylvan Theater on the grounds of the Washington Monument, and presentation and discussion of the Twenty Points document that Hank Adams had worked on in St. Paul. They also were planning spiritual services at Arlington National Cemetery and the Iwo Jima Memorial, where those on the Trail would commemorate Pima World War II hero Ira Hayes. Hayes, whose figure appears in the Iwo Jima statue, became famous for his heroics—but later, tragically, he drowned in a drainage ditch where, drunk, he had passed out. Other plans called for a four-hour "continuous parade" around the White House, designed to reenact processions of federal troops that were called out to impress Indian leaders of the past century when they visited Washington. This time, however, the Indians would be circling president Nixon. Organizers were inviting the president and Senator McGovern to speak later that evening at the Sylvan Theater.

A reporter asked Burnette where the demonstrators would stay.

"Churches throughout the city—we have already gotten a large number of calls from the good people of Washington asking Indians to stay in their homes," Burnette said.

The agenda, however, was already doomed. The next day, Burnette learned that the Park Service had denied permission for the services at Arlington National Cemetery and the Iwo Jima Memorial. The "churches throughout the city" was actually just one, and the Indians of the Trail of Broken Treaties would spend their week occupying, defending, and eventually laying waste to a place they never even intended to visit: the Bureau of Indian Affairs building.

As cars and buses continued to arrive at St. Stephen's Wednesday night, the Trail's leaders met at their temporary offices. The AIM people were furious. They confronted Burnette, demanding answers. "You wasted time playing Indian chief," said one, "wining and dining and acting big to the newspapers." Burnette angrily denied it, insisting Loesch had undone his arrangements. The meeting ended with no solutions, and the Trail's leaders returned to the church, where anger continued to simmer. The church basement overflowed with seven hundred exhausted Indians, their bedrolls spread on every available inch of space.

The church proved unacceptable, that much was clear, but no obvious alternative presented itself. At dawn, the caravan's spiritual leaders went to the White House, considered an appropriate place to decide the next move. They returned a few hours later, during the morning rush hour, and announced that everyone should go to the Bureau of Indian Affairs.

Why the BIA building? The schedule for the week of activities included meetings, vigils, and ceremonies at locations all over Washington, and the BIA hadn't been mentioned once. It seemed inconsistent with the language, spirit, and demands of the Trail. For Sid Mills and others who couldn't wait to leave the broken-down church, however, it made perfect sense. Mills thought, "Where the hell are we going to go? We're going down to our building. We're going down to the Bureau of Indian Affairs. We own that son of a bitch." So they went, and the caravan's final stop became the BIA headquarters. A member of the Trail with a bullhorn directed the cars and buses to park on side streets.

The unassuming, four-story building stands facing Constitution Avenue, not far from the Lincoln Memorial. It is a businesslike granite structure in a city of imposing marble, and though it offered few aesthetic rewards, 1951 Constitution Avenue had an impressive pedigree. During World War II, Ally leaders Charles DeGaulle, George Marshall, and Winston Churchill met there and charted Allied strategy. The Atomic Energy Commission moved in after the war, and the secret meetings America's nuclear scientists held there required the construction of a soundproof, bugproof room. When the AEC found better quarters in 1965, the Bureau of Indian Affairs moved in. BIA employees, the story went, gathered for clandestine meetings in the same high-security chambers used by Enrico Fermi and J. Robert Oppenheimer, to discuss not the mysteries of the atom, but BIA mismanagement and corruption.

Thursday morning, first by the score, then by the hundreds, Indians entered the building and settled in the main floor auditorium. They had lunch in the cafeteria, said hello to friends from back home who worked for the Bureau, and watched documentaries from the BIA film library. Upstairs, Trail leaders met with John Crow and Harrison Loesch. Loesch defended his infamous memo; he said he only wanted to prevent the use of federal money in assisting the caravan, and that he welcomed their presence in Washington. He also said the Trail's leaders told him they required no help with accommodations, only with meeting space in the evening which Loesch had arranged. The Trail leaders responded that they needed help now. Loesch promised to try, and said they could stay in the auditorium until he found housing.

It was not a riot or an occupation, but it was an uncertain situation that city and federal officials monitored closely. Next door, in the Interior Department auditorium, out of sight from the Indians, more than two hundred cops from the D.C. riot squad, the Federal Protection Service, and the Park Police waited for instructions.

Interior Department officials quickly found housing at Andrews Air Force Base and other government sites, at the Salvation Army, and even with the city's elusive churches and synagogues. Trail leaders dispatched teams to inspect the facilities.

By late afternoon over a thousand Indians were inside the building. Loesch, not wanting them at the BIA overnight, decided to offer them the use of a larger auditorium at the Labor Department five blocks away, until, hopefully, everyone relocated to the newly arranged housing.

Housing was still a priority, but it was no longer enough. The offer was put to a vote by the Indians and rejected, who demanded a meeting with a representative of President Nixon, preferably domestic affairs advisor Ehrlichman.

Loesch relayed the demand to the White House, and Ehrlichman assigned the meeting to Patterson, since his first choice, Leonard Garment, was out of town. The meeting would take place at eight that night. Reason and compromise appeared to be carrying the day. In a few hours the caravan would be ensconced in happier accommodations, a meeting would be held to iron out lingering distrust, and the Trail could begin the week of planned activities.

At five P.M., with a meeting with a Nixon representative secured, AIM leader and Trail spokesperson Dennis Banks held a news conference and told reporters that the Trail had accepted Loesch's offer of the Labor Department auditorium. His announcement was interrupted by the sound of screams and breaking glass. It came from the building lobby. GSA police in riot helmets had entered and told the

Indians to leave. A fight erupted, and when it ended five minutes later the police were in temporary disarray on the street, and the Indians, some bloodied and all furious, were barricading the entrance with desks, chairs, and file cabinets. They weren't going anywhere now.

Many of the BIA employees were still in the building. John Trudell, formerly of Alcatraz and now a rising star with AIM, helped one worker down a fire escape. Vernon Bellecourt escorted William Veeder, a non-Indian water rights expert who worked for the Bureau, through a window. The group, which had arrived in Washington to deliver the Twenty Points document to the White House and engage in nonviolent demonstrations, had instead repelled a police attack and were in the process of taking over a federal office building.

The wounded were taken to a nurse's station and bandaged up. The people inside started making themselves at home in the now empty offices throughout the building. They stacked typewriters and file cabinets at the tops of stairways, ready for people to throw them in the way of advancing cops. In raucous meetings in the auditorium, AIM leaders Russell Means and Dennis Banks emerged as the most compelling figures as the occupiers decided what to do next.

But what about the continuing negotiations for a peaceful exit? Had it all been a ruse to distract the people on the Trail from government plans for a forced eviction? Apparently not. Rather, the failed attack was the result of miscommunication. At one point on Thursday afternoon federal officials had made plans to stage the eviction at five, and not everyone heard that the plans were off. For the Indians inside, that hardly mattered. Police had assaulted them even as they made plans to leave peacefully.

The afternoon's events made a negotiating meeting that night in Loesch's office across the street from the BIA a rough one for Brad Patterson. He didn't learn of the police attack or that Indians now occupied the BIA building until he arrived. Harrison Loesch and Bob Robertson, who had negotiated at Alcatraz and was a key figure in the founding of the National Tribal Chairmen's Association, were also present. Russell Means and other Trail leaders immediately demanded Loesch's removal because of what they saw as his hostility to the Trail. The two remaining officials listened to the Indians for hours—insults, harangues, threats. As the meeting continued, re-

ports arrived that police in riot gear had surrounded the BIA building, appearing to be preparing to regain the building. That set off a
new round of heated rhetoric. For Robertson, veteran of Alcatraz,
the scene was all too familiar; for Patterson, it was a new and un-
pleasant experience. One activist announced calmly, "You know, Mr.
Patterson, we are going to die tonight."

Brad Patterson continued to feel confidence in the strategy he
and Garment had chosen to handle the Alcatraz occupation—others
in the White House had urged swift removal of the Indians, but he
and Garment had stuck to their course of low-key negotiation,
knowing that time was their ally and confrontation their enemy.
When, six months after the landing on Alcatraz, four students were
shot and killed at Kent State University in Ohio and campus protests
erupted nationwide, Patterson felt a strong sense of vindication for
his actions at Alcatraz. He had advocated negotiation over confrontation ever since.

If Alcatraz seemed fraught with potential disaster, this sudden
rebellion in Washington, D.C. had catastrophic possibilities that bordered on the surreal. Five days before the presidential election, Indian revolutionaries held a government building six blocks from the
White House, vowing to die rather than surrender. The casualties, if
it came to that, would likely include the Trail's scores of children
and old people.

Now and then Patterson left the angry meeting, which lasted
several hours, to consult with the White House. The General Services Administration, which had somehow found itself once more in
the bewildering position of devising military strategies to defeat Indian rebels, proposed tunneling in from the Interior Department
building, surprising the occupiers and then launching a simultane-
ous attack from the outside. Should they give the order? Robertson
and Loesch felt they should. Patterson voted no.

The person with most to lose decided the issue. President Nixon,
off campaigning, ruled against the assault and in favor of restraint.
The restraint option involved obtaining a court order Friday morning for the Indians' removal and continued talks.

The police retreated and disaster was averted. Patterson told the
Trail leaders that he believed the Twenty Points deserved careful

study, and tensions began to ease. Everyone agreed to talk more the next day. The Indians returned to their new home across the street.

Friday morning the occupiers swept the broken glass from the lobby. Some BIA employees arrived for work, but most stayed away. The White House filed suit in federal court for the removal of the Indians, while at the same time BIA Commissioner Bruce became involved in the search for housing. As the morning turned into afternoon, the government appeared to have found a solution when the Indians agreed to take the government up on its offer of a larger auditorium nearby at the Labor Department.

Then, unbelievably, something went amiss yet again. As the last caravaners left the BIA building, the first returned from the Labor building several blocks away, enraged. The auditorium, supposedly waiting and stocked with food, cots, and even showers, was locked. It seemed another double-cross, a mean-spirited trick to get the Indians out of the BIA. They quickly reoccupied the BIA building.

Perhaps only the BIA could have managed successive failures of this magnitude. The locked door was the result of a decision by a minor functionary who believed that only after everyone had left the BIA building could anyone enter the Labor Department.

The Indians unfurled a banner reading NATIVE AMERICAN EMBASSY across the BIA building. A tepee rose on the front lawn of the liberated territory.

Confusion, missed cues, bungled orders, and ineptitude were the occupation's hallmark. A court order requiring police to evict the Indians Friday evening prompted a new round of frenzied defense of the building. Some people barricaded doors with furniture and littered hallways with reports, memos, and other paperwork from filing cabinets. War paint appeared on the faces of Indian men. Occupiers assembled Molotov cocktails by the dozens; by the hundreds. They used so much gasoline that passersby could smell it from the street. Rumors alleged that bombs, ready to detonate, were inside. The message was clear: The government could retake the building, but only at enormous cost.

"Another 'Wounded Knee' was feared Friday night," read a *Washington Post* headline the next morning. The cops pulled back, as they had on Thursday, and as they would again. Inevitably, the court orders were all postponed, for another few hours or another day—then the madness would all start up again and the occupiers would fortify the building even more. Whenever one of those deadlines approached, warriors found their spears (which they had made from broomsticks and scissors) and stood in front of the building. On upper floors, others stood with weapons of their own—trash cans full of hot water, a fifty-pound pumpkin, pieces of office machinery—ready to rain down on attacking police.

Ralph Ware, a Kiowa, had been chosen by organizers at the Denver meeting in October to be one of the coordinators for the Trail. A month later, he stood on the steps of the BIA building, holding a club, waiting to be attacked by riot police. "I am not really a fighter," he said, "but these are my people." Ware was a mental health professional from Minneapolis. "It's going to take a lot for me to swing this club . . . it took me a long time to decide this."

As the occupation continued, the Native American Embassy became a magnet for Washington's counterculture, for radical celebrities like Dr. Benjamin Spock, celebrity radicals like Stokely Carmichael, and a local seventh-grade class conducting research for their project on Indians. Citizens of all races brought food and messages of support. Even Reverend Carl McIntire, a right-wing, pro-war publicity hound with his own radio station, stopped by to demonstrate his solidarity.

The BIA takeover was less a revolution than a conference planner's nightmare. It was a case of incompetent planning and appalling manners, a trifling event of no consequence; yet it somehow captured the essence of the BIA's failure to work with and for Indian tribes. Leaders of AIM, especially, seized the moment and cast themselves in starring roles of what had started as a multiorganizational effort. It seemed a media event dreams are made of, yet it attracted surprisingly little attention outside of Washington; *Time* magazine, for example, never mentioned it.

That it was a fiasco could hardly be denied, but there were also many memorable comic and ironic moments. First there was the cartography lesson: Room 219 of the BIA carried the designation "Rosebud Indian Movement's Department of War." The wall featured a map of Indian land that the office's new tenants had revised. Instead of the few patches of remaining reservations, it now included the entire United States.

In another twist, during the BIA takeover even the Bureau's Indian employees could participate. BIA Commissioner Louis Bruce, who had made statements sympathetic to the occupiers since their arrival in the capital, was a case in point.

Harrison Loesch, Bruce's superior at Interior and an opponent of Bruce's reforms at the Bureau, instructed the Commissioner to stay away from BIA headquarters, fearing his underling would embarrass the administration through further sympathy for the occupation. But on the third day of the occupation the Commissioner of Indian Affairs, who had been on the losing side of his own battles with the government, joined in the occupation of the building the federal government had put him in charge of. John Ehrlichman phoned from the White House and implored Bruce to leave. The place was about to be blown to smithereens. Bruce at first refused, Ehrlichman kept insisting, and finally Bruce agreed to leave.

To one of Bruce's employees who stayed much longer than her boss, the occupation was exciting. A Hopi who grew up in Nevada, Rose Robinson had been an employee at the Bureau since the 1950s. She toured the building during the weekend with her friend Evelyn Leading Fire. Some offices had been trashed, but there was still a semblance of order and discipline, of a kind. Occupiers welcomed the two women and even offered an assignment: to find Bob Burnette, who was staying at a private home in the upper-northwest part of town. Robinson and Leading Fire agreed to do it, and watched as a dour security person initiated them into their "security force" by solemnly tying Christmas ribbons around their arms and instructing them to eat the ribbons if they were captured. The two women found it all hilarious and struggled to keep from erupting into giggles.

Then there was the example of Clydia Nahwooksy, who with her husband Reaves had moved from Oklahoma to Washington and, while working at the Smithsonian, had loaned the occupation the emblematic tepee that had gone up on the lawn outside. At one point, she and Reaves even ate pizza in the Commissioner's office with some of the Black Panthers, Indian militants, and renegade Bureau employees in attendance. The Nahwooksys even brought their kids over. They explored the building, and their daughter made a sketch of gasoline bombs that were on the roof.

The hated Bureau actually became a Native American Embassy. Indians pored over the agency's documents, verifying their suspicions of BIA mismanagement. And, at least at the start, the caravan's security guards didn't turn away any Indian who wanted to come in.

The National Tribal Chairmen's Association held a press conference in Washington, D.C. on Monday, November 6, the day before election day. Clydia watched as the chairmen rose to denounce the occupiers. The NTCA contended that the protestors were not from reservations, were violent lawbreakers, or in some cases were naive, well-meaning people being used by irresponsible, self-styled Indian leaders who were elected by no one. But to Clydia, the tribal chairmen seemed to be the pawns. Robert Robertson, executive director of the National Council on Indian Opportunity which sponsored the NTCA, had flown some of them in for the express purpose of criticizing the militants as well as the reformers in the BIA, and provided them a sheet of "talking points" to use at the press conference. The NTCA believed that Bruce and his New Team had been destroying the Bureau for the last few years and that they were somehow responsible for the current crisis.

Militants disrupted the press conference, shouting that the chairmen were selling out their people for crumbs from Robertson's NCIO. While the insurgents wore feathers and black reservation hats, the NTCA's people dressed in suits as conservative as their politics. Clydia spotted a cousin stepping out of a hotel elevator with Robertson. As they made their way to the microphones, she confronted him. What did he plan to say? Her cousin mumbled a response, and Clydia angrily stalked out of the press conference.

Rose Robinson returned a final time after her adventure with Trail Security. She could see at once the occupation had begun fraying at the edges. She saw major vandalism, more files dumped in hallways, and more Molotov cocktails. The headquarters' huge collection of art had become a major casualty; she walked past slashed paintings on the walls and shattered pots in broken glass display cases. Robinson heard that some offices were being routinely trashed and she wanted to see if her office was one of those. It was.

She came to rescue her personal possessions, but it was too late for the one she treasured most. For ten years she had searched libraries to create an exhaustive index of books about Indians. Robinson kept careful notes about each title on colored index cards. The project was very close to her heart, which sank when she finally pushed open the door, jammed shut by the ankle-deep trash. Amid the debris were the tattered remains of her project, a few bits of useless color here and there. The rest had disappeared in the whirlwind.

She walked out, devastated by the sight, past the slashed paintings and shattered pots. She found a basket a friend had made for her next to some people who were asleep. She picked it up and left.

Time ran out for the Trail on Sunday night, November 5, two days before the election. Federal negotiators summoned caravan representatives to the Interior building and presented them with a document emphatically titled "Administration's Final Offer and Ultimatum." The Indians would leave by eight A.M. Monday; the government would provide the use of the BIA auditorium "at reasonable hours," an office with a phone for "local calls," and the Interior auditorium, which had showers; they would provide up to three trailers for cooking, which the GSA would hook up with electricity, but Indians would have to provide the stoves and gas; they would allow use of the BIA parking lot; finally, they would arrange for "one or two" representatives from the Trail to have a meeting with the Secretary of Interior. In the documents, the federal negotiators specifically rejected bus service and food.

In the Native American Embassy auditorium, the occupiers debated and rejected the offer. Twenty Points drafter Hank Adams, who was a lead negotiator for the protestors, phoned the government negotiators with the news. This decision, those officials told Adams, was extremely regrettable. Could he arrange to get the women and children out of the building, immediately? Adams said probably not, because the women and children had participated in the decision. The conversation ended, and a little while later the government disconnected the phone lines.

It was a bad turn and everyone knew it. The nearly constant

threat of attack, the roller-coaster mood swings, and the looming possibility that the bottles full of gasoline might actually be ignited became too much for the people inside to bear. It was psychological torture, and on the following day, the occupiers broke. On Monday afternoon the federal courts ruled for the government and ordered police to remove the Indians, effective at six P.M. The attorneys for the Trail believed that further appeals had little chance of success.

Inside the Bureau many of the occupiers had been watching a documentary on the fishing struggle in Washington when news came of the court's decision. "As Long as the Rivers Shall Run" featured graphic footage of state game wardens dragging Indian women across rocks. Hank Adams, who had been a central figure in the fishing struggles since he had worked with the National Indian Youth Council there in 1964, was in the film and had also produced it. The movie inflamed the audience, and when combined with news of the court ruling, their growing rage exploded. The Indians launched a ferocious wave of violence against the building. The earlier actions had been vandalism; this was war.

The ferocity of the vandalism could not be explained only by the fear of imminent attack. The looting and trashing was so widespread, so deliberate, that it pointed to a hatred on the part of many Indians for the documents because they were documents; records that must be destroyed because of what they and the building that housed them represented.

Hank Adams and a Mohawk spiritual leader named Francis Boots returned from the court to the BIA building in the late afternoon. What they saw shocked them both deeply. The two had been gone only a few hours, and in that space of time an orgy of destruction had occurred.

As they walked through the wreckage, Boots told Adams he felt "torn in two, right down the middle." He understood the reason for the actions of the frightened, enraged people in the building. Expecting attack from riot police, nerves frayed after days of being under siege, little sleep, and not enough food, the Indians chose to make certain the government's inevitable victory would be a costly one. He understood the motivation of their desperate act. At the same time, the ugly scene was an affront to the Mohawk's spiritual training and sense of discipline.

The destruction cast a pall over the occupiers. They became dispirited, and the mood changed from defiance to defeat. The people waited for the final, crushing police invasion, but it never came. At various times the building had felt like a festival of pan-Indian unity, a family reunion, a liberated zone of righteous anger and celebration. No longer. After the frightened, wild episode of destruction on Monday afternoon, the place had started to feel like a tomb.

Monday night the White House sent word they would agree to meet with a group from the occupation force. Leaders assembled a delegation of nine, including grandmothers, young people, and men still wearing the war paint from the threatened battle of earlier that day. Hank Adams led them to the Old Executive Office Building next to the White House, where the Indians negotiated the terms of their surrender.

Leonard Garment and Frank Carlucci represented the government, and listened as the Indians spoke of the reasons they came to Washington. They had little optimism that conditions for their families and communities would change. The Trail of Broken Treaties and the Twenty Points, one said, were but a slender thread of hope.

The government agreed to create a task force to study the Trail's grievances and proposals. In addition, the White House would formally respond to each of the Twenty Points. The concessions, if they could be called that, were easy ones for Garment and Carlucci to make. It quickly became apparent the main hurdles to an agreement were amnesty and financial assistance to help the Indians return home. Politically, the two issues were dangerous ones for the Nixon administration. Finally, Garment and Carlucci offered this to the Indians: "We will recommend that there be no prosecution for the seizure and occupation of the BIA building." The Indians accepted the less than binding language. Financial assistance was a less controversial matter, but the logistics were problematic. The money had to come from somewhere. It would take two more days to finalize the details, but the talks were oddly out of sync with the occupation. In spirit, it was already over. The people wanted to go home.

On Tuesday, a massive landslide returned Richard Nixon to the

White House for another term. He carried forty-nine states. As he addressed ecstatic supporters on television, some of the occupiers loaded furniture, artwork, and cartons of documents into trucks behind the BIA building. When Brad Patterson found out, he telephoned White House staffer Egil "Bud" Krogh, and insisted the trucks be stopped and the Indians arrested. Krogh was as hawkish as Patterson was liberal, and Krogh must have had trouble believing his ears. The two traded places as the law-and-order hard-liner told the liberal Patterson that such an action would be unwise given the offer of amnesty.

Some people had already left, but most waited until Wednesday afternoon when the travel money finally came through. The money had proved to be a vexing problem. Garment and Carlucci no longer had doubts about the wisdom of providing the funds; if they were ever in doubt as to finding a way to end the occupation quickly, they only had to remember the long duration of Alcatraz. The possibility of hundreds of destitute Indian militants wandering the streets of Washington for months was also a powerful incentive to help the occupiers return home. But apparently no White House safe of money existed for special emergencies. The solution they devised was oddly appropriate. The Office of Economic Opportunity had a generally positive reputation among Indians. It was the government agency on the front lines of the War on Poverty, and many welcomed its presence on reservations. The money would come from OEO.

The problem was that the OEO took weeks to process a grant and there was no time. The NCAI, however, received OEO money, and the White House prevailed on them to release their OEO grant as travel money to the occupiers. The NCAI was extremely reluctant to go along, and moreover they had nowhere near the needed amount in the bank. White House pressure carried the day, however, and the money changed hands at the Dupont Circle branch of the Riggs Bank on Wednesday afternoon, November 8. Federal officials handed $66,650 in small bills over to Vernon Bellecourt as the NCAI's newly elected Sioux executive director, Chuck Trimble, looked on. Trimble found the arrangement one of dubious legality. To him, the bank appeared to have agreed to an overdraft of the NCAI account based on the White House promise of eventual repayment by the OEO.

The cash fit inside two large envelopes. The bank offered Belle-court one of their guards to make sure the money arrived safely, but the AIM leader declined, saying, "We have our own security."

During the afternoon Indians lined up at the BIA auditorium and explained how much they needed to get home. Everyone who asked received something, usually between twenty and one hundred dollars.

The occupation had been a bold strike against colonialism, an attack on the very building where the BIA developed its hated policies. Yet the target was chosen not because of its strategic importance but because weary demonstrators had been unhappy with their rat-infested lodging and felt somehow the Bureau should make things better. It was the most important act of Indian resistance since the defeat of Custer at Little Big Horn, yet after all the vows of victory or death, everyone agreed to leave in exchange for gas money home.

On Wednesday night, November 8, before the occupation was completely over, Hank Adams paid a final visit to the building. Between the departure of the very last of the Indians and the reestablishment of government control, a deceptively quiet interlude settled over the building. It was quiet, but also dangerous. The place could still go up in flames, Adams thought, either by design or accident. For all he knew, provocateurs were already inside, waiting for the right moment to strike a match. To prevent this, Adams and the Trail's chief of security went through the building, room by room, to close off all areas but the ground floor where the remaining demonstrators were gathered.

Adams opened one office door to see someone rifling through papers. The man broke down in tears, explaining he was a bureau employee only trying to collect his personal possessions. He pleaded with Adams not to hurt him. His terror was so great that Adams had trouble assuring him he would not be harmed, by Adams or anyone else. The depth of the man's fear made Adams realize that it would be almost impossible for people to understand, much less sympathize, with the unleashed rage that tore through the building two days earlier. Surrounded by the frightening evidence of wholesale destruction, no wonder the employee begged for his life.

In another darkened room, they found a half-dozen teenagers drinking beer, indifferent to the news that their friends on the Trail were likely already on their way home. Adams gave them an angry lecture, and ordered them downstairs to the auditorium. The disturbing scene reminded him of another group of rowdy youth. Four years earlier, in Memphis, a peaceful march had turned ugly as belligerent young people, openly drinking and disdainful of nonviolent methods, sought confrontation with police. Martin Luther King had led that march, and his inability to control the angry kids had brought harsh criticism. King had left town but soon returned in the face of accusations that he had abandoned his people. King was assassinated in Memphis on April 4. For Adams, the memory was a painful one. He had been in meetings with the civil rights leader only days before the assassination.

After securing the building and seeing the last of the stragglers leave, Hank Adams walked out into the night.

One week after Bob Burnette's press conference remarks that spoke of spiritual lessons the caravan had to offer Americans, a sign in the BIA auditorium greeted those who would inventory the result of the occupation: "Gentlemen: we do not apologize for the ruin nor for the so-called destruction of this mausoleum. For in building anew, one must first destroy the old. This is the beginning of a new era for the Native American people. When history recalls our efforts here, our descendants will stand with pride knowing their people were the ones responsible for the stand taken against tyranny, injustice, and the gross inefficiency of this branch of a corrupt and decadent government. Native American Embassy."

Hank Adams, who saw color and shadow in a movement that increasingly could see only black and white, offered a quite different epitaph for the event. A few weeks later he wrote, "To some, we had defeated the building; to others, the building had defeated us."

For days, Bobbie Kilberg, a White House aide who worked on Indian issues, had been a courier of messages between presidential adviser John Ehrlichman and the occupiers. On the last day, amid the piles of debris outside the commissioner's office, one item left an indelible impression. It was a typewriter. Unlike other pieces of office equipment, it was not smashed or smeared with paint. Instead, some-

one had carefully twisted each of the typewriter's forty-four keys beyond repair. She thought about the slow, consuming anger such an
act required.

"Patient fury," she called it a few weeks later in an opinion
piece she wrote for the *Washington Post*. No friend of AIM or of law-
breaking, Kilberg nonetheless asked readers to consider the source of
the rage. She told stories of some of the people she had met in her
hours inside the Native American Embassy. She spoke of Josetts
Wahwassuck, a seventy-four-year-old Prairie Band Potawatamie,
who lived in a house without running water until only the year before, and whose son was beaten when he led a group to the local BIA
office seeking information on money legally theirs but held "in trust"
by the Bureau. She mentioned an Indian from Montana who spent a
year trying to obtain BIA approval to lease his land, until the lease
opportunity vanished. He wanted to start a business with the lease
income, and those hopes vanished as well.

Despite Kilberg's hope that the reasons Indian people came to
Washington was what the public and government officials would remember, the definitive images from the occupation were those of
broken toilets, raving graffiti, smashed furniture, and hallways littered with paper. The BIA thoughtfully provided tours for congressmen, for reporters, for Indian dignitaries, for, really, anyone at all.
Wind blew through broken windows, scattering paper down hallways
littered with debris. The building remained closed for weeks. It became a shrine to revolutionary hooliganism, a monument to the
error of militant Indian ways. The FBI was vigorously pursuing the
stolen documents around the country; yet weeks later documents inside the building were still so much trash.

If the government cared about the destruction, why didn't they
start repairing the damage? If the government saw BIA documents as
so precious, why weren't they sorting through the ones inside the
building? To the militants it was proof the government cared little
about the damage or the artwork or the documents. Rumors were always flying through the ranks of movement people about ways the
feds were trying to discredit them and create divisions within the
Indian world. This case seemed to show them doing just that, and
brilliantly.

On Monday, November 13, the government estimated the damage

at $2.2 million. The *Washington Post* noted that only twice in the 196 years of the Republic had greater destruction been inflicted on federal property. The first was the British Army's sacking of Washington in 1814; the second was the 1906 earthquake in California. (Government officials would later drastically revise the absurd figures downward, evidence that AIM had no monopoly on hyperbolic excess.)

At the beginning of the year, Vine Deloria had proposed an alliance that included AIM, NTCA, and NCAI. Now, people in the various organizations were not even speaking with each other. The family atmosphere—that allowed John Trudell to help a BIA employee escape, or Reaves and Clydia Nahwooksy to share pizza with AIM leaders in the Commissioner's Office, or BIA employee Rose Robinson to play Trail Security—was another casualty of the BIA takeover.

Leaders in the various groups established and confirmed their working perceptions of each other. AIM had become a gang of militant thugs. The NCAI was an increasingly inept and irrelevant collection of "hang around the fort Indians." The NTCA was a pawn of Bob Robertson's NCIO.

The year that had opened with visions of unprecedented unity ended with bitter recrimination.

Part Three

The Independent
Oglala Nation

Chapter 9

Border Town Campaign

hockwaves from the sacking of the BIA rattled Indian communities and raised fear in border towns across the country during the rest of 1972. Pieces of the building itself kept turning up in places near and far. On November 21, the FBI recovered paintings, books, and artifacts in Lawrence, Kansas. Two California Indians were nabbed on the streets of Washington with typewriters labeled "Bureau of Indian Affairs." The FBI was alerted in Clinton, Oklahoma, after a van carrying nine Indians turned over and the occupants refused treatment at the local hospital. A search of the vehicle uncovered office equipment from the BIA headquarters.

Paintings that a few months earlier had adorned government hallways now graced reservation homes. Baskets and pottery, liberated from stuffy glass cases, had not been stolen, but rather repossessed by their original owners. Or so it seemed to many of the people of the caravan.

The typewriters and artifacts were only minor spoils from the adventure in Washington. The caravan left town with tons of government documents, more than 20,000 pounds measuring 178 cubic feet.

Included were sixty-nine volumes of land allotment tract and deed books for the White Earth Chippewas of Minnesota and the Oneidas of Wisconsin. Also missing were the claim records of individual Indians from 1880–1930, organized by tribe and listing annuities, including per capita and pro-rated shares; General Accounting Office records on loan to the Bureau from the National Archives that detailed Navajo financial affairs from 1937–1951; and more than a thousand official personnel files of BIA employees. Those records, from an office of the Bureau few had ever heard of called the Office of Inspections, contained "administratively restricted files, inspection reports and irregularities, and FBI material."

Government documents were big news in the early 1970s. The release of the secret Pentagon Papers had been a national sensation two years earlier, and confirmed to many Americans that their government had lied to them about U.S. involvement in the Vietnam War. The theft of such a massive quantity of BIA documents indicated a desire on the part of occupiers to make a similar commotion. They planned to use the documents to educate tribes as well as to release them to the news media.

For AIM, whose members had played the major role in taking the files, the documents were the smoking gun in their case against the federal government, proof that whatever excesses the militants may have committed in November paled in comparison to the ongoing work of the true criminals: the Bureau of Indian Affairs itself.

The FBI soon tracked the largest cache of documents to North Carolina, home of the occupation's rowdiest contingent, the Tuscaroras. Agents made arrests and recovered the documents before the radicals' study could take place.

Nationally-syndicated columnist Jack Anderson wrote pieces based on the files, but the subject was nothing new to his readers—he had written about BIA mismanagement and corruption on other occasions. The Bureau, in fact, enjoyed a certain immunity to criticism since everyone who cared at all about the agency, and not many did, agreed the Bureau was a singularly inept organization, which is why one of its primary activities seemed to be a near-annual reorganization.

In the eyes of some Indian observers, the document heist was an exceptionally stupid and irresponsible action. The big losers, they believed, would be the tribes, who relied on government records to press for land claims and other issues. According to this theory, the BIA could now tell tribes key documents were missing even if they were not.

Vine Deloria, the Sioux writer and Indian affairs insider, and Hank Adams were as appalled as any government official at the destruction of documents. Deloria would argue in print that the seizure of the BIA did grave damage to important land, water, and treaty rights cases, and that in some instances this would make it much harder for tribes to fight the United States, and easier for bureaucrats to ignore important claims. He even suggested that unprincipled officials could claim documents had been destroyed when they had not been.

Hank Adams, who unlike Deloria had been inside the building and watched the successive waves of destruction, had never agreed with the removal of the documents. And in the weeks after the takeover he committed himself to arranging for their return. At a press conference in Washington in early January, he spoke candidly of "a division in the philosophies and personalities" of the movement. It had become splintered, he said, and suffered from a "great gap in the cohesiveness and coordination of activities."

All of that was true, but the document issue was a prime example of how fragile the coalition had been from the beginning. Adams found himself defending actions he personally disagreed with, a task he managed with considerable skill. The press would ask him about the criminal records of the AIM leaders, and he would talk of their rehabilitation, their years of gainful employment and service to their communities. Still, the Trail had become synonymous with crazed destruction, and Adams's efforts to redirect attention to larger issues proved unsuccessful.

The militants and their tactics, not federal policy, had become the issue. For Adams, this was perhaps the most painful casualty of the BIA occupation. He signed on to advance a new framework for Indian policy, and the Trail's Twenty Points—which he played the major hand in drafting—reflected a bold approach that, in substance, not only held treaty enforcement to be of central importance but even proposed reinstating treaty-making relationships between Indian tribes and the federal government.

The debate about treaties Adams and others had envisioned never materialized. When the White House made its official response on January 9, Leonard Garment and Frank Carlucci obviously saw no need to sugarcoat their curt dismissal of the proposals. First, they offered a stern lecture on the events of November: in their view an act which "served only to impede the progress already being achieved by the combined efforts of the administration and the responsible Indian community." They not only rejected the idea of reopening the treaty process—the heart of the Twenty Points—but said that even discussing such a proposal was a waste of time. "To call for new treaties is to raise a false issue, unconstitutional in concept, misleading to Indian people, and diversionary from the real problems that do need our combined energies," the White House statement read.

Also in the wake of the takeover, heads rolled at the Interior Department. In December, Nixon fired Commissioner Bruce—presumably for siding with the militants—and he dismissed Harrison Loesch and John Crow for their clumsy handling of the crisis in the early stages. Bruce's New Team of young reformers was also all but gone. Those who had fought for revolution from within had resigned or had been transferred out of Washington. The few that remained spent the winter in a ramshackle, barrackslike structure called Tempo 8. The offices accurately reflected their status in the new order; the place was so poorly heated that secretaries wore gloves even when typing, the phones were silent, and when it rained they had to arrange waste baskets under holes in the roof to catch the pouring water.

Though Garment and Patterson kept their jobs, conservative columnists excoriated them for their role in the takeover, accusing the two White House aides of being appeasement-minded liberals who undermined Nixon's hard (and popular) line against dissidents. Garment and Patterson also learned important new lessons in guerrilla theater. Court-ordered deadlines, they understood better than ever, played right into the hands of protesters by focusing media attention on the crisis. A strategy that appeared to be restrained and cautious may instead have prolonged the occupation. At Alcatraz, restraint carried the day and robbed the Indians of a confrontation in which the government could only have lost, at least from a public relations point of view. In Washington, however, that same restraint proved to be one of the militants' most effective weapons.

Mastering the intricacies of dealing with the radicals remained a challenge for the White House liberals. It would continue to bear close attention and study, and in the coming weeks there would be no shortage of opportunities for just that.

When not desperately trying to negotiate the return of the vast store of federal records stolen from the Bureau of Indian Affairs building, Hank Adams turned his attention to the condition of the documents that remained at the Bureau. He wrote to the president on November 22. "In the course of a survey of the BIA Building today," he said, "I was shocked that there had been no efforts made on the first and second floors to protect, recover, or restore documents and records that ostensibly are essential to a continuation of federal services to numerous Indian people. In fact, all papers are being exposed to greater disorder, disarray and damage under the practices adopted since the November 8 evacuation of that building."

Adams reminded the president of his own views of the destruction and theft of the records: "As one who has acted through all forms available to me for the protection of such materials during all the days of this month, I find the actions of departmental-level federal officials controlling this matter as being both unconscionable in the present instance and demonstrative of the uncaring attitudes and culpability which has characterized their actions during the same time period. I urge and respectfully appeal to you to direct that a higher standard of concern be invoked. . . ." Or, Adams said, "if the Administration is alternatively going to permit the departmental officials to pursue their 'the Indians be damned' policy with respect to these materials and other future actions, then that decision should be announced in order that Indian tribes and Indian people whose rights and interests are yet being disregarded, denied or sacrificed within the Bureau of Indian Affairs building may proceed to other legal recourse, remedies and protections, which may be required to be undertaken."

In spite of being a prime architect of an attempt at meaningful dialogue and negotiation that had resulted in spectacular failure, tremendous damage, and theft of documents, Adams managed to take the moral high ground and lecture President Nixon on how poorly his administration was caring for the trashed papers still lining the hallways.

Adams raised another issue in his letter, a situation that Indian insiders saw as increasingly dangerous. "With respect to the Pine Ridge Indian Reservation . . . ," he wrote, "it is my understanding federally-commissioned BIA [personnel] from a number of reservations are being used to comprise a private police force for the tribal chairman of that Sioux Tribe. Additionally, tribal funds are being used, wholly on [Oglala Sioux] Chairman Wilson's personal authorization, to hire and arm a band of 'special citizen deputies' to supplement and increase the strength of the federal police force. The focus of these forces appears to be tribal members of the Trail of Broken Treaties Caravan who are now attempting to return and remain in their home communities, but who are being threatened with violence and serious injury and harm by irresponsible tribal officials who are abusing their positions in a most flagrant and unacceptable manner."

The letter continued, "Also, I understand that Mr. Wilson has suspended all other tribal officials who are in disagreement with his actions—effectively has suspended tribal government altogether, except for his own command and personal dictates—and has declared that impeachment proceedings which had commenced against himself some time ago, as well as new tribal elections, cannot now be honored or held nor proceed to a constitutionally mandated conclusion."

Adams never received a reply. Clearly, the president's closest advisers at the White House had had quite enough of Indians for a while, and had no interest in getting involved in what seemed to be some petty dispute on Pine Ridge. Indeed, at a post-election meeting of high-level officials to map out strategies for Nixon's second term, Spiro Agnew suggested that he increase his vice-presidential efforts on behalf of Indians. Nixon, the son of Quakers and possessed of a soft spot for Indians, told Agnew to leave Indian issues alone. To him, the whole area had become, in words that would come back to haunt the administration, "A big loser."

Though nearly everyone else with the Trail had left town, Adams remained in Washington through the winter to try to accomplish something in the chilled political climate. His attempt to locate and return the BIA documents proved to be every bit as ill-fated as the dizzy scheme to remove them. Adams did manage to recover a large stash, but on January 31, 1973—the day before he planned to turn them over—the FBI arrested him, along with a reporter who worked as a researcher for Jack Anderson. The Justice Department dropped the charges a few weeks later, but even that small victory had little to do with Indian resistance. Instead, because federal agents had arrested a reporter, editorialists condemned the incident as a government attack on freedom of the press.

To a growing legion of disaffected Indian youth from both cities and reservations around the country, AIM was anything but a loser after D.C. Movement fashion came into its own, with young people wearing ribbons and patches on their Levi's, celebrating Alcatraz, Fort Lawton, the Trail of Broken Treaties, and other actions. The more you had, the better. For them, sacking Washington had felt righteous. Treated with contempt by bureaucrats in Washington and ignored by Nixon, this was exactly what many of the Indians expected. If the rhetoric of Dennis Banks and Russell Means seemed dangerous and irresponsible to some, it sounded entirely appropriate to those who faced the riot squads in D.C., armed only with chair-leg clubs.

To them and their admirers, AIM's star burned brighter than ever, and the battered caravan's exit out of Washington felt like something very close to a victory procession. The majority of Indians who participated in the Trail of Broken Treaties couldn't wait to get home; but for others the movement had become their home. Washington was not the end but one stop on a tour with no final destination. As Adams had predicted to the president, the growing legion made its way to South Dakota. But before they made it to Pine Ridge and Dick Wilson's troublesome tenure, they would put all the border towns in the region on alert.

Their focal point was Rapid City. Though it lies over a hundred miles from the most populated parts of Pine Ridge, Rapid City has always been as much a border town as an urban area for South Dakota's Indians. For the people of Pine Ridge, Rosebud, Cherry Creek, and other reservations, it is close enough to provide the kind of shopping not available on reservations. And the attitudes of local whites to Indians who came there to shop or to live was, in general, not much different from the attitude that led Raymond Yellow Thunder to his death in the border town of Gordon, Nebraska a year earlier, in February, 1972.

Area residents often drop the last half of Rapid City's name, perhaps a comment on the municipality's size and ambience. A big town more than a small city, from almost any downtown corner it offers pleasing vistas of the Black Hills, the centerpiece of Sioux spirituality and land claims ever since settlers discovered gold there and expelled the Sioux in the 1870s. With little industry, tourism is an essential part of the local economy. Clean air, good hunting and fishing, and a pioneer sensibility are the attractions. Mount Rushmore, sculpted into the Black Hills, is nearby, and the town of Custer, another big draw, is a short enough drive away to be almost a suburb. In Rapid, you are never far from a gun shop or a western clothing store. In the center of town is the Alex Johnson Hotel, featuring walls decorated with Indian designs, and headdresses behind glass cases in the lobby. Guests in more prosperous decades included presidents and royalty.

Rapid City that winter had not yet recovered from The Great Flood of 1972. In June, the heavens erupted and the suddenly furious waters of Rapid Creek ripped through the town and killed 231 citizens. The event devastated the rustic community of forty thousand. A policeman described the horror. "At one time, we had so many bodies we were sticking them in the post office truck, and everything was so confused, people hollering for help in the dark."

In the frozen months of the beginning of 1973, the community was still coming to terms with its grief. Rapid City was not in the mood for the scores of Indians from around the country who made the town their destination and base of operations. New arrivals joined the battalions from the Washington campaign to confront the king of South Dakota's border towns on the issue of its treatment of Indians.

In a way, the relationship was doomed from the start. Rapid lies within the boundaries of the Great Sioux Nation as defined by the Fort Laramie Treaty of 1868, and it exists because of the discovery of gold a few years later that doomed the treaty. Ever since, the Sioux have claimed the land as their own by right of treaty.

Indians fared badly in Rapid's planning and development. In the gold rush days, they lived in shacks near the railroad tracks by Rapid Creek. As the town grew it became apparent that the Indians were embarrassingly close to the business district, and they were relocated to some hills on the outskirts a comfortable distance away. When that land turned out to be the perfect location for a new junior high school in the 1950s, the Indians again had to move, this time miles away, on the prairie far from any transportation or shopping. This was the Sioux Addition, a collection of pink and blue and beige wood houses. Although its location seemed to promise an end to this new kind of urban relocation program, the city council and mayor once again underestimated their community's potential for growth. Interstate 90 came to South Dakota, and as fate would have it, the highway passed right by the new Indian ghetto. This in turn brought hotels, a new housing development, and even the Control Data Corporation to the neighborhood. Calvin Kentfield, a local novelist, wrote about the problem of the Sioux Addition and its inconvenient residents. He said that "many white citizens wish the Indians would disappear forever, forever vanish."

White residents of Rapid City had watched with growing concern the events in Gordon, Nebraska a year earlier, and the BIA occupation was major news in South Dakota. Now, instead of vanishing, the most violence-prone Indian organization in the country had targeted their city. To whites, it seemed a promise of chaos and disruption. The Indian leaders planning the event would characterize it as "sensitivity training."

Ron Petite, a local leader of AIM, announced the campaign—
which would soon expand to include towns across the state and in
Nebraska—at the beginning of January, 1973. The Executive Director of the Sioux Indian Emergency Care and Rehabilitation Center
in Rapid City, and a leader of the recently concluded Trail of Broken Treaties, Petite had also served as Associate National Director of
AIM. The local AIM chapter had asked its national parent organization to "put a freeze" on Rapid City. Petite said the campaign would
"literally chain up the doors of big business enterprises, federal
agencies and state and local community service agencies" through
protests and shutdowns.

He asked for federal hearings on discrimination in housing and
employment and misuse of federal flood appropriations. He blasted
the city for its treatment of Indian veterans. "All doors normally
opened have been slammed shut in their faces. The only doors the
Indian veteran finds open are racial discrimination, unemployment,
slum housing, broken families, suicide, alcohol and skid row," Petite
said, adding, "because of the crisis situation of Indian veterans in
Rapid City, we have no alternative but to turn to Indian people for
support."

Petite named a startling number of targets, including North-
western Bell Telephone, Black Hills Power and Light, First National
Bank of the Black Hills, K-Mart, Gibson's Discount Center, Piggly
Wiggly, Scooper Dooper, Safeway, Coca Cola Bottling Company,
Frontier Bar, Bronco Bar, the South Dakota Welfare Department,
HUD, the Community Action Program, St. John's Hospital, the Pub-
lic Health Service Hospital, Ellsworth Air Force Base, the Bureau of
Indian Affairs, local and state law enforcement agencies, the State
Division of Alcoholism, and the State Human Relations Commis-
sion. That added up to just about every business or governmental en-
terprise that ever touched Indian lives in Rapid City.

He also said that AIM had invited a similarly broad range of
groups to participate, ranging from the Nixon administration's National Council on Indian Opportunity to the Veterans of Foreign
Wars to the Native American Rights Fund, among others. The announcement said hearings would begin in a month, although Senator James Abourezk—a Lebanese American who had grown up on

the Rosebud Reservation and whom Petite said would be the one to sponsor hearings—claimed to know nothing about any of this. To many, it must have sounded like more empty threats from AIM people. But in fact, Petite's ambitious agenda, though not met in every detail, would largely come to pass.

First, however, AIM leaders had to get to Rapid—and that proved to be an adventure. The BIA occupation changed the movement's relationship to law enforcement permanently and profoundly. The televised images of Indians with clubs, the ruined bathrooms and the upended file cabinets, and the rumors of the entire building wired with Black Panther–supplied bombs, meant AIM held the attention of every police force within hundreds of miles of Indian country.

AIMsters, as they began to call themselves, often delighted in the outlaw image. But now, the guerrilla theater became more like a guerrilla war and less like stage-managed agitprop. Events in Washington confirmed them as a gang of hoodlums and nickel-and-dime terrorists in the eyes of many observers. The clever orchestration of anti-AIM statements from Indian leaders aligned with Bob Robertson's NCIO made it that much easier to paint the movement as a loose collection of jailbirds out to burn your town. Also, AIM's name appeared with increasing frequency in the Justice Department's secret directory of potential hot spots for subversive, violent actions around the country.

Russell Means had already experienced the new, tense atmosphere when he returned to South Dakota from D.C. He might as well have been wearing a bull's-eye on his back. In Scottsbluff, Nebraska, a town bordering Pine Ridge, AIM and Chicano activists (who had made significant steps toward collaboration with the Indian radicals) met for several days in January to plot common strategy. Police kept them under constant surveillance. On January 13, Scottsbluff police arrested Russell Means.

The trouble in Scottsbluff had begun at the Park Motel, where AIM conference participants were staying, after complaints of a loud party. Along with Means, police had also arrested Edgar Bear Runner of Pine Ridge. Dennis Banks issued a call for all chapters of AIM to "report and be prepared to liberate AIM officials." During his tense, first night in jail, Means claimed that a police sergeant threw a gun into his cell and told him to make a break for it. Rather than running that gauntlet, Means and Bear Runner got out the next day when AIM leader Carter Camp went to the jail and met their bail, and Russell told reporters his lawyers were flying in from Denver.

Two days after Means and Bear Runner were arrested, someone threw a firebomb through the window of Scottsbluff Junior High School. Later that night, police arrested John Two Birds Arbuckle, whom they suspected of having been involved in the bombing. In the course of the arrest, police discovered marijuana, automatic weapons, and materials for making a firebomb.

Russell Means told a news conference the next day that "We took on the federal government and we're not scared of the pigs in Scottsbluff County." Messages of all kinds, most as blunt as this one, were increasingly exchanged between AIM and law-enforcement officials throughout the region. AIM refused to back down. They proved they could bring in lawyers, the Justice Department, and national press to focus attention on redneck towns, just as they had in Gordon a year earlier. And towns like Scottsbluff made it clear they regarded AIM members not as civil rights workers but as hoods and criminals, and would deal with them accordingly.

Weeks later, in its plans to take over Rapid City, AIM sought to teach the white citizens some of the same hard lessons about respect and justice. As in Scottsbluff, the proposed subjects, for the most part, were not in the mood for such instruction. As far as most of them were concerned, AIM was a bunch of carpetbagging freeloaders, ex-cons who were quite clearly heading on a road straight back to prison. And the sooner the better.

In other regions of the country, people connected riots with the seasons, fearing that Memorial Day might signal the beginning of a "long hot summer" of civil unrest. In South Dakota, the long hot summer came during the bone-chilling weeks of January and February. The streets of Rapid and other towns in South Dakota would fill with young, angry Indians from around the country, who may have lost in earlier actions but were somehow never defeated. Those streets would also fill with some of the West's most macho cowboys—people who considered the term redneck a compliment, Indian protests a personal insult, and street fighting an interesting diversion. All the ingredients were present for an explosion, and trouble would have come to the Black Hills even if a white gas station attendant had not killed a Sioux man in a border town not far from Rapid City.

When Wesley Bad Heart Bull fell to the ground dying on the streets of Buffalo Gap—located off a dirt road fifty miles south of Rapid City and consisting of a post office, a liquor store, and a bank —on the night of January 21, not many people noticed. The killing involved disreputable citizens in front of a bar. Police arrested the accused, a white man named Darld Schmitz, and charged him with manslaughter.

A year earlier Raymond Yellow Thunder had died after a night of humiliation and beating at the hands of residents of a town not so different from Buffalo Gap. Much had changed in twelve months. The unprecedented response to Yellow Thunder had stunned whites and exhilarated Indians; but that demonstration already seemed modest and restrained after the events in Washington and the growing tide of anger now evident on reservations and in border towns in the region. The fury over Yellow Thunder centered in large part on precisely how and when the Oglala died. The fury over Bad Heart Bull had less to do with the details of his death than with the mounting support for AIM and impatience with business as usual in South Dakota.

The two cases were like night and day. Yellow Thunder was a gentle cowboy who loved horses and children and died at the hands of racists only because he was Indian; Bad Heart Bull had a record of nineteen arrests, and at the time of his death authorities were seeking him in connection with an assault a month earlier. The victim of that assault had suffered a torn windpipe and facial fractures.

But the issue wasn't Bad Heart Bull; it was South Dakota, and all that it stood for. And when it turned out that the case of Darld Schmitz would be decided in, of all places, Custer, the county seat, the stage was set for a new confrontation. Law enforcement agencies might as well have sent out invitations.

A riot fueled by the handling of the Bad Heart Bull case took place in Custer between snowstorms on February 6. AIM members had prepared for trouble. Indian cars rolled up from Rapid City, filled with AIM members from the Mother Butler Center, a charity where the rank and file were staying, who hated the very idea of Custer, South Dakota. In the trunks of some of those cars were Molotov cocktails. White citizens of Custer were ready, too. They knew all about the campaign in Rapid City and the takeover in Washington.

The agenda in Custer, nominally, was a meeting between concerned Indians and the county's District Attorney. Schmitz, the killer of Bad Heart Bull, was in custody but had not been formally arraigned. He was out on $5,000 bail after spending a single night in jail. Given the wildly varying accounts of what had happened—the only thing everyone agreed on was that the knifing took place in front of a bar, late at night, and all parties had been drinking—prosecutors were surprised to find themselves accused of letting Schmitz off easy with the manslaughter charge. Riot cops watched AIM. Townspeople watched, too, but kept off the streets, peering from windows behind locked doors.

At the hearing, prosecutors allowed only a handful of Indians inside the courthouse and denied AIM's request for a larger meeting. Indians on the courthouse steps contested that decision by trying to push their way in. To no one's surprise, Indians started fighting cops. Cops fought back, and in a flash tear gas and nightsticks flew. From inside the courthouse, Dennis Banks escaped the growing cloud of tear gas with a mad dash through a window. Indians charged the riot squad. Outside, on the courthouse steps, one trooper forced his nightstick around the neck of an older Indian woman. She was Sarah Bad Heart Bull, Wesley's mother.

The fighting lasted all afternoon. The cold and intermittent snow created difficulties for Indians who were attempting to torch police cruisers, but eventually they succeeded and two cars went up in flames. The Sheriff deputized white citizens and they joined the fray, as did officers of the state's Fish and Game Department. An absurdly small building that housed the local chamber of commerce—it was about the size of a hot dog stand—burned to the ground. It was an unimpressive feat to those familiar with the town, but on the wires and the evening news it sounded like a major incident.

Dozens of people were injured, none very seriously. Police ar-

rested twenty-two people, including Means, Banks, and Sarah Bad
Heart Bull. Others escaped, driving back to Rapid City frightened,
exhausted, bloody, bruised, and exuberant. Several of the cars
sported a bumper sticker that had become popular long before the
riot: CUSTER HAD IT COMING.

On Wednesday, February 7, one day after the riot, Custer awoke
to peaceful, snow-covered streets. The National Guard had been
alerted and was operating on a stand-by basis, although they had not
been called in during the riot itself. South Dakota highway patrol-
men converged on Custer. Members of the state Fish and Game Department kept a careful eye on the buffalo in Custer State Park that
evening. Reports came in of vandalism and robbery in places like
Hill City, Wyoming, as the demonstrators, according to authorities,
pillaged their way to their various homes.

Plenty of AIM people, though, remained in the state. When police held twenty-two of the Custer rioters in Rapid City, seventy-five
Indians gathered on Kansas City Street across from the Pennington
County Jail. Many of them carried clubs, and cops and highway pa-
trolmen surrounded the jail in defense. Smaller disturbances took
place later in the week at Main Street bars between Indians and
whites, and the town remained on edge.

But on Saturday, Banks had encouraging meetings with the
mayor and other officials; at least the beginnings of fulfilling Ron
Petite's promises for the campaign. Banks declared a moratorium on
further demonstrations. Also, he asked that the mayor close Main
Street bars for the next several days. Vernon Bellecourt spoke of an
AIM conference that was about to begin, a conference that would
hopefully open the door to further helpful discussions. He said "we
can make this conference a very meaningful, educational seminar to
explain our position. We will go into the churches on Sunday to talk
with the people to explain to them our purposes. If you want firm,
meaningful public discussion—we can do this." AIM spiritual leader
Leonard Crow Dog told city leaders, "We are not hoodlums, you
must know that."

A position paper from the city council's Public Safety and Parks
Committee outlined recommendations for improving Rapid City's
racial problems. The paper suggested that the Pennington County
Commissioners hire an Indian jailer, that the Council hire qualified

Indian personnel, that the Racial Conciliation Committee be expanded, and that bail and bonding procedures come under review.

But the recommendations also listed a set of demands that chilled relations between the city and AIM. The concessions were contingent on AIM leaders instructing their members not to come to the Black Hills, that AIM members who weren't Rapid residents return to their homes, that those who were local residents "refrain from any assembly on public property, streets or alleys or sidewalks without proper authority, and that some permanent Indian residents be appointed to a liaison committee to work with the mayor and the city council."

Banks understandably interpreted this as the council saying that they were unwilling to give Indians their rights until they were willing to leave town. At the opening of the conference Bellecourt had referred to, Banks announced that AIM would hold no further talks with the city council. He told the two hundred Indians at the conference, "the real question is when are they [white citizens of Rapid City] going to leave the Black Hills? When are they going to return where they came from? And when are we going to stop allowing them to congregate and arrest us?"

He did, however, leave one bridge unburned. The mayor, he said, seemed willing to negotiate, but a callous city council had reversed him. Banks said AIM was in the position of trying to work within the system, but wasn't getting the opportunity to do so.

"What has transpired in the past seven days will change the course of history," he said. "It will change the world's view of how it must now negotiate with Indian citizens in regard to their rights."

AIM would win this struggle, he said, not just because they had brought in attorneys from around the country, not just because they were tying up the South Dakota courts, but "because AIM has that kind of strength and spiritual guidance to withstand attacks by them."

Somehow, between the riots, near-riots, and arraignments, AIM managed to do more or less exactly what local AIM organizer Ron Petite had promised back in January. In the days following Custer, Indians met with Rapid City school administrators, city officials, and church leaders. Tensions ran high, but the street fighting ended. AIM leaders also met with the mayors of other towns, county commissioners, and state's attorneys. Outside the Fall River Courthouse in Hot Springs, townspeople watched as one hundred Indians sang the AIM song, while inside the city fathers met with Dennis Banks, the photogenic Chippewa many had already grown to hate.

Each side emerged to issue statements that were models of courtesy and diplomacy that would have done most international negotiations proud. One state's attorney said, "It was very productive and I was pleased with the seriousness of Banks and the others we met with. They all seemed concerned with getting to the root of the problem. I hope we can act to resolve these problems for the benefit of the whole community, both white and Indian."

The sight of mayors from hated, redneck towns like Fall River and Hot Springs, which had also become part of the statewide campaign, sitting down with Dennis Banks a week after the riot in Custer, must have startled Indians and whites in equal measure. Custer had sent a message, and that message had been received loudly and clearly by many whites. The starting point of the discussions would be that racism and discrimination exist and corrective measures must be taken. That in itself represented a major victory for AIM. Intimidation certainly must have been a factor as well.

The meetings also spoke volumes about the personal charm and charisma of Dennis Banks. Even rednecks in western South Dakota were not immune to the drama of a striking, articulate Indian leader, arriving with a full entourage of warriors, elders, a great many young women, reporters, and lawyers, with drums and haunting Lakota songs heralding his entrance. He could tell South Dakotans they had no right to be there (and Dennis was himself not Sioux but Ojibway) and hint at the possibility of arms and violence, but also sit down and discuss prospects for getting Law Enforcement Assistance Administration funding and the parochial details of county administration with the very officials he condemned.

In Rapid City, the focal point of what had become a regional campaign, Indians attended hearings on housing and civil rights, and at the same time organized shoplifting expeditions to keep everyone clothed and fed. Many of the town's merchants felt helpless in the face of the tinderbox atmosphere, and they ignored the pilfering, much of which occurred in plain sight.

At a meeting with the Superintendent of Rapid City Public Schools, Lakota spiritual leader Wallace Black Elk spoke of the sacred pipe and Lakota spiritual beliefs, holding the audience enthralled. He said the discussions were "A dream come true as we sit and talk . . . and not turn on each other with guns." Regarding educational issues, Russell Means argued that both white and Indian students were being cheated because Indians hardly appeared in history textbooks. Banks said no whites were qualified to teach Indians, and that Indian teachers should receive twice the salary of whites since they would be working as interpreters as well as teachers.

In the course of hearing testimony, people from AIM heard from Rapid City's Indian residents about the treatment they received in the town's bars, treatment that even included being drugged, robbed, and beaten, often with the knowledge of bar owners. On a freezing night in February, even as some of its leaders were speaking of conciliation with mayors and governors, some of AIM's rank and file, who were staying at the Mother Butler Center, launched a new offensive to deal with the problem—they would go in teams and wreak havoc on the redneck bars.

Regina Brave, an activist from Pine Ridge, carried out her mission perfectly. She and her comrades entered a targeted bar, the Pioneer, with clubs—and three minutes later left the place in pieces and its customers in shock. She led an all-woman team. The only man with them waited out back with the car running. They didn't bother with disguises since, as Brave put it, "They think we all look alike anyway."

Sirens filled the night, and her car picked up Indians running in every direction. Most of them had blown their assignments. "They panicked and ran," Regina noted without a trace of attitude. "They shouldn't have."

Three minutes in, three minutes out. She reflected on the experience. "I thought 'God it felt good,' you know? Dang I wouldn't have minded busting a few heads, too, but that wasn't why I was there."

And why was she there? "To say, hey we can do this and we can do it again. I think they learned a heck of a lot from that."

At the Golden Horn, in contrast, everything went wrong. Troy Lynn's Yellowwood team lost their leader Jess Largent, the only person in the team older than twenty-one, within moments. Troy Lynn, who lived in Denver, guessed that police had arrived and arrested him.

Five minutes later Troy Lynn and her sister were still standing around. They were there to destroy a bar in the name of all the Indians who had been mistreated there. But they were leaderless and inexperienced at the task at hand. They didn't know where to begin. The bartender noticed them and quickly surmised their intentions. He said they had no problems with Indians in this bar, and offered them free beer to prove it. "He tried to talk his way out having his bar broke up," she said.

Minutes dragged by without action, and finally Troy Lynn rallied her troops. "Me and my sister got everyone going, saying we were supposed to be out of there in three minutes, and here ten minutes had gone by." Curly Youpie, who also lived in Denver, rushed the stage, pushed aside a country and western band, and got on the microphone. "One, two, three, testing," he announced, and then started breaking up everything he could, using the mike as a weapon. Guitars and drums flew. "Then the place just went," Troy Lynn said.

No longer paralyzed, the militants at the Golden Horn picked up chairs and hurled them through the windows. Troy Lynn and her sister ran to the cash registers and even though both were cashiers, they couldn't get the machines open. They laughed at their ineptitude and finally just pushed them over. Even then, the registers failed to open.

Rushing out the back door they discovered that while they had been chatting with the bartender and wreaking mayhem, white cowboys had vandalized their car, slashed the tires, stolen the engine, and broken every window.

They ran out the front and found some of their friends spread-eagled on the street, a SWAT team's guns pointed at their heads. Retreating back into the bar they had just destroyed, they found most of the patrons still there. Many were Indians. As the Indian patrons left the bar, the commandoes mixed in with them. "We just mingled in with them and nobody told on us."

They walked right past the cops, and even got a ride back to Mother Butler Center. Others ran all the way back, and many were arrested. Troy Lynn journeyed to the hospital, where some of their number were taken after beatings by the police, and then to the jail. The temperature was way below zero, and she stood next to Lorelei Means, singing the AIM song until they were hoarse.

Pine Ridge was somehow at the center of AIM's rise, but had so far remained at the periphery of their statewide campaign. The reservation to the south and east of Rapid was a place of stark vistas, austere beauty, rolling hills, and lonely stands of pine trees, a place with ferocious winters and blistering summers. The Oglalas endured rampant poverty, epidemic alcoholism, and abysmal health care. The Indian Health Service, a scandal of an institution, routinely treated diseases on Pine Ridge that never occurred anywhere else except on other reservations.

The largest of the Sioux reservations, Pine Ridge was as rich in history as it was poor in almost everything else. A stunning number of celebrated Indians were Oglala, including Red Cloud, Sitting Bull, Crazy Horse, and Black Elk.

The Oglalas had led a successful war against the United States in the 1860s that ended with a peace treaty guaranteeing the Indians ownership of what is now western South Dakota. That guarantee became null and void when settlers began prospecting for gold in the 1870s. The Sioux fought again, this time to keep settlers and prospectors out of their territory, and in the summer of 1876 handed the United States a devastating defeat at a place the Indians called Greasy Grass. Reports of the battle took a week to reach residents of Philadelphia, New York, and Boston, arriving the very week America celebrated its one hundredth birthday. To most Americans, the battle was known as Custer's Last Stand, and the details of the engagement would be debated for a century. The decimated Seventh Cavalry won revenge thirteen years later at the Wounded Knee Massacre on Pine Ridge.

In the early 1970s Wounded Knee had become a subject of debate, controversy, and reflection among Americans, in large part because of a book by non-Indian, University of Illinois librarian Dee Brown, *Bury My Heart at Wounded Knee: An Indian History of the American West.* The book told its story from a point of view most Americans hadn't learned in school. In 1971, Brown's book became a publishing phenomenon, riding the best-seller lists for months. For many readers, the events Brown described from a century earlier had an implicit parallel with the war in Vietnam. Further, Pine Ridge had been a favorite of anthropologists and other academics for nearly a century. In the late 1960s they were joined by hippies seeking wisdom and spiritual guidance; growing numbers of tourists, in part because of Dee Brown's book, made the journey as well.

During 1972, after Yellow Thunder's death, activists on Pine Ridge had formed their own AIM chapters, and they joined forces with traditionals in opposing the rule of tribal chairman Dick Wilson. Complaints against him were numerous, including his alleged favoring of the mixed-blood residents of the town of Pine Ridge Village at the expense of the full-blood Oglalas who lived in the outlying districts, his securing of jobs and services for his friends and relatives and to mixed-bloods generally, and shutting his opponents out of tribal governmental processes.

The chasm between the factions was not a new one on Pine Ridge, but it had become especially bitter and personal under Wilson, even before AIM was involved. The Oglalas had proved better at creating leaders than followers, and even at their most cohesive moments, dissension was commonplace. Red Cloud, for instance, opposed Crazy Horse and Sitting Bull during the halcyon military days of the 1870s.

The new factor was AIM, which had been threatening since Washington, D.C. and Custer to turn its attention to Wilson and Pine Ridge. Dick Wilson, though, was not one to back down from threats, and had already promised to cut off Russell Means's braids if he dared venture on the Pine Ridge. And Russell Means had promised to do more than just visit; he boasted of his plans to succeed Wilson—a man he called a dictator, a liar, and a drunk—as tribal president in the next election.

On February 12, in response to the growing threats of an AIM confrontation on the reservation, sixty-five members of the elite Special Operations Group of the United States Marshal Service arrived on the reservation and set up a command post in Pine Ridge Village. The FBI and BIA increased their personnel at the same time; to residents it seemed the reservation had been invaded.

Impeachment proceedings against Chairman Wilson, which those from the traditional-activist side initiated, took place in this environment. Traditionals and AIM supporters saw the marshals in their blue jumpsuits as a force sent to protect Wilson. Pine Ridge had suddenly become a police state.

Wilson opened the impeachment hearings by showing a film. *Anarchy—USA*, produced by the John Birch Society, offered vivid, sometimes shocking images of violent revolution in China and Algeria and claimed that communists were behind the civil rights movement. Obviously, Wilson believed that AIM was part and parcel of this nefarious conspiracy.

The dissidents narrowly lost in their effort to remove the tribal chairman. Thus, legal efforts had failed, the sleepy village of Pine Ridge had become an armed garrison, and the traditionals feared a new round of threats and intimidation by a newly emboldened Wilson. Rumors flew, and informants variously told the government forces that AIM's rank and file (staying at the Mother Butler Center in Rapid) was on its way to the reservation, that AIM planned to assassinate a marshal, and that the militants were going to take over Pine Ridge Village.

On February 26, hundreds of all political persuasions turned out for a funeral on Pine Ridge for Ben Black Elk, the son of famed spiritual leader Nicholas Black Elk. He was a beloved and respected elder on the reservation. He was also perhaps the most photographed Indian in the world since he posed with tourists at Mount Rushmore in Sioux regalia. The tribe declared the day of the funeral a day of mourning, and BIA and other offices closed.

The BIA Superindentent, Stanley Lyman, planned to attend the funeral but chose not to, fearing his presence would seem provocative. In this he was probably right. AIM and traditionals left the funeral and gathered at a community building in nearby Calico. For hours, they debated their next course of action. The people split on a proposal to seize the village of Pine Ridge, but agreed to return the following day and take up the issue again.

It was fitting that the death of a Sioux elder would bring them together, because in the end it would be the elders and the militants who would stage a furious, desperate stand at Wounded Knee—bridging the century between the world Ben Black Elk's father described in *Black Elk Speaks* and the world the militants of AIM were fighting to create.

Chapter 10

The Independent Oglala Nation

n Tuesday afternoon, February 27, 1973, FBI surveillance tracked Russell Means as he drove a tan Cougar into Pine Ridge Village from Rushville, Nebraska. As Means stepped out of his car in the parking lot of the Great Sioux Nation supermarket, two men attacked and beat him. Poker Joe Noble and Glen Three Stars, the attackers, were associates of the Pine Ridge Tribal Chairman, and the thrashing was clearly Dick Wilson's way of saying "welcome home" to the AIM leader.

Since the BIA takeover four months earlier, the two rivals had traded long-distance insults through the press. Means called Wilson a drunkard, a liar, and a bootlegger. Wilson labeled Means a criminal and outsider, with no roots on the Pine Ridge, and promised to cut off the AIM leader's braids. The fight for political control of the reservation had complex roots in history, economics, and tradition, but it also had become a deeply personal struggle between two radically different Oglalas.

No one really expected Russell Means to get in his Cougar and drive back to Nebraska simply because he lost a brawl. If his politics and judgment were debatable, his physical courage was not. Means dusted himself off and later that evening joined other AIM leaders at Calico Hall, where the enemies of Dick Wilson gathered to discuss their next move in the wake of their unsuccessful attempts to impeach the tribe's elected leader.

The meeting promised to be critical. For the first time, the Oglala leadership formally invited AIM to take part in their deliberations. Although the movement had won a measure of respect on Pine Ridge in the twelve months since the breakthrough campaign to demand justice for Raymond Yellow Thunder, few on the reservation openly identified themselves as members.

A group of reservation activists called the Oglala Sioux Civil Rights Organization (OSCRO) spearheaded the recent impeachment effort. Though independent, they had strong informal ties with AIM, in particular with Russell Means.

For weeks the reservation had become dangerous for anyone who spoke out against the tribal government. The traditionalists at Calico believed that Wilson, having thwarted the impeachment effort, would bring a new wave of violent intimidation as the chairman sought revenge on his opponents.

The charged atmosphere on February 27 was both business as usual and completely unprecedented. Political crises and unpopular tribal chairmen were nothing new at Pine Ridge. The Sioux traditionally held a skeptical view of their leaders. The Oglalas revered Crazy Horse more than any other figure in their history, despite or perhaps because he refused to support treaty agreements Red Cloud and others had negotiated.

In more recent times, six previous chairmen had faced impeachment, just as Wilson had. Only one tribal chairman had ever been reelected in more than three decades of elective tribal government, and even that exception seemed to underscore the bruising nature of reservation politics, because the reelected leader had also been impeached on two separate occasions, fifteen years apart.

Politics on Pine Ridge had always been fiercely personal. With the tribal government virtually the only employer, and nepotism an accepted practice, the stakes for each election were enormous. Winning meant jobs for your friends and family, as well as a good chance of facing an organized attempt at being removed from office, and stiff odds on serving more than a single two-year term.

Wilson had appointed his wife director of the Head Start program and paid his brother to organize his inauguration, but those actions were not what made Wilson's tenure different. Pine Ridge had seen favoritism and incompetence before, but no previous chairmen had their own auxiliary police force acting as political enforcers. (Wilson's opponents gave the unit the derisive name "goons," and the name stuck like glue. Unable to shake it, they proudly accepted the term, claiming it stood for Guardians of the Oglala Nation.)

The presence of the goons, who acted as Wilson's bodyguards, dramatically changed the political landscape on the reservation. And suddenly, following the weeks of upheaval in Rapid and Custer, scores of federal marshals in blue jumpsuits joined them. The first contingent of marshals arrived on the reservation February 11, and over the following days their numbers increased to more than seventy-five. All were members of the elite Special Operations Group (SOG), the federal government's newly created rapid response strike force. A domestic version of the Green Berets, their activation required the specific approval of the president or the attorney general.

The marshals and their superiors at the Justice Department knew little and cared less about the factions on Pine Ridge. To the feds, the assignment of protecting federal property and personnel from marauding rebels was strictly a matter of law enforcement; officials would demonstrate their limited grasp of the reservation's political nuances by calling the tribal chairman "Chief Wilson." Officially, the Justice Department's role was neutral, but for the traditionals, any doubt about whose interests the federal government's armed presence served was settled with a glance at the sandbags and the .50-caliber machine-gun nest atop the Pine Ridge tribal office building, which created, in effect, a military compound.

The presence of the marshals and their attendant hardware stunned the Oglalas. People drove to Pine Ridge Village to see for themselves the machine gun. The normally sleepy complex had become a military installation. The dissidents named it "Camp Wilson."

As AIM's attention slowly turned away from Custer and Rapid City, from the killing of Wesley Bad Heart Bull and insensitive school boards to the disturbing reports of harassment and intimidation coming from Pine Ridge, they would find more than Wilson and his goons waiting for them. "Camp Wilson" existed to defend the reservation against the American Indian Movement.

The crisis on the reservation deepened in the last days of February, and so did activity inside the compound. Technicians transformed the Land Management office into a sophisticated communications center, and BIA employees laughed nervously as they tried on gas masks. Typewriters made way for rows of shotguns and tear gas canisters. Marshals and FBI agents huddled with the U.S. Attorney for South Dakota, sending hourly reports to their superiors in Washington. Intelligence streamed in constantly—rumors, illegal wiretaps, reports from highway patrols and police agencies throughout the Northern Plains. Even people on reservations several hundred miles away knew minute by minute what was happening on Pine Ridge.

At Camp Wilson no one knew the hour when AIM would bring its trademark chaos to Pine Ridge, but they knew it would be soon. Probably AIM itself didn't know when. This very unpredictability was part of what made AIM so dangerous. Since nearly destroying the BIA in Washington four months earlier, AIM seemed less a political organization than a force of nature. It had become a kind of prairie hurricane, wreaking havoc on one place until seemingly defeated and spent, only to inexplicably reappear weeks later somewhere else. Government operatives checked and rechecked their weapons and intelligence, and waited for the inevitable.

To the more than two hundred people jammed into Calico Hall, a community center that was a traditionalist stronghold a few miles away, AIM was a newcomer to a long-simmering battle. The chaos those who gathered there feared was the tribal government, not AIM, and speaker after speaker rose and shared personal experiences of harassment, intimidation, and unfair treatment at the hands of Wilson's government. Goons stood accused of criminal behavior including physical assault and rape.

The question on the floor was a simple one: What is to be done? The meeting began in the afternoon and continued for hours, fueled by frustration and anger. Representatives from each of the reservation's eight districts were present, as well as five traditional chiefs: Red Cloud, Iron Cloud, Fools Crow, Bad Cob, Kills Enemy. Often there were too many people to fit inside the building. The speaking occasionally gave way to drumming and singing, powerful words followed by powerful songs. Russell Means and Dennis Banks listened as one resident after another gave voice to their mounting anger and frustration. Often the testimony was in Lakota, and someone would translate for the two AIM leaders. Banks was Ojibway, and Means did not speak the language of his tribe. No translation was needed, however, to understand the fear and desperation in the eyes of so many of the speakers.

Pedro Bissonette, the charismatic young leader of OSCRO, was one of Wilson's most determined foes on the reservation, but his aunt Gladys gave one of the evening's most decisive speeches. For twenty minutes she spoke to her fellow citizens in Lakota. When she finished, she turned to the AIM leaders and addressed them in English. She told them that the Oglalas had lost their way. "For many years we have not fought any kind of war, we have not fought any kind of battle, and we have forgotten how to fight." She pleaded with them to bring AIM to Pine Ridge to help her people. By the time she ended her speech Gladys Bissonette was in tears.

Ellen Moves Camp, another Oglala mother, echoed Bissonette's words with her own impassioned address. She also demanded that the fight against Wilson continue. She spoke of the demonstrations against Wilson attended mostly by women and old people. Where are our men? she asked, where are our defenders?

To a movement whose credo had always been to stand with any Indian people who requested their assistance, AIM's answer to Ellen Moves Camp and Gladys Bissonette and the others at Calico could only be, yes. The Oglalas had made their request loud and clear, yet still no plan of action had emerged.

Some argued for the forcible eviction of the Wilson government from its offices in Pine Ridge, but the presence of the goons and the marshals turned that concept into a suicide mission. A takeover like that of the BIA headquarters would likely be met with machine-gun fire.

The five chiefs conferred among themselves, and then asked to meet with the AIM leaders and some of the key Oglala activists, about a dozen people in all. Stars burned in the winter night as the group crossed the highway to the Holy Rosary Catholic Church, where a priest granted them permission to meet in the basement.

The humble surroundings only seemed to underscore the gravity of their deliberations. The chiefs sat at one end of the room, old men of tremendous presence and dignity. They listened as the Oglala activists—Pedro and Gladys Bissonette, Ellen Moves Camp, Vern Long, Severt Young Bear, Edgar Bear Runner—again made the case for decisive action. Dennis Banks and Russell Means spoke last, pledging AIM's support in carrying out the chiefs' wishes.

Chief Frank Fools Crow never spoke English in public, though some claimed he understood it quite well. Fools Crow spoke Lakota. The young men of AIM did not, with few exceptions, speak their tribal languages. The old chiefs had everything the young bloods of the movement wanted: tradition and ceremony, wisdom and ancient knowledge. Those things had been denied the shock troops of the movement. To them it burned like the theft of something priceless, irreplaceable, and with it came a smoldering resentment they felt nearly every waking moment. This, more than any specific grievance, fueled their bold activism.

Yet the old men who barely spoke English needed the young men of AIM, who possessed power and knowledge of a different sort. This new warrior society spoke the fast language of distant cities. Their power came from hard times and fierce pride, the unlikely product of prison cells and drunk tanks, street demonstrations and liberal alliances. It made them different from the young men of Pine Ridge, the ones Ellen Moves Camp shamed with her pointed question, "Where are our defenders?"

The AIM people had spent most of their lives in another world from the stark, preindustrial beauty of Kyle, Wanblee, and Porcupine, and were changed because of it. They were back now, by their own choice, dog soldiers ready to stand with the Lakota. Their power could be reckless, unlearned, but it could also bring justice to a grief-stricken Oglala family and strike fear into the hearts of the city fathers of Gordon, Nebraska.

Perhaps the AIMs—this is what the old people called them, the AIMs—knew little of Oglala ceremonial life, but they held other secrets of immense value, exotic knowledge those who spent their lives on Pine Ridge could never obtain. They knew the home telephone numbers of New York lawyers, and understood the rituals of press cycles. They knew that television networks had bureaus in Chicago, and they knew ways journalists might be persuaded to charter planes to South Dakota. Russell Means and Dennis Banks knew how to bring the world to Pine Ridge.

Fools Crow finally addressed the small group. "Go ahead and do it, go to Wounded Knee," he said, adding that they would be protected there. "You can't get in the BIA office and the tribal office, so take your brothers from the American Indian Movement and go to Wounded Knee and make your stand there."

It was, arguably, the finest moment in AIM's brief and often troubled history. Together, the chiefs, the local activists, and AIM could accomplish what individually they could not, a synergy that perfectly realized the vision AIM always had for itself as a modern-day warrior society and defender of Indian communities. At times, the movement's concept of going anywhere, anytime, to stand up for Indian people sounded like empty rhetoric and resulted in embarrassing misadventures, but on that February night, AIM kept every promise it had ever made to itself and to Indian people.

Critics would accuse AIM of opportunism, using one reservation's troubles to make headlines for themselves. They suggested AIM took advantage of unsophisticated Indians who didn't know any better. Instead, the careful, deliberate process that ended in a church basement (a more appropriate venue for Indians plotting social change could scarcely be imagined—reservation or urban, they all knew church basements well), more accurately could be read as the Oglala people choosing to invite the American Indian Movement into Pine Ridge. No other organization could have responded to the Oglalas' political emergency. The national news media, the established Indian groups, the White House and Congress were beyond the reach of the citizens of Pine Ridge. Inviting AIM was a roll of the dice with uncertain results, but no one questioned that AIM would make things happen.

The chiefs left the meeting, and Russell Means took over. He suggested that no announcement be made of Wounded Knee to the hundreds across the road at Calico Hall. Wilson probably had informers there, and Means also believed some might panic and refuse to join the caravan if they knew the final destination. Instead, Means proposed they announce that the meeting would continue at a larger hall in Porcupine, a traditional stronghold eight miles past Wounded Knee.

The chiefs told them to take over Wounded Knee, but they didn't say how. Means knew how. He assembled a few carloads of trusted AIM warriors, veterans of previous campaigns in Scottsbluff, Nebraska, Custer, South Dakota, and Washington, D.C., and told them of the decision. He instructed them to leave Calico and go ahead of the caravan, and once at Wounded Knee to secure the guns and ammunition at the trading post.

A few minutes later the meeting at Calico ended, and the caravan, fifty-four vehicles strong, rolled through the winter night; old people and kids and tough guys and aunts and uncles. Red flags fluttered from some cars' antennas. When they drove through Pine Ridge, startled marshals and goons drew their guns, expecting a confrontation. But instead of stopping, the caravan drove straight through town, horns blowing. Agnes Lamont, a middle-aged teacher's aide, saw a streak of red lights heading east. She thought the cars were going to a dance.

Dennis Banks rode in the lead car with Chief Fools Crow, and on arrival at Wounded Knee, a hamlet of around one hundred residents, people from the car gathered at the mass grave for a prayer with movement spiritual leaders Pete Catches and Leonard Crow Dog. Patches of snow covered the ground, but strangely mild temperatures and a light breeze made the evening feel more like May than February.

Crow Dog had been thinking about the road from Pine Ridge to Wounded Knee, and about the distance between this century and the past century. He remembered that in 1890 Big Foot's band of Minneconjou had been traveling in the opposite direction, heading to Pine Ridge to surrender to federal authorities, knowing they would be arrested and chained on reservations.

To his comrades Crow Dog said, "Here we come going the other way. We're those Indian people, we're them, we're back, and we can't go any further. Wounded Knee is a place where we can't go any further."

Just as the prayers over the massacre victims concluded, a lightning raid struck the handful of buildings that constituted downtown Wounded Knee a short distance away. Within moments the village was theirs.

When Banks arrived at the trading post, he gave instructions not to touch anything. But it was too late, because by then almost everything was already gone. As Banks and the traditional spiritual and political leaders of the Oglalas stood at the cemetery, others in the caravan stormed the store, stripping it bare in moments, seizing guns, ammunition, food, and clothing. Frenzied Oglalas took pleasure in ransacking the place. Pedro Bissonette, the son of Gladys Bissonette who had made such an impassioned speech at Calico, put on a headdress from the museum and jumped on a display case, waving a handgun until he crashed through the glass top.

Two faces of the Wounded Knee occupation, the sacred and profane, were present from the first moments of the takeover. While some ransacked the trading post, others took over the Sacred Heart Catholic Church. One of the village's several houses of worship, Sacred Heart was a forlorn, white-steepled edifice at the top of a small rise, a short walk from the trading post. Means and others found the church's Jesuit priest inside, and led him away. The priest and the Gildersleeves, owners of the trading post, became hostages, and they were moved to one of the larger houses. A guard stood watch, both to prevent their escape and to keep anyone from venting their anger on the prisoners.

Marshals, the FBI, and BIA police had monitored the caravan's progress from the Calico meeting. At 7:55 P.M., the BIA police radioed the command post in Pine Ridge with news of a burglary in progress at Wounded Knee. The marshals notified FBI Special Agent in Charge, Joseph Trimbach. He and his agents arrived on the scene a short time later, and with the BIA police established roadblocks around the village. Militants with stolen guns fired on BIA police.

In the midst of the chaos, someone managed to get a list of demands to a Justice Department operative at the village, with the instruction: "Communicate this to whoever is in charge. We are operating under the Provisions of the 1868 Sioux Treaty. This is an act of war initiated by the United States. We are only demanding our country . . ."

Demands

I. Senator WILLIAM FULBRIGHT to convene Senate Foreign Relations Committee immediately for hearings on treaties made with American Indian Nations and ratified by the Congress of the U.S.

II. Senator EDWARD KENNEDY to convene Senate Sub-Committee on Administrative Practices and Procedures for immediate, full-scale investigations and exposure of the Bureau of Indian Affairs and the Department of the Interior from the Agency, reservation offices, to the area offices, to the central office in Washington, D.C.

III. Senator JAMES ABOUREZK to convene the Senate Sub-Committee on Indian Affairs for a complete investigation of all Sioux Reservations in South Dakota.

People we will negotiate with:

1. Mr. EHRLICHMAN of the White House,
2. Senators KENNEDY, ABOUREZK, and FULBRIGHT— or their top aides,
3. The Commissioner of the BIA and the Secretary of the Interior.

The only two options open to the United States of America are:

1. They wipe out the old people, women, children and men, by shooting and attacking us.
2. They negotiate our demands.

Signed:

Oglala Sioux Civil Rights Organization
President VERN LONG
Vice-Pres. PEDRO BISSONETTE
Secretary EDDIE WHITE WOLF
American Indian Movement Leader: RUSSELL MEANS

Before we took action this day we asked for and received complete direction and support of medicine men and chiefs of the Oglala Nation:

FRANK FOOLS CROW
PETER CATCHES
ELLIS CHIPS
EDGAR RED CLOUD
JAKE KILLS ENEMY
MORRIS WOUNDED
SEVERT YOUNG BEAR
EVERETTE CATCHES

The demands showed, in one way, how desperate the Oglalas were for redress of their grievances; so desperate they would pick up guns so that congressmen and senators would listen to them. Eyebrows might rise at the suggestion the Senate Foreign Relations Committee conduct hearings on Indian treaties, but Senator Fulbright told reporters he would consider holding such hearings. In Washington, congressional committees routinely convened to hear testimony on topics less compelling than Indian treaties.

The demands changed in the following days, with, for instance, the warriors inside Wounded Knee calling for the immediate removal of Wilson and for Secretary of State Henry Kissinger's presence on the scene. Although the details of their demands changed, the high card that Russell Means possessed did not. He dared the federal government to send an army to surround a few hundred Indians at the very site of the most infamous massacre the United States ever committed.

The final decisions on the government side rested with the White House. Baptized at Alcatraz, tested at the Bureau of Indian Affairs takeover, Bradley Patterson and Leonard Garment would once again do everything they could to pacify a militant Indian uprising. They had proven to be worthy adversaries to the militants. At Alcatraz they opened official talks with the student rebels, offered a package of glittering inducements, talked and waited, and then waited some more. When the right moment arrived, they had not hesitated to send in armed federal agents to remove the few remaining occupiers. In

Washington they had negotiated, threatened, and finally paid off the caravans in cash to leave town. The two White House aides were creative and unorthodox in their approaches to these crises, perhaps even as creative as their counterparts. Alcatraz and Washington had presented ample opportunity for disaster, and disaster, if not embarrassment, had been averted.

Forty months had passed since the November afternoon Richard Oakes jumped off a rich Canadian's yacht to jumpstart the Alcatraz occupation, but it seemed more like forty years. The horror of 1890 had always been there, usually lurking unspoken in the background, then suddenly recalled with shocking force. Stella Leach, the belligerent nurse at Alcatraz, answered government threats with promises of a Wounded Knee in San Francisco Bay. Two years later on the steps of the BIA headquarters, waiting for an expected attack by riot police, fearful occupiers armed with clubs fashioned from broomsticks and office furniture offered the same invocation. Russell Means had scrawled maps of Pine Ridge on a napkin in a New York City bar in 1970, explaining to Hank Adams the strategic importance of the reservation's most famous village.

Garment and Patterson had been successful because they followed one rule above all others, and that rule boiled down to this: no Wounded Knees. Now they had to prevent a Wounded Knee at Wounded Knee.

On Wednesday, February 28, as local residents ventured into Wounded Knee to fill their cars with gas from the trading post's pumps and to pick over what remained in the trading post and the museum, and defenders of the village fired shots at distant BIA police cars, the machinery of war rumbled to life and began making its way to South Dakota. By the first afternoon two armored personnel carriers moved into position near the roadblocks, and two Phantom jets zoomed low over the village on a reconnaissance mission.

By nightfall, the government had sealed off the village, and people inside wondered what they had gotten themselves into. The decision to make a stand at Wounded Knee provoked jubilation, but the spontaneous nature of that decision had left little time to ponder the consequences of the action. Ellen Moves Camp thought she would be there overnight, or at the most a few days. Wounded Knee was for her and the other traditionals a liberated zone on the reservation, the counterweight to Pine Ridge. In occupying it, they had hoped that meetings could take place without fear of goon intimidation, and perhaps they would be in a position to bargain with Wilson. She never imagined spending days inside the already seriously damaged buildings, encircled by hundreds of FBI agents and marshals.

As the mobilization took shape in the hills, and it became clear the government seemed to be neither on the verge of imminent attack nor staging a brief visit, leaders inside Wounded Knee stopped giving out their supply of gasoline and began making plans for an extended stay.

From a military point of view, it was a terrible place to defend. Located in the center of a small valley with few trees or other natural obstructions, the town was essentially a fishbowl. The few advantages it had for a long siege, a relatively well-stocked grocery store and a gas station, were both nearly depleted by the end of the first day.

A Wichita from Oklahoma named Stan Holder began planning the defense of the village using strategies he had learned in Southeast Asia. Holder's fighters were a volunteer militia, poorly armed and of uncertain training. Their weapons were a mediocre lot of hunting rifles, shotguns, and .22s. Russell Means had stopped on the way from Calico to borrow a hunting rifle from a Legal Aid attorney, and promptly broke the gun's stock when he attempted to smash through a locked door on the first night. A Kiowa named Bobby Onco, like Holder a vet from Oklahoma, had one of the few automatic weapons, an AK-47 brought home from Vietnam as a souvenir. The Soviet-designed assault rifle enjoyed a reputation as a far superior weapon to the unreliable M16 the Pentagon issued American soldiers. The M16 was prone to jamming, and the AK-47 was not.

The first afternoon of the occupation, FBI Special Agent Trimbach arranged to meet with Russell Means. Maeans gave Trimbach a list with the heading "Hostages, Wounded Knee, South Dakota." Eleven names followed, with their ages. They were residents of Wounded Knee, mostly white and elderly. Three were in their seventies, and two of the hostages were in their eighties. They were,

Means said, prisoners of war. Trimbach said the government would not leave the area, and surrender was Means's only hope. Means told the FBI agent that he was not afraid to die, but if he died the hostages would also die.

Wounded Knee received more attention during its first week than the entire previous decade of Indian activism combined. Alcatraz and the BIA takeover had been the subject of intense local interest in San Francisco and Washington, and sporadic national interest, but neither event had completely penetrated the national consciousness.

In contrast, the *New York Times* played Wounded Knee across the front page with banner headlines: ("Armed Indians Seize Wounded Knee, Hold Hostages"), with urgent reporting and photos of Indian gunmen at the church. The *CBS Evening News* with Walter Cronkite led with film of Russell Means issuing demands on a telephone call. *Time* magazine found the events surreal, as if "history had been hijacked by a band of revisionists armed with a time machine."

Alcatraz had won more attention than a decade's previous activism combined, but Wounded Knee had achieved that many times over. Whether a crime in progress or an act of national liberation, the event operated on rules of its own. If the Indians were living in a curious mix of old times and new, so too were others. On one of the first nights, a marshal, in a flak vest and steel helmet, stood on the perimeter with an FBI agent. The marshal said, "They're still roamin' out there, the Injuns. They'd love to get a whitey." In Gordon, Nebraska, where the new round of Indian trouble had first surfaced a year earlier, a waitress at the Western Cafe told a journalist her theory on who was behind the occupation. "Now, a trucker was in here last night, served nine years in the military and said he heard machine guns up there. You can't buy machine guns in this country, so that just goes to prove they're coming from Russia." She would not be the last to cite Bobby Onco's AK-47 as evidence of communist influence among the Sioux.

On Thursday, March 1, South Dakota's two Democratic United States Senators, George McGovern and James Abourezk, flew to Pine Ridge to investigate the situation firsthand. They spoke with the hostages and determined, in spite of press reports to the contrary, that they were free to come and go. Surprisingly, most elected to stay. "They don't want to leave because they consider that to be their home," McGovern announced.

Wilbur Reigert, eighty-two, told reporters "the fact is, we as a group of hostages decided to stay to save AIM (the "hostages" were, in fact, in sympathy with many of the militants' demands) and our own property. Had we not, those troops would have come down here and killed all of these people."

The resolution of the hostage crisis was a significant victory for the occupiers, clearing the way for more sympathetic press coverage, but the issue would haunt AIM's leaders and prevent an early settlement to the standoff.

On March 1, the daily White House news summary brought President Nixon news of the events in South Dakota. He vented anger not at the Oglalas or the American Indian Movement, but at the Bureau of Indian Affairs. Nixon read that all television networks carried lengthy accounts. One report noted that the "trading post was stripped of food, clothes, guns and Indian relics as Indians who say they'll die for [their] cause are attempt[ing] to force attention on what they say is corruption and mismanagement w-in BIA." Nixon circled BIA and wrote to Domestic Affairs Advisor John Ehrlichman: "E—when are we going to get action on this mess?"

For the BIA, still paralyzed from the November takeover of its Washington headquarters, the Wounded Knee occupation was a disaster. The BIA was slowly changing the way it worked with tribal governments, and what that meant in practice was ceding more of its power to the elected tribal officials. AIM rhetoric aside, the bureau was, through most of its history, a colonial agency. Everything that OSCRO and AIM wanted, namely to remove Wilson, flew in the face of how the agency was trying remake itself as a partner with tribal government. At other moments in history, the BIA would not have thought twice about removing a tribal chairman if such a move was seen to be in the Bureau's best interest. But doing so now would betray the Bureau's new mission of being a partner to tribal governments instead of their boss.

The BIA was only one of several government agencies with a stake in the outcome at Wounded Knee. The FBI, like the BIA, had its own claim to Pine Ridge. Several agents had permanent assignments to the reservation due to the federal government's jurisdiction over major crimes committed on reservation land. Their numbers increased to 150 as agents from around the country flew in.

The Justice Department had primary responsibility for finding a solution to the crisis. Its role seemed particularly schizophrenic, as it brought to Wounded Knee the negotiators, the marshals who kept the village in the sights of their automatic weapons, and the Community Relations Service, an almost independent agency that maintained communication with the occupiers and had a reputation among some as being too sympathetic to the radicals it was charged with pacifying. Dick Wilson already hated the CRS nearly as much as he hated AIM.

Against this powerful, if contentious, array of government agencies, the small band of Indian occupiers had their own differing agendas. The Oglalas at Wounded Knee were united in opposition to Wilson but divided on other issues. For some, his replacement in the tribal office building in Pine Ridge with one of their own would have been enough. For others, the ultimate goal of the campaign against Wilson was to fundamentally restructure the government on the reservation. They wanted a new system, one adapted from traditional Oglala culture and ways of governance.

For AIM, Wounded Knee represented a stand for all Indian people, everywhere. AIM would rise or fall as a movement based on what happened on Pine Ridge. Taking a page from American leftists who approvingly quoted Latin American revolutionary Che Guevara's prediction of "two, three, many Vietnams," AIM leaders spoke openly of other Wounded Knees in other places.

The movement's style was freewheeling as ever, with each of its national leaders having a moment in the spotlight, even though the takeover was primarily Russell's show; he was, after all, Oglala. But some days Dennis Banks would be clearly in charge, with Means in the background or having sneaked out of the village. Other times Carter Camp would be talking to the press and leading the nightly meetings, often taking positions more radical than either Means or

Banks. The Oglalas, officially, were the leaders; they had called in AIM and AIM was there to serve and not lead. But the Oglalas were rarely out front as spokespeople. The news media stood between these two unevenly matched forces—the feds and the Indians.

Reporters from around the world flocked to South Dakota. They compared notes at the Crazy Horse Cafe in Pine Ridge, hired locals to guide them across the hills through the scattered government positions for interviews with the militants, and wrote stories on how their coverage might be affecting events. Learjets flew into the tiny airport in Pine Ridge, shuttling that day's film to the television networks.

The unfolding drama of a few hundred Indians under siege by the military might of the federal government made for compelling television. The Sacred Heart Church, its white steeple rising against the stark plains, the young Indian men armed with feathers and rifles (sometimes on horseback), and the striking personalities of Dennis Banks and Russell Means became familiar sights on the evening news in March 1973.

AIM treated journalists who managed to creep past the marshals and FBI agents and enter the village like royalty, offering every hospitality available. The government tried to limit their access as much as possible.

As the occupation unfolded, journalists grew increasingly uneasy as they realized they were central players in the story they reported on, perhaps more so than any other major event in recent years. Wounded Knee, some reporters thought, was fundamentally different. Without the cameras, would there be an occupation at all?

From the start, both sides employed disinformation as a key tactic. Government spokesmen blandly lied to the press; AIM denied the hostages ever really were hostages. In reporting a firefight on March 3, for instance, the government told journalists that armored personnel carriers had taken positions two to three miles from the occupiers' bunkers. In one case, a reporter confronted a Justice Department Public Information Officer. He asked, "Newsmen that came out of there around noon today said that at least one of the APCs [Armored Personnel Carriers] came to a distance less than five hundred yards from the bunkers in Wounded Knee.... And that, by the way, has been documented on film. Don't you think that destroys your credibility telling us 'two to three miles away' when we have documentation on film that those APCs came to within at least five hundred yards of the bunkers?"

The Public Information Officer answered. "The federal authorities who are on the scene are taking those steps that they think are necessary in order to protect themselves as well as to perform their function and their mission, and they are not in any way taking offensive steps in terms of attacking or moving in . . ."

The reporter pressed the point. "Is it fair to assume that the Indians at Wounded Knee would do anything but try to take some counteraction if they see an APC approaching their bunkers? Isn't it reasonable to expect them to fire at the APC? Why should the marshals be surprised? That seems to be inciting an incident."

"We don't think it's reasonable to assume that anyone would fire at federal authorities. I think that's fairly clear," the government spokesman responded.

Intermittent gunfire kept both sides alert during the first days of the takeover, but neither side inflicted serious injury on the other. Few of the guns inside Wounded Knee could even reach most government bunkers, and ammunition was in short supply. Each night the occupiers organized people to cross through the federal lines and bring food and ammunition into the village. Marshals shot flares into the night sky to illuminate backpackers, often igniting fires.

The federal response continued to escalate. Fifteen more APCs quickly arrived to supplement the two already on the scene. Government spokesmen painted the effort as one to match the rebel firepower: They claimed the occupiers had an M60 machine gun. Reporters who crossed the government lines to confirm this found instead a supremely unimpressive collection of shotguns and hunting rifles, in addition to some pistols, knives, and screwdrivers. One journalist, presumably experienced in such matters, noted the Indians had the Molotov cocktails all wrong: They used soda bottles that were too thick to break properly. When asked about the M60, the warriors responded with laughter and comments like "I wish."

As the warriors inside the liberated town they had taken to calling "The Knee" endured smug criticism from reporters on their proficiency at bomb construction, and prayed that that night's ammunition run would be more successful than the previous night's, they wondered at the source of the equipment on the other side of the perimeter. With its fondness for rhetorical excess and an exaggerated sense of self-importance, AIM naturally harbored suspicions that the impressive military hardware arrayed against them was part of a secret, illegal government operation to use the Pentagon against civil disorders, probably managed by generals in a White House basement.

This seemed unlikely, since the Constitution prevented the military from being deployed against U.S. citizens without congressional action or an executive order. No journalist ever reported seeing a military uniform at Wounded Knee. The tanks and guns belonged, in fact, to the South Dakota National Guard, and the men who operated them were FBI agents and U.S. marshals. This in itself was vaguely insulting to the Sioux. They fought armies, commanded by generals like Custer and Sheridan, not glorified cops and G-men like Trimbach and Colburn. The Oglalas no doubt would have preferred that the government side wore the blue coats of the U.S. Army, ideally from the Seventh Cavalry

In fact, the paranoid suspicions turned out to be correct, although the details only became public long after the occupation had ended. Incredibly, the scores of reporters from around the world missed one of the occupation's biggest stories: the illegal presence of the military.

Military involvement at Wounded Knee began early. So early, in fact, it even preceded the occupation itself. On February 26, one day before the meeting at Calico Hall that ended with the takeover, marshals placed their first call to the Pentagon. General Alexander Haig authorized the deployment of the APCs and the use of the Air Force. From that moment on, the military played a central role in determining government strategy, concealing its presence with the simple yet brilliantly effective strategy of insisting that the colonels and generals sent to Pine Ridge wear civilian clothes at all times.

Stanley Lyman, the BIA Area Superintendent, kept a diary during the occupation, and recorded his impressions of one senior Pentagon official on the scene. "Colonel Potter: Deputy chief of staff of the Sixth Army. He is completely informal, sometimes looks like a duck hunter on vacation from hunting ducks. He has his desk clean all the time and never seems to be doing anything at all."

The two senior nonmilitary officials on the ground, Wayne Colburn of the U.S. Marshals and Joseph Trimbach of the FBI, conferred with Colonel Volney F. Warner, Chief of Staff of the Army's 82nd Airborne Division, in a four A.M. meeting on March 3 at Ellsworth Air Force Base near Rapid City. At that meeting, Warner's proposals on the crucial issue of rules of engagement (shoot to wound, he argued, not to kill), on negotiations (he was for them), and the use of the APCs for defensive purposes only, were accepted by Colburn and Trimbach.

The Pentagon, in a memorandum written to the Director of the Directorate of Military Support, offered this remarkably clear-eyed assessment of the occupation:

> C. The main objective of the Indians is to draw attention to their real or imagined complaints via national media coverage to stimulate public sympathy and congressional action.
>
> D. The Indians do not appear intent upon inflicting bodily harm upon the legitimate residents of Wounded Knee or upon the Federal law enforcement agents operating in the area, even though small arms fire has been exchanged between opposing forces.
>
> E. Because of its isolated geographical location, the seizure and holding of Wounded Knee poses no threat to the Nation, the State of South Dakota or the Pine Ridge Indian Reservation itself. However, it is conceded that this act is a source of irritation if not embarrassment to the Administration in general and the Department of Justice in particular.

The covert military conspiracy actually did have a code-name: Garden Plot.

The first round of talks between the Justice Department and the Indians took place on March 4 in a canvas tepee set up in the demilitarized zone between the village and the government roadblocks. The negotiations between Ralph Erickson, Special Assistant to the Attorney General, and the Oglala negotiating team went nowhere fast.

Erickson made clear that he would not grant amnesty. "We have a very grave and serious situation when people seize arms and take other people's properties. We could not close our eyes to the planning and execution of the takeover," he said on March 4. Even as the talks went on, so did arraignments in Rapid City for the seventeen people arrested for burglary and larceny in the first few days of the takeover. A federal grand jury impaneled in Sioux Falls seemed certain to return indictments.

What's more, the issue of the hostages continued to surface in the negotiations, with the implied threat of federal kidnapping charges. Conviction carried a maximum penalty of life in prison. The AIM leaders seemed resigned to facing criminal charges of some kind, but even the slight possibility of a kidnapping sentence promised to give the amnesty issue prominence.

For the United States, the difficulty was Dick Wilson, whom the feds ostensibly supported. The Justice Department frantically tried to work out a compromise on the issue of his tenure as tribal chairman. One proposed solution called for the government to endorse a recall effort initiated by Gerald One Feather, a former tribal chairman. This would give the anti-Wilson opponents another chance to remove the chairman through legal means, without the U.S. government directly intervening.

But even this was too much for the BIA and the Interior Department, which saw the occupation in quite different terms than Justice. Even a limited stand against Wilson would, one Interior official said, threaten other tribal governments.

Without a doubt, some in the Bureau would have been happy to see Dick Wilson vanish. He was no favorite of the area superintendent or those in Washington. But now, because AIM insisted on his removal, the Interior Department believed it had to take a position of solid support for a chairman it knew to be guilty of at least some of the charges made against him. To do otherwise would show that revolutions could take place on Indian reservations, and that Wounded Knee might, in fact, be only the first of many rebellions. *The New York*

Times summarized the profound concern Wounded Knee generated in Washington. The newspaper reported that "the Interior Department is known to fear that if the tribal governments can, in effect, be overthrown, the whole reservation structure may crumble."

As the talks continued, huge communications trucks moved into position behind the government perimeter, and the militants dug new trenches. Dennis Banks gave interviews wearing a pistol strapped to his waist, a leather-studded headband, and a beret featuring a Playboy bunny patch.

Dick Wilson grew impatient with the Justice Department's efforts and suggested he might take care of the situation himself. "I will not be responsible for holding my people back," he told reporters. "If necessary, I will join them with my guns." When asked the size of his army, Wilson answered "eight or nine hundred."

The eight or nine hundred never materialized. Wilson the individual, as opposed to all he represented to both sides, increasingly became a minor figure in the drama, fuming from the sidelines about both the "renegades, vagrants, intruders, knuckleheads" in Wounded Knee and the government officials who rarely consulted him.

To the occupiers, the government's proposals offered nothing more than the terms of a humiliating surrender. Essentially, they would have to check their weapons at a designated spot, walk out of Wounded Knee, and not face immediate arrest. (Women and children would not have to identify themselves, but the men would.) A federal grand jury could still prosecute anyone found to have committed criminal acts. Russell Means said it sounded like the offer they gave Big Foot, the Minneconjou chief the Seventh Cavalry gunned down eighty-three years earlier. On March 6, to the cheers of his comrades, Dennis Banks set fire to Erickson's proposal. The talks collapsed.

A last-ditch effort by the National Council of Churches to broker an agreement met with apparent success, but new firing began hours after its planned implementation. Each side accused the other of starting it. After the occupiers burned the agreement, Erickson told reporters he had had enough. "We find no basis on which we can negotiate further," he said on March 7, reading from a statement:

If the leaders at Wounded Knee are bent on violence, that is their concern, but I urge them now to send the women and children—both resident and nonresident—out of Wounded Knee before darkness falls tomorrow.

All of this may sound very melodramatic, but I assure you this is no melodrama. The failure of agreement on a peaceable solution—after every effort on behalf of the United States government—has created a very dangerous situation.

I cannot escape the feeling that the Indian leaders are bent on one of two courses—total capitulation by the United States Government to their illegal demands, or violence. It is no exaggeration to say the situation has become extremely grave.

He directed his principal aides, the U.S. attorneys for North and South Dakota, to return to their posts. "The United States marshals," he said, "and the Federal Bureau of Investigation will remain." He took no questions and left South Dakota for Washington.

In the village the next afternoon, the occupiers held a community meeting, kicked off with drumming and singing. Black smoke rose from a small bridge over Wounded Knee Creek that had been set ablaze with the goal of making an invasion more difficult. Those inside the perimeter camouflaged a U-Haul van used to transport warriors with mud and tumbleweed branches. Young Indians applied war paint and checked their ammunition.

As the sun began to disappear behind a stand of pine trees on a distant ridge, Dennis Banks roared into the village in a blue Cadillac Coupe DeVille. He announced the National Council of Churches had negotiated a cease fire. Darkness fell, and the tanks stayed at their positions on the hills surrounding Wounded Knee.

Meanwhile, at a hastily called news conference in Washington, Erickson announced that there would be no attack on Wounded Knee. The Justice Department, he said, "will make every effort to arrive at a peaceful conclusion to the tense and dangerous situation, but we must enforce the law and that we will do."

"We will not move into Wounded Knee tonight," he continued, without explaining the reasons for the about-face. Others, off the record, said that Erickson had never meant for his deadline to be an ultimatum. Two days later, the marshals packed up their ammunition, telephones, and rations and left.

Dennis Banks declared victory, and to cheers at a mass meeting promised Wounded Knee would only be the beginning. "We have won this war. But there are other wars to come. We have a war in Washington state, we have a war in Oklahoma. All these wars are next and the FBI and the Justice Department better lay their plans for those."

Where Dennis Banks saw victory, Russell Means saw defeat. Obviously, the Justice Department hoped their withdrawal would turn out the lights on the exasperating siege. Means believed federal police would arrest the occupiers as they left, and that the decision to lift the roadblocks was a clever ploy to take the wind out of the occupation. Talks would continue, but without the armed standoff and the media attention, the government had little incentive to consider AIM's demands. Means pleaded with the Oglalas to stay. Most left, but other Indians, overwhelmingly from other parts of the country, streamed into the village and took their place.

Journalists wrote that the siege had ended, and the federal officials prayed their stories held true, but two days after the withdrawal, Wounded Knee had a larger population of defiant Indians than it had before. The Justice Department's gamble failed.

With fresh troops and new supplies of food and ammunition, the occupiers issued a startling declaration: Their battered, flyspeck village was now the Independent Oglala Nation.

Their bold statement said "Let it be known this day, March 11, 1973, that the Oglala Sioux people will revive the Treaty of 1868 and that it will be the basis for all negotiations."

The occupation wasn't over. It had hardly even begun.

AIM members under arrest after February, 1973 protest in Custer, South Dakota.

Police guard Custer County South Dakota courthouse.

Armored Personnel Carriers at Wounded Knee.

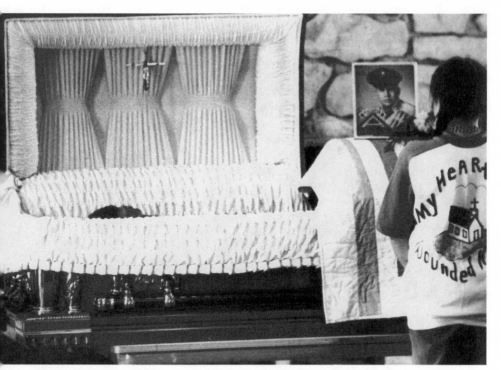

Mourner views the body of Buddy Lamont, killed during Wounded Knee occupation.

Russell Means, Dennis Banks, and William Kunstler at a 1974
Minneapolis press conference.

Vernon Bellecourt prepares for AIM convention at White Oak, Oklahoma, in July 1973.

Chapter 11

All Things Twice

he federal officials selected to investigate the Independent Oglala Nation's sovereign status were not diplomats, FBI agents, or lawyers, but, curiously, postal inspectors. In a move apparently designed to test the waters inside the village, six detectives from the postal service entered Wounded Knee Sunday morning, March 11, ostensibly responding to reports of mail tampering. The trading post served, in addition to its other services, as U.S. Post Office.

Their visit proved to be a godsend for Russell Means, who welcomed the opportunity to cut through the ambiguity of the last several days and project a harder edge to the national press. With news cameras rolling, he ordered the postal inspectors held at gunpoint, and in a harsh, shrill voice made clear that Wounded Knee was far from over. "If any foreign official representing any foreign power—specifically the United States—comes in here it will be treated as an act of war and dealt with accordingly." Spies, he said, would be "shot by a firing squad."

The postal inspectors, hands on their heads, were marched off to the Wounded Knee museum for a brief imprisonment. Dennis Banks told reporters, "We're going to establish here a symbolic Indian government and we're going to stay here indefinitely. We expect Indians from all over the country to help us in demonstrating our ability to rule ourselves." The scores of Indians who had arrived during the last several days would not be the last to stand with the Oglalas, he said, adding that caravans of additional volunteers were already heading to South Dakota from around the country.

The second confrontation of the day took place a few hours later. A van filled with warriors, returning to Wounded Knee from the nearby town of Manderson, reported that an FBI sedan pulled up alongside them and opened fire. One bullet blew a hole in the van's windshield. The warriors returned fire, hitting an FBI agent in the wrist. In the FBI's version of events, the agent and his partner were sitting in their car at a checkpoint when they were suddenly ambushed.

The two incidents put the occupation back on military footing and back on the front pages of the nation's newspapers. Fifteen APCs that had lumbered off to Nebraska reversed direction and returned to Pine Ridge. Federal lawmen rebuilt the perimeter they had disassembled only a few days before, and a call went out from the command post to reservation border towns for additional motel rooms.

The chief of the marshals, Wayne Colburn, looked at the disappointing results of the blockade removal experiment and said there would be a change in policy. "We're going to have to be a lot more hard-nosed about this than we were before. We have gotten no reasonable response from the AIM Indians and we have no reason to expect any reasonable response," he said.

The blockade was back, with a vengeance. The marshals planned to seal off Wounded Knee tighter than a drum. Reporters, hearing echoes of Indian policies of earlier centuries, asked if the new policy was designed to starve out the rebels, and Colburn seemed ready for their question: "We're sure planning to change their lifestyle."

Both parties agreed there was no point to a negotiating session on the morning of March 12. Colburn sent an aide to the place where the two sides held informal meetings, a rough barricade of sandbags and burned vehicles outside the village. The aide told Stan Holder,

Wounded Knee's defense minister, that the government believed "you have not been negotiating in good faith and there is no reason to have a meeting today." Holder couldn't argue with that. "Since we are an independent nation now we no longer recognize your authority and I have no authority on behalf of our country to negotiate with you. Any agreements made until now were made by me as an American citizen and are longer in effect." In reality, however, both sides still hoped for a settlement, and the pause in negotiations would be short-lived.

Some in AIM had argued they had scored a tremendous victory by gaining the world's attention and sympathy and forcing the government to back down. It was a moral victory, true, but one the movement could find ways to capitalize on, turning public sympathy into more concrete achievements. Continuing the occupation risked squandering the opportunities presented by this blaze of publicity if they failed to extract additional concessions from government negotiators.

Continuing the occupation also carried the obvious danger that the light, infrequent skirmishes between the two forces would turn into open warfare. So far, only two Indians had been wounded, and those wounds were slight. (In one of those cases, it was even the source of some amusement—a bullet had grazed the knee of a warrior.) But everyone knew the other side had firepower the village could never match, and even without a direct assault, federal bunkers could inflict devastating ruin on Wounded Knee.

If the Indians were going to declare victory and walk out, triumphantly, into the klieg lights of the television cameras and the arresting arms of federal lawmen, the best moment would have been during the weekend the government removed its roadblocks. That moment had passed. AIM and the Oglalas, knowing they could not hold out indefinitely, now needed to reach an agreement that would bring relief to Pine Ridge and force the United States to consider, in some way, the treaty and sovereignty issues at the center of the fight on the reservation.

The federal government had its own reasons for preferring a negotiated settlement. Another veiled threat of military action, after failing to pull the trigger on the last one, would probably have little credibility with either the Independent Oglala Nation or the press. Sealing off the village, the lifestyle change Colburn spoke of, might take weeks. The ring around the encampment measured fifteen miles in circumference, and even a force of three hundred marshals, FBI agents, and BIA police would not be enough to prevent some supplies from getting through. Even if this strategy worked it could be a disaster, in this strange contest where winning could be losing and losing could be winning. Starving out hundreds of Indians, many of them women and children, during a Dakota winter, might be as politically damaging as a military assault. Neither side felt the other had been serious about negotiations, but both, reluctantly, looked to a peace agreement as their best chance of winning.

A new envoy arrived from Washington on March 13, two days after the detainment of the postal inspectors and the wounding of the FBI agent. Ralph Erickson, the previous negotiator, had been replaced by Harlington Wood, an assistant attorney general for the Justice Department.

Wood set a new tone as soon as he landed in South Dakota. He insisted on meeting with the occupiers immediately, inside Wounded Knee. The FBI thought this a bad idea, warning he might be taken captive. Wood ignored them and went anyway.

With this decision Wood signaled that he would not treat the Indians as though they were simply common criminals. Wounded Knee responded with an elaborate show of protocol when they escorted Wood from the government checkpoint into the village for their first meeting. Two young Indians on horseback led the way. Russell Means, Leonard Crow Dog, and Carter Camp walked next to Wood. Two dozen fighters, most carrying rifles, completed the procession.

Ramon Roubideaux, AIM's attorney, was impressed. "It was quite a sight to see Wood stride into Wounded Knee. He took the bull by the horns and said he wanted to end this shooting. If there were more like him in government we wouldn't have any problems."

Dennis Banks, Russell Means, Clyde Bellecourt, Carter Camp, Pedro Bissonette, and Vernon Long made up the Wounded Knee negotiating team. Both sides called the session productive and businesslike, and said they would continue.

Another positive sign of progress came, ironically, in the first round of indictments returned by the federal grand jury in Sioux Falls. Although the grand jury issued thirty-one indictments for charges that included burglary, larceny, and civil disorder, they did not indict anyone for kidnapping. The panel continued to hear testimony—and the possibility existed that they could still charge AIM leaders for kidnapping—but at least for the moment the nightmare specter of lifetime sentences for Means, Banks, and the others seemed to recede.

In its second week, the occupation continued to win time on the evening newscasts and consume vast amounts of government resources. Yet it failed to break through to that highest level of emergency and become a crisis that required the personal attention of the president.

On March 13 President Nixon's most trusted advisors met to devise a political strategy for handling the situation. The strategy proposed by those experienced in Indian uprisings called for the now familiar techniques of labeling the protesters as not representative of the Indian community, and trotting out those leaders who supposedly were, as well as emphasizing the Nixon record of innovation and reform.

Indians had been a minor issue for those at Nixon's side on a day-to-day basis, a bone tossed to the liberals that paled in comparison to Vietnam, détente, and the economy. They saw no reason to elevate the issue now. In the minutes of the meeting, the president's no-nonsense right hand, H. R. Haldeman, penned his thoughts on the subject. Next to the topic heading "Wounded Knee" he wrote in large letters "don't worry about it." And across the top, he added "This meeting was a 100 percent waste of time."

Haldeman's political instincts seemed to be confirmed the next day, when President Nixon held a formal news conference. Reporters asked about China, Watergate, strategic nuclear weapons, and for the president's views on criminal penalties for the possession of marijuana, but not one asked about Wounded Knee.

That same day, a winter storm blew into South Dakota and dumped ten inches of snow on the reservation. Winds gusted to sixty miles an hour and windchills hit fifteen degrees below zero. Inside the village, the euphoric atmosphere of the previous weekend gave way to pneumonia and strict food rationing. The kitchen began serving one meal a day, and warriors left their bunkers to try their hand at cattle rustling. Three of the non-Indians surrendered to federal authorities.

The blizzard seemed a perfect complement to the marshals' new get-tough policy." The chief marshal, however, had to respond to the presence of dozens of permanent residents of Wounded Knee. They had stubbornly elected to stay, occupation or no occupation, and several of them needed insulin. The marshals allowed two cars into the village, loaded with food, fuel, and medicine. Dennis Banks, who had become anxious for the talks to resume, scoffed when the feds canceled a planned negotiating session because of the storm: "I've seen football games in worse weather than this."

The two sides talked again the following day, and at their conclusion Wood flew back to Washington for consultations. From his point of view, the negotiations had been frustrating, but not without some promise. He could not offer amnesty, or implementation of the 1868 Fort Laramie Treaty, but he could offer to align the Justice Department and its considerable resources on the side of those Pine Ridge citizens who felt victimized by Wilson's government.

Wood offered to flood the reservation with investigators from his agency's civil rights division, ready to file charges against Wilson's goons, or Wilson himself. U.S. attorneys could be assigned to prosecute civil rights violations. Even the marshals, now pointing automatic weapons at Wounded Knee, could remain on the reservation, ready to back up the Justice Department's teams of investigators and lawyers, becoming a force that would protect the Oglalas instead of Wilson.

For AIM and the Oglalas it was a tempting proposition. The basic issues were disarmament and amnesty. The AIM leaders had already reconciled themselves to the fact that amnesty would never be granted, and Means had started talking up the terrific political opportunity the inevitable trials would offer. Disarmament would come with an agreement. But the militants at Pine Ridge had not taken over Wounded Knee to battle the Justice Department. The fight was with the BIA and the Interior Department. To AIM, the marshals and the FBI men were essentially rented cops.

Although Dick Wilson's tenure as tribal president remained an obstacle, the new federal representative saw a possible solution. Wood listened carefully as Ramon Roubideaux spoke for the Oglalas about a new petition campaign underway asking for a referendum on Wilson's removal. It seemed to be a way to remove the tribal president through constitutional means. The Interior Department would not have to take any action against him, it would only have to remain impartial and allow the process to move forward.

Wood left South Dakota believing that he had reached a tentative agreement that called for AIM's disarmament and evacuation, and in return a high-ranking Interior official—preferably the head of the BIA—would meet with AIM the next day at Wounded Knee. All the government had to do was send somebody from Interior to talk to the Indians the day after they had disarmed. The package might as well have promised the immediate return of the Black Hills. In Washington, Wood ran into a buzz saw of opposition.

A few days earlier, Rogers Morton, the new Interior Secretary—in California receiving treatment for prostate cancer—issued a lengthy and passionate statement on Wounded Knee. He wrote "there has grown up in the wake of the black militant movement in this country a revolutionary Indian element. Dramatic violence is their pattern. The occupation of Alcatraz, Nike [missile] sites, the federal office building in Washington, the village of Wounded Knee and others all fall into it." Morton said some of their leaders are starstruck with self-righteousness, renegades, youthful adventurers "slipping from one expensive-to-the-taxpayers event to the next under a cloak of false idealism. The bloody past is the color of their banner, publicity is the course of their future."

As if anticipating Wood's proposal, Morton's statement continued, "There is one thing of which I am very sure. Nothing is gained by blackmail. You cannot run this government or find equitable solutions with a gun at your head or the heads of hostages. Any agency of government that is forced into a fast deal by revolutionary tactics, blackmail or terrorism is not worth its salt. These are criminal operations and should be dealt with accordingly."

Marvin Franklin, the BIA's acting director and former chairman of the Iowa tribe, announced that he would quit rather than sit down with AIM. Only after intense White House pressure would he agree to a meeting, and insisted it take place not in Wounded Knee but in Sioux Falls, on South Dakota's eastern edge. Resentful, he told reporters the whole thing was overblown and "not as serious as those Wild West movies on television would have you believe. All those people on the reservation are related and they all have a lot of fun."

Wood returned to Pine Ridge on March 17, walking past a federal checkpoint to hand Dennis Banks a dozen copies of the doomed agreement. "This is the best I could do," the Justice department lawyer said, sounding a note of regret. He thanked Banks personally for keeping the peace during the past days, and said "If you want to see me again, I'll come back at any time. It will be at your pleasure."

The peace ended that night when one of the heaviest firefights to date broke out. Hundreds of rounds of automatic weapons poured into the village. Tracer bullets lit up the sky. Warriors answered with their hunting rifles, and watched as the marshals unleashed their most lethal weapon, the .50-caliber machine-gun.

The M16 could kill a man, easily, even from five hundred yards, but the M50 was something else altogether. The M50 felt like it could knock down a house. The fearsome weapon was a modern version of the Hotchkiss gun, eighty years improved, and the Hotchkiss gun was what the Seventh Cavalry hauled up on one of the very hillsides now occupied by the APC that fired the M50. The bullets were huge, two inches in diameter, and left holes the size of softballs. They managed to terrify even when they missed, ripping into the frozen ground and tearing up pieces of earth like a plow.

The village felt lucky that night, even though a Chicano medic named Rocky Madrid took an M16 bullet in the stomach—he was going to be okay. No one panicked, the warriors performed with skill and discipline, and things could have been a lot worse.

On March 18, the Wounded Knee community voted down Wood's proposal, and offered a counterproposal that called for talks with a presidential emissary—to the Indians an approach more consistent with their sovereign status. The Interior Department, proving that it was still an agency of unvarnished colonialism, would not compromise on the issue of Wilson, not because of who he was but because of what he stood for.

The new arrivals who had streamed in during the government's temporary withdrawal had saved the occupation, but also brought new problems. Almost everyone during the first several days was Oglala and from the reservation. They were friends, comrades, relatives, or at least acquaintances. Similarly, the AIM people were known to Banks, Means, and the Bellecourts.

This changed dramatically after the roadblocks were lifted, and then reinstated. Scores of the Independent Oglala Nation's new citizens were not only not Sioux, they weren't even Indian. The showdown had captivated white leftists, eager to support this new and surprising armed struggle for national liberation, and members of the counterculture, who had always "liked Indians." Also arriving were contingents from the Vietnam Veterans Against the War, Chicanos, and a sprinkling of Asians and Blacks.

The Indians ranged from seasoned AIM members to students from the Institute of American Indian Arts in Santa Fe, New Mexico, who told reporters they drove up just to check things out. Richard Whitman, a Los Angeles college student, heard speakers give a firsthand account of the occupation and ask for volunteers to join them. When the militants drove back the same night, Whitman rode with them. A few days later he found himself assigned to a bunker, training his hunting rifle on federal agents.

Wounded Knee, to the outside world, was a startling, unlikely event—some called it heroic and brave, others quixotic and misguided—that had one message above all others. Indians are still here, and are still fighting. It was the same message proclaimed by the activists of the 1960s and the students who held Alcatraz Island, but it still struck many non-Indians as a new concept.

To Indians, however, it spoke in a determined and forceful way that touched all and moved many of them to action. Mary Brave Bird, a Lakota teenager present at Calico, described her emotions when she realized they were about to take over Wounded Knee. It was, she said, "an excitement choking our throats."

That same excitement choked at Richard Whitman's throat and thousands of other Indian people who would directly participate in the siege over the coming weeks. The flickering televised images of the warriors holding the United States at bay on the frozen, hallowed ground became a call to action.

Passamaquoddys in Maine burned tires on highways; Tuscaroras smashed windows on the main street of Lumberton, North Carolina;

Navajos marched on the federal building in Phoenix. On reservations far from Pine Ridge, teenagers laid out their jeans and bandannas, ready to steal away in the night and ride off with friends for a two-day journey in borrowed cars with noisy mufflers and uncertain durability.

For every person like Richard Whitman who defended the village by force of arms, dozens more put themselves at risk by hiking through the countryside, bringing food and ammunition to the warriors.

In Denver, a key center for Wounded Knee mobilizations, one woman had her Chevy Vega outfitted with a secret compartment to hold weapons. When law enforcement officials checked cars driven by Indians and young people heading anywhere close to South Dakota, her innovation made it through the searches.

Young Indian women took the lead in coordinating the demonstrations, the supply trains, and other logistical assistance. Most were not content just to provide support, and joined the occupation itself, sometimes for a few days, sometimes longer. They found at Wounded Knee solidarity, danger, and an exhilarating sense of freedom, among other things. At Christmastime, as 1973 drew to a close, so many had become mothers that the Indian community called their newborns the "Wounded Knee babies."

Oglalas furious at their tribal government had taken Wounded Knee, but the intricate local politics had been subsumed in greater meaning. Wounded Knee had declared itself a nation, a liberated territory, and this declaration had been greeted by the most powerful nation on earth with the threat of annihilation. Compared with this state of affairs, Wilson had as much to do with Wounded Knee as the seating policies of bus companies in southern cities had to do with the freedom struggle of African-Americans.

When the Oglalas declared Wounded Knee to be a sovereign nation, they formally sought the recognition and assistance from the Six Nations of the Iroquois Confederacy. On March 19, a delegation of chiefs arrived to convey their solidarity with the occupation.

That evening, Oren Lyons, the Onondaga chief who led the delegation, read from a statement issued by the Grand Council of Iroquois. Part of it addressed the U.S. government directly.

"You are concerned for the destruction of property at the BIA building and at Wounded Knee. Where is your concern for the destruction of our people, for human lives?" Lyons spoke of the Mohicans, the Pequots, of Sand Creek and Big Foot. "When will you cease your violence against our people? Where is your concern for us?" Lyons told of Indian lands flooded to make way for power projects, strip-mined by coal companies, and plundered of timber. "Compare the damage of the BIA and Wounded Knee against the terrible record and tell us that we are wrong for wanting redress. We ask for justice, and not from the muzzle of an M16 rifle."

The Grand Council's statement asked that the government withdraw the marshals and FBI agents, and not prosecute those involved in taking over Wounded Knee. The closing words were moving and eloquent.

> We have not asked you to give up your religions for ours.
> We have not asked you to give up your ways of life for ours.
> We have not asked you to give up your government for ours.
> We have not asked you to give up your territories.
> Why can you not accord us with the same respect? For your children learn from watching their elders, and if you want your children to do what is right, then it is up to you to set the example. That is all we have to say at this moment. Oneh.

The delegates remained at Wounded Knee for four days, and shared the Confederacy's views on sovereignty and nationhood. They left on March 23, and their exit was an impressive demonstration that Indian sovereignty could be more than political theory. The Iroquois issue their own passports, which the U.S. and Canadian governments honor at international borders because of treaties guaranteeing them free passage. The delegation walked straight through Federal Roadblock 1, unchallenged by the same marshals who for weeks had not hesitated to bar access to journalists and doctors. As the Iroquois left, they exchanged greetings with the militant black activist Angela Davis. She too came to Wounded Knee to show her solidarity, but never made it past the roadblocks.

As the occupation entered its third week, Leonard Crow Dog told his embattled, hungry community the Ghost Dance would be performed again the next morning.

Americans maintaining their hard-fought control of the western frontier in the late 1880s had to contend with a messianic, revivalist movement called the Ghost Dance. It promised that the dead would return; family members and buffaloes too. The movement swept the Plains, and starving, defeated Indians danced in a frenzy for days at a time, a spectacle that frightened the U.S. Army. Its leader was a Paiute visionary named Wovoka. (John Trudell chose that name for his son during the Alcatraz occupation.) The original Wovoka always wore a large black hat. It was said by Indians that if you looked into this hat, you would see the universe.

Crow Dog said the Ghost Dance would take place in the gully where Big Foot's people were killed. They would begin at dawn, barefoot, in the snow and mud, and dance in a circle for hours and hours, until the night returned. They would do this each morning for four days. Crow Dog explained why in his guttural, unexpectedly musical voice. "We're gonna unite together," he said, but achieving this unity would be hard. There would be "no rest, there's no intermission, no coffee break." Some might go into convulsions. If they do, "don't be scared. We won't call a medic—the spirit's gonna be the doctor." If someone falls, pick him up and hold hands, and keep going.

You will see clouds, he said, visions, and the visions will elevate you to another world. There you will see brothers and relations that have died. The Ghost Dance Spirit will appear. "We're not gonna go on a trip like on drugs. It starts physically and goes into spiritually, and then you will get into the power . . . we're gonna unite together as brothers—we're gonna Ghost Dance."

Crow Dog told them "everyone had heard about the Ghost Dance, but nobody ever seen it. That was something the United States of America prohibits—they're not gonna have no Ghost Dance, no Sun Dance religion, no Indian religion. But this hoop has to be not broken—for the whole unborn generations.

"So decide tonight if you want to dance with me tomorrow. You be ready."

Courage and stamina were not the only requirements. Special clothes were needed as well. A century earlier Ghost Dancers wore the sun and the moon and the stars on their backs, special shirts whose brightly painted images of the heavens possessed extraordinary power. Believers said the shirts made them bulletproof.

During the night women scoured Wounded Knee for material they could use, but fabric, like almost everything else, was in short supply. Instead the women found burlap and curtains, and turned the coarse material into Ghost Dance Shirts. They were painted by those who knew the old designs, and when they were finished the humble shirts were pronounced beautiful.

Forty men and women accepted Crow Dog's invitation. Russell Means was one of the forty, and shared his thoughts at a community meeting when the four days of dancing ended. "The white man says that the 1890 massacre was the end of the wars with the Indian, that it was the end of the Indian, the end of the Ghost Dance. Yet here we are at war, we're still Indians, and we're Ghost Dancing again. And the spirits of Big Foot and his people are all around us. They suffered through here once before, in the snow and the cold, and they were hungry, and they were surrounded at the time with the finest weapons the United States had available to them, brand new machine guns and cannons."

Big Foot's people, said Means, were "like a grandfather. It was time for them to go to sleep, but they had a child that was just born." For Means, this represented the generation born at the end of the last century, and he spoke of the events that shaped that child. "World War I came along, and the United States asked the American Indian if they would fight their war for them." The Indians who fought in Europe shared their knowledge of the globe when they returned home. Then, another war. "This time they not only took Indians into the army, but into defense plants all across America, and into the big cities." The history lesson became autobiography, at once the story of a people and the story of Russell Means, whose father left the reservation for work in a California naval base. "And we learned the ways of the white man, right here in this country . . . and brought that knowledge back for the use of our people." He recalled labor battles of the 1930s, anticommunism in the 1950s, the black rebellions of the 1960s—those events were lesson plans for the child born to Big Foot's people. We are that child, Means said, Oglala patriots unafraid to take up arms against the United States, and we are back.

They were also hungry. The parallels of eighty-three years earlier grew more acute with each passing day, as food supplies inside the village dwindled. Wounded Knee's population varied, but rarely dipped below two hundred, and feeding two hundred people proved to be a challenge as great as that of military defense or political strategy. The only way to get food into Wounded Knee was to bring it on your back.

Food came into Wounded Knee on the backs of volunteers, literally. There was no alternative. The trip for some began hundreds of miles away. When they arrived on Pine Ridge and made contact with occupation sympathizers, they usually assembled at a house eight or ten or fifteen miles from Wounded Knee. The reservation people crucial to making this underground railroad work risked as much or more as the ones who carried the supplies. Outsiders were deported from Pine Ridge, but the BIA police and Wilson's goons could take more severe action against residents.

The backpackers would set out in small groups at night, loaded down with forty or fifty pounds of food. Local Oglalas usually led them across the rugged terrain, but sometimes even they became lost. For the first five or six hours their enemies were freezing temperatures, darkness, steep inclines up riverbeds, and holes they couldn't see, a possible sprain with every misstep. When they neared the village, exhausted, they had to avoid federal marshals patrolling the area. Other officers launched flares to make their work easier. The flares cast an eerie light on the landscape, and forced the backpackers to hit the ground. The feds also had high-intensity searchlights, infrared detectors, jeeps equipped with xenon lights, and weapons with starlight scopes. Sometimes, after getting lost or not finding a way past the perimeter because of the patrols and the flares, dawn would arrive and force the backpackers to spend the entire day in a canyon. In daylight their chances of being arrested greatly increased.

Food was a weapon, and sometimes it also was a symbol. Beef "liberated" from white ranchers also contributed to the Wounded Knee kitchen, but these expeditions had their own dangers. Some ranchers had already been observed joining in gun battles between government forces and Indians, and if any of those ranchers caught

AIM militants poaching their cattle, one could only expect them to respond with gleeful and severe retribution.

One head of cattle prompted an incident that fascinated journalists. Young Indian men brought a cow into the village, and did not know how to kill or slaughter it. A cameraman for a television network showed them how.

The anecdote spoke volumes to reporters for whom the occupation, despite its moments of drama and heroism, had become increasingly disappointing. One editorial dismissed the Indians as more white than red. Indian demands were utopian, absurd. The rebels wanted to return to the nineteenth century, and when they didn't want to return to the nineteenth century they disappointed by doing mundane, twentieth century things like setting up an office for the Independent Oglala Nation and issuing newsletters. They were too Indian or not Indian enough, sophisticated manipulators of television or hopelessly romantic primitives. Indians should know how to butcher cattle, it was that simple. Any Indian who needed a television cameraman to butcher his cow could not be taken very seriously.

The government responded to the outpouring of support for Wounded Knee with an impressive national campaign of its own. Under the expansive terms of a controversial piece of legislation passed six years earlier, federal police arrested scores of individuals who tried to bring food into Wounded Knee. They arrested supporters in Nevada, Ohio, Oregon, and California, en route to Pine Ridge. In some cases they were political activists or students; in other cases they were Americans of no particular ideology, moved by the televised scenes. In almost every case they were shocked to find themselves arrested and often jailed for the possession of groceries, with the intent to cross state lines.

Opponents of the controversial legislation, passed in 1967, called it "the H. Rap Brown Act," a bitter nickname that referred to the Black Power activist who inspired its passage. The law gave the federal government wide authority, some argued unconstitutional authority, to stop and arrest people believed to be crossing state lines to take part in a civil disorder.

AIM had a special talent for creating sympathy for its actions, but at Wounded Knee that would not be enough. AIM needed both public opinion on its side—to stay the hand of crisis managers who might yet decide a military solution was the correct solution—and a coordinated resupply effort to keep the occupation alive.

The national crackdown against Wounded Knee's supporters mirrored a more aggressive strategy on Pine Ridge. On March 16, a hundred BIA police, FBI, and marshals stormed a house in Porcupine that served as a major link in the support network. The sweep resulted in the arrest and expulsion of seventy-five people. Some had traveled for days only to be stopped eight miles from their goal. The government net reached coast to coast, and seemed to be getting more effective by the day.

AIM had considerable experience at facing government barricades, court orders, and ultimatums. The movement was not easily frightened or intimidated, but this was their first siege. Each day at Wounded Knee was a victory of sorts, but time favored the government and not the Indians.

The arrival of a dozen backpackers in the morning prompted rejoicing for the occupiers. Often no one made it through, and that usually meant one of two things: The feds had arrested people during the night, or, even worse, no one had tried to make it to the village. Either way it was bad news.

One afternoon Dennis Banks gave reporters a firsthand look at the dismal state of the Independent Oglala Nation's kitchen. A dense fog had settled over the snow-covered ground, dreary weather that matched the atmosphere inside. Exhausted and bored fighters asked the visitors for cigarettes and fruit. Banks admitted the compound was almost out of food, and warned that if necessary, they would shoot their way past federal agents to acquire supplies.

Gun battles became more frequent in the days that followed the occupation rejection's of the Wood proposal. Furious exchanges lasting several hours took place on March 21 and March 22. The government told news organizations their safety could no longer be guaranteed. Reporters started leaving, and those who stayed found their access to the village limited.

For the occupation, the dwindling press corps was an ominous development, quickly followed by another. A few weeks earlier, one television reporter described Wounded Knee as "war games without the war." The clever line may have accurately described the first phase of the occupation, but it no longer applied, and he, like the other correspondents, were no longer around to cover the second phase. On Sunday evening, March 25, police found a key Wilson ally on the tribal council, Leo Wilcox, incinerated in his car on a highway near Scenic, just off the reservation. The first reports called the accident suspicious, and Wilson and others immediately concluded Wilcox's fiery death was a political assassination carried out by AIM.

A few days later a detailed investigation by coroners, fire marshals, and pathologists would rule otherwise, calling the death a result of asphyxiation, and the fire a freakish accident caused by a broken fuel line. They could find no evidence of foul play.

The report came too late to stop Wilson and his allies from acting on their rage, and the next morning, Monday, March 26, they established their own roadblocks around Wounded Knee, outside the federal government's roadblocks, and a few hours later made their presence felt. A judge in Sioux Falls had issued a decision a day earlier in favor of the newly created Wounded Knee Legal Defense/ Offense Committee, which asked that the federal government allow six cars, each with a lawyer, food, and medicine into the village. It was a small but important victory for AIM, and a defeat for the government. But Wilson announced the federal court order had no validity on Pine Ridge, and his new roadblock stopped the cars from going through. The marshals watched and did nothing.

A few hours later Wounded Knee saw the most intense exchange of gunfire yet, and the federal side took its first serious casualty. Lloyd Grimm, a marshal from Omaha, Nebraska, was hit in the chest. A helicopter brought him to a military hospital in Colorado. Grimm had no feeling in his legs; doctors said they didn't know if the paralysis was temporary or permanent.

Wounded Knee's security forces felt certain Grimm was hit by his own side's crossfire, the result of overzealous and poorly coordinated shooting by the marshals, FBI agents, and BIA police. This theory could not be proved, but it gained in credibility when the government failed to release information on the bullet.

Monday evening, March 26, the firing resumed, and it lasted all night. The incoming fire hit no one inside the village, but the occupation nonetheless suffered a devastating defeat at Wounded Knee's most vulnerable moment: The last of the network television crews packed up and left. As if to underscore the village's sudden isolation, the last telephone line went down during the night.

The next evening Dennis Banks and Russell Means secretly left the village and by morning had made the hundred-mile journey to Rosebud, the neighboring Sioux reservation. AIM had supporters at Rosebud—Crow Dog lived there, for example—and unlike Pine Ridge it could operate openly. The two AIM leaders found volunteers and supplies waiting at Rosebud, and organized new supply lines into Pine Ridge.

Banks and Means returned the next day to confront the new headaches of Wilson's roadblock and the lack of news reporters. They also learned that Hank Adams, their ally in the Trail of Broken Treaties six months earlier, had arrived in Pine Ridge bearing a new proposal on behalf of Leonard Garment and the White House.

Wounded Knee disappeared from the newscasts and the front pages at the end of March, but it had not been forgotten. On March 25, nearly four thousand people attended a mass at New York's Cathedral of St. John the Divine in support of the occupation. Indians from throughout the northeast made up half of the audience. Singer Buffy Sainte-Marie performed, and Reverend Vine Deloria, Sr., father of the more famous writer and activist Vine Jr., offered a sermon.

"May your cause be heard by all the people in America," said the Very Reverend James P. Morton. During the mass, Reverend Morton prayed for forgiveness for the crimes of the American state against American Indians. Morton's prayer sounded like indictments read by a prosecutor: "the racism of our ancestors ... forcing Native Americans to accept our culture ... violating their gravesites ... destroying their lands with our mining industry ... being entertained by movies celebrating their genocide," and after each one the congregation responded with the chant "Lord God forgive us."

A service of another kind took place a few days earlier in Los Angeles. Actor Marlon Brando had been famous for decades, but never more so than in early 1973. *The Godfather* had been a critical and commercial triumph, and the steamy *Last Tango in Paris* had generated more controversy than any movie in years.

With hundreds of millions watching the Academy Awards broadcast, Brando declined his Academy Award for *The Godfather*, and sent an Apache actress named Sacheen Littlefeather in front of the cameras to explain why. (Brando himself had planned to be at Wounded Knee during the award ceremony, but this effort failed.)

Demonstrations continued in scores of cities, both in the United States and abroad. The U.S. State Department promptly cabled its embassies with instructions on how to respond to demonstrations and inquiries about the oppression of Native Americans. The United States Information Agency warned that "If Indians are killed, we can surely expect sharp and widespread foreign condemnation of this U.S. government action. It would come at a particularly unpropitious time, giving Arab governments an excuse to fog up the terrorist issue."

On April 1, a Harris Poll confirmed the obvious. Ninety-three percent of Americans were following the occupation, and fifty-one percent said they supported the Indians. The support may have been a mile wide but it also seemed no more than an inch deep. It meant that government attempts to portray the occupiers as criminals and hooligans failed, but it did not translate into support for AIM, reform efforts in Congress, or recognition of treaties. The sympathy for the occupation was just that; sympathy. The government had surrounded a few hundred Indians in South Dakota with tanks and guns, and most Americans vastly preferred that the government not use the tanks and guns to kill those few hundred Indians, especially not at the same place where such an event had already taken place once.

The world knew of the Oglalas' stand and perhaps even sided with them, but it couldn't force the government to withdraw their tanks, it could only keep them from advancing. What was the value of such support? The question presented itself as the village endured hardship, and even the date of the poll—April 1—seemed to mock the good news it carried.

Wounded Knee seemed to be a place where everything happened twice. At times, the Ghost Dance and the machine guns, the army and the political agendas seemed like ghostly apparitions or cheap imitations of historical events. Political theater, some called it. Destiny and prophecy, countered the militants.

Even the one truly modern touch, the presence of electronic media that brought the siege into millions of living rooms, had its own antecedents. Wounded Knee had been a sound stage for cameras once before. In 1911, twenty-one years after the massacre, Buffalo Bill re-created the events of 1890 with a huge cast and an unprecedented budget. He enlisted General Nelson Miles as his technical advisor, and convinced the Department of War to donate eleven thousand troops. He hired Oglalas who had survived the events of December 1890 to play themselves in the most expensive, ambitious movie yet made.

The night before shooting the massacre itself, rumors swept the Indians at the camp that the guns might not be fake, and they might be firing bullets and not blanks. The filming of the massacre, using army troops and massacre survivors, was almost too much for some of the Indians to bear, and many wept as they pretended to die in front of Cody's cameras. The film became the victim of Cody's vanity and the pressures of history and current events. It disintegrated under the pressure, and a few decades later only a tiny fraction of the film survived. For its day Cody's movie was a docudrama, an epic, an honest effort to make sense of terrible events.

Wounded Knee was as stark and plain as the prairie bluffs, as mysterious and complex as the suddenly changing weather. December 1890 was undeniably a massacre that claimed the lives of more than three hundred Indians, but it was also a terribly botched, almost accidental massacre in which twenty-eight American soldiers died as well.

Stanley Lyman spent March 29 attending Leo Wilcox's funeral and providing illegal support to the Wilson roadblock. The BIA superintendent at Pine Ridge came from a Quaker background and had spent his life working with Indians. He was an ardent supporter of the Bureau's new approach of supporting tribal government, and since the occupation at Wounded Knee had begun a month earlier he had become increasingly angry at the way the officials from Washington paid more attention to AIM than to the elected representatives.

Lyman loved to tell people, feigning exasperation, that it was he who was a puppet of Wilson, not the other way around. When Lyman approved the tribal president's resolutions that banned the American Indian Movement from the reservation, or ordered the removal of the National Council of Churches and all outsiders from Pine Ridge, he saw this as carrying out the federal government's policy of self-determination.

He also liked Wilson, and did everything he could to support the man who came off so badly to the national press and the liberal churches. Dick Wilson was a plain-speaking man who only felt comfortable in the mixed-blood society of Pine Ridge Village. He wasn't one of those tribal chairmen always flying off to speak at national conferences or testify in Washington. The tribal president sported a Marine haircut, an impressive paunch, thick glasses, and a blue windbreaker. He was often described, accurately, as a plumber by trade, but by the time outsiders were through profiling him the phrase "former plumber" sounded like "convicted felon," only worse. He possessed a sort of anti-charisma and practiced counterdiplomacy. A reporter asked him, at one crucial moment during the siege, what he planned to do next. Wilson answered, "I think I'll have a drink."

Wilson may have not cornered the market on sophisticated sloganeering or stylish dressing—unlike Russell Means and Dennis Banks, who looked like movie stars, and spoke even better than they looked—but he was a crafty and effective politician. He rose to the top in the bitterly competitive arena of Sioux politics, successfully outmaneuvered his opponents on the tribal council, and still enjoyed considerable support on the reservation. He was the elected leader of one of the largest and most politically important reservations in the country, and that carried a lot of weight in national Indian politics. He also had an impressive family; brother James had a Ph.D. and a high-ranking job in Washington, D.C. with the Office of Economic Opportunity.

Wilson, along with his family and the marshals who rarely left their sides, lived in secret locations off the reservation but he joined Lyman on March 29 to attend the funeral of his friend Leo Wilcox, the councilman who perished in the bizarre auto accident a few days earlier. One of the last coversations with Wilcox had taken place five weeks earlier, in the tense days immediately before the occupation. Dick Wilson, Wilcox, and Lyman were in the BIA building. The three men shared a quiet moment together during a lull in the crises.

Wilcox spoke of a recent, very strange experience on Mount Rushmore. He had been walking near the top of the mountain and slipped, falling very close to the top of one of the huge carved faces. Suddenly a man appeared and helped him up, though he somehow did this without ever touching Wilcox. Standing up, Wilcox noticed which president they were on top of. It was Jefferson. This stranger—a big man, Wilcox remembered—then walked into the thin air above the marbled president and dissapeared.

Wilcox also spoke of coming upon four AIM people on a vigil in the Black Hills, and as he watched them a snake crawled by one of the four. The snake, Wilcox said, meant danger; danger from AIM.

Often people tried to make sense of Pine Ridge by pigeonholing its citizens. They were called Christian or traditional, full-blood or mixed-blood, sellout or militant. Leo Wilcox—the man who led the campaign to revoke the Congressional Medals of Honor awarded for the carnage at Wounded Knee in 1890—was a Dick Wilson ally, but he was also a man who studied to become a medicine man and believed in the power of dreams and visions. His life offered powerful evidence that the Sioux of Pine Ridge could not easily be classified.

At the church hundreds came to pay their respects. Lyman, Wilson, and other mourners left the church for the final good-bye at the nearby cemetery. The landscape was a study in brown, with no sign of spring in sight. Dust blew at the cemetery. The site bordered something improbable: the brown fairways of the reservation's golf course. (Larger than Delaware, Pine Ridge had the same number of golf courses as supermarkets—one.)

The service started, then stopped. Someone had forgotten to bring the Oglala Sioux flag to place on the casket, and Dick Wilson had to retrieve one from the tribal office. When the ceremony resumed a man played taps on the horn, badly, Lyman thought, and then the hymn "The Land Was Fairer Than Day" was sung in Oglala.

Golfers played on, untroubled by the funeral of a key political figure a few yards away, or the armed standoff twenty miles over the hills. Lyman counted the number of people who played golf during the time they buried the councilman. Twenty.

A marshal asked Lyman, back at his office, how the funeral was, and Lyman thought, that's a hell of a question. Among the issues demanding Lyman's attention that day were the results of an energetic campaign by anxious school children in Miami. They had collected twelve thousand pounds of canned goods for the besieged Indians at Wounded Knee, but so far had no success in getting the food out of Florida. Someone from the campaign had enlisted the director of the Young Men and Young Women's Hebrew Association to find a solution, and when he reached Lyman by phone, the superintendent tried to explain the occupation from his point of view, without much luck.

Lyman proposed that instead of going to the occupation force—a group of outsiders, acting against the tribal government, he insisted—the six tons of canned goods be donated to the Felix Cohen Home for the Elderly. The caller seemed dumbfounded by the complexity of the Indians versus Indians situation.

Lyman next turned his attention to the roadblock Wilson had established a few days earlier. Although a federal judge ordered supplies into Wounded Knee, the tribal roadblock continued to keep them out. The same federal judge ordered the federal agencies to provide no support to this roadblock, which he considered illegal, but Lyman believed the tribal roadblock had more justification for being there than the Justice Department did, and certainly more than AIM, who Lyman felt started the trouble in the first place.

Wilson's roadblocks were guarded by swaggering young guys, usually brandishing rifles and often drinking openly. They won few popularity contests, frightening reporters and even showing little respect for the federal agents, but Lyman had a soft spot for the people AIM called goons. He had sent BIA police cars to the roadblocks so they would have radio communication. The federal judge found this violated his orders, so Lyman reluctantly had the cars recalled. But he vowed to help his friends at the illegal roadblock in other ways. They were on twenty-four-hour-a-day duty, and often had trouble getting meals delivered at night. Lyman resolved to have some of the federal agents' stockpiled C rations delivered to his friends, each and every day they were out there.

No doubt the judge in Sioux Falls would frown on this, but Lyman didn't care. Rumor had it that the liberals of the Community Relations Service shared their C rations with AIM, which was also illegal, and there was little doubt that reporters and the National Council of Churches people did the same.

The men on the government barricades dined on C rations only when they were on duty, and sometimes managed more interesting fare even at their bunkers. Sometimes they had cookouts, and the tantalizing aroma of the marshals' sizzling steaks became a form of psychological warfare against the hungry warriors. When their shifts ended, most of the federal agents not only retired to hotels, hot showers, and restaurant meals, but as the siege went on some earned "R and R" at the Hot Springs Country Club or at similar venues in Colorado.

Some, however, were bivouacked at a school on Pine Ridge. Agnes Lamont, a teacher's aide at the school, cooked for the students and the marshals both. At one lunch, a marshal complimented her fry bread and asked for a recipe. She questioned him about why he was on Pine Ridge, and voiced her opinion that he and the others were there to protect Wilson.

To make room for the marshals and FBI agents, the six- and seven-year-old boys moved to another dormitory and doubled up. The reservation's vast distances made this and other facilities a boarding school during the week. Sometimes the inquisitive kids would volunteer breathless reports on what they discovered at the agents' barracks: "Mrs. Lamont, there's some guns in there. There's some guns in there and some shells in there and there's some whiskey in there."

Agnes Lamont had joined demonstrations against the tribal president and the BIA superintendent, and had a personal connection to Wounded Knee—both past and present. Lamont's only son Buddy, a Vietnam vet, had joined the others at Wounded Knee. He had been employed with the tribe, but lost his job when he spoke out against Wilson. When the roadblocks came down after the first week, Agnes brought him clothes, food, and aspirin. She asked him to come home, at least for a few days. Buddy told her he couldn't, that he had to stay. The massacre was also a part of her family history. She knew of the events from her mother, who was twelve years old in 1890 and had survived the carnage. Her mother's aunt and uncle were killed.

On March 31st, Wounded Knee and the U.S. government, resumed their negotiations. The discussions were contentious but productive, with both parties relieved that the Interior Department and the BIA were no longer direct participants. The Indian delegation saw the new arrangement as one consistent with their declarations of sovereignty, and the U.S. side had removed the major stumbling block in reaching previous agreements.

Five days later, under a brilliant April sun, Russell Means, Clyde Bellecourt, Carter Camp, and Pedro Bissonette signed an agreement in a ceremony that self-consciously echoed treaty signings of the 1870s. The Oglalas would get their meeting with the White House. The Justice Department would go after criminal activity on Pine Ridge. Auditors would examine the Pine Ridge Tribal government's books.

Frizzell, the lead negotiator from Washington, smoked the sacred pipe in a tepee with the chiefs and the AIM leaders. Indians watching the ceremony nudged each other and pointed to the sky. Eagles wheeled high over the valley, a fortuitous and powerful sign.

There were smiles, handshakes, poses for the cameras, and a few minutes later Russell Means boarded a red helicopter and flew northwest to Rapid City. Since he had achieved a small measure of fame in the last few years, Means already insisted that anyone who invited him to speak or attend a conference had to provide first-class tickets.

The ride had elements of first-class travel. Means was the most important passenger and he left in impressive style, having successfully concluded negotiations with the United States to the applause and cheers of his people. It was almost perfect, and would have been, except that the red helicopter was taking Russell Means to the Rapid City Jail. The marshals who rode with Means offered nothing in the way of refreshments—no peanuts or soft drinks—instead they insisted on placing handcuffs on their prisoner.

His arrest was part of the agreement, a sacrifice Means willingly made for the cause of Oglala sovereignty. The settlement called for Means to be booked in Rapid City, but released so he could attend a meeting in Washington in two days with Leonard Garment. Leonard Crow Dog and Tom Bad Cob also were part of the Oglala delegation. That meeting would set the terms for the White House conference on the 1868 treaty, which would take place sometime in the third week of May. When this first initial meeting concluded satisfactorily, Means would call Dennis Banks, still in the village, and the remaining occupation force would lay down their arms.

AIM called it a victory, and in a way it was, as much as anything could be that resulted in the immediate arrest of one of the occupation's leaders, and the certain prosecution of many others. Some in the federal government openly called AIM and the Oglalas criminals and opposed any negotiations, but the April 5th Agreement, as it was called, granted AIM an official meeting with a representative of the president of the United States.

That alone was impressive, and there were additional concessions to AIM as well, including audits of Wilson and the promise that the Justice Department's Civil Rights Division would build cases against the goon squad. Maybe AIM didn't win everything it wanted, but it did better than many observers could have imagined. There was no amnesty and Russell Means's arrest was a hard pill to swallow, but on the other hand, no one had died.

It was over and everyone seemed relieved. Dennis Banks was not in the picture and was not a signer to the agreement, but Means and Camp and Clyde Bellecourt were. The warriors had defended the village against automatic weapon fire, kept their community intact against blizzards, hunger, sickness, and the influx of adventurers, hippies, and revolutionaries.

Cob, Means, and Crow Dog arrived in Washington on Friday night. The meeting for the following morning suddenly turned troublesome. Garment's people understood the April 5th agreement in a very different way than the Oglalas. The White House position was that Means would order the evacuation of Wounded Knee before the meeting started. The Oglalas understood it to be exactly the opposite.

Incensed, Means held press conferences in his hotel lobby, charging the White House with a double-cross. Means asked reporters to use their common sense. "Why," he asked, "would I do it any other way?" The White House stood firm. The agreement disintegrated. At Wounded Knee, Dennis Banks, saying he never believed in the agreement in the first place, announced the occupation would continue.

Free on bail, Means found time to testify before the Indian

Affairs subcommittee, whose chairman, Rep. James Haley, excoriated Means for the BIA takeover and Wounded Knee both. Haley told Means: "you should have never been allowed in Wounded Knee. You should be in the federal penitentiary right now."

Means suffered the abuse with poise, and the *Washington Star* wrote that the AIM leader "had the presence of a tall sturdy pine tree . . . unyielding calm and confident." The committee members, the account said, were "like saplings in comparison as Means refused to give an inch or be provoked, and gave them a taste of what federal negotiators at Wounded Knee have faced."

A few days later he left Washington for a national speaking tour to raise money and build support. The occupation went on, but without Means. The view from the helicopter was his last look at the Independent Oglala Nation.

Chapter 12

Hundred Gun Salute

A s the focus shifted to Washington and the April 5th agreement slowly fell apart, Wounded Knee enjoyed a period of relative peace. Entire days passed without exchanges of gunfire between the two sides.

The cordon around the village remained tight, however, and fewer and fewer backpackers made it through. By the second week in April, federal agents had arrested nearly 140 people for charges directly connected with the occupation, usually obstructing a federal officer in the performance of his duty. Two stubborn individuals, having once been arrested in March and ordered to return to their California homes, reappeared in April and were again arrested. A judge, displeased to see them again, reset their bail, and the two were now incarcerated in Rapid City. Dozens more had been arrested as far away as Nevada, Wyoming, and Oregon and charged under the riot statute.

There was another piece of bitter legal news: A jury in California returned its verdict in the voluntary manslaughter trial of the man who shot and killed Alcatraz leader Richard Oakes. Oakes's assailant was found not guilty.

245

Wounded Knee itself was rife with frequent reports of unusual events. Warriors on patrol told of seeing riders on horseback who would suddenly vanish. Villagers sometimes heard singing but could see no singers. Bullets slammed into the canvas cover of the sweat lodge and bounced off, falling harmlessly to the ground below.

One marshal reportedly had been removed from duty because of things he had seen at Wounded Knee. He told Rev. John Adams of the National Council of Churches that "one night he kept hearing cries and screams and he thought he saw Indians approaching his bunker. He shot at them and shot at them but they kept coming. They finally disappeared." Indians told the minister there was no mystery to any of it. Those people, they said, "are the victims of Wounded Knee—they're all around here."

Though the warriors had business to attend to—the maintainance of the health clinic, the reinforcement of the bunkers, the discussion and rejection of government proposals at community meetings—the hallmark of life inside Wounded Knee, more than anything else, was a stupefying boredom. It was a siege, a waiting game, a chess match. Nobody was going anywhere, and for most hours of most days there was absolutely nothing to do.

The community did not seem a good place to get married or have kids, but both things happened anyway. On April 11 the Independent Oglala Nation saw the birth of its first child (named Pedro after the local activist Pedro Bissonette), and the next day Annie Mae Pictou and Nogeeshik Aquash, two Indians from Canada, were married in a ceremony conducted by Wallace Black Elk.

Stanley Lyman, the BIA superintendent at Pine Ridge, would probably not have been invited to either event even if he were in town, but as it happened he spent April 11 to 14 in Brigham City, Utah, meeting with other BIA directors to devise strategies to respond to the militant threat. Specifically, they discussed creating a special BIA force that could respond to AIM rebellions on other reservations. The force would be modeled after the U.S. Marshal Service.

At the Salt Lake City airport, en route home, Lyman instantly recognized one of the AIM leaders—he wasn't sure which one—entering the lobby. The AIM leader stopped to greet two black men. As the Indian leader and the two men conversed, Lyman noticed an FBI agent he knew standing nearby. The agent seemed reluctant to talk with Lyman, and Lyman realized the agent was not there by accident but instead carrying out surveillance. He told Lyman the AIM leader was Clyde Bellecourt, and one of the men he had been talking with was a Black Power activist named Stokely Carmichael. Apparently, Bellecourt was out raising money and rallying public support for the occupation.

Lyman felt the resurgence of a powerful emotion he had first experienced only a few weeks earlier. He had watched from a hillside as marshals placed Russell Means in handcuffs at the April 5th signing ceremony, and felt a surge of sheer hatred. Lyman considered Means brilliant, resourceful, and charismatic, but could barely contain his joy at seeing him in chains. It was an unsettling emotion, one he felt again as he watched the FBI agent spy on Bellecourt as Bellecourt talked with Stokely Carmichael. Indian affairs, in Lyman's experience, had been free from anything approaching that level of rancor and hostility. He couldn't remember ever feeling so angry at any Indian person in all of his years with the BIA.

The anger, which had seemingly erupted out of nowhere, had changed Lyman's world completely. He had always seen his role as a partner in helping Indians improve their lives, and never imagined his job would ever include meetings like the one he just attended. He flew back to South Dakota with commitments for a quarter of a million dollars worth of military hardware for use on the reservation.

Meanwhile, as the Pine Ridge superintendent's plane landed in Rapid City, two carloads of occupation supporters left town with supplies and a mission of their own. In Porcupine, they joined up with others and waited nervously in a two-room safe house for darkness to fall. The group included warriors who helped run the supply operation from Rapid City, a woman who operated one of the occupation's military radios, and Oglalas who wanted to visit their families.

Some of the fourteen had set out by foot the night before. At two in the morning a sudden blizzard cut their visibility to almost nothing, and left them disoriented. They continued on for three agonizing hours, and finally one of their group saw lights in the distance.

APCs, someone said. But the lights were from cars on a highway. Instead of reaching Wounded Knee they had circled back to Porcupine. They returned to their safe house, exhausted and laughing at themselves.

When they set out again the next night, Sunday, April 14, the weather was clear and they were joined by others. Not everyone could manage the fifty-pound loads, and a few people had to abandon their packs to keep up with the others. At one point, the group had to lay motionless in a gully for two hours when APCs were heard nearby. They finally moved on, and at sunrise on Monday morning walked over the last ridge and looked down at the encircled village. The group walked straight through the federal line and then the Indian bunkers, across Wounded Knee Creek and behind the Catholic Church. No one stopped them.

People came running from the Wounded Knee bunkers to meet them, delirious. "Welcome home!" they said, happy to see comrades, and even more thrilled to see their backpacks crammed with groceries. It was the largest shipment to make it through in nearly two weeks. They were heroes, saviors, and like others who had made the treacherous journey they spent most of the day sleeping. Some were going to leave right away and do it all again, while others planned to stay. Frank and Morningstar Clearwater, a couple who had hitchhiked from North Carolina, were among those who decided to stay.

The next morning, at dawn, something even more astonishing happened. Food fell from the sky. People who heard the sound of aircraft looked up to see ten parachutes fluttering to the ground, and three Cessna planes flying low away from the village. The bundles contained the usual beans, coffee, rice, and powdered milk, but also chocolate, ham, prunes, and cashews. People ripped open the packages, laughing and crying. Gladys Bissonette and others in charge of the Wounded Knee kitchen oversaw distribution, making sure that the families in the cluster housing unit received a share of the food.

A few moments later, the feds detected the planes and the FBI sent its helicopter, nicknamed "Snoopy," aloft to investigate. The pilot radioed a description of the ten packages as "leather cases," round and about three feet in length. The description suggested shipments of ammunition and guns instead of potatoes and flour, and is a possible explanation for the helicopter's next action. An Indian family, permanent residents of Wounded Knee, walked back to their house with a cart loaded with goods from the air drop. The helicopter fired on them, not hitting anyone, but prompting Wounded Knee security to return fire.

Law enforcement officers on the perimeter opened up in response, and one of their bullets ripped through the walls of a small church that served as the Hawk Eye bunker and smashed into the back of Frank Clearwater's skull. He had been sleeping in the church-turned-bunker and had been awake only a short time. A woman from the bunkers squad pressed a clean shirt to his head and spoke to him, but he was unconscious. His blood covered the floor.

Forty-five minutes passed before he could be taken to the clinic, a half-mile away, and snipers continued to fire at the three women and three men who carried the stretcher and waved a mop handle to signal a truce. It would be an hour more before a helicopter arrived to take Clearwater to a Rapid City hospital. He was unconscious but alive. Three other people inside Wounded Knee were wounded during the hours of shooting that morning and afternoon, though none as seriously as Clearwater.

At first, Morningstar Clearwater stayed inside Wounded Knee, fearing arrest if she tried to stay with her husband. A few days later, fearing that Frank was near death, she made her way to the federal roadblocks, where marshals immediately arrested her. She spent the night in the Pine Ridge jail. The cell had no bed, and her only food was a bowl of corn mush, a few spoonfuls of beans, and some crackers at night. She was thirty-seven years old and three months pregnant.

When Morningstar Clearwater was released a day later, she told reporters about conditions inside Wounded Knee: "The people are starving, they don't have cover, they don't have food, they don't have nothin'."

Dennis Banks called the airlift a new beginning for Wounded Knee, even if it had come at a terrible cost. He said they had been on the verge of surrender, but the ten parachutes convinced him and the others that the world had not forgotten about them and they should not give up. The shooting of Frank Clearwater, a man who risked his life to aid people he did not even know, was a reason to fight on, not to give up.

The flight had been carried out by a group of antiwar activists from Chicago, and they included a printed message in their precious cargo that explained why they did it:

Manifesto of the Wounded Knee Airlift

To the Independent Oglala Nation and their friends at Wounded Knee:

Your struggle for freedom and justice is our struggle. Our hearts are with you.

To the people of America:

The delivery of these packages of food to the courageous people in Wounded Knee is being carried out by a number of Americans who have worked, and continue to work, to end American aggression in Indochina.

The buffaloes that gave life to the Sioux were killed by American rifles, just as the rice that gives life to the Vietnamese was destroyed by American chemicals and bombs. But the people of Indochina are moving steadily toward freedom and independence and so too are the people who were the first Americans.

In a devastating sign of both public disinterest and the success of new government restrictions on the media that remained at Wounded Knee, the dramatic and bloody events merited vague reports of between ten and twenty seconds in length on the evening newscasts on April 17, the night of the firefight, and the next day.

The occupation faced new adversity on all fronts in the following days. The blockade tightened even further as marshals stepped up their roving patrols in the hills around Wounded Knee. By the end of the week they had arrested nearly fifty backpackers. Frank Clearwater lived, but just barely. Doctors at St. John's McNamara Hospital called his condition grave.

Also, supporters from around the country had gathered at Crow Dog's on the Rosebud Reservation and were preparing to march the seventy miles to Wounded Knee, bringing food and medical supplies. The march had been planned weeks before, and organizers had optimistically predicted a turnout of thousands. Instead, 150 supporters, led by AIM's Vernon Bellecourt, set out on April 22 on the grimly titled "March for Survival."

The journey recalled dangerous civil rights protests in Mississippi or Alabama a decade earlier, with new wrinkles thrown in for added excitement. As if by design, the March for Survival offered increasing levels of peril from a variety of adversaries. To arrive at Pine Ridge from Rosebud, they had to march straight through Bennett County, considered by Indians to be one of the most racist areas in South Dakota. After Bennett County and the cowboy town of Martin, they would encounter Dick Wilson and his goons. And after that, three hundred federal lawmen and a war zone.

The marchers, however, never made it past level one. When they left the friendly confines of the Rosebud reservation and entered Bennett County, the March for Survival found eighty BIA police and federal marshals standing across the highway. An FBI helicopter hovered above, and fifteen FBI agents were stationed nearby. A BIA policeman read a restraining order from the Pine Ridge tribal court banning the marchers from entering Pine Ridge.

Normally, an Oglala Sioux tribal court order would have no more standing in Bennett County than in Zurich, and probably less. On this occasion, it had the full backing of the federal government. The audacious maneuver prompted reporters to ask how the Justice Department's Hellstern justified sending his officers to enforce a patently unconstitutional tribal court order on land under South Dakota's jurisdiction.

The assistant attorney general offered a startling legal opinion that under other circumstances, would have gladdened the hearts of Lakota patriots everywhere. "Although it appears on the map as part of the state's jurisdiction, Bennett County has historically been a part of the Pine Ridge Indian Reservation," Hellstern said. "A very strong case can be made that the tribe has jurisdiction in Bennett County."

This generous interpretation of Sioux sovereignty from an important government lawyer would have provoked much hilarity among the Oglalas holed up at The Knee, who argued a very strong case could be made that the tribe had jurisdiction over all of western South Dakota as well.

The protest marchers didn't have much to laugh at, however. Vernon Bellecourt and the others had no choice but to turn back. That night, many of them tried to hike through the hills into Wounded Knee, but few succeeded, and federal police had one of their best nights yet, arresting seventy people in the Pine Ridge countryside.

The evermore formidable curtain around Wounded Knee did not prevent Agnes Lamont from helping her granddaughter prepare the bundles she and her friends would smuggle past government lines. Lakota women kept the food trains going even during the hazardous days of late April. On this occasion Agnes went with her granddaughter and others part of the way. "I took them over in the afternoon," she said in describing the experience.

> I took them on the north side of Wounded Knee. They sat there and waited until dark and they went in. I prayed for them and I sang a song that people sing when the enemies are around coming for them. With that song, the enemies couldn't come even if they have three or four guns. So I sang a song for them and I thought, 'Well, I will just wait.'
>
> 'Do your best to get back in,' I told them. Some hungry little children were in there. I left and came home.
>
> They got in though. On the way they got lost and gave the howl or whistle that let them into Wounded Knee. It's our belief, our spiritual belief, that they were being guided into Wounded Knee. They got into Wounded Knee at dawn and they walked in front of the soldiers where they were camping, but no one was up. The Great Spirit held their eyes closed so they didn't see them. So they walked right in there.

In Washington, Attorney General Kleindienst asked the Defense Department for more assistance, and General Alexander Haig responded by assembling a "preposition package" at Fort Collins, Colorado. This specialized group had training in nonlethal chemical warfare and included two air ambulance crews, two physicians, a chemical training team, and communications and logistics specialists. The "package" waited on standby in Fort Collins for the order to take the village. A lieutenant colonel from the unit was dispatched to

Pine Ridge to make a first-hand assessment on the possible effectiveness of chemical weapons at Wounded Knee. The day after the almost fatal firefight, government bunkers were issued M-79 grenade launchers equipped with gas grenades.

The nation's most famous dove seemed to welcome their use. South Dakota's George McGovern, perhaps the most liberal member of the U.S. Senate, wrote Attorney General Kleindienst on April 21 urging new measures to end the crisis: "I am convinced that we are now faced with two alternatives within the next couple of weeks: either a carefully planned action by trained law enforcement officials to arrest those illegally occupying Wounded Knee, or a much more dangerous effort to dislodge the AIM militants by angry private citizens in the area." The "angry private citizens" McGovern referred to were a band of Wounded Knee's permanent residents who, fed up with the federal government's inability to end the crisis, had established their own roadblock around the village, in effect replacing the Wilson roadblock that had been removed with the signing of the April 5th agreement. Other village residents denounced them as Wilson supporters who were not, in fact, permanent residents of Wounded Knee.

The number of participants had always been dizzying, but with this latest development it bordered on the surreal. On the federal side there were now BIA police from reservations around the country, Pine Ridge BIA police, U.S. marshals, FBI agents, Justice Department aides, the peacekeepers and mediators of the Community Relations Service (CRS), and officers from the Sixth Army, still in their duck-hunting clothes. Wilson had his famous auxiliary police force and other assorted volunteers. Vigilantes and ranchers operated on a freelance basis, firing from trees and riverbeds into Wounded Knee, hoping to provoke firefights between the Indians and the federal police—a tactic that in recent days enjoyed consistent success.

Technically, chief marshal Colburn was the highest ranking government official on the scene, the overall general of the forces arrayed against the rebels. But the agencies had rarely worked together, and never during a lengthy siege against armed Indians in a South

Dakota winter. The FBI men sometimes had trouble taking orders from a marshal, so much so that Colburn insisted on putting some of his men in bunkers with the FBI agents.

Political differences became apparent as well. The FBI men, unlike the marshals, had a particularly close relationship with the goons, and AIM supporters claimed the goons had been seen with automatic weapons that could only have come from federal agents.

The greatest source of tension, though, remained between the tribal government and the people from Washington sent to resolve the crisis. Kent Frizzell rarely consulted Wilson or the BIA's Lyman about his plans, and when he did Frizzell sometimes ended up shouting that the whole tribal government should be shut down and put in receivership.

Since the failure of the April 5th agreement, the government's lead negotiator had been Stanley Pottinger, the fifth envoy from Washington to try—and fail—to end the stalemate. He left South Dakota on April 22, leaving his deputy Richard Hellstern, thought to be a hard-liner, in charge. Pottinger expressed his frustration about the rising tensions. "What would the public reaction be if the government uses tear gas to clear the noncombatants out of Wounded Knee and two or three of the militants are killed? Would they have their second massacre of Wounded Knee?"

Pottinger's question about a tear gas attack did not seem to be a rhetorical one. One day later, the military team waiting for instructions at a Colorado army base received new orders. The unit was placed on six-hour standby alert. New supplies of tear gas arrived in Pine Ridge from Quantico, Virginia and Fort Ord, Washington.

A plan for retaking the village was finalized and leaked to the press. The plan, one newspaper said, "calls for the dropping of leaflets urging all non-combatants to leave Wounded Knee several hours in advance of the time set for the assault. If the assault becomes necessary the armored helicopter would spread nausea gas and smoke over the area, marshals wearing flight jackets would follow, some walking and some in APCs."

On April 23, the enforcers of the new roadblock barred the Justice Department's CRS from entering the village. Wilson's forces considered the CRS a direct AIM ally, accusing it of entering Wounded Knee in vehicles with full gas tanks and returning with the tanks nearly empty. CRS denied the charges. When the roadblock turned back the Justice Department officials at gunpoint, the self-appointed vigilantes had finally crossed a line Colburn could no longer ignore. He ordered his troops to take the roadblock and round up the vigilantes for arrest. John Hussman, an arrestee, told reporters that an FBI agent had tried to stop Colburn from making the arrests. He also said that FBI agents and BIA police had been working together to staff the vigilante roadblock for almost two weeks.

The arrests prompted a crisis between Wilson, the FBI, and the Justice Department. Intense negotiations took place on Pine Ridge that eventually involved Patrick Gray, the FBI's acting director. A compromise was finally reached. Essentially, the goon roadblock had become openly and officially part of the FBI's roadblock.

News of the compromise somehow failed to reach the three top federal officials on the scene in time to prevent a near catastrophe on Tuesday evening, April 24. Frizzell, Hellstern, and Colburn approached the disputed roadblock, and an Indian teenager with a shotgun rapped on their car and said "Roll down the window." The young Indian did not recognize the government officials, and thought they might be with the hated CRS.

The three inside the car found the existence of the roadblock an affront, and the sight of a teenager pointing a shotgun at them more than they could take. Colburn bounded out of the car with his automatic weapon, and aimed at the kid and his shotgun. From the shadows an FBI man appeared and asked everyone to put away their guns. The teenager said, "I will lower mine when he lowers his."

Hellstern was forced to give an account of the incident at a news conference two days later. He described the men at the tribal roadblock as "hot under the collar," adding that "words were exchanged, and weapons raised, but fortunately cooler heads prevailed." Chairman Wilson stood next to Hellstern at the news conference and offered a more vivid description. Holding his fingers barely apart, he said "We came this far from shooting Frizzell and Colburn." The accidental assassination of the three highest ranking federal officials at Wounded Knee by allies of the very tribal government hundreds of

U.S. agents had been defending for six weeks would have been difficult to explain, and would have provided a strong incentive for improved coordination.

As the federal contingent and its various allies sorted out their
uneasy truce, the weather turned chaotic and unpredictable in the
usual way of spring in the Northern Plains. Thunderstorms and hail
one day, snow and thirty-five-mile-per-hour winds the next. The
dismal weather reflected something of the mood of those inside
Wounded Knee, who were experiencing a bit of leadership shortage,
a rare and perhaps unprecedented occurance for any AIM activity.
Russell Means was still out on bond traveling around the country
trying to raise money and build support for the occupation. Clyde
Bellecourt and his brother Vernon were doing the same. Pedro Bissonette, the Oglala leader, had recently left the village but he was expected to return in a few days. Dennis Banks and Carter Camp
remained inside, and Leonard Crow Dog had finally returned from
Washington.

Then, on April 25, Frank Clearwater died. He was forty-seven
years old. Wounded Knee leaders declared a four-day period of
mourning. The next day a firefight began in the afternoon—started,
according to those inside Wounded Knee, by vigilantes who fired
into the village and sometimes into the government positions. Eventually government bunkers responded with their own volleys into
Wounded Knee.

Aware of the disarray on the government side and believing that
Colburn might not be receiving accurate reports on the role of the
vigilantes, Wounded Knee security radioed the government bunkers
and asked to meet with the chief marshal. The government radioed
back that Colburn would try to arrange a meeting the next day.

Some warriors inside the village would probably have liked
nothing better than to open up on the federal bunkers for hours at a
time, but ammunition was nearly as scarce as food. Everyone knew
this: the marshals, the goons, and the mysterious third party that
kept the shooting going. The last thing the absurdly overmatched
Wounded Knee's fighters could afford was extended gun battles. The
villagers were, in fact, desperate to maintain the latest cease-fire.

But at ten that evening, in a valley with acoustics so extraordinary that even the sound of someone chopping firewood could sound like gunshots, the fighters at Wounded Knee heard something new come over the government radio. A voice counted down "four, three, two, one, GO!" and a few seconds later fifty aerial flares turned night into day. Fire rained on the bunker the rebels had named Little Big Horn, as anonymous gunmen opened up from the hills on both government and insurgent positions.

Gunfire continued through the night. Chaos ensued. APCs, outfitted in recent days with the .50-caliber guns, hunted warriors on patrol. Goons coordinated their movements with the marshals. The government radio personnel calmly discussed the location of the third party with Wounded Knee security, advising the village's fighters on where to look for the targets who were firing on both the government and Wounded Knee. The government, for the first time, used tear gas against the village. Warriors who had survived tours of duty in Southeast Asia looked at each other and shook their heads when it was over, wondering how so many in the village managed to survive. The village took thousands of rounds during thr firefight. The battle finally ended Friday afternoon. The government side suffered no casualties.

Inside Wounded Knee, there were injuries. One man had been shot through both legs, another in the hand, and a woman received lacerations from flying glass. The fourth casualty was the most serious. Buddy Lamont had been shot and killed. A bullet pierced his heart and shattered the stock of his rifle, ending his life and, effectively, the Wounded Knee occupation. On the same day in Los Angeles, FBI agents arrested Russell Means for violating the terms of his bond. In Rapid City, Pedro Bissonette was arrested and held without bail when he asked for a hearing on Wounded Knee–related charges from March.

Except for the formal closures of Lamont's and Clearwater's funerals, it was pretty much the end. In the days following Buddy Lamont's death, the shattered buildings matched the feeling inside Wounded Knee. As a result of the firefight, the village's electricity was cut off. Wounded Knee had no power, no telephone, no running water, and very little food.

Sunday night, April 29, brought cold rain and further disaster when a kerosene lamp ignited curtains in the trading post, setting it ablaze. Aided by strong winds, the fire burned for hours as the occupiers hauled buckets of water through rain and mud in a futile, exhausting effort to save the building.

The next evening President Nixon tried to put out fires of his own with a televised address to the nation on Watergate. Disclosures in recent weeks had moved the scandal from a minor incident that mainly fascinated people in Washington to a national obsession, and growing talk of impeachment had forced the President to take extreme measures. He announced the resignations of his two closest aides, H. R. Haldeman and John Ehrlichman, and of Richard Kleindienst, the Attorney General. He also fired John Dean, the disloyal White House counsel who had met with prosecutors, and replaced him with Leonard Garment.

Garment, so instrumental in representing the administration in the Alcatraz and BIA takeover situations, had new priorities. But he still kept in touch with his emissary Hank Adams. Adams felt betrayed by Garment after the BIA takeover, but that didn't really matter. Both Garment and Adams still wanted to prevent the striking of the match.

On Monday, April 30, as Nixon prepared for his speech and villagers surveyed the ruins of the trading post, a twenty-one-car procession left Rapid City with the body of Frank Clearwater. It was still raining as the caravan traveled on Highway 40 through the Badlands before entering Pine Ridge.

Morningstar Clearwater had asked permission for her husband to be buried at Wounded Knee. Wilson denied her request, explaining that because Clearwater was not Oglala he could not be buried on the reservation. One occupation supporter ridiculed Wilson's reasoning, referring to other non-Oglalas interred on Pine Ridge: "Guess we'll have to dig up all those white people." Mrs. Clearwater finally agreed to have her husband buried on Crow Dog's property on the Rosebud Reservation, but insisted on having a wake on Pine Ridge at Chief Fools Crow's house.

When the caravan reached Pine Ridge, a BIA policeman stopped the cars and read a tribal order that granted permission for the body of Frank Clearwater, his wife, and Oglalas to enter, but denied permission for everyone else. Each car was inspected and handed a copy of the rain-soaked order. Half of the cars were found to contain non-Oglalas and turned back. To his opponents it was Wilson at his most odious.

At Fools Crow's, the coffin was placed in a tepee and covered with a blanket, as the mourners, mostly people who never knew Clearwater, shared hot cherry soup and beef stew. The next day Clearwater was buried on Crow Dog's land at Rosebud.

The rebellion's two fatalities were almost perfectly chosen opposites. Everyone on the reservation knew Buddy Lamont, and his death touched even those who hated AIM and hated the occupation. He was not a big talker, or one of the Vietnam vets who spoke approvingly of Ho Chi Minh. Nor did he self-consciously try to wrap himself in the nineteenth century mystique of the Lakota warrior. He was just Buddy, Agnes's only son, a local kid who had worked for the tribal office until he disagreed with their politics. Buddy Lamont's death moved people because everyone knew him and he had spent his life on Pine Ridge. Frank Clearwater's death moved people because no one knew him—he had been at Wounded Knee only a day.

On May 1, the warring parties resumed their talks. This time, instead of a tepee, the negotiations were held in two school buses inside the DMZ. It was an awkward venue. In March, if the two sides frequently talked past each other, they were at least facing one another. In the school buses they couldn't even do that.

In one bus the occupation's military leaders conferred with the chief of the U.S. Marshals and Assistant Attorney General Hellstern. Political talks were underway in the other school bus, where Frizzell desperately tried to convince eight designated Oglalas to end the occupation.

Verona Crow Dog, Leonard Crow Dog's sister, told Frizzell that if he would only send the White House representatives to Wounded Knee for serious talks then perhaps the occupation could end. Frizzell told her that would not be easy, and took the opportunity to update the Oglalas on recent Washington developments. "Do you know what's been going on at the White House the last day or two? Attorney General Kleindienst resigned, and will be replaced by Elliot Richardson, who is now Secretary of Defense. Mr. Ehrlichman and Mr. Haldeman resigned, on the immediate staff of the president. And John Dean, the attorney or special counsel to the president, resigned. So I really don't know if they can scare up eight bodies around the White House to come out here. Mr. Kissinger has got so many problems over in Vietnam with that treaty that was signed, that he can't possibly come here. Things are happening so fast back there I can't tell you who they would send or how many."

Gladys Bissonette and the other Oglalas continually turned the discussion back to the treaty of 1868, while the government only wanted to talk about disarmament, just as they had wanted to in the March negotiations. Frizzell was willing to promise almost anything if only the Indians would lay down their weapons. "All of those fears that you have, aren't going to be resolved as long as you have the confrontation here at Wounded Knee. If we can end this, we will have the guns available to protect you. We'll keep a residual force of FBI and marshals. We'll set up a police station right down in Wounded Knee. But we can't do it as long as you're down there and all of our officers are engaged in a warlike action . . . I'm willing to give you a meeting in Washington, here, wherever you want it, with representatives of the White House to discuss any and all matters on an agenda regarding the 1868 treaty . . . but I can't do that as long as the arms are in Wounded Knee." Frizzell pleaded with the Oglala negotiators to meet him "half-way."

Frizzell's tone became more urgent. "The Secretary of the Interior, I've talked with him, he agrees with me. The Attorney General of the United States agrees with me, the White House agrees with me, but they're all of one mind: 'This thing can't go on indefinitely. You've got one more chance . . . and if you don't get it across, then the hard decisions are going to be made.'" Frizzell wanted to be sure Gladys and the others understood what he meant. He was the good cop. The bad ones had itchy fingers on big guns, and they would make April's firefights seem like sparklers at a kid's birthday party. "I don't know how to tell you any plainer. I don't want that hard decision to be made."

The school bus negotiations resolved little. The Oglalas would not meet Frizzell "half-way." When they spoke of beatings by Wilson's goons or the centrality of the Fort Laramie Treaty, Frizzell answered with homilies about the good and bad politicians in his home town. He told them you have to get rid of the bad ones, but peacefully. You can't go down to city hall with guns. "Those in city hall," he told them, "control the police, and you're going to be met with resistance every time."

As the Oglalas saw it they had tried to remove their bad politician through legal means, only to see Wilson preside over his own impeachment hearing. They had not surrounded the tribal offices in Pine Ridge, it was the federal government that had surrounded them. "We are tired," Gladys said. "We don't care if we die here. We can't even turn in our complaints. We turn in our petitions—there's nothing done." Dick Wilson, she continued, gives orders and the entire U.S. government listens. "The Indians, we never get listened to."

As if to prove the point, on May 2, a Rapid City jury completed its deliberations in the trial of Darld Schmitz, the white man who stabbed Wesley Bad Heart Bull in a reservation border town five months earlier. The jury acquitted Schmitz of second degree manslaughter. Sarah Bad Heart Bull, Wesley's mother, and dozens of other Indians still faced riot charges from the melee in Custer in February.

On May 3, the Lakota chiefs sent the White House a proposal that called for the establishment of a Presidential Treaty Commission. Two days later, Hank Adams, sent by Garment, arrived with the agreement. Although Adams was a personal envoy of the President of the United States, he was still *persona non grata* on Pine Ridge, and in his earlier visits Wilson had ordered Adams's expulsion from the reservation. Adams's mission to resolve the crisis had become public knowledge, and Wilson's antipathy had not lessened, so a rendezvous was arranged at the edge of the reservation. Frank Fools Crow and a hundred others gathered near a fence. Hank Adams handed the letter over a barbed-wire fence to Fools Crow, who came to the meeting attired in buckskin and a headdress.

The letter from Garment promised Fools Crow that the White House would agree to send representatives to a meeting on Pine Ridge to discuss the treaty in the third week of May, and also get tough with Wilson, who had so far treated Garment's mission with undisguised contempt. Garment had been unable even to get his emissary on the reservation, so it remained unclear how he proposed to take these measures against Wilson. But Fools Crow and the other leaders accepted the proposal. Only Buddy Lamont's funeral remained.

The funeral finally took place under gray skies on the afternoon of Sunday, May 6. Spring had not yet arrived; despite the calendar, the day was cold. Wilson's tribal government had insisted only Lamont's family would be permitted through the roadblocks, but more than one hundred people came to the village that afternoon. Buddy Lamont lay in the coffin in the Church of God, wrapped in the contradictions of his life. He was dressed in his army uniform from Vietnam, wearing moccasins and beadwork. His hands held a pipe. Two flags covered his coffin, from each of the nations in whose service he had fought. One was the American flag. The second was the Wounded Knee flag. It read "Wounded Knee, 1890–1973," with colors of red, yellow, black, and white, representing the four races and the four directions.

"This is the only son I have," Agnes Lamont told the small crowd. "I have nothing but girls, only this." She remembered when he said he wanted to go to Vietnam. "He didn't have to go and fight. They told him he didn't have to go. And I told him he didn't have to go, I need him at home. 'No, mom, what should I do at home when the rest of them are going?' I prayed nothing will happen, I will see my son alive. And God must have answered my prayers—he came home alive.

"And again, when he joined this, when the roadblocks were open, I met him right out here. He's a big eater, he loves to eat. I brought him food for two days. I asked him to go home. 'I need you at home,' I said. 'Well, mom, maybe you need me, but,' he said, 'I'm here for a good cause.' He said, 'Watch now, we're going to win. We're going to come to the top. And you're going to be happy. All the people will be happy. So in the end we will win—you remember that,' he said . . . And that's the last I saw of him."

Dennis Banks, who gave the eulogy, said Buddy Lamont died a warrior's death. The fighters said farewell with a hundred-gun salute, and then he was lowered into a grave near Big Foot and the others who fell eighty-three years earlier.

Final agreement on the remaining details—principally on the one issue the federal government cared most passionately about, disarmament—came that night. The stand-down would take place in two days, on May 8.

Of AIM's leaders, only Dennis Banks and Carter Camp were still at Wounded Knee, and neither signed the agreement. Banks issued a written statement explaining his reasons. "I have reviewed the agreement and find that the document falls outside the protection of the U.S. Constitution. I will submit to the arms laying down because the chiefs and headmen have agreed. Also, AIM's job is done here. It must be understood that AIM was called on to aid these Oglalas in their struggle against repressive government forces."

Leonard Crow Dog and Carter Camp chose to surrender a day early. Both men were handcuffed, shackled, and chained, and at their arraignment in Rapid City bail was set at $70,000 for Camp and $35,000 for Crow Dog. They were required to post the entire amount, in cash or collateral, and neither could. High bail, and even chains, for gun-toting AIM leaders might be expected, but Indians found Crow Dog's treatment shocking. His spiritual practice forbade him from even carrying weapons, and they could not imagine a white religious leader being handled the same way.

The night before the stand-down Dennis Banks and dozens of others somehow eluded the federal perimeter, whose troops were in maximum alert just to prevent such a possibility. A Navajo warrior named Lenny Foster sought spiritual guidance for the group's journey, and they managed to pass within a few feet of the marshals and somehow avoid detection.

As Dennis Banks, Lenny Foster, and the others raced through the hills hoping to be as far from Wounded Knee as they could before sunrise, buses pulled up in front of border town motels and began ferrying government lawmen into position for the standdown.

At 7:00 A.M. the armored personnel carriers once again withdrew from their positions. Occupiers and feds slowly walked away from their bunkers. A helicopter carrying an Oglala headman flew from government bunker to government bunker to verify that no agents remained.

Television networks returned to cover the final hours of the drama, but only CBS managed to get in, and they could only observe the beginning of the stand-down before they were discovered and then arrested by the marshals. The rest were kept miles away and saw nothing of what happened.

The final moments of the occupation did not end on a note of grace or dignity. Instead, marshals used two warriors as metal detectors, ordering them to sit on the front of a jeep as it surveyed the area for land mines. Arvin Wells, an occupier designated to assist marshals in their inspection of the village, watched as they removed the AIM flag from the church steeple and replaced it with the U.S. flag. The marshals—the ones chosen for this assignment all seemed to have been Green Berets—insisted that Wells and the other occupiers observe the victory ceremony that accompanied the change in flags. The ceremony ended with the firing of automatic weapons.

The rest of the occupiers were at the main federal roadblock, where they stood in line and waited to be fingerprinted, interviewed, photographed. If they had outstanding warrants, they were arrested and taken to Rapid City. Supporters from the reservation offered encouragement, and the AIM song—the song given to AIM by grateful Lakotas in appreciation for the Raymond Yellow Thunder campaign—rang out as the warriors waited in the hot sun for their processing and their school bus ride to Rapid City. Also on the bus were the four men from the CBS crew.

Careful protocols had been worked out in the accords on access to the village, which were designed expressly to prevent carloads of Wilson supporters from racing into the shattered hamlet. The protocol failed grotesquely. The CRS in particular expressed outrage at the Wilson people's rampage in its reports, but no one else on the government side seemed concerned.

The television crews offered graphic footage of mindless destruction. The village looked as if it had been in the middle of a war zone for six weeks, which was shocking enough, but the press tours focused on demented acts of vandalism. Dick Wilson, as if unaware of the role his supporters may have played, offered commentary from behind his dark glasses, expressing little surprise at what he saw. "These hoodlums and clowns—that's how they live."

The damage included the theft and desecration of religious objects belonging to Wallace Black Elk and Leonard Crow Dog. The occupiers had made special arrangements to preserve the objects, which were intact when the insurgents left and trashed after the tribal government once again controlled the town.

The occupiers turned in their weapons as the agreement called for, but they turned out to be, in Hellstern's words, "a lot of old crap." Even he seemed a bit amused by the toy bow and arrow set, the plastic M16s, the carved wooden rifles, and the rusting .22s. Still, he wasted no time in declaring victory, telling the press "We've broken AIM." He also shared his views on lessons for future Wounded Knees: "I would like to see law enforcement people deal with these things as they would a bank robbery."

Gladys Bissonette, for one, was not ready to admit defeat. "Well, for myself, I think this was one of the greatest things that ever happened in my life. And although today is our last day here, I still feel like I'll always be here because this is part of my home. We didn't have anything here, we didn't have nothing to eat. But we had one thing—that was unity and friendship amongst sixty-four different tribes and that's more than I could say that the Pine Ridge Reservation has ever had in my life. I have never seen anything like this and although we were half-starved here, we didn't mind it. We were all happy together and it is kind of sad to see everyone leave but we know we'll all be together again, soon."

Stanley Lyman, the BIA superintendent, stopped by Wounded Knee on the afternoon of May 8. He surveyed the burned trading post and the scattered debris of all kinds—clothing, discarded weapons, food, and spent cartridges. Yellow tractors were already at work knocking down the bunkers. The occupation had been a nightmare for Lyman. The reservation had been invaded not just by the AIM troublemakers but also by federal officials who usually ignored and patronized him. He was sickened at the cost of the government's operations, knowing how far that money could have gone to meeting the desperate human needs of the reservation.

He noticed, for the first time, that amid the trash and destruction green grass had sprouted. Looking up, he saw the American flag fly-ing right-side-up from the church, and his mood brightened. At last the ordeal was over, and Pine Ridge could finally get back to normal.

The events of the last ten weeks had shaken him to the core. The unquenchable rage of Indians he thought he knew raised profound doubts. He had to face the reality that many of the ten thousand Oglalas truly despised the tribal government, and his role in sup-porting it. The next day, when the news summary told President Nixon the occupation had ended "with nary a shot fired," he jotted instructions for his aides to send "Congrats to our people who han-dled this."

On May 17, the Oglalas finally got their White House meeting. Leonard Garment sent his aide Brad Patterson. The agreement called for five White House aides, but only Patterson and one other member of the delegation were from the White House. The others were from different agencies.

Patterson later called it "a symbolic solution for a symbolic oc-cupation. When those guys picked Wounded Knee—what a place!" Patterson told Fools Crow and the others that treaties were a dead letter. But the trip was successful in another respect, as Patterson re-membered this pivotal moment in Lakota history: "Some bad things were breaking in Washington, I think some Watergate exposures were coming up. Then all of a sudden the papers came out with pic-tures of this old Indian chief escorting me by the hand. He grabbed my hand and hauled me across the field, me and my briefcase and him in his feathers. It turned out that was one of the more favorable pictures of the Nixon administration around that time. It was a guy willing to listen to the Indians."

Listening to the Indians entailed only a polite nod when they brought up sovereignty or colonialism. If the Indians wanted to talk about a treaty from a hundred years ago, government officials would gladly promise to discuss the possibility of a treaty commission. Those demands, like the promise that high-level administration offi-cials would read and respond to the Twenty Points in Washington at the Trail of Broken Treaties, were the easy issues.

To traditional Oglalas, the meeting was a faint glimmer of hope that something might yet come from the extraordinary sacrifices made during the previous two months. To Brad Patterson, it was a photo-op. Two documents written on May 4 provide strong evidence that some in the capital believed Wounded Knee was far more than symbolic. The defeated occupation managed to raise national security concerns at the highest level in Washington. Prior to a final resolution of Wounded Knee, a Justice Department options memo prepared exclusively for the Attorney General concerned itself with what course the government should take if Frizzell's final mission failed. Further talks, beyond the current round, would likely be unsuccessful, the memo stated, because "remaining in Wounded Knee offers to the Indians the following advantages: a) continuing publicity regarding the Indians' cause and the objectives of AIM; b) enhances the fundraising capacity of AIM; provides a lever to extract additional unilateral concessions by the U.S.; maintains the possibility of an incident that will increase public sympathy for the Indian cause."

The government could do nothing more in the way of concessions. Everything had been on the table except for payment of ransom, amnesty, and the suspension of the tribal government. Reversing policy on any of those items would invite "dissident groups to create other incidents similar to Wounded Knee;" and "the credibility of the U.S. to enforce the law would be gravely impaired."

The weak and hungry occupiers would have been fascinated by this unintentionally flattering assessment of their strength and capabilities: "Unilateral withdrawal by U.S. forces probably would lead to expansion of the territory controlled by the AIM militants. Such expansion could include areas of the Rosebud Reservation as well as areas adjacent to Wounded Knee. This would increase the likelihood of guerrilla warfare involving all the Indian factions as well as the neighboring ranchers."

The memo ended with this recommendation: If the Frizzell mission has not succeeded by May 8, "the U.S. Marshals and the FBI will be given permission to terminate the Indian occupation of Wounded Knee by whatever force they deem necessary."

Wyman Babby, Stanley Lyman's boss, wrote the same day to a senate staffer organizing hearings into Wounded Knee. He also viewed AIM as an organization capable of extraordinary achievements. Babby argued that the Wounded Knee occupation "has crystallized revolutionary movement in the United States," and that where blacks and students had failed "to capture the national sympathy needed to support such an effort, the American Indian Movement has succeeded. We now see all minority groups attempting to bind themselves together in a national movement using Wounded Knee as the catalyst."

The memos were unmailed valentines of a sort to AIM's national leaders. The memo writers apparently had confidence that even though by the end of the takeover in May those leaders were either already in jail or facing numerous charges that carried lengthy prison sentences, they were possessed of such resourcefulness they might still manage to carry out new, large-scale occupations in surrounding reservations and, concurrently, guide the second American revolution.

AIM, which had always found ways to do so much with so little, could be proud that in the final, grim hours of the Wounded Knee takeover, they still managed to frighten government officials with visions of guerilla warfare spreading across the Plains.

During the spring and summer months of 1973, the village once again became a popular tourist attraction. Burned fields, military debris abandoned by the federal lawmen, and the occasional tattered white parachute hanging from a tree provided evidence that the strange rebellion in the Dakotas really happened. Visitors gazed into the lonely terrain and tried to visualize where the Indians and the American troops of both the first and second Wounded Knees had made history.

For Indian people, the movement's grand entry had raised dizzying hopes of respect for treaties and sacred lands, but also of a new kind of person, a new kind of democracy, and a new kind of Indian future. Those hopes lived on even as the memory of the seventy-one day siege faded. The season of occupations may have ended in defeat at Wounded Knee, but with those occupations a door had been opened, and with it a world of new possibilities.

Epilogue

IM had promised the Lakota revolution on Pine Ridge would be only the beginning, but the seventy-one day uprising instead marked the high tide of the most remarkable period of activism carried out by Indians in the twentieth century.

Wounded Knee proved to be the final performance of AIM's daring brand of political theater. As quickly as Indian radicalism had exploded on the national stage, it faded, disintegrating under the weight of its own internal contradictions and divisions, and a relentless legal assault by federal and state governments. In the months and years following the dissolution of the Independent Oglala Nation, Indians once again became a flickering, intermittent presence in the public affairs of the United States.

As should be clear by now, AIM was never the whole of the Indian movement. But the organization's decline marked the turning point for the rest of Indian activism. That fall came with breathtaking suddenness. Two months after the stand-down at Wounded Knee, the movement held its annual convention in White Oak, Ok-

269

lahoma, convening for the first time in the state with the largest Indian population. It was a crucial test of AIM's assertion that it had
wide support throughout Indian country. The meeting was a poorly
organized and sparsely attended disaster. Then, in August, on the
Rosebud reservation in South Dakota, an altercation among several
AIM people resulted in one national leader shooting another. Carter
Camp was the shooter, and Clyde Bellecourt the victim. Bellecourt
did not press charges, and Alcatraz leader John Trudell, invisible
during Wounded Knee but recently elected National Chairman,
lamely implied the government was somehow involved. The incident
caused severe damage to AIM's already fraying reputation. In October, the Oglala leader Pedro Bissonette was shot and killed in a
shoot-out with BIA police on Pine Ridge.

As AIM unraveled, the Justice Department launched an unprecedented legal assault on movement leaders, followers, and supporters. During the seven weeks of the Wounded Knee occupation,
the federal government arrested 562 people on charges directly connected to the siege. Dozens more were arrested in riot conspiracy
charges across the country.

The unique feature of the government's prosecution lay in its decision to bring to trial every possible case it could, without undue
concern for winning convictions. "AIM's most militant leaders and
followers, over three hundred, are under indictment, in jail or warrants are out for their arrest. But the government can win even if no
one goes to prison," argued Colonel Volney Warner in a succinct description of the government's legal strategy.

It was a brilliant move, and a major departure from government
practice in other high-profile cases against other radicals of the era.
It recognized that immobilizing AIM was more important than
putting any individual behind bars. Even a well-organized and financially stable group would have withered under the pressure and expense of defending so many of its members; for AIM the task was
overwhelming.

Trials took place for two years in South Dakota, Nebraska, and
Iowa, often at the same time. Staff from the valiantly named
Wounded Knee Legal Defense/Offense Committee survived on food
stamps. In Sioux Falls, WKLD/OC headquarters was an empty

apartment building scheduled for demolition, and in Lincoln the legal committee lived and worked at the barracks of an abandoned Air Force base out of town. The trials became a bizarre coda to Wounded Knee, where government lawyers prosecuted Indians for crimes ranging from sedition to cattle rustling. The proceedings were almost invisible, often covered only by local newspapers. AIM argued it was the subject of the largest mass political trial in United States history, but few were listening.

The Wounded Knee trials did, however, provide one last moment of stardom for Banks and Means. Government prosecutors decided to try the pair together, apart from other leaders, and the case was scheduled for St. Paul. The two AIM leaders, aided by William Kunstler, turned the courtroom into a stage. They effectively put the federal government on trial, introducing evidence and calling witnesses who spoke vividly of the harsh conditions on Pine Ridge. The proceedings captivated the Twin Cities for months in early 1974. When the judge dismissed the charges because of government misconduct, the national spotlight again briefly shined on Means and Banks.

Even with that success, the trials bankrupted the movement and placed AIM permanently on the defensive. Miraculously, with severely limited resources, WKLD/OC managed to win 92 percent of the cases, yet as Colonel Warner predicted, the government emerged as the real victor.

Even the trials that resulted from the riots in Custer extracted a heavy toll on AIM. The killer of Wesley Bad Heart Bull, whose death had been a key trigger in the events that led inexorably to Wounded Knee, won acquittal during the final days of the occupation. Russell Means, Dennis Banks, and others in AIM still faced riot charges for Custer, as did Sarah Bad Heart Bull herself. Wesley's mother, photographed by news cameras with a South Dakota riot stick across her throat on the courthouse steps that snowy afternoon in February 1973, saw her case finally reach trial in 1974. She was convicted and sentenced to one to three years in prison. At her sentencing, a judge reluctantly granted her twenty-four hours to make arrangements for her children.

The legal offensive against AIM not only bankrupted the movement, but the Justice Department negotiators also reneged on their promise to prosecute the Pine Ridge goons. Despite their pledge to bring an end to the reign of terror on the reservation, no indictments were ever returned against the goons. In fact, political violence increased on Pine Ridge, and a low-level civil war raged in a desultory fashion for more than two years after the occupation.

It was the very outcome feared by AIM, and the reason it considered the Justice Department's offer to stay on the reservation and keep the Wilson forces in check. But when the occupation ended and AIM's most pressing battles took place in the courtroom, the goons once again had the upper hand and used the opportunity to settle many scores against movement activists and their allies.

Three women who were among the strongest and most eloquent supporters of the rebellion paid the highest price. Agnes Lamont, who never wavered in her opposition to the Wilson government, lost her only son during the occupation. Gladys Bissonette, whose passionate speech at Calico moved many to tears, lost her son Pedro in a gun battle with BIA police six months later. Ellen Moves Camp— another fiercely articulate activist who negotiated for the occupation force with senior Justice Department officials—saw her son Louis, under intense pressure from the FBI, testify against Russell Means and Dennis Banks in the St. Paul trial.

Apart from legal battles, there were other obstacles that worked to prevent AIM from making itself relevant to large numbers of Indian people: government surveillance and infiltration. Most people in AIM assumed that the movement had its share of government informers; its informal style and lack of rigid structure made the group easy to monitor. But few imagined just how compromised AIM was until Douglass Durham, Dennis Banks's trusted lieutenant who carried the title of Director of Security, held a press conference in 1975 and announced he had been working for the FBI for two years.

By then Russell Means had been arrested thirteen times, was free on bonds totaling $130,000, and could look forward to eight separate trials. Dennis Banks was a fugitive. Leonard Crow Dog, Carter Camp, and Stan Holder were convicted of Wounded Knee charges and sent to federal prison.

Yet for all the disorganization, AIM still commanded the respect of many Indian people. Even Vine Deloria, one of AIM's frequent critics, found himself impressed at the way AIM was regarded on one South Dakota reservation after he visited in June, 1973, shortly after Russell Means had been freed on bail.

The Standing Rock Sioux tribe held a two-day meeting to discuss a proposal that all elected tribal council members hold discussions with their constituents at least once a month. Major Indian organizations were invited to participate. So too, Deloria wrote, was AIM.

Deloria and other experts offered a pessimistic view of the political outlook for the Sioux. They told the reservation people that lobbying in Congress was necessary to prevent efforts to weaken their treaty rights, but that even with effective lobbying it was likely those rights would be steadily eroded.

Means arrived on the second day. He introduced the AIM singers, who performed the AIM song in honor of Raymond Yellow Thunder. He prayed and invoked the name of Black Elk. Means began his speech by reviewing the efforts of the Sioux to win justice from the United States for more than a century. He argued that Lakota people must win their treaty rights by any means possible. He said AIM won at Wounded Knee, because kids on Pine Ridge now play "AIM and Goon Squad" instead of "Cowboys and Indians", and all the boys wanted to be AIM and none wanted to be the goon squad.

Deloria wrote of his reaction to this talk. "As I was listening to Russell Means I continually looked around the room to see the faces of the people as he spoke. Almost every face shone with a new pride." It was, he said, "a beatific vision of the tribe as it should be, not as it had become through a century of betrayal. Old men sat entranced and nodded ever so slightly at the different points Russell discussed.

"I came away from Means's speech with the feeling that Russell is a terribly important man to our tribe. He may be the greatest Lakota of this century and his ability to light the eyes that have been dimmed so long is probably more important for us than anything that anyone else can do. I think it is the pride in living that many Indians have lost and in the manner of clarity of Russell Means's speech many Indian people found that pride and also found a strength they did not know they had possessed."

He ended his paean to Russell Means saying "we should cherish this man as one of our greatest people. History has a way of leveling all the honors of a century and allowing the truly great figures to emerge from the shadows as they really were.

"I am thankful that in my time I have been allowed to know three great Indians—Clyde Warrior, Hank Adams, and Russell Means. If we had a hundred like them we would now rule the world. But every race is given only a few people of this stature in each century. I still have fundamental disagreements with Russell in a number of areas and I am still keenly aware that the problems of enforcing treaties are more complicated than anyone believes. And I am not likely to be in the ranks at the next AIM protest because I don't think that they are very well planned events.

"But I cannot remain silent because of disagreements over strategy and allow a chance to go by to honor as best I can a man who gave to my tribe even for a brief moment, a vision of something better than what we had. If Russell Means has faults, and we all do, he also has talent and dedication which greatly outweigh the faults and which in my mind make him one of the great Indians of our time."

As if to underscore Deloria's point, Means somehow managed to run for tribal president against his nemesis Dick Wilson in February 1974, even as he stood trial in Minnesota, and forced Wilson into a run-off. Wilson narrowly won that election. Means attributed his loss to voter fraud. The U.S. Civil Rights Commission investigated Means's complaints and found so many violations it called for a new election. Wilson declined to take their advice. In that election, as in so many other movement crusades, Means could claim a moral victory.

Apparently, to most in AIM, that moral victory was enough. There has been surprising public and private interest in gaining a more careful measure of the movement's success and failure. The movement failed dismally in transmitting to later activists the lessons of its campaign of popular struggle. The result was that although most in Indian country would agree AIM had a profound impact on the lives of Indian communities in the 1970s, few could agree on what that impact was. There was remarkably little dialogue about what to keep and what to discard in the continuing struggle for Indian empowerment.

One of the few critiques came in a penetrating analysis delivered fifteen years after AIM's high tide. Fittingly, it came from the executive director of the National Indian Youth Council in a speech to students. Jerry Wilkinson was a Cherokee in his forties who led a group composed of young people of the Southwest. He reveled in contradictions and provided no shortage of them in his critique. To Wilkinson, it was Procter and Gamble who provided the most devastating evidence of the Indian movement's decline into irrelevance. He noted the consumer products giant had named a new toothpaste AIM, adding wryly that it was "perhaps the greatest slap in the face the white society has given us in the past fifty years."

He praised the movement for making Indians visible, for emboldening tribal leaders who previously had been afraid to criticize the government, for instilling pride in Indian people. Most people, he said, were at protest events "not primarily to correct a wrong but to make a personal identity statement and assert their pride in being Indian."

He also noted the most frequent criticisms of the Indian movement leaders. Many complained that they "gave big speeches about the earth and the sacred Indian way by day and then got drunk or took dope in the disco by night," made fantastic claims for Indian religion, or misappropriated church grants. But Wilkinson added that although valid, these were not the crucial failings.

Wilkinson focused his critique instead on what he considered the movement's two main weaknesses. "It did not create a tradition of people relentlessly, ceaselessly, and uncompromisingly pursuing a long-range goal," he said. "There were plenty of manifestoes with plenty of demands but these are not what moved people." He contrasted the movement's lack of clear goals with the success of the civil rights movement in winning passage of the voting rights legislation. For Indians, "it was generally more important to throw these [demands] in somebody's face than to get them to act on it."

Wilkinson argued the movement's second major failing was that it became "terribly anti-intellectual. Everybody was for sovereignty, the Indian way, and traditional religion, but there were as many ideas about what these things were as there were people involved. Anyone raising questions about these things was highly suspect."

Wilkinson spoke of NIYC's files from the early 1960s, full of lengthy, thoughtful letters from Clyde Warrior, Herb Blatchford, and Mel Thom debating the future direction of their organization. By the late 1960s, Wilkinson said, the telephone replaced correspondence, and Indian leaders rarely wrote letters or articles. "Intellectual growth in the Indian community over the last twenty years has been next to zero. Without an intellectual base we cannot build strength or consensus in the Indian community or achieve the capacity to critically assess ideas and people so as to determine what to do next."

Wilkinson said he understood the reasons the movement had not built an environment filled with sharp political debate. Such discussions might have ended up "splitting hairs . . . This may have been right but in retrospect I think not. I think such reflection would have been healthy in creating ideas and bringing more tolerance for people with different ideas," he said. "For what we have now is the legacy of a movement in which people fought and even died for, ideas as still undefined in people's minds."

He ended his address with familiar exhortations for "a new kind of warrior," who could work hard and gain skills of the modern world to support his community, adding that this new warrior would also benefit from "intangibles the last movement sorely lacked, things like tolerance, kindness, good humor."

Wilkinson's point about the ambiguous nature of the movement's history was sharply underscored by the historical ignorance of his own audience. Few of the young people who heard Wilkinson that night in 1987 knew of the people he spoke of from the early 1960s. The people Wilkinson considered heroes of Indian resistance—Warrior, Thom, and Blatchford, for example, Indian leaders who were as proud of their academic training and intellectual skills as they were of their radical activism—were largely forgotten.

Most of those young people knew of AIM's glory days, but were confused in the details. By the late 1980s an AIM dog soldier named Leonard Peltier had arguably become more famous than any AIM leader. Peltier was serving two life sentences after being convicted of murdering two FBI agents in a 1975 shoot-out on Pine Ridge. A national campaign that gave him equal billing with Nelson Mandela toured college campuses, and documentaries cast him as a symbol of Indian resistance. He was often referred to as an AIM leader, though he would be more accurately described, before the shoot-out, as a not particularly beloved AIM regular. The 1975 incident and Wounded Knee, though two years apart and occurring in vastly different circumstances, had become conflated with time, and Leonard Peltier, to many young Indian activists, was vaguely understood to be a key AIM leader who was framed for shooting FBI agents during the occupation of Wounded Knee. Thus, even Wounded Knee itself, AIM's premier accomplishment, had become hazy, another "undefined idea in people's minds."

AIM won attention, but what did the attention win? The occupations from Alcatraz to Wounded Knee illustrated both the vast possibilities and the stark limitations of a politics based on symbols and media. AIM could highlight a problem, but failed to make a compelling case for its own vision of change. The Indian movement consistently underestimated its opposite numbers, and failed to grasp that others could also master the dramaturgy of guerrilla theater. At Alcatraz, Washington, and Wounded Knee, the moment came when Indians said "meet our demands or kill us." Garment and Patterson understood that if they massacred Indians the government would be the loser. They knew the Indian leadership was rarely united, and took advantage of the fact that the demands were often contradictory. They knew time, in every case, was on the federal government's side, and that if they could just keep talking eventually the rebel forces would tire. For all the charisma and savvy of AIM's leaders, in the end they found themselves outmaneuvered at their own game by White House aides.

The movement's three and a half years in the spotlight were, however, more than a show of guerrilla theater tactics. It was also a season of struggle for power and respect, for treaty rights and personal validation, for economic and political justice. Most importantly, it gave thousands of Indians a *raison d'être*, an opportunity to be important to their own communities.

Indians found a way to be more than a footnote and to force fundamental reassessments of what it meant to be Indian, of American history, of each other, and of their communities. The victory was uncertain at best, but for a brief, thrilling period of time no one quite knew what to expect of Indian communities.

In the years that followed, the Indian movement built on its experiences and matured in some respects, but it rarely demonstrated the kind of bold, imaginative strokes of genius that, for a brief season at the end of the 1960s, were poised to change everything.

If the movement's success in bringing pride to Indian communities was undisputed, it was also evident that it achieved few tangible accomplishments. AIM's leaders, on the other hand, pursued a range of careers with a curiously American sort of vigor and optimism.

Russell Means ran for vice president with a pornographer, ran for president as a Libertarian, built alliances with the right-wing religious leader Reverend Moon, picked up a rifle to fight the Sandinistas in Nicaragua, became a movie star, and still managed to command respect on reservations throughout Indian country. Dennis Banks declared himself a born-again capitalist. Clyde Bellecourt was sent to prison in the late 1980s for selling LSD to undercover agents. Vernon Bellecourt became a tireless advocate for Indians among progressives, and made several highly publicized trips to Libya. John Trudell abandoned politics and made interesting, jangly records of his poetry. Although Means was the only AIM leader to have a career in Hollywood, Trudell and Banks had several film credits as well. John Trudell has released the most recordings, although Russell Means also tried his hand in that arena. His CD featured a track called "Nixon's Dead Ass."

In late 1993, one faction of what remained of the American Indian Movement called for a people's tribunal to place Vernon and Clyde Bellecourt on trial for "being in collusion with the U.S. government in passing bills of genocide." Both Bellecourts showed up for the trial and strenuously contested the charges.

For the rank and file, in important respects little had changed. The Pine Ridge Reservation's civil wars ended, but it ranked in the 1980 and 1990 census as the poorest jurisdiction in the United States.

In December of 1990, Oglalas staged a 150-mile ride on horseback through bitter temperatures to remember and heal the wounds of the massacre of 1890. Former goons and former AIM members sought common ground in their shared spirituality forgiving each other for the pain of 1973, vowing to work together for the future of their people.

Cultural revival swept Indian communities, but it was also criticized by some as diluting tribal differences into a generic, pan-Indian culture almost as harmful as assimilation.

The Indian movement was an edgy, unpredictable creature that challenged American power in a way not equaled this century before or since. In the decades that followed, activists have tried and failed to re-create its passion and drama.

The days when Indian people invented meaning and community, stormed into the most notorious prison in the world, or fought the U.S. military machine for seven weeks as the world watched are, two decades later, like a shimmering mirage across a desert floor.

Indians in the 1990s are ubiquitous—in movies, in advertising, in New Age boutiques, and as spiritual and environmental role models. Their political space, however, has dramatically receded. Indian radicals still carry the torch of the 1970s, but their actions are by comparison timid, predictable, and barely noticed. Hardy militants carry picket signs at Super Bowls and World Series, and petition the White House for executive clemency for Leonard Peltier, and the era when Indians seized the attention of the world is so distant as to seem more legend than history.

It was a spectacular ride, all the more exciting because no one really knew where they were headed. The fast times had more than their share of brilliant mistakes, misguided strategies, and foolish bravado. It also was a time of hope and idealism when Indians could imagine a university rising from the wreckage of a prison, when a bureaucratic fortress could become a Native American Embassy, when a desperately poor and repressive reservation might become a free and independent nation.

That a few thousand who fought to bring power and visibility to the most ignored population in the United States failed to win all they dreamed can hardly be surprising. That they came so close is the miracle.

Notes

Chapter 1: Leap of Faith

1   Running without lights: Edward Castillo, interviewed by Robert Allen Warrior, Rohnert Park, California, July 20, 1993. Since this interview, Castillo has published a nearly identical account of his experiences at Alcatraz, Edward D. Castillo, "A Reminiscence of the Alcatraz Occupation," *American Indian Culture and Research Journal* 18 (4, 1994): 111–22.

1   felt like a soldier: Castillo interview.

1   November 20, 1969: Memorandum from Tom Hannon to file, 20 November 1969, box 3, Correspondence and Documents (8 of 16 [1 of 2]), Records Relating to the Disposal of Alcatraz Island, 1961–73 (J-California-786), RG 269, General Records of the General Services Administration, Region 9 Regional Office, San Francisco, National Archives–Pacific Sierra Region, San Bruno, California (hereafter GSA).

2   Castillo and the other passengers: Castillo interview. Other details about Castillo's journey across the Bay are from the same interview.

2   warming themselves: Castillo interview.

2   Garcia ... and ... Turner: Anthony Garcia, interviewed by Robert Allen Warrior, tape recording, Berkeley, California, January 4, 1994. The authors contacted Turner on a number of occasions, but were not able to arrange an interview.

3   people whom the educational system neglected: Most of the available literature on the occupation makes this point, see especially Garcia interview; Castillo interview; Jeff Sklansky, "Rock, Reservation, and Prison: The Native American Occupation of Alcatraz Island," *American Indian Culture and Research Journal* 13 (2, 1989): 39ff.; and Steve Talbot, "Indian Students and Reminiscences of Alcatraz," *American Indian Culture and Research Journal* 18 (4, 1994): 93–102. For an account of statewide Indian educational organizing, see Jack D. Forbes, "The Native Struggle for Liberation: Alcatraz," *American Indian Culture and Research Journal* 18 (4, 1994): 127.

3   "Anthony," said Turner: Garcia interview.

3   instructions to bring warm clothing: Garcia interview.

4   white and red helicopter: Garcia interview; Castillo, "A Reminiscence," 117.

4   worked together for months: For accounts of the planning, see Garcia interview; Quitiquit interview; LaNada Boyer, interviewed by Robert Allen Warrior, Fort Hall, Idaho by telephone, tape recording, September 28, 1994. See also LaNada Boyer, "Reflections of Alcatraz," *American Indian Culture and Research Journal* 18 (4, 1994): 77–9 (In writing this chapter, the authors used a nearly identical manuscript version of this essay that Ms. Boyer provided to them in January, 1993). Tim Findley, a reporter for the *San Francisco Chronicle* who knew about the planning, gives a great amount of credit to a woman Oakes worked with at San Francisco State ("Alcatraz Recollections," 66). In his recent dissertation about the occupation, Troy Johnson identifies the woman, based on Findley's notes, as Marlene Sharon (p. 98). Johnson, "The Indian Occupation of Alcatraz Island, Indian Self-Determination and the Rise of Indian Activism," (Ph.D. dissertation, UCLA, 1993, p. 91).

5   seventy-eight young Indians: The most reliable scholarly sources place the number of occupiers on November 20 at seventy-eight, seventy-nine, or eighty. Edward Castillo (see interview) recalls that the count taken the day of the landing was seventy-eight. See

also Johnson, "Indian Occupation," p. 143; and John Dominic Garvey, "The Government and the Indians: The American Indian Occupation of Alcatraz Island 1969–1971 (master's thesis, San Diego State University, 1993), p. 34. For accounts of the meetings the first days, see Castillo interview; Boyer interview; Quitiquit inter-view; Garcia interview; and Dennis Jennings, interviewed by Robert Allen Warrior, San Francisco, California, tape recording, January 6, 1994.

5   He would be their representative: While Oakes seems to have had the strong support of large number of the occupiers, many people were not, in fact, overly impressed with his leadership, while others opposed the very idea of having a spokesperson at all.

5   Richard Oakes: Richard Oakes, "Alcatraz is Not an Island," *Ramparts*, December, 1972, 35–41.

5   "I was working": Oakes, "Alcatraz is Not an Island," 35.

5   his second job: Oakes, "Alcatraz is Not an Island," 36.

6   San Francisco State College: Oakes, "Alcatraz is Not an Island," 36–7.

6   traveled the state in 1969: Oakes, "Alcatraz is Not an Island," 37–8. The full story of the development of Native American Studies at San Francisco State College in 1969 has not been written. For one account of the subject, see Luis M. Kemnitzer, "Personal Memories of Alcatraz, 1969," *American Indian Culture and Research Journal* 18 (4, 1994): 103–9. Kemnitzer recalls that American Indian students were not originally a part of the Third World Strike at SFSC and were added in later as a part of the La Raza group. A promising set of documents that tells at least part of the story is in the papers of Allan Miller (Seminole), box 4, files 20–32, Alcatraz Collection, San Francisco Public Library, San Francisco, California (hereafter SFPL).

6   Bay Area Indian community: For discussions of the Bay Area Indian community in the 1950s and 1960s, see Joan Ablon, "Relocated Indians in the San Francisco Bay Area," in Deward Walker, ed., *The Emergent Native Americans: A Reader in Culture Contact* (Boston: Little, Brown, 1972): 712–27 [reprinted from *Human Organization* 23 (Winter, 1964): 296–304]; and Adam Fortunate Eagle [Nordwall], *Alcatraz!*

Alcatraz! The Indian Occupation of 1969–1971 (Berkeley: Heyday Books, 1992), 19–26. Fortunate Eagle's book is a cause of controversy among many of those who occupied Alcatraz, since the author was involved almost strictly with the mainland part of the occupation. As an overall history of the occupations of Alcatraz, it indeed leaves much to be desired, but it is a fairly reliable account of Nordwall's activites before and during the occupation. See also Gerald Brown, interviewed by Paul Chaat Smith, Denver, Colorado, by telephone, tape recording, October 23, 1993; and Newspaper Articles Which Concern Native Americans (*San Francisco Chronicle* 1950–1965), Newsclippings, Community History Project, Oakland Intertribal Friendship House, Oakland, California.

6   departure from earlier policies: for extended analyses of the Indian Reorganization Act and its consequences, see Vine Deloria, Jr. and Clifford Lytle, *The Nations Within: The Past, Present and Future of American Indian Sovereignty* (New York: Pantheon, 1984); and Francis Paul Prucha, *The Great Father: The United States Government and the American Indians* (Lincoln: University of Nebraska Press, 1984), 917–1012; for interesting first-person accounts of the IRA and its effects, see Kenneth R. Philp, ed., *Indian Self-Rule: First-Hand Accounts of the Indian-White Relations from Roosevelt to Reagan* (Salt Lake City: Howe Brothers, 1986; reprint Logan: Utah State University Press, 1995), 28–109. For an account of Indian policy published by the federal government, see S. Lyman Tyler, *A History of Indian Policy* (Washington, D.C., United States Department of the Interior, Bureau of Indian Affairs, 1973).

7   Truman appointed Dillon S. Myer: For the fullest account of Myer's tenure as head of the Japanese American interment program and as Indian Commissioner, see Richard Drinnon, *Keeper of Concentration Camps: Dillon S. Myer and American Racism* (Berkeley: University of California Press, 1987).

7   a policy ominously named termination: Myer has been perhaps the most notorious of those who led the charge on the termination policy, but he is far from the only U.S. official to play a part in its design and implementation. For discussions of some of the others who developed and promulgated the policy, see Donald Fixico, *Termination and Relocation: Federal Indian Policy, 1945–1960*, esp. 158ff on the disastrous years of the policy after Myer under Commis-

sioner Glenn Emmons. Also, the policy could not have worked without the cooperation, and sometimes impetus, of those in Congress see Prucha, *The Great Father*, 1041ff. See also Prucha, *Great Father*, 1013–84 and Philps, *Self-Rule*, 112–85.

7   a related policy called relocation: Drinnon, *Keeper*, 240. Relocation was first proposed in the Meriam Report of 1928, was initiated on a small scale during the Depression and World War II, but wasn't a major feature of federal Indian policy until the 1950s. For detailed analysis, see Fixico, *Termination and Relocation*.

8   "have the advantages": Drinnon, *Keeper*, 242.

8   "in our . . . language" : Drinnon, *Keeper*, 240.

8   "Hitler and Mussolini": Drinnon, *Keeper*, 194.

8   replaced by a banker: Prucha, *Great Father*, 1041.

8   thirty-five thousand Indians moved: This is an approximate figure. Prucha reports 33,466 participants in the relocation program between 1953 and 1960. *Great Father*, 1082.

8   program rarely lived up to the promises: See, among others, Gladys Ellenwood, interviewed by Robert Allen Warrior, San Francisco, California, tape recording, April 7, 1993; Fixico notes many of the struggles relocatees faced, often without the aid of the bureaucrats who were supposed to be helping them (*Termination and Relocation*, 134ff). Prucha argues that many of these hard luck stories are exaggerations, but also contends that they contain more than an element of truth (*Great Father*, 1083).

9   Adam Nordwall: Fortunate Eagle, *Alcatraz! Alcatraz!*, 12, 23.

9   one of the local leaders: Fortunate Eagle, *Alcatraz! Alcatraz!*, 25ff

9   Intertribal Friendship House in Oakland: Fortunate Eagle, *Alcatraz! Alcatraz!*, 25. The Intertribal Friendship House's Community History Project has a fine collection of historical materials regarding the Bay Area Indian community.

9   United Council: Fortunate Eagle, *Alcatraz! Alcatraz!*, 26.

10   Nordwall and others took notice: Fortunate Eagle, *Alcatraz! Alcatraz!*, 14.

10   Fort Laramie Treaty of 1868: Fortunate Eagle, *Alcatraz! Alcatraz!*, 14.

10   March 8, 1964, forty Indians: Fortunate Eagle, *Alcatraz! Alcatraz!*, 15.
Russell Means offers his version of this story in *Where White Men
Fear to Tread: The Autobiography of Russell Means*, (with Marvin J.
Wolf), (New York: St. Martin's Press, 1995), 105ff. See also "Sioux
Stake Claim on the Rock," *San Francisco Chronicle*, March 9, 1964.

10   saw the action as a publicity stunt: Fortunate Eagle, *Alcatraz! Alcatraz!*, 15.

11   stories about the event: Fortunate Eagle, *Alcatraz! Alcatraz!*, 14–15.
Russell Means points to the press attention garnered by the brief
occupation as the moment he learned the impact of direct action
protest (*Where White Men Fear*, 106–7).

11   lawsuits to acquire title: For an account of the Sioux claim on Alcatraz based on the 1864 treaty, see Johnson, "Alcatraz," 64ff.

11   H. Lamar Hun . . . proposed: Findley, "Alcatraz Recollections," 63;
Fortunate Eagle, *Alcatraz! Alcatraz!*, 39ff. For one example of how
deeply many people in the Bay Area opposed the Hunt plan, see
"Dear Friend" letter from Alvin Duskin, December 22, 1969, San
Francisco Islands, Alcatraz, Indians, Magazines, San Francisco
Public Library, San Francisco, California.

12   planned to write up a proposal: Fortunate Eagle, *Alcatraz! Alcatraz!*, 38ff.

12   they talked up the idea: The extent to which Oakes and Nordwall
knew one another in the months leading up to the occupation is
unclear. Nordwall indicates that the two met in late October, (Fortunate Eagle, *Alcatraz! Alcatraz!*, 49). Oakes, in his *Ramparts* article,
distances himself from Nordwall ("Alcatraz is Not an Island," 38).
Chronicle reporter Tim Findley, who knew both men before the occupation, is unclear as to their relationship, and his suggestion that
Nordwall might have been Oakes's mentor seems improbable ("Alcatraz Recollections," 63).

12   San Francisco Indian Center burned: Fortunate Eagle, *Alcatraz!
Alcatraz!*, 40. Findley reports that most Indian people in the Bay
Area community believed the fire to have been set by "Samoans,"
as part of a "turf war in the Mission District" ("Alcatraz Recollections," 63).

13   Nordwall briefed the reporters: Fortunate Eagle, *Alcatraz! Alcatraz!*,
50; Findley, "Alcatraz Recollections," 63–4. While both of these

sources agree that a large number of reporters were present that night, Findley also says that various political leaders, perhaps even current San Francisco Mayor Willie Brown and Senator Diane Feinstein, were there. Findley, further, doesn't record Nordwall speaking to the group as a whole.

13   the student leader handled himself badly: Fortunate Eagle, *Alcatraz! Alcatraz!*, 109. Findley corroborates that Oakes drank heavily at the party, but doesn't indicate that he risked embarassing himself or the Nordwalls more than any of the other revelers ("Alcatraz Recollections," 64).

13   an action independent of Nordwall's: Oakes, "Alcatraz is Not an Island," 38. Nordwall/Fortunate Eagle portrays the actions as more unified than does Oakes, but he does little to account for just how much animosity toward him existed among many of the student leaders and others in the local Indian community. As Findley, a family friend and adopted son of Fortunate Eagle recently said, "Adam sometimes still embarrasses me with his reckless self-confidence and his certainty that everybody is bound to like him and his ideas. I think sometimes he is unaware that there are people who don't take him seriously" ("Alcatraz Recollections," 62).

14   let attorneys like him: Garcia interview.

14   Garcia loved order: Garcia interview.

14   Oakes grew impatient: Garcia interview. See also Findley, "Alcatraz Recollections," 66ff.

14   students filled blackboards: Quitiquit interview. See also Garcia interview; Boyer interview.

14   Nordwall drove: Fortunate Eagle, *Alcatraz! Alcatraz!*, 52ff.

14   "Where the hell are the boats?": Fortunate Eagle, *Alcatraz! Alcatraz!*, 53.

15   film crews . . . in position: Fortunate Eagle, *Alcatraz! Alcatraz!*, 53. See also, Findley, "Alcatraz Recollections," 67.

15   three-masted schooner: Fortunate Eagle, *Alcatraz! Alcatraz!*, 54.

15   the sound of cannons: Fortunate Eagle, *Alcatraz! Alcatraz!*, 56; Tim Findley, "Fourteen Indians Invade, Claim Alcatraz," *Chronicle* November 10, 1969.

15   would be no landing: Fortunate Eagle, *Alcatraz! Alcatraz!*, 54–5.

16   Oakes . . . jumped over the railing: Oakes, "Alcatraz is Not an Island," 38; Fortunate Eagle, *Alcatraz! Alcatraz!*, 57. See also Johnson, "Indian Occupation," 111ff.

16   Another one, then two more: Various sources place the number of those who jumped overboard at four or five. See Findley, "Fourteen Indians"; Oakes, Alcatraz is Not an Island, 38; Fortunate Eagle, *Alcatraz! Alcatraz!*, 57–8; Johnson, "Indian Occupation," 111–18.

16   He swam desperately: Oakes, "Alcatraz is Not an Island," 38. Sources are at odds as to whether those who jumped overboard actually swam to the island or were rescued from the frigid water and strong current. Adam [Nordwall] Fortunate Eagle contends that only one person, an Eskimo student named Joe Bill, was able to make it, and only then because he waited until the boat was in a more favorable position than when Oakes jumped. (*Alcatraz! Alcatraz!*, 57–8; and conversation with Robert Allen Warrior, Alcatraz Island, November 20, 1994). Joe Bill himself, however, has claimed that the others made it, as has Ross Harden, another of those who jumped. See Johnson, "Indian Occupation," 111–18. Tim Findley, whose byline appears on the *Chronicle* story about the November 9 attempt on this island, states in his article that the "four or five stalwarts" made it to the shore ("Fourteen Indians," 1). More recently, though, he has claimed, like Fortunate Eagle, that only Joe Bill made it ("Alcatraz Recollections," 67). The most revealing government account of the event supports the contention that four people made it to the island (Memorandum from Richard Laws, November 19, 1969, Box 3, Correspondence and Documents [8 of 16 (1 of 2)], GSA).

16   back at Fisherman's Wharf: Fortunate Eagle, *Alcatraz! Alcatraz!*, 58. See also Johnson, "Indian Occupation," 113–15.

16   Findley's story: Findley, "Fourteen Indians."

16   Oakes and thirteen others returned: Findley, "Fourteen Indians," 1; Fortunate Eagle, *Alcatraz! Alcatraz!*, 58. Some confusion exists as to when this landing and overnight occupation occurred. At some unknown point during the occupation, November 14 rather than November 9 began to be cited as the date when the fourteen occupiers spent the night (see, for instance, General Fact Sheet, Pro-

motional Materials—Forms, Box 3, File 27, SFPL). However unreliable daily newspaper reports might be, they cannot report events before they happen. Thus, November 9 seems an incontrovertible date for both the circling of the island and the later fourteen-person overnight occupation.

17   scouting expeditions: Findley, "Invaders Say 'We'll Be Back,'" *Chronicle* November 11, 1969.

17   he traveled to UCLA: Oakes, "Alcatraz is Not an Island," 38–9; Castillo interview; Jennings interview.

17   Nordwall . . . would be out of town: Fortunate Eagle, *Alcatraz! Alcatraz!*, 71; and Boyer interview. Boyer makes the same assertion in the manuscript version of her written account, but the published version does not include the two paragraphs in which she discusses her dissatisfaction with Nordwall ("Reflections of Alcatraz," ms version, 15; cf. published version, 79).

Chapter 2: We Won't Move

18   Coast Guard blockaded the island: Tim Findley, "Indians Reinforced—U.S. Delays Action," *Chronicle* November 22, 1969; and "The Rock Blockaded—Indians Vow to Stay," *Chronicle,* November 23, 1969.

18   land at the dock: Garcia interview.

18   making Alcatraz liveable: Quitiquit interview; Castillo interview. See also *Chronicle* reports from November 21–30.

19   "That's exactly what": Quitiquit interview.

19   Oakes as their spokesperson: Quitiquit interview; Castillo interview; Jennings interview; Garcia interview.

19   agreed to have a coordinating council: see typed list of committee members, Council Memoranda, Box 1, File 29, SFPL. This is no doubt one of several early organizational configurations during the first days of the occupation. See also Johnson, "Indian Occupation," 156ff.

19   the well of anarchism: Jennings interview; Castillo interview.

19   the group elected Ed Castillo: Castillo interview; One written record of island leadership from early in the occupation shows Castillo as one of seven members of a "Central Co-Ordinating [sic] Committee," with someone else listed in charge of a security and dock committee (Typed list of committee members, Council Memoranda, Box 1, File 29, SFPL).

19   Those with a stash: Quitiquit interview; Jennings interview; Castillo interview.

19   sit and watch the sunset: Castillo interview; Quitiquit interview.

19   "Here we are": Quitiquit interview.

20   they were the "invisible Americans": Tim Findley, "Invaders Claim Rock is Theirs," *Chronicle,* November 21, 1969.

20   San Francisco Board of Supervisors: Tim Findley, "A Tribal Feast on Alcatraz," *Chronicle,* November 27, 1969.

20   cast of the musical *Hair*: Findley, "Tribal Feast."

20   donations of food, clothing, and money: See various items in Correspondence, Inward, Donations, Box 1, File 6, SFPL and Correspondence, Inward, Donations of Money, Box 1, File 7, SFPL. See also Findley, "Tribal Feast"; Oakes, "Alcatraz is Not an Island," 39; Quitiquit interview; and Kay Boyle, "A Day on Alcatraz with the Indians," *New Republic,* January 17, 1970: 10.

20   she moved . . . into the warden's house: Quitiquit interview.

20   in charge of feeding: Quitiquit interview. Quitiquit points out that she worked with Linda Aranaydo, a Creek woman who is listed as in charge of the cooking committee during the early part of the occupation (see typed list of committee members, Council Memoranda, Box 1, File 29, SFPL).

21   blank, army-green logbook: Quitiquit interview.

21   press clippings from . . . England: See, for example, John Strand, "We've Captured Heap Big Wigwam!" *Saturday Titbits* (U.K.), San Francisco Islands-Alcatraz-Indians-Magazines, SFPL.

21   Gladys Ellenwood . . . from Idaho: Ellenwood interview.

22   "pretty much on my own": Ellenwood interview.

22   Alcatraz would become an extension: Ellenwood interview; Fortu-
      nate Eagle, *"Alcatraz! Alcatraz!,"* 77ff.

22   a sea of cooked turkeys: Ellenwood interview; Castillo interview;
      Marshall Schwartz, "Alcatraz Gathering of Indian Tribes," *Chron-
      icle,* November 28, 1969.

22   Bratskellar's . . . had volunteered: Schwartz, "Alcatraz Gathering."

22   Castillo . . . greeted those coming across: Castillo interview.

23   Adam Nordwall on its prow: Castillo interview.

23   Oakes had become a celebrity: Lynn Ludlow, "Oakes Has One
      Goal for Alcatraz: Unity," *Chronicle,* December 7, 1969; Findley, "Al-
      catraz Recollections," 65; Earl Shorris, *The Death of the Great Spirit:
      An Elegy for the American Indian* (New York: Simon and Schuster,
      1971), 272.

24   "We're only young people": Ludlow, "Oakes Has One Goal."

24   "It's hard to say": Ludlow, "Oakes Has One Goal."

24   "We have the ultimate punishment": Ludlow, "Oakes Has One
      Goal."

24   "a sad neglect": Council on Interracial Books, *Chronicles of American
      Indian Protest,* 314–15.

24   "I speak as a youth": Council on Interracial Books, *Chronicles of
      American Indian Protest,* 315.

25   one Seneca was startled: Pete Jemison, interviewed by Paul Chaat
      Smith, Washington, D.C., tape recording, November 11, 1993.

25   "Everywhere I went": Jerry Burns, "Alioto Says $2 Million Fee
      'Low,'" *Chronicle,* December 6, 1969.

25   newspapers reported: "Schooling and Plumbing," *Chronicle,* De-
      cember 4, 1969.

25   Creedence Clearwater Revival paid for: See, among others, Boyer,
      "Reflections of Alcatraz," ms version, 19. The name of the boat
      before the rock band bought it for Indians of All Tribes was the
      Bass Tub.

25   One concert took place at Stanford: "Benefit for Alcatraz," De-
      cember 18, 1969, tape recording, Pacifica Radio Archives, North

Hollywood, California. December 18 appears to be the date that Pacifica stations broadcast the tape of the concert. The *Chronicle* reports the concert as scheduled for December 13 at 8 P.M. (see Dale Champion "Burton's Plea on Alcatraz Indians," *Chronicle,* December 12, 1969).

25–6   the church is the focal point: Jane Stanford, the wife of university founder Leland Stanford, apparently took great care to make the church the center of the campus. Conversation with Joyce Cook, former staff member at Memorial Church, Stanford University, May 15, 1995.

26   "I would like to invite": "Benefit for Alcatraz."

26   "why we are not leaving": "Benefit for Alcatraz."

26   "This is going to become": "Benefit for Alcatraz."

27   "your government thinks": "Benefit for Alcatraz."

27   The opening act was Malvina Reynolds: "Benefit for Alcatraz."

27–8   headliner was Buffy Sainte-Marie: Benefit for Alcatraz. For lyrics to Sainte-Marie's songs, see *The Buffy Sainte-Marie Songbook* (New York: Grosset and Dunlap, 1971).

28   "Ladies and gentlemen": "Benefit for Alcatraz."

28   "Thank you," Oakes began: "Benefit for Alcatraz."

28   He read the Alcatraz Proclamation: Several versions of the proclamation, which no doubt have undergone several revisions over time, have appeared in print. The version we have used here comes from Fortunate Eagle, *Alcatraz! Alcatraz!*, 44–8. It differs slightly from what Nordwall read at the Stanford concert (see "Benefit for Alcatraz"). For another published version, see Council on Interracial Books for Children, *Chronicles of American Indian Protest* (Greenwich, Conn.: Fawcett, 1971), 310-13.

30   piles of it remained dockside: Jennings interview; Quitiquit interview.

30   "It felt like the monthly commodities": Oakes, "Alcatraz is Not an Island", 39.

31   Street punks and winos. See Shorris, *Great Spirit*, 239ff.

31   Castillo held out: Castillo interview.

31   Anthony Quinn or Jonathan Winters: Castillo interview. See also Tim Findley, "The Indians Claim Alcatraz Victory," *Chronicle* December 9, 1969; and "Surprise Visitor on Alcatraz," *Chronicle*, December 15, 1969.

32   did their share of partying: Castillo interview.

32   Castillo finally broke: Castillo interview.

32   Christmas on Alcatraz: Findley, "A Vital Indian Meeting on Confederation Plans," *Chronicle*, December 24, 1969;"A Hanukkah Gift to the Indians," *Chronicle*, December 8, 1969; Quitiquit interview.

32–33 "In the hall far below": Boyle, "A Day," 11.

33   pan-Indian conference: A large set of documents from the conference, including notes from group discussions, can be found at Council Minutes, December 23, 1969 (Conference Notes), Box 1, File 32, SFPL. For one personal account of the conference, see Ruth Dial, "Alcatraz Revisited," unpublished essay.

33   "most important conference": Findley, "Vital Indian Meeting."

33   Colin Wesaw knew none of this: Colin Wesaw interviewed by Paul Chaat Smith, by telephone, tape recorded April 21, 1993.

33-34 Oakes seemed kind and generous: Wesaw interview.

34   While in line: Wesaw interview.

34   a new semester . . . beckoned them: Wesaw interview.

34   "They would come to the island": Quitiquit interview.

34   a brilliant, astonishing metaphor: Sklansky makes this point ably in his "Rock, Reservation, and Prison."

Chapter 3: Fancydance Revolution

37   "What it amounts to": Stan Steiner, *The New Indians* (New York: Harper and Row, 1968), 68, 72. Much of the material Steiner used in writing about Warrior in his book came from a single interview. See Clyde Warrior, interviewed by Stan Steiner, Tahlequah, Oklahoma, tape recording, September, 1966, Stan Steiner papers, Special Collections, Green Library, Stanford University (hereafter

Steiner papers). As of this writing, many of the tapes from this collection have been transferred from reel-to-reel format to audiocassette and are available at the Archive of Recorded Sound, Stanford University, Stanford, California.

37 patience as opposed to unrest: For characterizations of American Indian politics in the period before 1969, see Deloria, *Nations Within*, 198f., Jack Forbes, *Native Americans and Nixon: Presidential Politics and Minority Self-Determination* (Los Angeles: American Indian Studies Center, University of California, Los Angeles, 1981), 25–9; and Alvin Josephy, Jr., *Now that the Buffalo's Gone: A Study of Today's American Indians* (New York: Knopf, 1982), 215–28.

37 National Congress of American Indians: For accounts of the rise of NCAI, see Vine Deloria, Jr., "The Rise of Indian Organizations," in Jennings Wise, *The Red Man in the New World Drama: A Politico-Legal Study with a Pageantry of American Indian History*, rev. and ed. and with an intro. by Vine Deloria, Jr. (Washington, D.C.: W. F. Roberts, 1931; New York: Macmillan, 1971), 371–8; Prucha, *The Great Father*, 1012; and Dorothy R. Parker, *Singing an Indian Song: A Biography of D'Arcy McNickle* (Lincoln: University of Nebraska Press, 1992), 106–9.

38 Many could lay claim: Clyde Warrior is not related to the coauthor of this book, Robert Allen Warrior. Clyde Warrior is featured in a number of books about the period, but almost all of the accounts show little change over time in his story and are mainly concerned with the impact he made as a national youth leader. See Steiner, *New Indians*, 65-72; Josephy, *Buffalo's Gone*, 224; and Vine Deloria, Jr., *Custer Died for Your Sins: An American Indian Manifesto* (New York: Macmillan, 1969), 277. See also Robert Allen Warrior, "Clyde Warrior: Ponca Activist and Writer," in Frederick Hoxie, ed., *Encyclopedia of the American Indian* (New York: Houghton-Mifflin, forthcoming).

39 Clyde Warrior posed: Postcard, family papers of Clyde Warrior, Santa Fe, New Mexico (hereafter Warrior papers).

39 fancydance champion: Della Warrior interview; Bernard Kendall, letter to Robert Allen Warrior, August 8, 1995. See also Hank Adams interview.

39 photo . . . downing a Nehi: Photograph, Warrior papers.

39   work at Disneyland: Adams interview. Followup conversation with Della Warrior, December, 1994. Oklahoma Indians working at Disneyland was not all that unusual in the period. See Jennings interview.

39   How . . . can you revive something: Clyde Warrior interview. One example of the kind of statement Warrior argues against here is Richard Oakes, *Chronicles of Indian Protest*, 314–15.

39   Born in 1941: Della Warrior interview.

39   the Poncas had been batted around: For Ponca travails in the nineteenth century, see Thomas Henry Tibbles, *The Ponca Chiefs: An Account of the Trial of Standing Bear* (1880; Lincoln: University of Nebraska Press, 1972); and Dorothy Clarke Wilson, *Bright Eyes: The Story of Susette La Flesche, an Omaha Indian* (New York: McGraw-Hill, 1974).

40   Poncas have produced . . . fancydancers: Della Warrior interview; conversations between Robert Allen Warrior and Browning Pipestem, Stanford, California, handwritten notes, June 17–19, 1995. See also Carter Revard, "Ponca War Dancers," in *Ponca War Dancers* (Norman, Okla.: Point Riders Press, 1990), 53–9.

40   he learned the protocol: Adams interview. See also, George Big Eagle [Crossland], interviewed by Paul Chaat Smith, by telephone from Alexandria, Virginia, tape recording, January 13, 1995.

40   summer program: For accounts of the Boulder workshops, see workshop brochures and publicity, assorted documents from Murray Wax to Robert Allen Warrior, December 1993 (hereafter Wax documents). See also Dorothy Parker, *Singing an Indian Song: the Life of D'Arcy McNickle* (Lincoln: University of Nebraska Press, 1990), 181–7.

40   unwritten rule: Jeri Red Corn, interviewed by Robert Allen Warrior, Norman, Oklahoma by telephone, tape recording, November, 22, 1993.

40–41   Southwest Regional Indian Youth Council: Information on this group comes from a conversation between Alfonso Ortiz and Robert Allen Warrior, Santa Fe, New Mexico, April 11, 1994.

41   "What I Would Like": Clyde Warrior papers.

41 bombarded with the opposite message: Jeri Red Corn interview; Della Warrior interview; Adams interview.

41 "Indian people must change": Pipestem conversations.

41–42 Warrior's bid to become president: Pipestem conversations.

42 "The sewage of Europe": Pipestem conversations.

42 "It's painful,": Pipestem conversations.

42 in the middle of a whirlwind: For accounts of the Chicago meeting, see Laurence M. Hauptman and Jack Campisi, "The Voice of Eastern Indians: The American Indian Chicago Conference of 1961 and the Movement for Federal Recognition," *Proceedings of the American Philosophical Society* 132 (4, 1988): 316–29; Parker, *D'Arcy McNickle*, 188–93; and Deloria, "Indian Organizations," 374f. For accounts of the founding of the NIYC, see Kathryn Red Corn, interviewed by Robert Allen Warrior, Pawhuska, Oklahoma by telephone, tape recording, December 28, 1993; and Steiner, *New Indians*, 28–38.

43 "With the belief that we can serve": Thom's statement is reprinted as an appendix to Steiner, *New Indians*, 304–5.

43 groups like the United Scholarship Service: Adams interview; Elizabeth Clark Rosenthal, interviewed by Robert Allen Warrior, Santa Fe, New Mexico, tape recording, April 11, 1994. For an account of the founding and work of the USS, see Elizabeth Clark Rosenthal, "American Indian and Spanish-American Students Seeking to Bridge a Gap," reprinted from *Mount Holyoke Alumnae Quarterly*, Spring 1967, Wax documents. Correspondence to and from USS Executive Director Tillie Walker can be found in Wax documents.

43 annual meetings on Indian reservations: Adams interview.

43 summer meeting at Fort Duchesne, Utah: Adams interview. Marlon Brando with Robert Lindsey, *Brando: Songs My Mother Taught Me* (New York: Random House, 1994), 375.

44 Negro causes carried little credibility: Adams interview; Della Warrior interview.

44 Warrior was the loudest advocate: Adams interview.

44   the group's winter meeting: Adams interview.

44   fishing tribes . . . battled . . . over . . . rights to fish: For accounts of the history of the fishing struggle in the Pacific Northwest, see Deloria, *Indians of the Pacific Northwest: From the Coming of the White Man to the Present Day* (New York: Doubleday, 1977); *Uncommon Controversy: Fishing Rights of the Muckelshoot, Puyallup, and Nisqually Indians,* a report prepared for the American Friends Service Committee (Washington: National Congress of American Indians, 1966; rev. ed. Seattle: University of Washington Press, 1970).

44   Hank Adams, who would: Adams interview.

44   Public Law 280: For a discussion of the history and impact of P.L. 280, see Deloria, *The Nations Within,* 192ff.; Prucha, *The Great Father,* 1044–6.

45   Adams . . . was outraged: Adams interview.

45   Though still a teenager: Adams interview.

45   By 1963, though, he had vast doubts: Adams interview.

45   worked as a liaison: Adams interview; Deloria, *Pacific Northwest,* 162ff.

45   The Youth Council . . . arrived: Adams interview. Janet McCloud, interviewed by Robert Allen Warrior, by telephone from Franks Landing, Washington, tape recording, January 11, 1994. Hunter S. Thompson, "Marlon Brando and the Indian Fish-In," In Thompson, *The Great Shark Hunt: Gonzo Papers,* vol. 1 (New York: Summit, 1979), 440–6. Steiner, *New Indians,* 48–64.

46   when a star like . . . Gregory or . . . Fonda: See, for instance, Robert C. Lee, "Dick Gregory Goes Fishing," *The Nation,* April 25, 1966, 487–9. See also "NAACP Legal Defense," Pacifica Radio Archives, North Hollywood, Calif., April 10, 1969.

46   Some local people were dissatisfied: McCloud interview. See also Adams interview for a rebuttal. These two activists from the Pacific Northwest have a long-standing dispute.

46   where Indians fit into the OEO: Deloria, "Social Programs of the 60s," in Wise, *Red Man,* 379–88; James Wilson, interviewed by Stan Steiner, Steiner papers; program from the Capital Conference on

Poverty, May, 1964 in Wax documents; and Philps, *Indian Self-Rule*, 219–27.

46   National Congress . . . undergoing wholesale changes: See Deloria's description of his work at USS and selection as executive director of NCAI in Vine Deloria, Jr., *Custer Died for Your Sins: An American Indian Manifesto* (New York: Macmillan, 1969), 270–1. Hank Adams contends that Clyde Warrior was a major force behind Deloria's ascent to national leadership. See Adams interview.

46   Deloria, who had grown up: See: Robert Allen Warrior, *Tribal Secrets: Recovering American Indian Intellectual Traditions* (Minneapolis: University of Minnesota Press, 1994), 31ff. for a review of biographical materials on Deloria.

47   In a 1966 interview: Vine Deloria, Jr., interviewed by Stan Steiner, Steiner papers.

47   making a network of their own: McCloud interview; Gerald Vizenor, interviewed by Robert Allen Warrior, Berkeley, California, tape recording, July 22, 1993.

47   Deloria . . . encouraged them: Deloria interview, Steiner tapes.

47   "You meet the Great White Father": Clydia Nahwooksy, interviewed by Robert Allen Warrior, from Lincoln, Nebraska, by telephone, tape recording, November 9, 1993.

47   In certain ways: Clydia Nahwooksy interview; Reaves Nahwooks, interviewed by Robert Allen Warrior, from Lincoln, Nebraska, by telephone, tape recording, October 31, 1993. Reaves dropped the letter *y* from the end of his last name when he was ordained as a Baptist minister.

48   "tear our note up": Reaves Nahwooks interview.

49   "Well, I don't have time": Clydia Nahwooksy interview.

49   "How can this change?": Clydia Nahwooksy interview; Reaves Nahwooks interview.

49   an institution gone terribly awry: For analyses of the history of the Bureau, see, among others, Prucha, *The Great Father*, and Edgar S. Cahn, ed., *Our Brother's Keeper: The Indian in White America* (New York: New Community, 1969). Warrior's friend Browning Pipestem was an associate editor of the book.

50   commission and task force reports: A list of these reports appears in Cahn, ed., *Brother's Keeper*, 187ff.

50   got out of the Bureau for good: Reaves Nahwooks interview.

51   series of hearings the NCIO planned: Reaves Nahwooks interview; for a report on these hearings, see Richard G. Woods and Arthur M. Harkins, "An Examination of the 1968–69 Urban Indian Hearings Held by the National Council on Indian Opportunity" (five parts), Training Center for Community Programs, University of Minnesota, Minneapolis, June 1971.

51   "These guys were really confronters": Reaves Nahwooks interview.

51   worked to establish an "Indian Desk": Reaves Nahwooks interview. For discussions of the emergence of Indian desks in the federal bureaucracy, see Deloria, *Nations Within*, 197; and Josephy, *Buffalo's Gone*, 226.

52   The Nahwooksy home: Clydia Nahwooksy interview.

52   "Which One Are You?": *ABC: Americans Before Columbus* 2 (December 4, 1964); reprinted as an appendix to Steiner, *New Indians*, 305–7. Warrior apparently used this essay as the basis for at least some public presentations. See Clyde Warrior, speech at Wayne State University, February 1966, tape recording, Warrior papers. A remastered version is available at the Archive of Recorded Sound, Stanford University, Stanford, California.

53   the outrageous alternative: Clyde Warrior interview; Adams interview.

53   he had married Della Hopper: Della Warrior interview.

54   a field researcher for Murray Wax: Murray Wax, interviewed by Robert Allen Warrior, St. Louis, Missouri, by telephone, tape recording, December 14, 1993.

54   In an interview in 1966: Clyde Warrior interview.

54   "I . . . see an alliance": Clyde Warrior, Wayne State speech.

55   Indian people "are not free": Clyde Warrior, "We Are not Free," in Alvin M. Josephy, Jr., ed., *Red Power* (New York: McGraw-Hill, 1971), 71–7.

56 Warrior's lack of productivity: Wax says Warrior never produced material for the project. Other evidence shows, though, that Warrior did, in fact, work on the project and taped notes from his fieldwork. In these taped notes, Warrior records his attempts to carry out research on Indian education in area schools, attempts that were thwarted by school administrators who knew of Warrior's notoriety. Robert Dumont, with whom we were unable to arrange an interview for this book, accompanied Warrior on these forays. Warrior narrates the story of their travails in a typically droll and frustrated manner. Starting with the second report, Warrior signs off as "Agent 49." See Clyde Warrior, field notes from Tahlequah project, tape recording, October 1966, Warrior papers. A remastered version of this recording is available at the Archive of Recorded Sound, Stanford University, Stanford, California.

56 ministrations of Tillie Walker: Bill Center, a local man who was something of a parental figure to Clyde Warrior, was instrumental in getting him into treatment the second time. Della Warrior interview; Pipestem conversations; Adams interview. Tillie Walker declined to be interviewed for this book.

56 "Clyde is back": Letter from Murray Wax to Tillie Walker, October 29, 1967, Wax documents.

57 He fell off the wagon: Della Warrior interview.

57 Anita Collins, died . . . Della Warrior interview.

57 "I hurt all over": Pipestem conversations.

57 Clyde took seriously ill: Della Warrior interview. See also Kathryn Red Corn interview.

57 Area Indian people: Della Warrior interview.

57–8 Della . . . did a giveaway: Della Warrior interview. The telegrams are in Warrior papers.

58 "A Fresh Air of New Indian Idealism": Clyde Warrior's grave, along with those of his mother Anita Collins and many other relatives, is near the southern end of the Ponca cemetery southeast of Ponca City, Oklahoma.

58 "prophet of Red Power": Steiner, *New Indians*, 66.

58 "And, as I see it": Steiner, *New Indians*, 71. cf. Clyde Warrior interview.

59 headed out for Vietnam: For one perspective on American Indians and Vietnam, see Tom Holm, *Strong Hearts, Wounded Souls* (Austin: University of Texas Press, 1996).

59 Hank Adams had watched: Adams interview. Press release from Poor People's Campaign, Warrior papers.

59 "his life was in the song": Adams interview.

Chapter 4: Life As a Metaphor

60 sharing a boat to Alcatraz: Adams interview.

61 To Adams, the majority: Adams interview.

61 could speak quite eloquently: See, among others, Richard Oakes, "Alcatraz is Not an Island"; Boyer interview; Adams interview.

61 lack of organization and coherence: Adams interview; Pipestem conversations. Pipestem remained involved with the occupation for over two months. Negative comments toward his counsel, attributed to LaNada Means, were made at a meeting on the island in early February (Minutes of General Meeting February 6, 1970, Box 1, File 34, Council Minutes, SFPL.)

61 And Alcatraz had become: For specific accounts of some of the accidents, see Tim Findley, "Child Badly Injured in Fall on Alcatraz," *Chronicle* January 6, 1970; and Tim Findley, "Alactraz Dissension Grows," *Chronicle,* January 7, 1970.

62 That became the dividing line: For accounts of these differences, see Boyer interview; Castillo interview; Quitiquit interview; Fortunate Eagle, *Alcatraz! Alcatraz!*; and Memorandum from T. E. Hannon to file, January 5, 1970, Box 15, Correspondence, Confidential "A," GSA.

63 described by some as an intellectual: Castillo interview; Garcia interview.

63 without a sighting of Richard: See Findley, "Alcatraz Dissension."

63 a dispute broke out: Findley reported this dispute to GSA Regional Administrator Tom Hannon on January 5, 1970 (Hannon

memo to file, January 5, 1970). See also Tim Findley, "Factionalism and Feuds," *Chronicle*, January 8, 1970.

63   Quitiquit said she had: Quitiquit interview.

64   "They were looking for anything": Quitiquit interview.

64   Oakes still maintained an apartment: Hannon memo to file, January 5, 1970.

64   stubborn perseverance of a tepee: Stella Leach, interviewed by Anna Boyd and Irene Silentman, Alcatraz Island, tape recording, February 4, 1970, Box 20, File 44, Doris Duke American Indian Oral History Project, Center for Southwest Research, University of New Mexico, Albuquerque (hereafter UNM).

65   a tragedy struck: Hannon memo to file, January 5, 1970. See also Findley, "Child Badly Injured."

65   had been home: Findley, "Alcatraz Dissension."

65   to send a message to Oakes: Hannon memo to file, January 5, 1970; Castillo interview; Garcia interview. Richard Oakes, according to one source, strongly contended that Yvonne's fall had not been an accident. See Sidney Mills, interviewed by Robert Allen Warrior, Franks Landing, Washington, by telephone, tape recording, December 16, 1994.

66   "Kids could go in": Quitiquit interview. A number of people who seemed to know Anne Oakes well indicated that she would prefer not to answer questions about this sensitive issue. We hope that is true. Regardless, we also hope it is clear that we have reached no conclusions. Hannon memo to file, January 5, 1970.

66   She finally succumbed: "Girl Dies after Fall on Alcatraz," *Chronicle*, January 9, 1970.

66   a devastating two-part series: "Alcatraz Dissension," and "Factionalism and Feuds."

67   slipped off the island: See Castillo interview; Garcia interview; Quitiquit interview, Boyer interview.

67   Yvonne was buried: "Girl Dies."

67   pay for her shroud: Notes on an intact stenographer's pad, n.d. Box 1, File 33, Council Meetings, SFPL.

67 only to pick up his belongings: Oakes, "Alcatraz is Not an Island," 40. Oakes seems to have muddled the dates a little here, perhaps as a way of avoiding talking about the power struggle and money controversies.

67 Kunzig decided: Garvey, "Government and the Indians," 22.

68 Hannon returned to his office: Garvey, "Government and the Indians," 23.

68 The White House had taken over: Garvey, "Government and the Indians," 23.

68 Leonard Garment was actually: Leonard Garment, interviewed by Paul Chaat Smith, Washington, D.C., tape recording, February 10, 1995.

68 with his assistant Brad Patterson: Bradley Patterson, interviewed by Paul Chaat Smith, Washington, D.C., tape recording, July 9, 1993.

68 Garment knew that in Alcatraz: Garment interview.

69 a federal response to Alcatraz: Garment interview; Patterson interview; Bradley H. Patterson, Jr., *The Ring of Power: The White House Staff and its Expanding Role in Government* (New York: Basic Books, 1988), 72ff.

69 Garment and his allies saw opportunity: Garment interview; Patterson interview.

69 Nixon revered his coach: Roger Morris, *Richard Milhous Nixon: The Rise of an American Politician* (New York: Henry Holt, 1990), 120, 133–35, 324, 608, 744; Richard Milhous Nixon, *RN: The Memoirs of Richard Nixon* (New York: Grosset and Dunlap, 1975), 19–20. For Quaker history in Indian affairs, see Prucha, *Great Father*, 499–500.

69 indifference to domestic affairs: Bobbie Green Kilberg, interviewed by Paul Chaat Smith, McLean, Virginia, tape recording, October 4, 1993.

70 Garment kept in close touch: Garment interview; Patterson, *Ring of Power*, 73. See also Letter from Leonard Garment to Mr. and Mrs. John [sic] Oakes, January 9, 1970, Correspondence, Confidential "A," Box 15, GSA.

70 federal task force: Garment interview; Patterson interview; Patterson, *Ring of Power*, 73f.

70   National Council on Indian Opportunity: At some point, Indians of All Tribes obtained a copy of the executive order that established the NCIO ("Copy of Executive Order," March 6, 1968, NCIO, Box 3, File 15, SFPL). See also Patterson interview; Robert Robertson, interviewed by Paul Chaat Smith, Smithfield, Virginia, tape recording, December 1, 1993. The records of the NCIO are available at RG-75, National Archives, Washington, D.C. (hereafter NCIO).

70   a seven-member council: These elections took place around the time of Yvonne Oakes's death (Steno pad notes, SFPL).

70   most controversial was Stella Leach: For Stella Leach's power struggle with Richard Oakes and discussion of her temperament as a leader, see Shorris, *Great Spirit*, 235f.

71   John Trudell: The tapes from Radio Free Alcatraz are available at the Pacifica Radio Archives, North Hollywood, California.

71   LaNada Means: Boyer interview; Boyer, "Reflections of Alcatraz"; see also Quitiquit interview.

72   the Alcatraz Kid: "The Rock Blockaded—Indians Vow to Stay," *Chronicle*, November 23, 1969.

72   Bob Robertson had a disarming way: Robertson interview.

73   "One would have to search": Robert Robertson, memorandum to file, Subject: Alcatraz Negotiations, January 10, 11, 12, 1970, Alcatraz folder, NCIO.

73   Robertson found it interesting: Robertson, Alcatraz Negotiations.

74   The Indians wanted to talk about receiving title to the island: Robertson, Alcatraz Negotiations.

74   "If we can render foreign aid": Robertson, Alcatraz Negotiations.

74   "died for the cause": Robertson, Alcatraz Negotiations.

74   Robertson said the government would be willing: Robertson, Alcatraz Negotiations.

74   LaNada Means insisted that Robertson join her for dinner: Robertson, Alcatraz Negotiations.

75   "reason is a commodity": Roberston, Alcatraz Negotiations.

75   Robertson stayed in close touch with Tom Hannon: Robertson interview.

75   "only real change": Robert Robertson draft memorandum to Spiro Agnew and Leonard Garment, January 26, 1970, Alcatraz folder, NCIO. For the photographs from Hannon's visit, see Photographs, first file of seven, Box 9, GSA.

76    $170,000 just to get: Minutes of General Meeting February 6, 1970.

76   took up the full range of issues: Minutes of General Meeting February 6, 1970.

76   Means finished her proposal: Proposal and budget, Proposals for Funding, Box 4, File 4, SFPL.

77   banned reporters: Fortunate Eagle, *Alcatraz! Alcatraz!*, 120.

77   A flattering spread in *Look*: "America's Indians: Reawakening of a Conquered People, *Look,* June 2, 1970).

77   Merv Griffin flew out: Fortunate Eagle, *Alcatraz! Alcatraz!*, 120.

77   He asked for more time: Robertson interview.

78   he brought a new proposal: "A Proposal for Indians of All Tribes, Incorporated," March 31, 1970, Box 4, Folder 3, NCIO. See also J. Campbell Bruce, "Indianized Alcatraz Park," *Chronicle*, April 1, 1970, sec. 1; Robertson interview.

78   "protect the symbolic value": "A Proposal"; Robertson interview.

79   largely crafted before the occupation: Bruce, "Indianized Alcatraz."

79   "symbols of arrival, like flags on the moon": Shorris, *Great Spirit*, 242.

80   Robertson felt bitter disappointment: Robertson interview.

80   "I noticed one man": Statement by Lt. Gilbert Shaw, April 3, 1970, Alcatraz folder, Box 5, NCIO.

81   "The government's proposal is nothing": Reply to counterproposal, April 3, 1970, Alcatraz folder, Box 5, Folder 4, NCIO.

82   "only ten Indians": Typed notes, Council Minutes, May 7, 1970, Box 1, File 38, SFPL.

82 "Al Miller made a motion": Typed notes, Council Minutes, May 7, 1970, Box 1, File 38, SFPL.

82 "take over the island completely": Memorandum recording daily report of caretaker Don Carroll from Thomas N. Scott to file, Daily Reports, May 6, 1970; Memorandum recording daily report of caretaker Don Carroll from John A. Peters to file, Daily Reports, May 18, 1970, GSA.

82 "extremely abusive": Memo, May 6, 1970. Carroll reported that Oakes and company were drunk, but on several occasions in his daily reports he overstated such things. Sid Mills, in his account, doesn't mention alcohol, and he seems a more reliable source. Sidney Mills interview.

82–3 As the month wore on: See Don Carroll's daily reports to GSA officials in May 1970, Daily Reports, Box 14, GSA. The reference to a Nixon address on the occupation is from May 21.

83 Carroll planned: Memorandum recording daily report of caretaker Don Carroll from Thomas N. Scott to file, Daily Reports, May 25, 1970. For Carroll's checking of his radio, see Memorandum recording daily report of caretaker Don Carroll from Thomas N. Scott to file, Daily Reports, May 20, 1970. See also Tim Findley, "Alcatraz to be Converted Into National Park," *Chronicle* May 28, 1970.

83 The occupiers gathered: "Alcatraz," May 31, 1970, Pacifica Radio Archives, North Hollywood, California; and Perry Carroll, "Indians to Fight the Alcatraz Park," *Chronicle,* June 1, 1970.

Chapter 5: The Monument Tour

87 "I believe": Johnson, "Indian Occupation," 296–97.

88 "If those Indians": Johnson, "Indian Occupation," 297.

88 "They have no reason": Johnson, "Indian Occupation," 297.

88 targets of Indian protest: For readings of the period, see Vine Deloria, Jr., *God is Red* (New York: Grosset and Dunlap, 1973), Means, *White Men Fear*, 3–56; 149–78; Josephy, *Buffalo's Gone*, 215–63; and Warrior, *Tribal Secrets*, 26–41.

89 urban communities of Indians: The literature on American Indian urbanization is quite extensive and always growing. See, among

many others, Fixico, *Termination and Relocation*; and Woods and Harkins, *An Examination of the 1968-69 Urban Indian Hearings.*

89   the Seattle Indian community: Bernie White Bear, interviewed by Robert Allen Warrior, Seattle, Washington, by telephone, tape recording, December 7, 1993; Ramona Bennett, interviewed by Robert Allen Warrior, Tacoma, Washington, by telephone, tape recording, January 15, 1993; Sid Mills interview; Suzette Mills, interviewed by Robert Allen Warrior, Franks Landing, Washington, December 16, 1994; Sue Morales, interviewed by Robert Allen Warrior, Tacoma, Washington by telephone, May 16, 1994; Hank Adams interview.

90   the land was theirs: White Bear interview. Gaining the land, of course, was not without its ups and downs. See Lawton-M156, American Indian Press Association News Service story, May 15, 1971, News Service chronological and subject files, archives of the American Indian Press Association (AIPA), temporarily in possession of the authors (hereafter AIPA); and Lawton-N241, AIPA News Service Story, November 24, 1971, AIPA. AIPA News Service stories were coded by: story slug, month, day of the month, and the sequential number of how the story appeared on that day. The abbreviations for the months are, in sequence, JA, F, MR, A, M, JU, JY, AU, S, OC, N, D. In the above example, M156, M represents May, 15 represents the fifteenth day of the month, and 6 represents that this is the sixth story the News Service issued on that day. The news releases do not indicate the year of publication other than by story content.

90   Bruce Oakes: Bruce Oakes, interviewed by Paul Chaat Smith, Boston, Massachussetts, by telephone, handwritten notes, December 1, 1993.

90   "What I'd very much like to do": "Summer Work Study Project Report," 21–3, Wax documents.

90–1   "Without transportation": "Summer Work," 22.

91   He saw the news of Alcatraz: Bruce Oakes interview.

91   occupation of Ellis Island: Bruce Oakes interview. See also Boyer interview; Adams interview.

92   Bruce returned to the car: Bruce Oakes interview.

92 "Tell Merv Griffin": Bruce Oakes interview.

93 A spectacular inferno: Charles Howe, "Indians Deny They Set Alcatraz Fire," *Chronicle*, June 3, 1970.

93 Trudell took to the airwaves: Broadcasts from Alcatraz, reels 28, 29, 30, Pacifica Radio Archives, North Hollywood, California.

93 LaNada Means survived: Boyer, "Reflections of Alcatraz," 82ff. Boyer does not provide a date for the fire. One possibility is a fire that occurred April 26, 1970. See Thomas Scott memorandum to file, April 28, 1970, Box 14, Daily Reports, GSA.

94 "I gathered my blanket": Boyer, "Reflections of Alcatraz," 83.

94 *Ramparts*, a leftist magazine: Peter Collier, "Red Man's Burden," *Ramparts* 8 (February 1970): 26–38.

94 Jane Fonda saw it: Boyer interview; Boyer, "Reflections of Alcatraz," 86.

95 A fight erupted: "Richard Oakes and a Clash of Cultures," *Chronicle*, June 17, 1970.

95 Bruce heard the news: Bruce Oakes interview.

95 A Tuscarora leader: Doug Boyd, *Mad Bear: Spirit, Healing, and the Sacred in the Life of a Native American Medicine Man* (New York: Simon and Schuster, 1994), 43–4. See also Boyer, "Reflections on Alcatraz," 81.

96 would not talk to Bruce: Bruce Oakes interview.

96 fired back a response: Copy of Lou Trudell letter to Schultz, Correspondence—Outward, Box 1, File 24, SFPL. See Boyer, "Reflections of Alcatraz," 87.

96 Ghost Dance movement in the 1880s: A mostly reliable account of the Ghost Dance and the Wounded Knee Massacre is Rex Alan Smith, *Moon of the Popping Trees* (Lincoln: University of Nebraska Press, 1975). A recent addition to the literature is Conger Beasley, Jr., *We Are a People in This World: The Lakota Sioux and the Massacre at Wounded Knee* (Fayetteville: University of Arkansas Press, 1995). See also Robert Allen Warrior, "Dances with Ghosts; Pain and Suffering on the Big Foot Trail," *Village Voice* January 16, 1991, 33–7.

97   Herb Caen learned of the plan: Peter Blue Cloud, ed., *Alcatraz is Not an Island* (Berkeley: Wingbow Press, 1972), 69.

97   protesting at the Gallup Ceremonial: NIYC apparently invited occupiers from Alcatraz to work as security people during their protests. See "NIYC Demonstration: Gallup Ceremonial," *Americans Before Columbus* 2 (August 3,–December 1970): 1, 5, Box 23, NIYC file, UNM.

98   he was a walking contradiction: See Adams interview. A collection of original articles and reprinted articles from local, regional, and national newspapers about Hank Adams and the fishing rights struggle in the Pacific Northwest can be found in *The Renegade: Official Publication—Survival of American Indians Association* in reel 37, *Periodicals by and about North American Indians, 1923–1981* (Washington, D.C.: Congressional Information Service, 1981).

98   after being among those: Adams interview.

98   the real indication: Adams interview.

99   He never sensed: Adams interview.

99   Adams had his first long conversation: Adams interview. In his recent autobiography, *Where White Men Fear to Tread*, Russell Means does not recount this story.

99   AIM, which had started: See, among many others, James S. Olson and Raymond Wilson, *Native Americans in the Twentieth Century* (Provo, Utah: Brigham Young University Press, 1984), 167.

99   Means and Adams spun out theories: Adams interview.

100–1 organizations having nothing to do: See Deloria, "The Rise of Indian Organizations." See also, among many, Press release, January 7, 1971, AIPA; Coalition—JU012, AIPA News Service story, June 1, 1971; Law—JU022, AIPA News Service story, June 2, 1971; Scout—JU141, AIPA News Service story, June 14, 1971; Women—JU192, AIPA News Service story, June 14, 1971; *Indian Voices: The Native American Today; A Report on the Second Convocation of Indian Scholars* (San Francisco: Indian Historian Press, 1974), v; Means, *White Men Fear*, 194.

101   articles and books: Vine Deloria, Jr. makes this criticism and discusses specific publications in *God is Red*, 39–56.

101   "We weren't reborn": Philps, *Indian Self-Rule*, 261.

102   a conference at the Airlie Center: Robertson interview; John Jollie, confidential memorandum to Robert Robertson, March 5, 1971, Airlie House folder, Box 2, NCIO.

102   months of hearings on urban issues: Reaves Nahwooks interview; Woods and Harkins, *An Examination of the 1968–69 Urban Indian Hearings.*

102   "tranquility, gentle beauty": Brochure, n.d. Airlie House, Warrenton, Virginia.

102   The Indians arrived: Jim Burress, interviewed by Paul Chaat Smith, Warrenton, Virginia, handwritten notes, October 11, 1993.

102   Some of the 150 participants came with the expectation that they would be meeting with the president or vice president: Burress interview.

102   "ungentlemanly behavior": Richard Ross memorandum "For the record," January 12, 1971, Airlie House folder, Box 2, NCIO.

103   "truculent, pugnacious": Ross memo January 12, 1971.

103   The real trouble: Ross memo January 12, 1971.

103   "Many of the so-called door guards": Ross memo January 12, 1971.

104   "Two saddle blankets were stolen": Ross memo January 12, 1971.

104   *The Washington Post* ran: "Vandalism Mars Indian Conference," *The Washington Post*, December 17, 1970, Airlie House folder, Box 2, NCIO.

104   the NCIO called the meeting a success: Draft press release, December 17, 1970, Airlie House folder, Box 2, NCIO.

105   Bob Robertson . . . was growing weary: Robertson interview.

105   "Thanks for item": Tom [Hannon] to Robert Robertson, December 28, 1970, Airlie House folder, Box 2, NCIO.

105   missed all the excitement: Boyer, "Reflections of Alcatraz," ms. version, 33.

106   She stayed with Edgar Cahn: Boyer, "Reflections of Alcatraz," 87.

106   her new friend Ethel Kennedy: Boyer, "Reflections of Alcatraz," 87.

106   boomeranged when: Boyer, "Reflections of Alcatraz," ms version, 33.

106   she reported to her colleagues: Boyer, "Reflections of Alcatraz," 87.

107   "He has taken cases": Boyer, "Reflections of Alcatraz," 87.

107   She returned to the island: Boyer, "Reflections of Alcatraz," 87.

107   Her time away: Boyer, "Reflections of Alcatraz," 87.

108   "This letter": Unsigned letter, April 19, 1971, Box 1, File 26, Correspondence—Outward—Letters to be Mailed (sealed) [opened], SFPL.

108   meeting that ended the occupation: Garvey, "Government and the Indians," 135.

109   afternoon of June 11: Paul Avery, "Alcatraz is 'Recaptured' by Armed U.S. Marshals," *Chronicle*, June 12, 1971.

109   "long, 19 months takeover": "End of a Squalid Sit-In," *Chronicle*, June 15, 1971.

110   watched a report: Castillo interview.

Chapter 6: Yellow Thunder

112   The police found him: Anthony Ripley, "Five Held in Death of Dakota Indian," *New York Times*, March 5, 1972.

112   Yellow Thunder's death would be different: Richard La Course, "Sensitizing the Community," Raymond—MR281, part 3 of 3, AIPA News Service story, March 28, 1972, AIPA.

113   a fifty-one-year-old cowboy: Richard La Course, "Violent Death of a Silent Man," Raymond—MR281, part 1 of 3, AIPA News Service story, March 28, 1972, AIPA.

113   town had a bad reputation: B. Drummond Ayres, Jr., "White Man's Town Bows to Angry Indians," *New York Times*, March 20, 1972.

113   the coroner reported: Ripley, "Five Held"; "Death of Indian Sparks Protest," *New York Times*, March 8, 1972.

113   only after morticians: La Course, "Violent Death."

113–14   Those details were as follows: Trial—MR242, AIPA News Service story, March 24, 1972, AIPA. Ludder, who claimed not to have struck the victim, testified against the Hare brothers and Bayliss.

114   whites who had witnessed: Ripley, "Five Held."

114   Later that night: Trial—MR242, AIPA.

114   angry rumors: These rumors, in many ways, overshadowed what were clearly horrific, provable details. See La Course, "Violent Death"; Ripley, "Five Held"; "Death of Indian."

114   the family sought assistance: Robert Anderson, Joanna Brown, Jonny Lerner, and Barbara Lou Shafer, eds., *Voices from Wounded Knee, 1973, in the Words of the Participants* (Akwesasne, via Rooseveltown, New York: Akwesasne Notes, 1974), 13.

114   "Sonny, we don't": *Voices*, 13.

115   people from Porcupine: For an account of communities in the Medicine Root District at Pine Ridge, including Porcupine, see Vine Deloria, Jr., "The Country Was a Lot Better Off When the Indians Were Running It," *The New York Times Magazine*, March 8, 1970 (reprinted in Josephy, *Red Power*, 243–4; and Warrior, "Dances With Ghosts."

115   meeting with other activist Indian organizations: Urbans—JA251, AIPA News Service story, January 25, 1972, AIPA; Council—MR051, AIPA News Service story, March 5, 1972; Committee—MR052, AIPA News Service story, March 5, 1972, AIPA; "Urban Indians Form Unit for Equality," *The New York Times*, March 7, 1972, sec. 1; Means, *White Men Fear*, 194–5.

115   He got a storekeeper: *Voices*, 13. See also Means, *White Men Fear*, 194–5; and Severt Young Bear and R. D. Theisz, *Standing in the Light: A Lakota Way of Seeing* (Lincoln: University of Nebraska Press, 1994), 158–9; Birgil Kills Straight, interviewed by Robert Allen Warrior, Kyle, South Dakota, tape recording, December 27, 1990.

115   Young Bear returned: *Voices*, 13.

115   streets of the whiskey town: "Death of Indian"; Richard La Course, "Boycott as a Human Rights Tool," Raymond—MR281, AIPA News Service story, part 2 of 3, March 28, 1972, AIPA.

116   As a result of the protests: La Course, "Boycott"; B. Drummond Ayres, Jr., "Inquiry Ordered in Indian's Death," *The New York Times*, March 9, 1972; "Morton Sets Investigation," *The New York Times*, March 9, 1972.

116   "cruel practical joke": La Course, "Violent Death."

116   second autopsy confirmed the first: "Autopsy Shows No Torture," *The New York Times* (hereafter NYT), March 10, 1972.

116   "It wasn't as bad": La Course, "Violent Death."

116   smoked a Lakota pipe: Ayres, "Inquiry Ordered."

116   "The spell has been broken": Ayres, "White Man's Town."

116   "I think people": Ayres, "White Man's Town."

117   "Yellow Thunder wasn't the first": Ayres, "White Man's Town."

117   In the aftermath: William Wertz, "Massive Gathering at Pine Ridge Planned," *Rapid City Journal*, March 12, 1972. This article is included in a valuable, though incomplete, collection of articles from various publications arranged in files by subject (e.g. American Indian Movement, Russell Means, Dennis Banks, Wounded Knee) in the vertical file at the Rapid Public Library, Rapid City, South Dakota.

118   Wounded Knee Trading Post: "Indians Damage Trading Post at Wounded Knee," *Rapid City Journal*, March 10, 1972.

118   Lakotas hated few places: Regina Brave, interviewed by Paul Chaat Smith, Albuquerque, New Mexico, by telephone, tape recording, July 23, 1993.

118   "It was terrible, terrible": "Indians Damage."

119   "It's just like the rest": "Indians Damage."

119   "a signal turning point": La Course, "Sensitizing."

119   "The central AIM effort": La Course, "Sensitizing."

122   "urban Indians": Deloria, *Custer*, 248.

123   July of 1970: For an insightful discussion of the July, 1970 message and the policies that came before it and after it, see the essay by Philip S. Deloria (followed by statements from others who worked in Indian affairs during the period), in Philps, *Indian Self-Rule*, 191–218. See also Kilberg interview; Patterson interview; Garment interview; Robertson interview; and H. Richard Haldeman, *The Haldeman Diaries: Inside the Nixon White House*, the Complete Multimedia Edition, (Santa Monica, California: Sony Electronic Publishing Company, 1994).

123   a proposal called Resolution 26: Vine Deloria, Jr., "Toward a Common Indian Front," Deloria—JA132, AIPA News Service story, January 13, 1972, AIPA.

124   NIYC still had an active: See, for example, NIYC—F123, AIPA News Service story, February 12, 1972, AIPA.

124   "the great concern": "Reservation Tribal Chairmen's Conference," AIPA News Service story, February 22, 1971, AIPA .

124   "It appears that": "Reservation Tribal Chairmen's Conference."

125   "NCAI is not the only organization": Deloria, "Common Indian Front."

126   the support of the NCAI convention: Deloria, "Common Indian Front."

126   Both of them believed: Warrior, Wayne State speech; Deloria, "Indian Activism," 397–8.

Chapter 7: The American Indian Movement

127   250 Indians . . . who met: Bill Zimmerman, *Airlift to Wounded Knee* (Chicago: Swallow Press, 1976), 118f. See also Fay G. Cohen, "The Indian Patrol in Minneapolis: Social Control and Social Change in an Urban Context," Ph.D. dissertation, University of Minnesota, June 1973, 46. Cohen reports that around fifty people were active in the organization in its early days.

128   Minneapolis and St. Paul: For general readings of the Minneapolis and St. Paul Indian communities and organizations, see Cohen, "Indian Patrol," n.33, 34–43; Nancy Shoemaker, "Urban Indians and Ethnic Choices: American Indian Organizations in Minneapolis, 1920–1950," *Western Historical Quarterly* 19 (4, 1988): 431–47; Gerald Vizenor, *Wordarrows: Indians and Whites in the New Fur Trade* (Minneapolis: University of Minnesota Press, 1978); Gerald Vizenor, interviewed by Robert Allen Warrior, Berkeley, California, tape recording, July 22, 1993.

128   AIM Patrol: Cohen, "Indian Patrol," esp. 55–99.

128   The founders and leaders: Cohen, "Indian Patrol," 45–6.

128   Dennis Banks was sent: Zimmerman, *Airlift*, 110–1, 116–9.

129   "Demonstrations are not the Indian way": Gerald Vizenor, *The People Named the Chippewa: Narrative Histories* (Minneapolis: University of Minnesota Press, 1984), 128. See also Vizenor interview.

129   "It had a tremendous impact": Zimmerman, *Airlift*, 118f.

130   Once out of prison: Zimmerman, *Airlift*, 119.

130   "willing to give you": Zimmerman, *Airlift*, 120.

130   Bellecourt had a different: Peter Nabokov, ed., *Native American Testimony: A Chronicle of Indian-White Relations from Prophecy to the Present, 1492–1992* (New York: Viking Penguin, 1991), 373.

131   Bellecourt caught Banks's attention: Zimmerman, *Airlift*, 119.

131   November, 1969 meeting: Cohen, "Indian Patrol," 49–50.

132   national Indian conferences: Cohen, "Indian Patrol," 93; Lehman Brightman, interviewed by Robert Allen Warrior, Pinole, California, by telephone, tape recording, October 27, 1993. The 1969 convention in Albuquerque seems to be one event at which militant protests became a major issue for NCAI. See transcript of NCAI panel featuring Mad Bear Anderson and Lee Brightman, Albuquerque, New Mexico, October, 1969, Box 20, Folder 1, UNM.

132   urban Indian leaders: Means, *White Men Fear*, 147.

132   born on the Pine Ridge: Means, *White Men Fear*, 21, 22.

132   Vallejo, then San Leandro: Means, *White Men Fear*, 36, 38, 44, 45ff., 51ff, 56ff., 62.

133   drifted down to southern California: Means, *White Men Fear*, 66–135.

133   In 1967 he moved: Means, *White Men Fear*, 136–48; Josephy, *Buffalo's Gone*, 236.

133   AIM leaders actively recruited him: Means, *White Men Fear*, 149–61, 176ff.

135   dance instructor: Means, *White Men Fear*, 99.

135   "made things up": Dick LeGarde, interviewed by Paul Chaat Smith, Mahnomen, Minnesota, by telephone, tape recording, October 28, 1993.

135   a growing set of local chapters: Means's Cleveland chapter was the first one outside of the Twin Cities. Milwaukee and Denver soon followed (Zimmerman, *Airlift*, 120).

136   "It figures": *Newsweek*, January 31, 1972. See also "Horse-feathers" Feathers-JA291, AIPA News Service story "Light Feature," January 29, 1972, AIPA.

136   "Dear D.J. and National Board Members": Russell Means, open letter to Dennis Banks and National Board of AIM, Russell Means, subject file, AIPA.

137   "you can't resign": LaGarde interview.

139   AIM leaders met: Leonard Crow Dog and Richard Erdoes, *Crow Dog: Six Generations of Sioux Medicine Men* (New York: Harper-Collins, 1995), 171; Robert Burnette and John Koster, *The Road to Wounded Knee* (New York: Bantam, 1974), 197; Means, *White Men Fear*, 223.

139   "This shall be our finest hour": Burnette, *Road*, 198.

140   a caretaker for a YMCA camp: Oakes-SP261, AIPA News Service story, September 26, 1972, AIPA.

140   "What took you so long?": "Indian Activists May Be Unified by Slaying," *The Washington Post*, November 26, 1972.

140   a traveling college: Sid Mills interview; Suzette Mills interview.

141   "If Richard Oakes": Hank Adams, "Richard Oakes and the Sea of Violence," Legacy-SP262, AIPA News Service editorial, September 26, 1972, AIPA.

141   In the midst of the somber mourning: Sid Mills interview; La-Garde interview. See also Vine Deloria, Jr., *Behind the Trail of Broken Treaties: An Indian Declaration of Independence* (New York: Delacorte Press, 1974), 46.

142   worked independently: Adams interview; Sid Mills interview.

142   disparate elements gathered: Richard La Course, "Trail of Broken Treaties—Planning the Caravans," Caravans DC121, AIPA News Service story, December 12, 1972, AIPA.

143   "cause civil disorder": *BIA, I'm Not Your Indian Anymore* (Mohawk Nation via Rooseveltown, New York: Akwesasne Notes, 1973).

143 Mills made the trip: Sid Mills interview. See also "The Trail of the Broken Treaty," Pacifica Radio Archives, North Hollywood, California.

143 Bellecourt sought assistance: Richard La Course, "Trail of Broken Treaties—On the Road to St. Paul," Caravan-DC234, AIPA News Service story, December 23, 1972, AIPA.

143-4 "In honor of our heroic warriors": La Course, "Road to St. Paul."

144 midnight attempt to seize the Fort Sill Indian School: La Course, "Road to St. Paul."

144 caravans made their way slowly toward St. Paul: La Course, "Road to St. Paul."

144 The group held sessions: Adams interview; Sid Mills interview.

145 had a nagging concern: LaGarde interview.

146 a polite letter: Dennis Banks to Richard Nixon, October 4, 1972, Trail of Broken Treaties folder, NCIO; Leonard Garment to Dennis Banks, October 1972, Trail of Broken Treaties folder, NCIO.

146 Patterson, who worked for Garment: Patterson interview.

146 it seemed terribly unfair: Patterson interview; Garment interview; Robertson interview.

146 Bruce's lieutenants: Josephy, *Buffalo's Gone*, 232.

147 Robertson made a prediction: Robertson interview.

148 "Legislation is now being used": "Indians Off to a Barbecue," *Sarasota Journal*, n.d., in NCAI folder, NCIO.

Chapter 8: The Native American Embassy

149 Wednesday afternoon, November 1: John Tiger, Chronicle-NV092, AIPA News Service story, November 9, 1972, AIPA; Robert Treuer, "Seven Days in November; The Anatomy of a Native Uprising," *Washingtonian* (May 1978): 74.

149 traveling for days, some for weeks: La Course, "On the Road to St. Paul." See also "Chronology of Events," *Legislative Review* 2 (November 1, 1972): 2.

149   Those expectations were dashed: Treuer, "Seven Days," 74.

150   arranged for Black Panthers: Treuer, "Seven Days," 75.

150   Loesch's memo: Treuer, "Seven Days," 74. See also La Course, "Road to St. Paul"; Burnette, *Road*, 199m; and Patterson, *Ring of Power*, 76.

151   "It is time to fulfill a prophecy": Transcript of press conference with Robert Burnette, Washington, D.C., October 30, 1972, Trail of Broken Treaties folder, NCIO.

151   "We have already sixty-five Indians": Burnette press conference transcript.

152   activites the Trail had planned: Burnette press conference transcript. See also Harold M. Gross, "The Judicial Proceedings," *Legislative Review* 2 (November 1, 1972): 47.

152   "Churches throughout the city": Burnette press conference transcript.

152   services at Arlington: These services were important to the organizers because their intent was to honor American Indians who had been heroes in the United States military—especially Ira Hayes, a Pima man who helped raise the flag at Iwo Jima in World War II. He was feted as a hero upon his return, and died inauspiciously of alcohol-related causes years later. *Not Your Indian*, 17. Services of a limited nature did occur during the week of protests. See "Inside the Native American Embassy," *Indian Voice* (March 1973): 8.

152   "You wasted time": Treuer, "Seven Days," 97.

153   "Where the hell are we going": Sid Mills interview.

153   an impressive pedigree: Richard La Course, Building-NV243, AIPA News Service story, November 24, 1972, AIPA.

153   Indians entered the building: Treuer, "Seven Days," 98ff.; Tiger, Chronology.

153   The offer was put to a vote: Treuer, "Seven Days," 100.

154   the sound of screams and breaking glass: Treuer, "Seven Days," 100f.

154   helped one worker down a fire escape: Big Eagle interview.

155 Bellecourt escorted William Veeder: Treuer, "Seven Days," 100–1.

155 The wounded were taken: Adams interview; Sid Mills interview; Patterson, *Ring of Power*, 76.

155 the result of miscommunication: Hank Adams, "Trail of Broken Treaties: Information and Fact Sheet," typescript manuscript, November 20, 1972, Trail of Broken Treaties folder, NCIO.

155 negotiating meeting that night: Treuer, "Seven Days," 100–2; Patterson, *Ring of Power*, 76.

156 "we're going to die tonight": Patterson, *Ring of Power*, 76.

156 Patterson continued to feel confidence: Patterson interview; Patterson, *Ring of Power*, 72-78.

156 Nixon, off campaigning, ruled against: Treuer, "Seven Days," TK

157 Friday morning the occupiers: Treuer, "Seven Days," 102f.

157 A court order: Lance Gay and Michael Satchell, "Siege by Indians in Sixth Day," *Washington Star-News*, November 7, 1972.

157 "Another 'Wounded Knee'": Paul Hodge, "Another 'Wounded Knee' Was Feared Friday Night," *The Washington Post*, November 5, 1972, sec. 1.

158 magnet for Washington's counterculture: Donald P. Baker and Raul Ramirez, "Officials, Indians Parley on Protest," *The Washington Post*, November 5, 1972, sec. 1; Treuer, "Seven Days," T/K.

158 "Rosebud Indian Movement's": *Crow Dog*, 174.

159 Rose Robinson had been: Rose Robinson, interviewed by Paul Chaat Smith, Washington, D.C., tape recording, October 23, 1993.

160 press conference: Material for this press conference is in Trail of Broken Treaties folder, NCIO.

160 Clydia watched: Clydia Nahwooksy interview.

160 Militants disrupted: Clydia Nahwooksy interview.

160 Robinson returned a final time: Robinson interview.

161 "Administration's Final Offer": Adams, "Information."

162 federal courts ruled for the government: Adams, "Information."

162   watching a documentary: Adams interview.

162   "torn in two": Adams, "Information."

163   Adams led them: Adams, "Information."

163   "We will recommend": Adams, "Information."

164   cartons of documents: Adams, "Information"; "Indians Call Files from BIA Ransom," *The Washington Post,* November 9, 1973, Metro sec.

164   money would come from OEO: Adams, "Information."

164   NCAI was extremely reluctant: Statement of Charles Trimble, *Legislative Review* 2 (November 1, 1972): 28–29.

165   Adams paid a final visit: Adams, "Information."

166   a half-dozen teenagers: Adams, "Information"; Adams interview.

166   "we do not apologize": Richard La Course, "In the Caravan's Wake—an Unstable Status Quo," *Legislative Review* 2 (November 1, 1972), 12.

166   "To some, we had defeated": Adams, "Information."

167   "Patient fury": Bobbie Greene Kilberg, "Indian Affairs Hearings: Beyond the Destruction," *The Washington Post,* December 2, 1972.

167   government estimated: Michael Satchell and Toni House, "BIA Damage Hits $1.9 Million," *Washington Star-News* November 10, 1972, sec. 1.

Chapter 9: Border Town Campaign

171   Pieces of the building: "FBI Finds Missing Art in Kansas," *The Washington Post,* November 21, 1972, sec. 1; Raul Ramirez, "Probe Begun on Return of BIA Paintings," *The Washington Post,* November 14, 1972, sec. 2; Donald P. Baker, "Stolen BIA Artifacts, Documents Recovered," *The Washington Post,* November 15, 1972.

171   tons of government documents: Richard La Course, Documents-AP131, AIPA News Service story, April 13, 1973, AIPA; Lance Gay, "Indians Go with 'Incriminating' Files," *Washington Star-News* November 9, 1972.

172   The FBI soon tracked: La Course, Documents.

172   Anderson wrote pieces: For a review of the series by Anderson, see Anderson-DC152, AIPA News Service story, December 15, 1972, AIPA.

174   "served only to impede": "U.S. Rejects Indian Demands, Says Nixon Supports Reforms," *The Washington Post*, January 11, 1973.

174   heads rolled: Bruce-DC102, AIPA News Service story, December 10, 1972, AIPA.

174   Tempo 8: Donald Baker, "BIA Shakeup: 189 Out in Cold," *The Washington Post*, March 8, 1973, sec. 1.

174   conservative columnists excoriated: See, for instance, Rowland Evans and Robert Novak, "The Nixon Permissiveness," *The Washington Post*, November 27, 1972.

177   "A big loser": Haldeman, *Haldeman Diaries*.

178   "At one time": Calvin Kentfield, "A Letter from Rapid City," *The New York Times Magazine*, April 15, 1973.

179   Fort Laramie Treaty of 1868: For a discussion of the treaty, see, among others, Roxanne Dunbar Ortiz, *The Great Sioux Nation: Sitting in Judgment on America, An Oral History of the Sioux Nation and Its Struggle for Sovereignty*, (Berkeley: Moon Books, 1977).

179   Indians fared badly in Rapid's planning and development: Kentfield, "Letter from Rapid."

180   "put a freeze": "AIM Asked to 'Put Freeze on City' for 'Mistreatment of Indian Veterans,'" *Rapid City Journal* (hereafter *RCJ*) January 5, 1973.

180   "literally chain up": "AIM Asked."

180   "All doors normally opened": "AIM Asked."

181   Justice Department's secret directory: See Memorandum and attached report from Benjamin Holman to the Acting U.S. Attorney General, 1973, Tension, Racial folder, Box 13, the papers of Benjamin Holman, Hoover Institution Archives, Stanford, California. Holman, the highest-ranking African-American in the Nixon Administration, was director of the Community Relations Service of

the Justice Department. Documents from previous years on the same subject in the same folder give no mention of potential problems from American Indian radical groups. In the memo above, Indians are listed first, with Holman stating that the country could expect "Continued high tensions in many locations with special problems anticipated among the American Indians."

181   Scottsbluff, Nebraska: "AIM Charges Follow Police Charges," *RCJ*, January 15, 1973. For another account of events in Scottsbluff, see Means, *White Men Fear*, 239ff.

182   "report and be prepared": "AIM Charges."

182   firebomb through the window: "Another AIM Leader Arrested in Scottsbluff," *RCJ*, January 16, 1973.

182   "We took on": "Minority Confrontations."

183   Wesley Bad Heart Bull: Rolland Dewing, "South Dakota Newspaper Coverage of the 1973 Occupation of Wounded Knee," South Dakota History 12 (1, 1982): 60–3.

184   Indian cars rolled up from Rapid City: Mary Crow Dog with Richard Erdoes, *Lakota Woman*, (New York: Grove Weidenfeld, 1990), 122.

184   The agenda in Custer: Zimmerman, *Airlift*, 114–16.

184   fighting lasted all afternoon: Crow Dog, *Lakota Woman*, 119–21.

185   Several of the cars sported a bumper sticker: Crow Dog, *Lakota Woman*, 122.

185   one day after the riot: Harold Higgins, "Rapid City Situation Tense," *RCJ*, February 7, 1973.

185   "we can make": Harold Higgins, "AIM Sets Moratorium on Violent Activities," *RCJ*, February 11, 1973.

185   "We are not hoodlums": Higgins, "AIM Sets Moratorium."

185   A position paper: "AIM Angry with Council; Midwest Conference Continues Here," *RCJ*, February 13, 1973.

186   "the real question": "AIM Angry with Council."

186   "What has transpired": "AIM Angry with Council."

186 Indians met: "Coalition to Work on Race Issues," *RCJ*, February 16, 1973.

187 Outside the Fall River Courthouse: Harold Higgins, "Hot Springs Discussion 'Productive,'" *RCJ*, February 16, 1973.

187 "It was very productive": Higgins, "Hot Springs."

187 merchants felt helpless: Gerald Vizenor, *Crossbloods; Bone Courts, Bingo, and other Reports*, (Minneapolis: University of Minnesota Press, 1990), 171.

188 "A dream come true": Sally Farrar, "AIM, School Officials," *RCJ*, February 21, 1973.

188 redneck bars: Brave interview; Troy Lynn Yellowwood, interviewed by Paul Chaat Smith and Robert Allen Warrior, Wounded Knee District School, Pine Ridge, South Dakota, February 27, 1993.

191 *Bury My Heart*: Dee Brown, *Bury My Heart at Wounded Knee: An Indian History of the American West* (New York: Holt, Rinehart, 1971).

191 Complaints against him were numerous: *Voices*, 14ff.

191 promised to cut off Russell Means's braids: *Not Your Indian*, 34.

192 Special Operations Group: Document from Karen Northcott, *U.S. v. Casper*, Lank, White Star, Red Feather, and Bill, appeal April, 76. Wounded Knee files. Northcott was an investigator for the defense in many trials that followed Wounded Knee. Her files document many of the specifics of covert U.S. government activities during the takeover.

192 *Anarchy—USA*,: "Current Reservation Trouble has Long History," *RCJ*, February 28, 1973. See also *Voices*, 26.

192 dissidents narrowly lost: *Voices*, 25–31.

192 Ben Black Elk: Stanley Lyman, *Wounded Knee: A Personal Account* (Lincoln: University of Nebraska Press, 1991), xxiif. "Ben Black Elk is Dead: Fifth Rushmore Face," *NYT*, February 24, 1973.

Chapter 10: The Independent Oglala Nation

194 drove a tan Cougar: *Voices*, 31.

195 joined other AIM leaders: Means, *White Men Fear*, 252.

195   a measure of respect: For one account of AIM's activities on Pine Ridge before Wounded Knee, see Philip D. Roos et al., "The Impact of the American Indian Movement on the Pine Ridge Reservation," *Phylon* 41 (1, 1980): 89–99.

195   Oglala Sioux Civil Rights Organization: *Voices*, 26.

195   had faced impeachment: Lyn Gladstone, "Efforts Made to Impeach Last Six Tribal Presidents," *RCJ*, March 8, 1973.

196   Head Start program: *Voices*, 20–1 . See also, Means, *White Men Fear*, 237.

196   The first contingent of marshals arrived on the reservation February 11: *Voices*, 15.

196   specific approval: *Voices*, 24

196   "Chief Wilson": "Armed Indians Seize Wounded Knee, Hold Hostages," *NYT*, March 1, 1973; Lyman, *Wounded Knee*, 123.

196   People drove to Pine Ridge Village: Lyman, *Wounded Knee*, 3. See also *Voices*, 31.

197   Technicians transformed: Lyman, *Wounded Knee*, 3–5.

197   Calico Hall: Several participants and other eyewitnesses have given accounts of the meetings at Calico Hall. For the most part, the accounts corroborate each other. See Crow Dog, *Crow Dog*, 187–8; Young Bear, *Standing*, 149–51; Means, *White Men Fear*, 252–3; *Voices*, 26ff.; Gerald Vizenor, *Interior Landscapes: Autobiographical Myths and Metaphors* (Minneapolis: University of Minnesota Press, 1990), 235–36; Zimmerman, *Airlift*, 125f.

198   "For many years we have not fought any kind of war": Zimmerman, *Airlift*, 125–6.

198   "Where are our men": Means, *White Men Fear*, 253; *Voices*, 31–2.

198   Some argued: Dewing, *Wounded Knee*, 97; Young Bear, *Standing*, 150.

199   crossed the highway: Means, *White Men Fear*, 252–3; Young Bear, *Standing*, 150.

200   "Go ahead and do it": *Voices*, 31.

201   suggested that no announcement: Means, *White Men Fear*, 253.

201   carloads of trusted AIM warriors: Means, *White Men Fear*, 257ff.

201   fifty-four vehicles strong: *Voices*, 31.

201   a streak of red lights: Ortiz, *Great Sioux Nation*, 48.

202   "Here we come": Zimmerman, *Airlift*, 127.

202   a headdress from the museum: Means, *White Men Fear*, 258.

202   monitored the caravan's progress: *Voices*, 31–2.

203   "Communicate this": *Voices*, 34.

204   demands changed: see, for instance, "Indians Offer Accord," *NYT*, March 4, 1972; "A Suspenseful Show of Red Power," *Time*, March 19, 1973, 17.

204   rested with the White House: Patterson, *Ring of Power*, 78ff.

205   fill their cars with gas: Means, *White Men Fear*, 261.

205   armored personnel carriers: "Armed Indians"; John Kifner, "Federal Force Rings Wounded Knee; FBI Car Hit," *NYT*, March 3, 1973.

205   thought she would: *Voices*, 31.

206   supply of gasoline: Means, *White Men Fear*, 261ff.

206   Holder began planning: *Voices*, 76f. Means, *White Men Fear*, 258–9.

206   "Hostages, Wounded Knee, South Dakota": *Voices*, 38.

207   The *CBS Evening News*: Television news broadcasts from the period to the present are available at the Television News Archive, Vanderbilt University, Nashville, Tennessee. Descriptions of newscasts are available in monthly volumes in the *Television News Index and Abstracts*, a guide to the videotape collection of the network evening news programs in the Vanderbilt Television News Archive (Nashville: Joint University Libraries). The library of the Freedom Forum First Amendment Center in Nashville holds a compilation of broadcasts involving Wounded Knee.

207   "history had been hijacked": "Raid at Wounded Knee," *Time*, March 12, 1973, 21.

207   "They're still roamin' out there, the Injuns": John Kifner, "Indians at Wounded Knee Free Eleven Held for Two Days," *NYT*, March 2, 1973.

207   "Now, a trucker": Kifner, "Free Eleven."

208   "They don't want to leave": *Voices*, 39.

209   primary responsibility: For an insightful analysis of the inter agency tensions during Wounded Knee, see Ed Howder memorandum to Leo Cardenas, June 16, 1973, Box 13, File 9, Holman papers.

210   Reporters from around the world: See Neil Hickey, "Was the Truth Buried at Wounded Knee?" (four parts), *TV Guide*, December 1, 8, 15, and 22, 1973.

210   compelling television: See *TV News Index*, and Wounded Knee compilation, Freedom Forum.

210   journalists grew increasingly uneasy: Hickey, "Was the Truth Buried?"

210   "Newsmen that came out": *Voices*, 48.

211   Fifteen more APCs: "Federal Offer is Spurned by Indians as Talks Go On," *NYT*, March 6, 1973.

212   the illegal presence of the military: *U.S. v. Casper*.

213   "Colonel Potter": Lyman, 36.

213   senior nonmilitary officials: *U.S. v. Casper*.

213   in a memorandum: *U.S. v. Casper*.

213   Garden Plot: *U.S. v. Casper*.

214   "a very grave and serious situation": "Indians Get Offer on Ending Seizure," *NYT*, March 5, 1973.

214   arraignments in Rapid City: "Seven Arraigned in Reservation Incidents," *RCJ*, March 6, 1973; "Three Arraigned on Charges from Wounded Knee," *RCJ*, March 7, 1973.

214   a recall effort: "Accord reported at Wounded Knee," *NYT*, March 10, 1973.

214   a limited stand against Wilson: "Indians' Truce Ends as Talks Collapse," *NYT*, March 7, 1973.

215   "the Interior Department is known to fear that if the tribal governments can, in effect, be overthrown, the whole reservation structure may crumble.": "Indians' Truce."

215   communications trucks moved into position: "Indians' Truce."

215 Banks gave interviews: "Indians' Truce."

215 "I will not be responsible": *Voices*, 46.

215 "renegades, vagrants, intruders, knuckleheads": "Tribal Chairmen Support Wilson," *RCJ*, March 6, 1973.

215 offer they gave Big Foot: *Voices*, 45.

215 "We find no basis": "Indians Given Till Tonight to Leave Wounded Knee,"*NYT*, March 8, 1973.

216 occupiers held a community meeting: "U.S. and Indians Reach Ceasefire,"*NYT*, March 9, 1973.

216 "will make every effort": "U.S. and Indians Reach Ceasefire."

217 "We have won": John Kifner, "U.S. Removes Roadblocks in Wounded Knee Vicinity," *NYT*, March 11, 1973.

217 Russell Means saw defeat: Means, *White Men Fear*, 271–72.

217 "Let it be known": *Voices*, 55.

Chapter 11: All Things Twice

218 "If any foreign official": Bill Kovach, "F.B.I. Agent Shot as Indians Warn U.S.," *NYT*, March 12, 1973.

219 "We're going to establish": Kovach, "Agent Shot."

219 The second confrontation: Kovach, "Agent Shot"; *Voices*, 58.

219 back on military footing: Bill Kovach, "U.S. Again Blocks Roads to Isolate Wounded Knee," *NYT*, March 13, 1972.

219 "We're going to have": Kovach, "Blocks Roads."

220 two Indians had been wounded: "U.S. and Indians Reach Ceasefire," *NYT*, March 9, 1973.

221 A new envoy: Bill Kovach, "U.S. Relaxes Blockade at Wounded Knee, but Storm Hampers New Parleys," *NYT*, March 15, 1973.

221 elaborate show of protocol: *Voices*, 112.

221 "It was quite a sight": Terry De Vine, "Negotiations Halted by Storm; Indians Low on Supply," *RCJ*, March 15, 1973.

221   negotiating team: Lyman, *Wounded Knee*, xxxiii.

221   first round of indictments: De Vine, "Negotiations."

222   formal news conference: Transcript of Nixon press conference, *NYT,* March 16, 1973.

223   pneumonia and strict food rationing: Kovach, "U.S. Relaxes."

223   "I've seen football games": Kovach, "U.S. Relaxes Blockade."

223   flood the reservation: *Voices*, 112–3.

224   new petition campaign: *Voices*, 113.

224   "there has grown up": C. B. Rogers Morton, Department of Interior press release, March 1973, Wounded Knee file, NCIO.

225   "not as serious": "Twin Stalemates," *Time,* March 26, 1973.

225   "This is the best": Zimmerman, *Airlift*, 207.

225   The peace ended: *Voices*, 114.

225   M16 could kill: *Voices*, 114–16; Means, *White Men Fear*, 253.

225   village felt lucky: *Voices*, 114.

225   new arrivals: See video compilation of Wounded Knee evening news reports.

226   Whitman, a Los Angeles college student: Richard Whitman, interviewed by Paul Chaat Smith and Robert Allen Warrior, Wounded Knee District School, Pine Ridge, South Dakota, February 27, 1993.

226   "an excitement choking": Mary Crow Dog, *Lakota Woman*, 123.

227   Chevy Vega outfitted: Yellow Wood, interview.

227   "Wounded Knee babies": Yellow Wood interview.

228   "You are concerned": *Voices*, 94–5.

228   an impressive demonstration: *Voices*, 95.

228   Angela Davis: *Voices*, 97; "Angela Davis is Turned Back In Effort to Visit Wounded Knee," *NYT,* March 24, 1973.

229   "We're gonna unite": *Voices*, 88–90.

230   "The white man says": *Voices*, 89–90.

231   backpackers would set out: Zimmerman, *Airlift*, 235; Mary Crow Dog, *Lakota Woman*, 134–5.

231   entire day in a canyon: Zimmerman, *Airlift*, 235.

232   One head of cattle: John Kifner, "At Wounded Knee, Two Worlds Collide," *NYT*, March 24, 1973; Mary Crow Dog, *Lakota Woman*, 134.

232   One editorial: "No More Massacres," *NYT*, March 30, 1973.

233   marshals stormed a house: Bill Kovach, "Outsiders Headed for Wounded Knee Are Arrested," *NYT*, March 18, 1973.

233   Banks gave reporters: Martin Waldron, "Judge Allows Food for Wounded Knee," *NYT*, March 26, 1973.

233   Furious exchanges: *Voices*, 118–21.

234   incinerated in his car: "Charred Body Found in Car Unidentified," *RCJ*, March 26, 1973; "Wilcox Death Ruled by Asphyxiation," *RCJ*, March 27, 1973.

234   established their own roadblocks: "Sioux Seize Road into Wounded Knee, Vow to Starve Militants," *NYT*, March 27, 1973.

234   issued a decision: allow six cars, each with a lawyer, food, and medicine into the village: Waldron, "Judge Allows Food."

234   Grimm, a marshal from Omaha: Terry Woster, "Shot Marshal Remains in Serious Condition," *RCJ*, March 27, 1973.

234   government failed to release information on the bullet: *Voices*, 128.

234   firing resumed: *Voices*, 128.

235   secretly left the village: Means, *White Men Fear*, 283ff.

235   "May your cause": George Vecsey, "Indians Celebrate Special Mass Here," *NYT*, March 26, 1973.

236   Brando declined: Brando, *Songs*, 403–4; "Brando Has Long Backed Rights of Racial Minorities," *NYT*, March 28, 1973; Marlon Brando, "That Unfinished Oscar Speech," *NYT*, March 30, 1973. See also Corrections, *NYT*, March 31, 1973.

236   "If Indians are killed": Patterson, 79.

236   Harris Poll: Zimmerman, *Airlift*, 210.

237   Buffalo Bill re-created: Andrea I. Paul, "Buffalo Bill and Wounded Knee: The Movie," *Nebraska History* 71 (4, 1990): 182–90.

237   Leo Wilcox's funeral: Lyman, *Wounded Knee*, 39, 41.

238   "I think I'll have": *Voices*, 47.

238   Wilson along with his family: Konnie LeMay, "Twenty Years of Anguish," *Indian Country Today*, February 25, 1993.

239   very strange experience: Lyman, *Wounded Knee*, 15.

239   danger from AIM: Lyman, *Wounded Knee*, 15.

239   Wilcox . . . was a Dick Wilson ally: Lyman, *Wounded Knee*, 41.

239   hundreds came: Lyman, *Wounded Knee*, 39.

239   A marshal asked Lyman: Lyman, *Wounded Knee*, 33.

241   Sometimes they had cookouts: Lennie Foster, interviewed by Paul Chaat Smith and Robert Allen Warrior, Rapid City, South Dakota, tape recording, February 26, 1993.

241   some earned "R and R": Lyman, *Wounded Knee*, 119.

241   "Mrs. Lamont": Ortiz, *Great Sioux Nation*, 50.

242   signed an agreement: William K. Stevens, "Indians and U.S. Sign Agreement at Wounded Knee," *NYT*, April 6, 1973.

242   Indians watching the ceremony: Stevens, "Indians and U.S."

242   boarded a red helicopter: Stevens, "Indians and U.S."

243   Banks was not in the picture: Zimmerman, *Airlift*, 211.

243   Garment's people: *Voices*, 143–52.

243   "Why," he asked: Means, *White Men Fear*, 288

244   "you should have never": "Sioux Faces Hill Probers, Is Adamant," *Washington Star*, April 10, 1973.

Chapter 12: Hundred Gun Salute

245   A judge, displeased: "Indictments or Hearings Next for Wounded Knee Occupation Suspects," *RCJ*, April 14, 1973. *New Republic*, July 21, 1973.

245   a jury in California: "Y.M.C.A. Aide is Acquitted in Slaying of Indian Leader," *NYT,* March 17, 1973.

246   "one night he kept hearing": *Voices,* 188.

246   birth of its first child: Mary Crow Dog, *Lakota Woman,* 161–3.

246   married in a ceremony: conducted by Wallace Black Elk: *Voices,* 164–5.

246   Salt Lake City airport: Lyman, *Wounded Knee,* 82–3.

247   supply operation from Rapid City: *Voices,* 171–3.

247   Some of the fourteen had set out by foot: *Voices,* 173.

248   joined by others: *Voices,* 173.

248   "Welcome home!": *Voices,* 174.

248   sound of aircraft: see, among many, Zimmerman, *Airlift,* 276.

249   into the back of Frank Clearwater's skull: *Voices,* 177; Zimmerman, *Airlift,* 277–8.

249   "people are starving": "Wife of Injured Indian Says He Was Lying Down When Shot in the Head," *RCJ,* April 22, 1973.

249   new beginning: Zimmerman, *Airlift,* 272.

250   a printed message: Zimmerman, *Airlift,* 273.

250   evening newscasts: *Television News Index.*

250   arrested nearly fifty: "Nineteen Arrested in Effort for Indians," *The Washington Post,* April 23, 1973.

250   supporters from around the country: *Voices,* 202. See also Bob Fell, "March from Rosebud to Wounded Knee Set," *RCJ,* April 22, 1973.

251   restraining order: Martin Waldron, "Wounded Knee Shooting Victim Dies," *NYT,* April 26, 1973; "70 in Rosebud March Halted," *RCJ,* April 25, 1973.

251   "Although it appears": Terry De Vine, "Tribal Residents More Impatient," *RCJ,* April 26, 1973.

252   "I took them over": Ortiz, *Great Sioux,* 50–1.

252   "preposition package": *U.S. v. Casper.*

253   M-79 grenade launchers: Lyman, *Wounded Knee*, 95.

253   "I am convinced": "McGovern Urges Justice Action at Wounded Knee," *RCJ*, April 22, 1973.

253   permanent residents who were fed up: Martin Waldron, "Indians Set Up New Roadblock at Wounded Knee," *NYT*, April 25, 1973.

253   agencies had rarely worked together: Bill Kovach, "U.S. Agencies Squabble on Wounded Knee Moves," *NYT*, June 9, 1973.

254   shut down and put in receivership: Lyman, *Wounded Knee*, 110.

254   "What would the public": Martin Waldron, "Deteriorating Situation at Wounded Knee is Described as 'Brother against Brother, Sister against Sister'," *NYT*, April 23, 1973.

254   six-hour standby alert: *U.S. v. Casper.*

256   New supplies of tear gas: Martin Waldron, "Dispute over Indian Burial Worsens at Wounded Knee, *NYT*, April 30, 1973.

254   "calls for the dropping": Waldron, "Dispute over Burial."

255   John Hussman, an arrestee: Lyn Gladstone, "Man Arrested at Roadblock Says FBI Agents Were Assisting Them," *RCJ*, April 27, 1973.

255   "I will lower mine": Lyman, *Wounded Knee*, 113–24.

255   "hot under the collar": De Vine, "Tribal Residents."

256   Clearwater died: "Shooting Victim Dies."

256   firefight began in the afternoon: *Voices*, 204–5.

256   security radioed: *Voices*, 206.

257   "Four, three, two, one, GO!": *Voices*, 206.

257   Goons coordinated: *Voices*, 204–9.

257   Inside Wounded Knee, there were injuries: *Voices*, 204–21; Zimmerman *Airlift*, 320–2.

257   Lamont had been shot and killed: Martin Waldron, "Shot Kills an Indian at Wounded Knee," *NYT*, April 28, 1973.

257   terms of his bond: "Means Arrested after $25,000 Bond Revoked," *RCJ*, April 28, 1973.

257 Bissonette was arrested: "Bissonette Being Held without Bail," *RCJ*, April 28, 1973.

258 kerosene lamp: *Voices*, 222.

258 televised address: Bob Woodward and Carl Bernstein, *The Final Days* (New York: Simon and Schuster, 1976), 458.

258 Garment, so instrumental: *Voices*, 231.

258 "Guess we'll have to": *Voices*, 222.

258 caravan reached Pine Ridge: John Kifner, "Body of Slain Indian is Taken to Sioux Reservation," *NYT*, May 1, 1973.

259 warring parties resumed their talks: *Voices*, 226.

259 "Do you know": *Voices*, 226.

260 turned the discussion: *Voices*, 226-30

260 "All of those fears": *Voices*, 226.

260 "The Secretary of the Interior": *Voices*, 227.

260 "I don't know how to tell you any plainer": *Voices*, 227.

261 "Those in city hall": *Voices*, 226.

261 "We are tired": *Voices*, 227.

261 jury acquitted Schmitz: Dewing, *Wounded Knee*, 62.

262 lay in the coffin: *Voices*, 232.

262 "This is the only son I have": *Voices*, 233.

263 Dennis Banks, who gave the eulogy: *Voices*, 232.

263 "I have reviewed": Zimmerman, *Airlift*, 325–6.

263 night before the stand-down: Foster interview.

263 buses pulled up: "Occupation of Wounded Knee is Ended," *NYT*, May 9, 1973.

263 At 7:00 A.M.: "Occupation of Wounded Knee is Ended."

264 only CBS managed to get in: "Occupation of Wounded Knee is Ended."

264 The final moments: Whitman interview; *Voices*, 241.

264 Arvin Wells: *Voices*, 240–2.

264 main federal roadblock, where they stood in line and waited to be fingerprinted, interviewed, photographed: Lyman, *Wounded Knee*, 140–4; *Voices*, 244.

264 offered encouragement: *Voices*, 244; Lyman, *Wounded Knee*, 140–4.

264 the CRS in particular: Howden memorandum.

265 "These hoodlums and clowns": Zimmerman, *Airlift*, 328.

265 "a lot of old crap": "Indians Lay Down Arms," *RCJ*, May 8, 1973.

265 "We've broken AIM": "Not with a Bang," *Newsweek*, May 21, 1973.

265 "Well, for myself": *Voices*, 244.

265 a nightmare for Lyman: Lyman, *Wounded Knee*, 135–44

Epilogue

273 Deloria wrote: Vine Deloria, Jr., "Russell Means: New Indian Hope," *Indian Voice* 3 (5); 5–6.

275 Wilkinson was a Cherokee: Gerald Wilkinson, "The Indian 'Red Power' Movement: Alive, Dead, or Just Sleeping?" *Americans Before Columbus*, 17 (2, 1989), 1ff.

Index

Credits

The Rock: AP Wide World Photos.

Richard Oakes: *San Francisco Chronicle*.

LaNada Means: AP Wide World Photos.

Clyde Warrior: *Ponca City News*.

Alcatraz Quarters: Archive Photos.

Enjoying a sunny moment at Alcatraz: Archive Photos.

Alcatraz press conference: AP Wide World Photos.

John Trudell: AP Wide World Photos.

Clyde Bellecourt: AP Wide World Photos.

Dennis Banks: AP Wide World Photos.

Russell Means: AP Wide World Photos.

Dennis Banks helps escort women and children from building: AP Wide World Photos.

The Trail of Broken Treaties waits for possible police attack: Archive Photos.

After declaring BIA headquarters the native American Embassy: Archive Photos.

An aerial view of the Sacred Heart Catholic Church: UPI/Corbis-Bettmann.

Graffiti lines hallway of BIA building: AP Wide World Photos.

Hank Adams: AP Wide World Photos.

Leonard Garment: AP Wide World Photos.

AIM members under arrest: AP Wide World Photos.

Police guard Custer County South Dakota courthouse: AP Wide World Photos.

Armored Personnel Carriers at Wounded Knee: AP Wide World Photos.

Mourner views the body of Buddy Lamont: AP Wide World Photos.

Russell Means, Dennis Banks, and William Kunstler: AP Wide World Photos

Vernon Bellecourt: AP Wide World Photos.

Cities in
the Sand

The Dial Press
New York
1973